EDUCATION

HEATH
PHYSICAL SCIENCE

Authors **Louise Mary Nolan**
Science Teacher and Science Department Chairperson
John F. Kennedy Memorial Junior High School
Woburn, Massachusetts

Wallace Tucker
Science Consultant, Writer, and Lecturer
Harvard-Smithsonian Center for Astrophysics, and
University of California, Irvine

Consulting Author Zelda D. Tetenbaum
Science Teacher
Hinsdale Junior High School
Hinsdale, Illinois

Content Consultants Stephen S. Barshay CHEMIST
Assistant Professor of Chemistry
Rhode Island College
Providence, Rhode Island

Mario Iona PHYSICIST
Professor of Physics
University of Denver
Denver, Colorado

D.C. Heath and Company
Lexington, Massachusetts   Toronto

Executive Editor: Roger R. Rogalin
Project Editor: Caroline N. Stevens
Production Coordinator: Donna Porter

Series Design: William Tenney
Book Designer: Cornelia L. Boynton

Cover Photo: Tom Magno

Teacher Consultants

Kathleen Carlig
Science Teacher
Dirksen Junior High School
Calumet City, Illinois

Barbara P. Groshens
Science Teacher
North Penn Junior High School
Lansdale, Pennsylvania

Barbara Hicks
Science Department Chairperson
Sylvan Hills High School
Atlanta, Georgia

Dr. John Ignacio
Science Supervisor
Irvington Public Schools
Irvington, New Jersey

Richard T. McKnight
Director of Science/Health
Waltham Public Schools
Waltham, Massachusetts

Nancy T. Watson
Assistant Professor
Burris Lab School
Ball State University
Muncie, Indiana

Series Consultants

Napoleon Bryant
Professor of Education
Xavier University
Cincinnati, Ohio

James H. McGill
Science Department Chairperson
Hill Country Middle School
Austin, Texas

Sister Rita Meredith, O.P.
Former Science Teacher
St. Agnes High School
Rockville Center, New York

Richard Merrill
Curriculum Specialist
Mt. Diablo Unified School District
Concord, California

William D. Thomas
Science Supervisor
Escambia County Schools
Pensacola, Florida

Reading Level Consultant

J & F
Milton D. Jacobson, Founder
Charlottesville, Virginia

Field Test Teachers

Grateful acknowledgement is given to the teachers and students who participated in field tests for this program.

ARIZONA
Harold Pruitt, Pima Middle School, Scottsdale

CALIFORNIA
L. Meyer, C. W. Tewinkle Middle School, Costa Mesa
Catherine Baird, Rancho San Joaquin Intermediate School, Irvine
Patrick Croner Venado Middle School, Irvine
Patrick Gleason, Vista Verde School, Irvine

ILLINOIS
Kristin Ciesemier, Naperville North High School, District 203, Naperville
David Klussendorf, Michael Sommers, Jefferson Junior High School, District 203, Naperville
Jean Kriebs, Butler Junior High School, Oakbrook
Kelly Douglas, Wilson Middle School, Rockford

INDIANA
Nancy Watson, Burris Lab School, Ball State University, Muncie

MASSACHUSETTS
Brian Flaherty, Ronald Gomes, Plymouth Carver Intermediate School, Plymouth
Warren Phillips, Nathaniel Morton Elementary School, Plymouth
Paula Garten, Russell Magee, Middle School East, Salem
Alan Chasse, North Intermediate School, Wilmington
Joseph Gilligan, West Intermediate School, Wilmington
Priscilla Lockwood, Wilmington High School, Wilmington

MISSOURI
Beverly Edwards, Visual and Performing Arts Center, St. Louis
Marie Globig, Investigate Learning Center, St. Louis

NEW JERSEY
Joan Camarigg, Eisenhower School, Freehold
Susanne Flannelly, Joseph Herman, Barkalow School, Freehold

NEW YORK
John Spring, Trinity Lutheran School, Hicksville
Sam Alaimo, Hoover Middle School, Kenmore
Elaine Johnson, Kenmore Middle School, Kenmore
James Morgan, Benjamin Franklin Middle School, Kenmore
Edith Newfield, Hendrick Hudson High School, Montrose
A. Charles Rossi, Blue Mountain School, Peekskill
Alan Goodman, Pamona Junior High School, Suffern

PENNSYLVANIA
Anna McCartney, Tidioute Junior/Senior High School, Tidioute

TENNESSEE
Jo Quarles, Jefferson Middle School, Jefferson City
Ted Frisby, Westwood Junior High School, Manchester
Peggy Mason, Gary Mullican, Central Middle School, Murfreesboro

TEXAS
Mary Jane Vasquez, Lake Travis Junior High School, Austin

TABLE OF CONTENTS

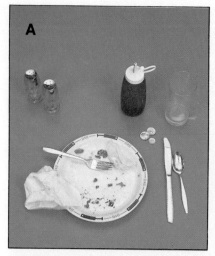

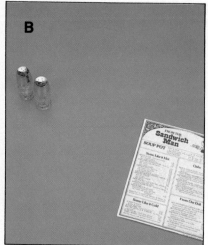

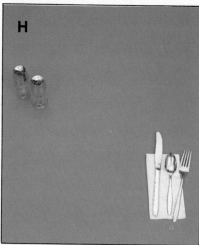

Physical Science at First Glance

You live in exciting times. Frontiers are opening up all around you, from the depths of the ocean to the heights of space to the microworld of electronics. To get the most from these times, maybe even to survive them, you need to learn as much as you can about the world. What is it made of? How does it work? How can the matter and energy available to the planet earth be used to make life better for everyone?

The purpose of this book is to help you explore the answers to some of these questions. You will use a branch of knowledge called physical science.

In the next few pages you will learn a method of thinking about the world and everything in it. It is called the scientific method. It is used not only by scientists. Anyone at all who is curious about the world may find it a valuable method.

Figure 1.1 Look at the nine photographs very carefully. Can you put them in the correct order?

1.1 What Is Physical Science?

You will find out
- what science is;
- how facts and theories are used in science;
- what physical science is.

What is **science?** The answer is simpler than you might think. Science is a method of organizing curiosity. The scientific person asks questions and tries to understand the world in an organized, orderly way.

Science questions can be about almost anything: Why does an apple fall down from a tree and not up? What is the world made of? What causes measles? You may ask about anything at all as long as you are truly curious to know the answer and go about searching for the answer in an organized, orderly way.

To be scientific, you must follow some rules. Here is the main rule: If you gather some information to help answer a certain question, other people must be able to understand how you got your information. They must then be able to gather similar information on their own. That is, other people must be able to repeat what you have done and get the same results.

Do You Know?
According to George Bernard Shaw, "Science is always simple and always profound. It is only the half-truths that are dangerous."

Figure 1.2 Which statements are facts? Which are opinions?

For example, the observation that the average annual rainfall at the Honolulu, Hawaii, airport is greater than that at the Los Angeles, California, airport is scientific information. This is because the observation can be tested by someone else. On the other hand, suppose someone reports that little green creatures from outer space are moving more clouds over Honolulu and causing more rain there. This observation is impossible to check out (at least it has been so far!) and is therefore not scientific.

Observations that can be checked out, or scientific observations, go by a much shorter, simpler name: **facts.** Facts are the building blocks of science. These blocks are held together by **theories,** or ideas that explain groups of facts.

Figure 1.3 It is easy to understand why people years ago theorized that the earth was flat. A view such as the one above clearly suggests that. Later theories correctly suggested that the earth was round.

One of the most successful theories in the history of science is Isaac Newton's theory of gravitation. Using a few simple rules, he was able to explain how apples and other things fall to earth, how the moon moves around the earth, and how the planets move around the sun.

Any good scientific theory not only explains and connects facts but also makes predictions. A theory makes predictions that should lead scientists to new ideas in the future. These predictions cannot be fuzzy ones of the kind found in fortune cookies, such as "you will meet an interesting friend tomorrow." They must be exact.

If a theory does not make predictions that can be tested, it is not a very good theory. Otherwise people have no way to agree on whether a theory was right or wrong. A good theory sets itself up as a target to be shot down if possible. In fact, as people's understanding of the world has deepened, almost all theories have turned out to be wrong in one way or another.

Some theories are so badly wrong that they have to be thrown out completely. For example, today the theory that the earth is flat is known to be wrong. Other theories, such as Newton's theory of gravitation, are wrong only under certain extreme conditions—near black holes in space, for example. Such theories can continue to be used as long as people understand that they are not correct under all conditions.

Figure 1.4 Many theories about the earth were developed in myths. An Eskimo myth offered a theory to explain the formation of rivers: A raven carrying water in its mouth spilled that water. It fell to the earth forming rivers.

Science is not a rigid body of laws carved in stone. Science is a way of doing things, a way of learning about the universe, a way of being curious. What really counts is the method of asking questions, making careful observations, coming up with answers, and testing these answers with more questions and observations.

Scientists do not have all the answers to all the scientific questions. They have not yet asked all the right questions either. They probably do not have any final answers. But today's scientists have better answers than they had in years gone by, and they will have still better answers in the years to come. Who knows? Maybe you will come up with some better answers yourself. Just by being curious about the world, you can take part in the adventure of search and discovery that makes science so exciting and important.

Figure 1.5 The same process that produces energy on the sun is being studied by physical scientists here on Earth.

Physical science is that branch of science that searches for answers to questions about matter and energy. Why is a fire hot? How is electricity generated? Where does the sun get its energy? All these questions involve matter and energy, and so they are questions for physical scientists.

Study Questions for 1.1

1. What is any method of organizing curiosity called?
2. What are the building blocks of science? How are they held together?
3. What is physical science?

1.2 Why Is Physical Science Important to You?

You will find out
- why the study of physical science is important.

Physical science is basic to understanding how things work. In fact, physical science is basic to understanding everything from simple machines, such as hammers and wheelbarrows, to computers and nuclear power plants. If you have ever wondered what causes rainbows or what causes stars to shine, you can expect to find an answer through physical science.

The information learned through physical science has helped to make life better for a great many of the people on earth. This information has made it possible for scientists to do things that your ancestors never dreamed of. Scientists have put astronauts on the moon, landed a machine on Mars, and built a computer that will fit into a pocket.

Figure 1.6 Recent developments in physical science: *top left:* An ultrasound study of a baby before birth; *top right:* Scientists using lasers; *bottom left:* Photograph of Saturn's rings; *bottom right:* A semiconductor chip

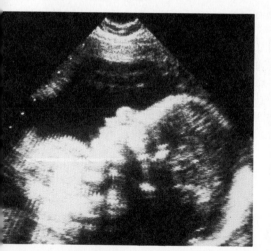

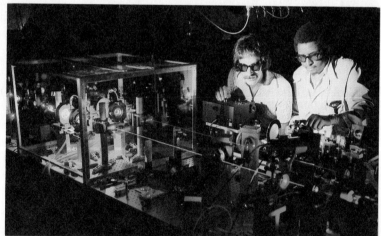

More than a billion people alive today owe their lives to agricultural and medical **technology** brought about by research in the physical and life sciences. Because of the tremendous progress that has been made, people sometimes forget that technology is just a tool, not a miraculous cure-all. Technology is simply a way of applying scientific discoveries to the real world.

The advances in science and technology are not entirely free of problems. People still have to worry about where to find enough energy to run machines, what to do about the pollution that these machines cause, and how to live with the challenges of nuclear power.

Science and technology may be in part responsible for many of the problems that face people today. But this is not the fault of science and technology themselves. Whether science and technology help or hurt people depends on how wisely people use them.

Some of you may want to do more than acquire a general knowledge of physical science. You may want to become an expert in one of the many fields of physical science and to make your living that way. If so, you will have a choice of any one of hundreds of interesting careers. Table 1-1 lists a few of these from A to Z.

Table 1-1 Physical Science Careers from A to Z

A	Aeronautical engineer, astronomer, audio engineer	**J**	Jig and fixture builder, jet engine mechanic	**R**	Rubber chemist, radar designer
B	Biomedical engineer	**K**	Kettle operator, kiln operator	**S**	Solar heating engineer, safety engineer
C	Crystallographer, chemist	**L**	Laboratory supervisor, laser technician	**T**	Teacher, transportation planner
D	Demolition specialist, draftperson	**M**	Mechanical engineer, materials scientist	**U**	Utilization engineer, ultrasound technologist
E	Environmental analyst, electrical engineer	**N**	Nuclear physicist, nuclear reactor safety inspector	**V**	Vacuum technologist, volcanologist
F	Foundry metallurgist, flight engineer	**O**	Optician, oceanographer	**W**	Welding engineer
G	Geologist, geophysical prospector	**P**	Pharmacist, physicist, petroleum engineer	**X**	X-ray technician, X-ray astronomer
H	Health physicist, hydraulic engineer	**Q**	Quality control engineer, quarry supervisor	**Y**	Yeast culture developer
I	Industrial designer, instrumentation technician			**Z**	Zanjero

Study Question for 1.2

List three ways that the discoveries of physical science have improved your life.

1.3 Thinking as a Scientist

You will find out
- the four steps of the scientific method;
- some qualities of a good scientist.

If you want to think the way a scientist does, the most important thing you must do is to be curious about the world. Why is the sky blue at noon and red at sunset? What causes static on radios?

The next thing you must do is to believe that the world can be understood, that there are some rules that nature follows. These rules can be discovered and understood by anyone willing to make the effort.

Figure 1.7 The four steps of the scientific method

Finally, you must do something about your curiosity and your belief. What a scientist does can be summarized in these four words: *observe, analyze, synthesize,* and *test*. These four steps are what is meant by the **scientific method** of investigation.

For thousands of years people have had a sense of wonder and a belief in an order in nature. But it was less than four centuries ago that the scientific method was developed. The first person to make this method popular was Galileo Galilei, an Italian who has been called the father of physical science. Galileo developed the scientific method when he studied how the earth's gravity affects the way things move.

Figure 1.8 After you observed the photographs on the first page, you analyzed and synthesized your observations. You might have determined a logical order by studying only the milk. The milk makes sense in the order above. What other items suggest that the milk theory is wrong?

The first thing Galileo did was **observe**; that is, he recorded either mentally or in writing the things he noticed. The story goes that Galileo first became interested in the laws of motion when he was in a cathedral. While he was there, a small earthquake set in motion a chandelier attached to a long chain. It moved much like a giant pendulum. Galileo timed the swings with his pulse beat and noticed that each swing of the pendulum seemed to take the same amount of time. This happened even though the distance the chandelier swung got smaller with each swing.

Galileo was interested in far more than pendulums. He wanted to find out how things move under the influence of gravity. He built test tracks and rolled balls of different sizes down them. Time after time he rolled the balls. Time after time he measured and recorded the results. In this way he observed the motion of bodies under carefully controlled conditions. In other words, Galileo performed **experiments,** or measurements and tests under controlled conditions. As you will see, experiments are the backbone of science.

The next step was to **analyze** the observations, that is, to organize them in one way or another. For example, Galileo might have analyzed his observations by noting that the balls rolled down the tracks faster when the track was tilted at a steeper angle.

Do You Know?
Dr. Joseph Bell, who was supposed to have been the model used by Arthur Conan Doyle for Sherlock Holmes, once said, "Most people see, but they do not observe."

Figure 1.9 You test the milk theory from page 9 by following other items such as the hamburger and the salad. By using all four steps of the scientific method, you conclude that the correct order is as shown above and a second glass of milk must have been involved.

The third step was to **synthesize** [SIN-thuh-syz], that is, to put the observations together in a new way and come up with a **hypothesis** [hy-PAHTH-uh-sis] that explains the observations. A hypothesis is really just an educated guess based on a few observations at hand. It is the first step in the synthesis. The next step in the synthesis is just a more educated guess, or theory. It is based on more work and more observations. Galileo's synthesis was the theory that objects of lighter weight fall just as fast as objects of heavier weight.

The last step of Galileo's scientific investigation was the **test,** or the check of the theory's predictions against new observations. This came, according to one story, when Galileo dropped a cannonball whose weight was relatively heavy and a musket ball of much lighter weight from the Leaning Tower of Pisa in the presence of a doubting crowd of onlookers. The crowd was amazed when both objects hit the ground at the same time.

These four steps—observe, analyze, synthesize, and test—are part of every scientific method. In most cases not all steps are performed by the same person. One group of scientists may do the experiments and make the observations. Another group may analyze the observations. Still another may synthesize the observations into a theory. Many times there is more than one theory, and it may take years to come up with a test to decide which theory is better. For example, there are several theories about how the earth and the other planets were formed, but until there are more observations of the other planets, scientists may not be able to decide between the different theories.

These four steps do not apply only to science. In fact, you go through them all the time, day in and day out. For example, suppose someone puts a cup of soup in front of you. You observe that steam is rising from the cup. You also observe that steam is not rising from a glass of cool milk. By analyzing this and other observations you put these facts together, or synthesize them, to conclude that the cup of soup is hot. Being a true scientist, you take a sip of the soup and find that it is hot, thereby proving your theory!

Good scientists have several qualities that set them apart. First, they ask good questions. These are often the simplest questions. But if Galileo had asked, as did many people in those days, how to turn lead to gold, he might have worked very hard with little result.

Second, good scientists are patient, careful, and honest in collecting observations. Incorrect observations are worse than useless. They can cause others to work very hard to explain observations that can be misleading. Scientists must report exactly what is observed even if it disproves their own theory.

Third, good scientists are able to make bold guesses about laws that bind the observations together. When Galileo put forth his theory, he was going against strongly held ideas. Since these ideas had been around for over a thousand years, almost everyone took them for granted. Yet he was right and the others were wrong.

Figure 1.10 An artist makes very careful observations of a painting's subject.

Study Questions for 1.3

1. List and describe the four steps of the scientific method.
2. List three qualities of a good scientist.

1.4 The Laboratory

You will find out
- what a laboratory is and its role in science;
- the steps in a laboratory experiment.

The first business of science is to collect facts. Facts are the building blocks with which to construct theories, and they provide the final judgment as to whether those theories are suitable or not.

If you are an astronomer or a geologist, you collect most of your observations through a telescope or in the field. But if you are a physicist or a chemist or an engineer, you will collect observations in controlled tests or experiments. Most of the time these experiments are performed in a room where the testing equipment is set up and where conditions such as temperature, amount of light, and volume of gas can be carefully controlled. Such a room or building is called a **laboratory.**

The laboratory, or lab, is the workshop of science, the place where the action begins and ends. It is where observations that result in new theories are collected, tested, and retested. When you are doing an experiment in the lab, you should think of that lab as a workshop or testing ground. But your lab should not look like many workshops, with sawdust on the floor and tools scattered around. It should look more like an operating room with a place for everything and everything in its place.

The two most important words to remember when going to work in the lab are BE CAREFUL. Careless work in the lab is worthless. It could also cause serious injury to you or your fellow workers. Certain procedures or steps should be followed in every lab experiment.

1. Think what you are going to do in the lab before you go there. PLAN AHEAD. Read the procedure for the activity in your book. If you are doing an experiment that is not in your book, jot down what you plan to do. Then make a chart to record your observations.

2. Record in your notebook the date, the time, the place, the kinds of observations you intend to make, and the equipment you will use.

Figure 1.11 A safe laboratory is necessary for collecting observations and testing theories.

3. Organize your equipment.

4. Perform the experiment, observing the results.

5. Record your observations. If you don't keep a record, you may as well not have done the experiment.

6. Put the equipment back where you got it.

ACTIVITY

How Can These Students Be More Careful?

Materials
plain white paper
felt pens

Procedure

In the picture some students are doing something that is dangerous. What are they doing wrong?

Questions

1. For each mistake, what rule should the students have followed to have a safe lab?

2. Create a poster to illustrate one of the rules.

Study Questions for 1.4

1. Why is the lab called the workshop of science?

2. List the steps you should follow in a lab experiment.

1.5 Measurement

You will find out
- the standard units of measurement in the metric system.

You learned earlier that the building blocks of science are scientific observations, or facts. If they are to be of any use to a scientist, the observations must be expressed in numbers. That is, they must be **measurements.** For example, it is not good enough to say that a large, heavy object moved over a long distance in a short time. Specific measurements give a more accurate picture of the size of the object than the words *large* and *heavy.* **Mass** is the measurement of the amount of material in an object. **Volume** is a measurement of the amount of space an object takes up. It is better to say that an object whose mass is 2,500 kilograms and volume is 1.2 cubic meters moved 510 meters in 5.4 seconds.

In making observations, words such as *long, hot, light,* and *big* are not useful. These words mean different things to different people. If mass, volume, length, temperature, and time are described in measurements instead of words, misunderstandings can be avoided. It is important that all measurements be taken by everyone in the same way. Such standards of measurement are necessary to make observations clear and understandable.

Figure 1.12 The word *far* means different things to different people.

Standards of measurement are so important to science that many countries have large laboratories whose main task is to build and maintain precise standards of measurement. In the United States there is a National Bureau of Standards with laboratories in Washington, D.C., and Boulder, Colorado.

The system of measurement used in laboratories in this country and around the world is the **metric system.** The metric system is a decimal system of measurement based on the **meter** as the unit of length, the **kilogram** as the unit of mass, and the **liter** as the unit of volume.

The metric system was first used in France. Here the meter was defined as one ten-millionth of the distance from the North Pole to the equator along a line passing through Paris. Today the meter is defined as 1,650,763.73 times the wavelength of orange-red light given off by the element krypton 86. In less precise units the meter is about equal to the height of a doorknob above the floor. For most measurements you don't have to have krypton 86 on hand. You can do quite well with a reasonably straight ruler, tape measure, or meterstick.

The standard for a kilogram is defined as the mass of a particular block made of platinum and iridium, which is preserved at Sevres, France. Exact duplicates exist at the National Bureau of Standards and in other institutions around the world. A kilogram has a mass about equal to that of a brick. Mass can be measured by comparing the object you are measuring with carefully constructed masses.

Figure 1.13 Some metric measurements

22°C

355 mL

1.5 min

52 kg

500 m

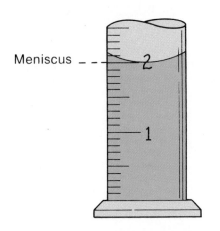

Meniscus

Figure 1.14 Observe a graduated cylinder at eye level. Read the volume at the bottom of the meniscus.

When you measure the volume of a substance, especially a liquid, you use a unit of measure called the liter. One liter is a cube 0.1 m on each side and contains one thousand cubic centimeters, or 1,000 cm³, as they are abbreviated. Since 1 cm³ is one thousandth of a liter, it is often called a milliliter.

Liquid volumes are measured with a graduated cylinder, which is much like a kitchen measuring cup. To find the volume, observe the level of the liquid and read the marks on the cylinder. For thin cylinders the liquid surface may be curved. Read the bottom of this curve, or the **meniscus** [me-NIS-kuhs], to get the volume.

You can measure the volume of solid objects by using this convenient fact: When the object is immersed in water, it will raise the water level by an amount equal to the volume of the immersed object.

ACTIVITY How Do You Find the Volume of an Irregular Object?

Materials
water
100 mL graduated cylinder
nail
marble
pebble
paper towel

Procedure
1. Copy the chart.
2. Gather all the materials.
3. Fill your graduated cylinder with water to 50 mL.
4. Carefully drop the nail into the graduated cylinder.
5. Observe the level of the water. Record this level in your chart.
6. Repeat the procedure with the marble, and then the pebble.

Questions
1. What was the original level of the water in the cylinder?
2. What was the level of the water after you added the nail?
3. How much did the nail cause the water to rise?
4. What is the volume of the nail?
5. In your chart record and label the volume of the other two objects.

Object	Volume of Water and Object	Volume of Water at Start	Volume of Object
nail		50 mL	
marble		50 mL	

The temperature scale in the metric system is based on the freezing and boiling points of water. The freezing point of water is given the value of zero degrees Celsius, or 0°C for short. The boiling point under standard atmospheric pressure is 100°C. A Celsius or Centigrade degree is one-hundredth the difference between 0° and 100°.

The metric unit of time is the **second.** The second was originally defined in terms of the earth's rotation as 1/86,400 of one day. Now the second is defined with atomic clocks that have an accuracy of about one second in 3000 years. Thanks to the marvels of solid state physics, split-second digital stopwatches with an accuracy of one second in about two weeks are available at reasonable prices.

The metric system has gained worldwide acceptance by scientists because it is easy to make larger or smaller units from the standard units. You simply multiply or divide by ten or powers of ten. Prefixes are used for each multiplication by ten, hundred, etc., and for each division by ten, hundred, etc.

Do You Know?
The small slice of quartz crystal in an electronic digital watch vibrates over 56,000 times a second.

Prefix	Abbreviation	Meaning
kilo	k	1000
hecto	h	100
deka	da	10
deci	d	.1 (1/10)
centi	c	.01 (1/100)
milli	m	.001 (1/1000)

Figure 1.15 Some common metric prefixes

Suppose, for example, you wanted to say one thousand meters in a simpler way. Just attach the prefix *kilo*, which stands for a thousand, to *meter*, and you have one kilometer, or a thousand meters. Likewise you could write one thousandth of a meter by putting the prefix for one thousandth *milli* in front of *meter* to get millimeter, one thousandth of a meter.

Study Question for 1.5

What are the metric units of measurement for mass, length, volume, and time?

What Did You Learn?

- Science is a way of learning about the universe, a method of organizing your curiosity.
- The building blocks of science are facts. Theories are ideas that connect groups of facts.
- Physical science is that branch of science that deals with the study of matter and energy.
- Physical science is important because it is basic to understanding how things work.
- The four steps in the scientific method are observe, analyze, synthesize, and test.
- The two most important words for lab work are *be careful.*
- The six steps in performing an experiment are (1) plan ahead, (2) record date and conditions, (3) organize equipment, (4) perform experiment, (5) record observations, and (6) put equipment back where it belongs.
- Measurements are observations expressed as a certain number of units.
- The system of measure used by scientists is the metric system. In this system the primary units—mass, length, and volume—are measured in terms of kilograms, meters, and liters.

Key Terms

science
facts
theories
physical science
technology
scientific method
observe
experiments
analyze
synthesize
hypothesis
test
laboratory
measurements
mass
volume
metric system
meter
kilogram
liter
meniscus
second

Biography

Galileo Galilei   (1564-1642)

Galileo was born in Pisa, Italy. He began training for a medical career but soon switched to mathematics and natural philosophy, which is what people called physical science in those days.

Galileo was a person who did many things well. He was a fair musician, an excellent writer, a brilliant lecturer, and one of the best scientists of all time. He was also good at making things.

In 1609 a man arrived in Italy with a new instrument said to be of great use for both military and shipping purposes. The instrument was called a telescope. He offered to sell it to the Grand Duke, but the Duke refused and sent a description of it to Galileo instead. A month later Galileo, who had never seen the instrument, presented the Grand Duke with a telescope three times more sensitive than the one offered for sale!

Galileo made over a hundred telescopes and was the first person to use a telescope to study the moon, the sun, the planets, and the stars. With it he discovered the moons of Jupiter, craters on the earth's moon, and sunspots. His work in astronomy proved beyond doubt that the earth moves around the sun.

Galileo's writings about his astronomical discoveries made him famous. He also faced a problem that many early scientists faced. Many powerful leaders refused to accept Galileo's new methods and ideas.

Because of his quick mind and his biting sarcasm, Galileo seldom lost an argument. But this time it was different. Because of his ideas, Galileo was sentenced to life in prison and spent the last eight years of his life under house arrest. It was there that he wrote the books on motion, which laid the foundation for the modern method of exploring science.

TO THINK ABOUT AND DO

Vocabulary

Select the term in parentheses that correctly completes each sentence.

1. The building blocks of science are called (facts, hypotheses, theories).
2. The branch of science that deals with matter and energy is (astronomy, meteorology, physical science).
3. When scientists record mentally or in writing the things they notice, they are performing the step of the scientific method called (analyze, synthesize, observe).
4. When scientists organize their observations in order to interpret them more easily, they are performing the step of the scientific method called (analyze, observe, test).
5. An educated scientific guess that is based on a few observations is a (hypothesis, theory, fact).
6. The basic unit used to measure volume in the metric system is the (second, liter, meter).

What Do You Remember?

1. What is science?
2. Distinguish among hypothesis, theory, and fact.
3. List three advances of physical science that have made life easier.
4. Describe how Galileo used each step of the scientific method.
5. What are the qualities of a good scientist?
6. Why is the laboratory so important to a scientist?
7. What are the two most important words to remember when working in the lab?
8. What is the basic unit used to measure mass in the metric system?
9. Explain how you would change 45 kilograms to milligrams.

Applying What You Have Learned

1. a. How long is the line in cm? In mm?

b. What is the diameter of the ball in cm?

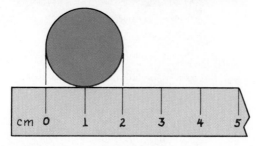

c. What is the volume of the rock in mL?

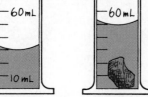

2. How would you use a balance to determine the mass of 1000 mL of water?

3. If you are given a meterstick, two wooden blocks, and a basketball, how would you find the diameter of the ball?

4. What would you do if you saw someone with long hair leaning near a lighted Bunsen burner?

Research and Investigation

Choose a scientific theory currently making the news. How did it evolve from a hypothesis? What experiments were done to prove it?

Motion, Force, and Energy

Matter, Energy, and Motion

2

Think about anything in this world. Other people can't be sure what you are thinking. But if you are thinking about something in this world, they can be sure of one thing. You are thinking about matter, energy, and motion. If you think about other people, they are matter. So are rocks, buildings, dogs, cats, bikes, water, and air. If you think about a song, that is the energy of waves moving through air, which is matter.

Matter gets from one place to another or changes from one substance to another because of energy. Energy is involved, for example, when a burning log changes to ashes and smoke. In other words, energy can cause things to happen to matter.

Matter is in constant motion whether you see it or not. The wind blows; a leaf falls; you use your brain to solve a puzzle. In each case, matter is in motion, and energy causes that motion to occur.

Figure 2.1 What are some examples of matter and energy in the photograph?

2.1 Matter and Energy

You will find out

• what matter is;
• the three states of matter;
• what energy is;
• how energy changes from one form to another.

Anything that has mass and takes up space is **matter.** Since visible light waves, radio waves, and X rays do not take up space, they are not matter. But almost everything else around you is.

Scientists classify matter into three different states—**solids, liquids,** and **gases.** A solid has a definite shape. Ice, rocks, tin cans, glass bottles, and wood are examples of solids. If you set any of these on a table, it will not change. In fact, you can place a solid in a bowl or roll it on the ground, and it still won't change. If you hit a solid with a hammer, it might bend or break into smaller pieces, but these smaller pieces will keep their shape unless other forces act on them.

Figure 2.2 Can you identify an example of each of the three states of matter in this photograph?

A liquid, on the other hand, does not have a definite shape. If you pour water from a pitcher into a glass, its shape changes from that of the pitcher to that of the glass. If you then pour the glass of water into a bowl, the water will spread out and take the shape of the bowl. Crayons left in the sun too long, water, gasoline, and mercury are examples of liquids.

ACTIVITY

What Are the Characteristics of Liquids?

Materials
graduated cylinder
water
containers of
    different shapes
paper towels

Procedure

1. Mark the containers A, B, and C and observe the shape of each container.

2. Pour 100 mL of water into the graduated cylinder.

3. Pour the water from the cylinder into container A, then into B, and then into C. In each case note how the water changes.

4. Now pour the water back into the graduated cylinder. Observe the amount of water you have now.

Questions

1. How do containers A, B, and C differ?

2. Was the volume of the water changed as you poured it from A to B to C? How do you know? Hint: Try pouring the water back into the graduated cylinder after you pour the water into each container.

3. Copy and complete the graph.

4. Explain how this experiment shows that liquids have a definite volume but can change their shapes.

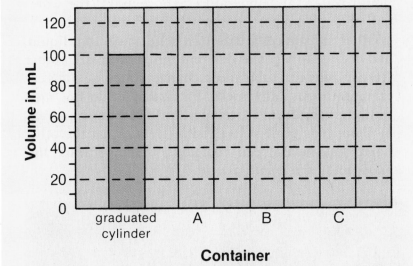

A liquid, like a solid, does have a definite volume. A hundred milliliters of water take up the same volume whether the water is in a bottle, in a glass, or spilled on a tabletop. And if you add 50 mL of milk to the water, you'd better make sure that there is room for it. The milk will take up the same amount of space, 50 mL, whether it is mixed with the water or not.

Figure 2.3 The scent of a skunk expands to fill the space available.

A gas has no definite shape or volume. It spreads out to fill the space available to it. Imagine you are at one end of a room and someone spills a bottle of perfume at the other end. Some of the perfume will change to a gas, and pretty soon you will be smelling it at your end of the room. The perfume gas spread out and filled all the space available, the whole room.

Many scientists recognize a fourth state of matter that is quite different from most matter found on the earth. It is called the **plasma** state. It occurs when the temperature of a gas becomes very high. Some of the gas particles break apart into electrically charged pieces. The outer layers of stars are in the plasma state.

Most matter can exist in any one of the common states—solid, liquid, or gas. For example, think of a pail of water. Most of the water will be ice if the temperature is below 0°C. Above that temperature there will be only liquid water. At temperatures above 100°C the water will change to a gas, commonly called water vapor.

Other substances freeze to a solid, melt to a liquid, and change to a gas at different temperatures. In other words, different substances change states at different temperatures. Many rocks, for example, do not melt until they are heated to temperatures of many hundreds or thousands of degrees Celsius. Helium, on the other hand, has never been cooled to a temperature low enough to turn it into a solid.

Figure 2.4 The three common states of water

Figure 2.5 Some solids with different properties

The temperature at which a particular substance changes states is a **property** of that form of matter. A property is a quality or characteristic of a substance and can be used to identify it. Other properties of matter include color, hardness, smell, whether it will burn, and whether it will mix with other substances.

As you move deeper into the study of physical science, you will keep coming back to two basic ideas: matter and energy. You know that matter is the stuff that the world is made of. But what is **energy?** Energy is the capacity to move matter from one place to another or to change matter from one substance to another. Put another way, energy can make things happen to matter.

One of the most important things to know about energy is that it never disappears. It simply changes form. A simple experiment can illustrate this changeability of energy. Try lifting a book about half a meter above the surface of your desk. It takes energy stored in the muscles of your body to lift the book. At first some of this energy is changed into the motion of the book. But now the book is not moving. So what happened to the energy? It is in the form of **potential energy,** or the energy of position. Potential energy is stored energy which can be released when matter moves. This energy can be released by simply letting go of the book.

When you let go of the book, it begins to move. The potential energy is changed into **kinetic energy,** or the energy of motion. In less than a second the book slams against the desk top. Where have the book's potential energy and kinetic energy gone? They have gone into the energy of sound waves and some heat energy.

Figure 2.6 The roller coaster has kinetic energy.

ACTIVITY

Materials

toy car
6 books
1 board
3 milk cartons

What Is the Effect of Height on Potential Energy?

Procedure

1. Slant your board by resting it against one book.

2. With the milk cartons, build a tower at the bottom of the board.

3. Place the car at the top of the board and allow the car to roll down it. Repeat this step.

4. Raise the board by placing three books under it and rebuild the tower.

5. Place the car at the top of the board and allow the car to roll down it. Repeat this step.

6. Repeat the experiment but increase the height of your hill by using six books to raise the board.

Questions

1. How did the height of the hill change in your experiment?

2. What kind of energy did the car have at the top of the hill?

3. What kind of energy did the car have as it was rolling down the hill?

4. When did the car have the least energy—at one book, three books, or six books? When did the car have the most energy?

5. Copy and complete the chart.

6. How does height affect the amount of potential energy in a body?

7. How did this experiment show that energy can be converted to other forms?

Height (number of books)	Amount Milk Cartons Moved (least, most)
1 book	

Figure 2.7 In the home, people benefit from different forms of energy.

The amazing thing about energy is that you can actually make it change from one form to another. You can light a fire and change the energy stored in wood into heat energy. Or you can flip a switch and change electrical energy into light. As a result you can do things that would put the magicians in the fairy tales to shame.

The key to technical progress has always been the ability to control and use energy. Prehistoric people started the progress when they learned to release energy in a controlled way by burning wood. They used the energy from the burning wood to keep warm, cook food, and make tools.

Today energy is used in many forms. People use energy to keep warm and to cook food. They use it also to change dark to light, to move themselves all over the planet, and to send astronauts and machines into space.

Do You Know?
The energy released by the space shuttle's three main gate engines is 23 times the Hoover Dam's output.

Study Questions for 2.1

1. What is matter?
2. List the three common states of matter and give an example of each.
3. What produces changes in matter?
4. Give an example of energy changing from one form to another.

2.2 Speed and Velocity

You will find out
- how to get the average speed of an object;
- the difference between speed and velocity;
- how to combine two or more velocities.

How do you describe the effects of energy on matter? To do this, scientists talk about matter that's in motion. They measure how fast a particular piece of matter is moving. For example, scientists need to know how fast a satellite must move in order to stay in a certain orbit. They also need to know how that motion is changing.

Figure 2.8 Over short distances a cheetah can reach speeds of 110 km/hr.

The **speed** of an object is a measure of how fast it is moving. You can find the speed of an object by measuring the distance the object has traveled and dividing by the time it took to travel that distance. For example, if you travel 80 kilometers in one hour, your speed is 80 kilometers per hour. If you travel 160 kilometers in two hours, your speed is still 80 kilometers per hour. Suppose you travel 40 kilometers in half an hour. What would your speed be?

$$\text{Speed} = \frac{\text{distance}}{\text{time}}$$

This formula gives the average speed. It does not tell the whole story of stops and starts, of slowdowns and speedups. Nor does it tell which direction the object is traveling in.

Do You Know?
A woodpecker's beak reaches speeds of 2,000 km per hour.

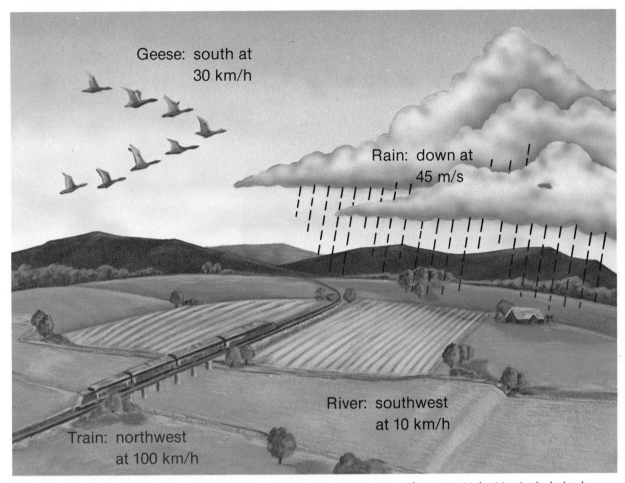

Geese: south at 30 km/h

Rain: down at 45 m/s

Train: northwest at 100 km/h

River: southwest at 10 km/h

Figure 2.9 Velocities include both speed and direction.

The **velocity** [vuh-LAHS-uh-tee] of a body is a measure of both the speed of the body and its direction of motion. For example, suppose that in one hour's time an automobile travels 80 kilometers north along a highway. The speed of the automobile is 80 kilometers per hour. The velocity is 80 kilometers per hour due north. If the automobile had been traveling east, the speed would have been the same, but the velocity would have been 80 kilometers per hour due east.

It is especially important for air traffic controllers to know the velocities of the airplanes whose motion they control. Their job is to keep the airplanes from running into each other. For this reason they continually tell pilots the positions and velocities of other aircraft in the area.

Figure 2.10 The combined velocities of the boat and the river tell you how fast the boat is moving downriver.

Sometimes you may also need to know how to combine two or more velocities. Suppose, for example, you are on a boat moving down a river that flows at a speed of 10 km per hour. How fast will the boat go downstream? To find the answer, you add the velocity of the boat, 40 km per hour downstream, to the velocity of the river, 10 km per hour downstream, to get 40 + 10 = 50 km per hour downstream. In general, if you want to combine velocities that have the same direction, you simply add the speeds.

Figure 2.11 The combined velocities of the girl and the escalator tell you how fast the girl is moving upstairs.

Chapter 2 / Matter, Energy, and Motion

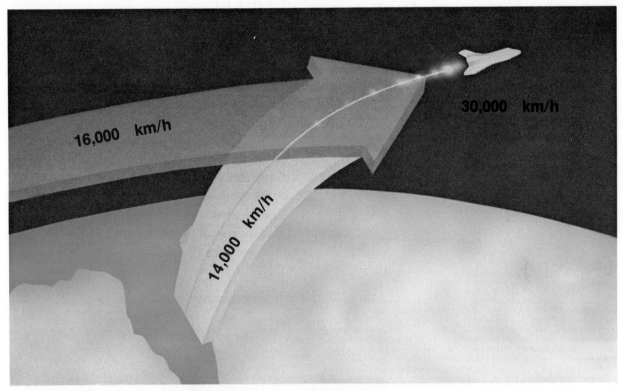

16,000 km/h

30,000 km/h

14,000 km/h

Figure 2.12 A rocket launched in the direction of the earth's rotation picks up an extra 16,000 km/hr.

Space scientists use this addition of velocities to their advantage when they launch rockets in the same direction as the rotation of the earth. By launching a rocket in the direction of the rotation of the earth, scientists pick up an extra 1,600 km per hour, the speed of the rotation of the earth at Cape Canaveral in Florida. This means that less fuel is needed to get up to the speed of about 30,000 km per hour, the velocity required to put a rocket on a course for the moon or beyond.

Study Questions for 2.2

1. What is the average speed of an ice puck that travels 10 m in 5 s?
2. What is the difference between speed and velocity?
3. A plane is moving 640 km per hour east in a wind current that is moving 80 km per hour east. What is the velocity of the plane?

2.3 Acceleration

You will find out
- how to describe the changing velocity of an object;
- why a body moving at a constant speed can be accelerating;
- how falling objects accelerate;
- what is meant by terminal velocity.

Velocity tells you about the average motion of an object during a certain period of time. But it does not tell you about all the stops and starts that happen when the object picks up speed, slows down, or changes direction. This change of velocity divided by the time during which the change occurs is called the **acceleration** [ak-sehl-uh-RAY-shuhn].

Acceleration = change in velocity ÷ time

Figure 2.13 A bobsled accelerates every time it changes either speed or direction or both.

For example, suppose a car moves from a dead stop to twenty meters per second in five seconds. That is, the car went from zero meters per second to twenty meters per second in five seconds' time. If the car moves along a straight path, the average acceleration during this time interval is (20 m/s − 0 m/s) ÷ 5 s = meters per second each second or 4 m/s/s. That is, the car is picking up speed at a rate of four meters per second every second. Suppose now that the driver of the car brakes the car and slows it down. In this case, the car's speed has decreased. This change in velocity to a decreasing speed is called **deceleration.** You can find the deceleration of an object by using the same formula as that for acceleration.

Figure 2.14 Cars and trucks accelerate and decelerate frequently.

Since acceleration measures changes in velocity and velocity has direction as well as speed, a body can be accelerating even if its speed is constant! For example, even if the driver takes a corner at a constant speed, the automobile will be accelerating, since it is changing direction. The sides of racetracks are usually sloped upward to furnish an extra force to accelerate the cars as they go around a curve.

What do autumn leaves, sky divers, and hailstones have in common? They are falling toward the surface of the earth. There is a fact about all falling objects that may surprise you. It was proved by Galileo centuries ago. If you dropped a marble and a bowling ball at exactly the same instant from the top of the Washington Monument, both would hit the ground at the same time. This fact amazes many people who expect the heavy bowling ball to fall faster. Even though the bowling ball is much heavier, both objects fall through the air at the same velocity. Thus, they strike the ground together. That is what Galileo proved when he dropped a cannon ball and a musket ball from the Leaning Tower of Pisa.

Figure 2.15 Objects of different weight fall at the same rate.

Falling objects all accelerate in the same way. Any object falling near the surface of the earth will accelerate 9.8 m/s/s. This means the velocity of an object will increase by 9.8 meters per second every second it is falling. Take for example an apple dropped from the roof of a 20-story building. Before the apple is dropped, its velocity is 0 m/s. One second after the apple is dropped, its velocity is 9.8 m/s. After two seconds the apple has accelerated to 9.8 + 9.8, or 19.6 m/s. After another second the apple's velocity is 19.6 + 9.8, or 29.4 m/s. As the apple continues to fall, it continues to accelerate by 9.8 m/s every second. A falling brick would accelerate the same way. So would a nickel, a person, and a sack of potatoes. All falling objects accelerate 9.8 m/s for each second they fall.

Figure 2.16 A falling object accelerates at a rate of 9.8 m/s/s.

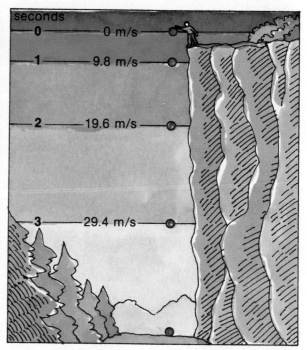

Can objects falling through air keep accelerating as long as they are falling? The answer to this question is no. Every falling object, if it is falling long enough, reaches a **terminal velocity.** Once this velocity is reached, the object will not accelerate any more. It will continue to fall at a constant rate, its terminal velocity.

Figure 2.17 An open parachute encounters a large amount of air resistance.

What causes a falling object to reach a terminal velocity and to stop accelerating? To understand the answer to this question, imagine you have dropped a feather and a pebble. The pebble may be heavier than the feather, but all falling objects accelerate at 9.8 m/s/s. Both should reach the ground together. However, the pebble will probably fall faster. It will touch the ground first not because it is heavier but because of its shape. The air an object falls through provides resistance to the falling motion of the object. A feather encounters much more air resistance than a pebble. It falls more slowly. If the feather and pebble were falling in the absence of air, a vacuum, both would fall at the same velocity. There can be no air resistance when there is no air. It is air resistance that causes falling objects to stop accelerating and reach a terminal velocity.

Study Questions for 2.3

1. The velocity at which a car is moving changes from 20 m/s south to 30 m/s south in 10 seconds. Find the acceleration of the car.
2. How can a body moving at a constant speed be accelerating?
3. A package is dropped from a helicopter. Find the velocity of the package after 5 seconds.
4. What causes a falling object to stop accelerating?

2.4 Momentum

You will find out
- what momentum is;
- how to find the momentum of an object.

Velocity and acceleration tell you a lot about the motion of an object, but they don't tell you the whole story. For example, suppose you rolled a Ping-Pong ball down a bowling alley at a speed of six meters per second. The Ping-Pong ball would just bounce off the bowling pins. On the other hand, a bowling ball moving at six meters per second would send the pins flying!

It is clear from these examples that the velocity and acceleration of an object are not the only important things to know about its motion. You must also consider the **momentum** [moh-MEHN-tuhm]. The momentum of an object is the mass of the object multiplied by its velocity.

$$\textbf{Momentum} = \textbf{mass} \times \textbf{velocity}$$

An object with a larger mass has more momentum and can exert a larger force than an object of smaller mass even if the velocity of the two objects is equal. This is one reason you cannot bowl a strike with a Ping-Pong ball. Even if a bowling ball and a Ping-Pong ball are traveling at exactly the same velocity, the bowling ball will have much more momentum. It will exert a larger

Figure 2.18 The ball with greater mass has greater momentum.

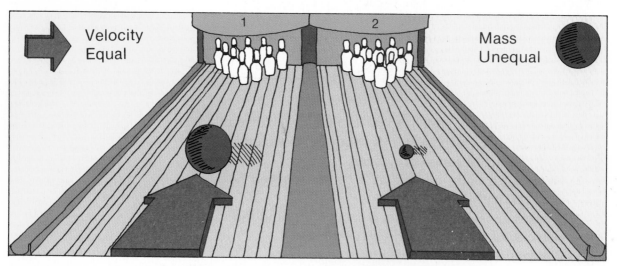

force and be able to knock down the pins. The bowling ball has greater momentum because it has more mass. In general, if two objects are moving with the same velocity, the one with more mass will have greater momentum.

The reverse is also true. If two moving objects have the same mass, the one with the greater velocity will have more momentum. Consider, for example, two bowling balls of the same mass, 6 kg, moving in the same direction. If the first ball has a velocity of 3 m/s down the alley and the second ball has a velocity of 6 m/s down the alley, what is the momentum of each? For the first ball the momentum is

$$6 \text{ kg} \times 3 \text{ m/s, or } 18 \text{ (kg) (m)/s.}$$

For the second ball the momentum is

$$6 \text{ kg} \times 6 \text{ m/s, or } 36 \text{ (kg) (m)/s.}$$

The second ball has greater momentum because it has greater velocity.

Figure 2.19 The ball with greater velocity has greater momentum.

Study Questions for 2.4

1. What is meant by the momentum of a moving body?
2. What is the momentum of a 3-kg rock moving at 4 m per second?

What Did You Learn?

- Anything that has mass and takes up space is matter.
- The three common states of matter are solids, liquids, and gases.
- The fourth state of matter is a high-temperature gas called a plasma.
- Energy is the ability to move matter and produce changes in it.
- Energy changes from one form to another but never disappears. For example, potential energy, or the energy due to position, may change to kinetic energy, or the energy of motion.
- The speed at which an object is moving is found by dividing the distance the object travels by the time it takes to travel that distance.
- Velocity gives both the speed of an object and the direction in which it is traveling.
- To combine two or more velocities that are in the same direction, you must add the speeds.
- An object's acceleration is found by dividing the change in its velocity by the time that is required for that change to occur.
- The change in velocity to a decreasing speed is called deceleration.
- Falling objects accelerate at 9.8 m/s/s.
- When falling objects reach terminal velocity, they continue to fall but do not accelerate.
- Air resistance causes falling objects to stop accelerating.
- The momentum of an object is its mass times the velocity at which it is moving.

Key Terms

matter
solids
liquids
gases
plasma
property
energy
potential energy
kinetic energy
speed
velocity
acceleration
deceleration
terminal velocity
momentum

Biography

Gottfried Wilhelm Leibniz (1646–1716)

Leibniz was a German mathematician noted for his idea of the kinetic energy of motion. Today he is even more famous for his invention of calculus. Calculus is a mathematical method of dealing with rates of change, such as accelerations, for complicated motions. Today calculus is used in every field of physical science to calculate velocities and accelerations and to deal with other changing quantities.

Leibniz was not the only inventor of calculus! Isaac Newton, an Englishman who lived at the same time as Leibniz, also invented a method for calculating rates of change that was almost identical to Leibniz's. It was apparently a coincidence that both men came up with the same idea at the same time. Neither man believed it was a coincidence, however. Each accused the other of stealing his ideas. The quarrel became so bitter that English and German scientists joined in the dispute on the sides of their countrymen. An international commission of scientists was then set up to investigate. The commission decided that both men had made their discoveries independently. Nevertheless, the bad feelings between Leibniz and Newton remained until they died.

Leibniz was involved in politics and philosophy as well as science. He got into many bitter arguments in these fields as well. As a result, he had few friends. When Leibniz died at the age of 70, only one person attended his funeral. This happened even though Leibniz was one of the most brilliant scientists in Germany.

TO THINK ABOUT AND DO

Vocabulary

Match each term in column A to the phrase that describes
it in column B.

<table>
<tr><td colspan="2">A</td><td colspan="2">B</td></tr>
<tr><td>1.</td><td>acceleration</td><td>a.</td><td>anything that has mass and takes up space</td></tr>
<tr><td>2.</td><td>kinetic energy</td><td>b.</td><td>matter that has a definite shape and volume</td></tr>
<tr><td>3.</td><td>plasma</td><td>c.</td><td>distance divided by time</td></tr>
<tr><td>4.</td><td>solid</td><td>d.</td><td>ability to move matter or to change it into another substance</td></tr>
<tr><td>5.</td><td>gas</td><td></td><td></td></tr>
<tr><td>6.</td><td>speed</td><td>e.</td><td>mass times velocity</td></tr>
<tr><td>7.</td><td>velocity</td><td>f.</td><td>the change in velocity during a given time</td></tr>
<tr><td>8.</td><td>momentum</td><td>g.</td><td>property of motion that takes speed and direction into account</td></tr>
<tr><td>9.</td><td>matter</td><td></td><td></td></tr>
<tr><td>10.</td><td>energy</td><td>h.</td><td>a fourth state of matter found in the outer layers of stars</td></tr>
<tr><td></td><td></td><td>i.</td><td>energy of object in motion</td></tr>
<tr><td></td><td></td><td>j.</td><td>state of matter with no definite shape or volume</td></tr>
</table>

What Do You Remember?

1. Name the three common states of matter. Describe the shape and volume of each state.
2. What is the name of a fourth state of matter making up the outer layers of stars?
3. Give an example of the way energy may change from one form to another.
4. A car travels 192 kilometers in 8 hours. What is its average speed?
5. A boat is sailing at 48 km per hour downstream on a river whose current is moving 16 km per hour downstream. What is the resulting velocity of the boat?
6. A car increases its velocity from 16 km per hour to 88 km per hour in six seconds. What is its acceleration?
7. Why does a truck traveling 88 km per hour have greater momentum than a car traveling at the same speed?

Applying What You Have Learned

1. A rock, a can of orange soda, and a helium balloon are all alike in some ways and different in others. How are they alike? How are they different?
2. Paul drove to the store with his mother. This graph shows the speeds at which the car moved. Use the graph to explain what happened in terms of acceleration, deceleration, and constant speed.

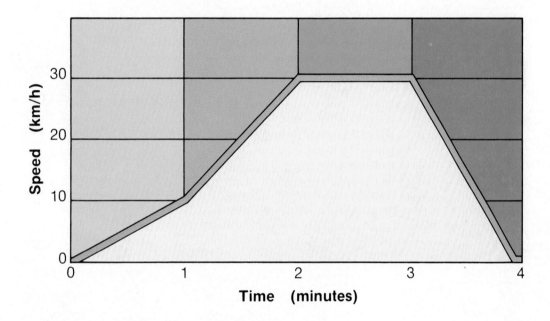

Research and Investigation

1. Parachutes are used to decrease the speed of falling objects. They can also be used to slow down race cars. How does a parachute reduce the speed of a fast-moving object? Will a larger parachute reduce the speed more than a smaller one?
2. If a balloon is put into a bell jar and a vacuum pump is used to remove the air from the bell jar, what will happen to the balloon? Why? What will happen if air is pumped into the bell jar? Why? What does this tell you about the volume of a gas?

Forces

3

What holds bridges up but can also cause bridges to collapse? What causes cars to speed up as well as slow down? What drives electric current through wires and water through pipes? What pushes you into the air when you jump and causes you to come down to earth again? Forces do! Forces give energy to matter and put it into motion.

The action of forces explain many circumstances that are familiar to you. When you ride up in an elevator, the elevator floor presses hard against the bottom of your feet. When the elevator goes down it feels as if the floor is pulling away from your feet. If the car you are riding in stops suddenly, your body lurches forward. If that same car rounds a corner at a relatively high speed, your body leans to the side. When you blow up a balloon and release it, the balloon shoots through the air as it empties and falls.

In this chapter you will find out how the idea of forces helps in understanding why things happen the way they do.

Figure 3.1 The Golden Gate Bridge in California

3.1 Gravitational Forces

You will find out
- what is meant by the universal law of gravitation;
- how gravity changes with mass and distance;
- how weight and mass are different.

A **force** is a push or a pull that is exerted on matter. Whenever the car, plane, or elevator in which you are riding changes its rate of motion, you may feel this push or pull. You could say that force is the cause of motion. It speeds things up, slows things down, and pushes things around corners.

Physical scientists have identified several basic forces in nature. In this lesson you will learn about one of the most important forces—**gravitational force.** Gravitational force is the attraction between the earth and all the objects on it. When you drop a book, for example, gravitational force causes the book to fall to the ground rather than to remain floating in the air. When you jump off a diving board, gravitational force causes you to fall into the water.

Figure 3.2 Gravitational force moves skiers downhill and swimmers into the water.

Figure 3.3 Gravitational force keeps the moon in orbit around the earth.

Gravitational force acts between all objects in the universe as well. The gravitational force between the sun and the earth, for example, keeps the earth in its orbit. In the same way, the gravitational force between the earth and the moon keeps the moon in its orbit. It took the genius of the English mathematician Isaac Newton to realize that the force between the earth and the moon acts in the same way as the force between the earth and an apple. In fact, Newton is said to have come up with this idea while sitting under an apple tree and watching an apple fall to the ground.

Newton's **universal law of gravitation** states that the force of gravitation is present between any two objects in the universe. The amount of gravitational force that one object exerts on another depends on two things: (a) the masses of the objects and (b) how far apart they are.

If you cruised around the solar system, passing by each planet at the same distance, you would soon find that the gravitational pull of a massive planet such as Jupiter is far stronger than a less massive one such as Pluto. The strength of an object's gravitational pull depends on its mass.

As you travel away from the earth, you are affected less and less by the earth's gravitational pull. As your distance from earth increases, the gravitational pull decreases. If you travel far enough, you will not be affected

Figure 3.4 The amount of gravitational force increases as the mass of the objects involved increases.

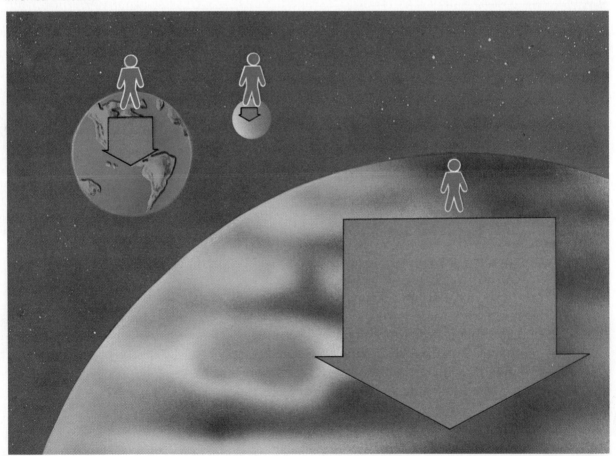

by the earth's gravitational pull at all. In other words, gravitational pull between two objects depends on the distance between the objects. The closer the objects, the stronger is the gravitational pull.

Objects anywhere on the earth's surface are about the same distance from the center of the earth. For this reason, the earth's gravitational pull on an object depends only on the object's mass. The greater the object's mass, the greater is the gravitational pull. The measure of this pull on an object is the object's **weight.** When you stand on a scale, you are measuring the amount of gravitational pull on your mass. Scientists use the **newton,** abbreviated N, as the unit of weight.

It is important to remember that weight and mass are not the same. Mass is a measure of the amount of matter in an object. Mass is measured on a balance, not a scale, and the units are grams. The mass of an object is not changed by changes in gravitational force. Weight is affected by gravity. It increases when the gravitational force increases and decreases when the gravitational force decreases.

If you go on a diet, you say you want to lose weight. That's not really what you want. What you really want is to lose mass. You would lose a lot of weight very quickly if you could leave earth and go to the moon. The moon's gravitational pull is weaker than the earth's so your weight would be less. However, you wouldn't look any thinner. Your mass would still be the same because the amount of matter in your body didn't change. Your clothes would fit just as they did on earth where you weighed more.

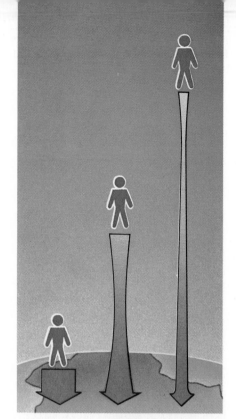

Figure 3.5 The amount of gravitational force decreases as the distance between the objects involved increases.

Do You Know?
A locust can jump more than 17 times the length of its body. In only a fiftieth of a second, the muscles in its two rear legs must exert a force more than a hundred times its weight.

Study Questions for 3.1
1. According to the universal law of gravitation, which objects have gravitational pull?
2. Explain why the gravitational pull at 12,000 km from the center of the earth is only a fraction as strong as at the surface of the earth.
3. How is weight different from mass?

3.2 Electric Forces

You will find out
- how like and unlike charges behave toward each other;
- how electric forces affect matter.

Figure 3.6 Lightning results from the action of electric forces.

Gravitational force is not the only force that can act between objects. To find out how another force behaves, run a comb through your hair or across a wool sweater. Then hold the comb just above some tiny pieces of torn newspaper. The paper is attracted to the comb. This attraction is caused by **electric forces.** The ancient Greeks observed the behavior of electric forces when they rubbed amber, a hard yellow-brown resin, with a cloth. The amber then attracted bits of straw. Our word *electricity* comes from the Greek word for amber *elektron*.

You have just seen that electric forces cause objects such as the comb and the paper to be attracted to each other. Whenever an object is affected by electric forces in this way, scientists say the object has acquired an **electric charge.**

In most cases objects are made up of particles with equal numbers of positive and negative electric charges. Scientists call objects with equal numbers of positive and negative charge **electrically neutral objects.** Sometimes, however, this balance between equal numbers of

Figure 3.7 Electric forces can affect your hair.

positive and negative charges is upset. This happened, for example, when you ran the comb through your hair. The comb got some negative charge from your hair. The comb, then, ended up with more negative than positive charge, or a net negative charge.

The electric force on an electrically neutral object is zero. If two objects have opposite net charges, the electric forces will cause them to be pulled toward each other. In other words, opposites **attract.** In the case of the comb and the paper the excess negative charge was attracted to the opposite, or positive, charge in the paper. On the other hand, two objects may have the same net charges. In this case, they will push each other apart, or **repel** each other.

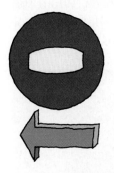 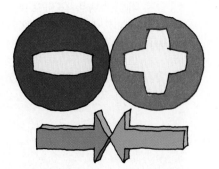 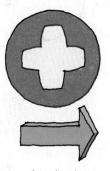

Figure 3.8 Like charges repel each other. Opposites attract.

In most objects, the number of positive and negative charges is about equal, so the object is almost electrically neutral. For this reason, the electric forces between two objects are usually small. Electric forces are still important, though, because they also determine the forces *inside* matter. For example, electric forces give steel its strength and rubber bands the ability to stretch. Electric forces cause glue to stick and muscles to tense. In fact, most of the forces that are not due to gravity can be traced to the electric forces between the charged particles that make up matter.

Study Questions for 3.2
1. Do like charges attract or repel? Unlike charges?
2. What are three examples of ways that electric forces affect matter?

3.3 Balance of Forces

You will find out
- when a state of equilibrium exists;
- how to locate an object's center of gravity.

Have you ever played tug-of-war? What happens when your team applies more force than the other team? The rope and the other team are pulled forward. Motion occurs because the pulling forces are no longer balanced. As long as your team and the other team pull with the same force but in opposite directions, neither the rope nor the teams move. These equal forces in opposite directions have canceled each other. In other words, the sum of these opposing forces is zero. The sum of the opposing forces is called the **net force.** When the net force is equal to zero, scientists say that a state of **equilibrium** [ee-kwuh-LIHB-ree-uhm] exists.

Figure 3.9 The opposing forces of the dam and the water cancel each other. A state of equilibrium exists.

Understanding how to get forces in equilibrium and how to keep them there is very important. An engineer who designs bridges must make sure that the bridge can provide enough force to balance the weight of the bridge and the weight of any vehicles that might cross over it. A dam must be strong enough to withstand the pressure of the water that the dam is holding back.

If the net force on an object is not zero, the object will start to move. In fact, the moving object will accelerate until another force comes into play and brings about an equilibrium. For example, a book resting on a desk top is in equilibrium because the gravitational force pushing down on the book is balanced by the desk top pushing up on the book. In other words, all the forces acting on the book add up to zero.

Suppose you exert another force on the book in order to lift it. The equilibrium will be destroyed, and the book will move.

Figure·3.10 *left:* A state of equilibrium exists. *right:* The state of equilibrium is destroyed.

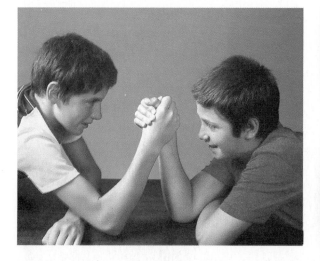 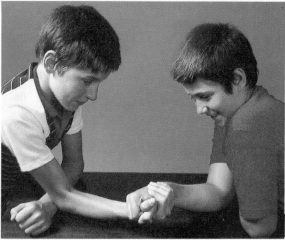

The earth's gravitational force pulls downward on every particle in an object. In order to find the forces necessary to keep an object in equilibrium, you do not need to consider every particle in that object. You can always assume that all the gravitational forces act on the object at a single point, the object's **center of gravity.** This is the point around which an object's weight is evenly placed.

ACTIVITY

Materials

cardboard
scissors
nail
ring stand
clamp
thread
weight such as a
    paper clip or
    pebble
paper punch
ruler

How Is the Center of Gravity Found?

Procedure

1. Cut a piece of cardboard into a shape similar to the one on this page.

2. Around the edge of the cardboard, punch five holes, evenly spaced. Number the holes 1 to 5.

3. Try to balance the cardboard flat on your fingertip.

4. Cut a piece of thread 30 cm long.

5. Tie the weight to one end of the thread and make a loop in the other end.

6. Set up the ring stand, clamp, and nail as shown.

7. Place the cardboard on the nail at hole 1.

8. Place the loop of the thread in front of the cardboard on the nail.

9. Make a dot where the thread hits the bottom of the cardboard.

10. Remove the thread and cardboard and use a ruler to draw a straight line from the dot to hole 1.

11. Repeat steps 7 through 10 using each of the four remaining holes.

Questions

1. What do you notice about the five lines that you drew? Try to balance the cardboard on your fingertip by placing your fingertip at the place where the five lines cross.

2. What point have you found?

3. Why do objects balance at their center of gravity?

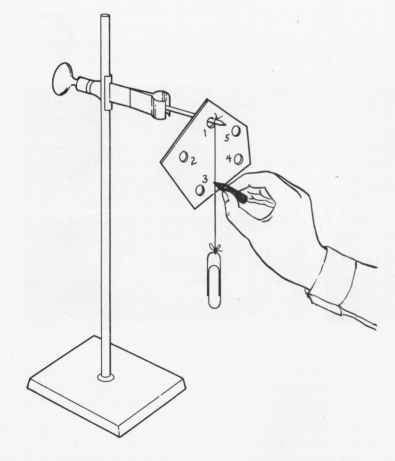

The center of gravity of a regularly shaped object, such as a cube or a sphere, is easy to find. It is in the exact center of the object. The center of gravity of an irregularly shaped object is more difficult to find. It is the place on the object where the object can be balanced without any tendency to rotate.

In a stable equilibrium an object is usually supported with its center of gravity as low as possible. If the object is not supported in this way, a small force will cause the body to move to a new position where its center of gravity is lower. A top-heavy vase, for example, tips over because its center of gravity is high. More of its weight is near the top of the vase than is safe for it to be stable. The center of gravity of a weighted punching bag is low, because most of its weight is below the middle. It does not easily tip all the way over.

Figure 3.11 The athlete's center of gravity changes as her position changes.

Study Questions for 3.3

1. Does a state of equilibrium exist in a tug-of-war game in which one team pulls with a force of 150 N and the other team pulls with the same force in the opposite direction? How can you tell?
2. How do you know when you have found an object's center of gravity?

3.4 The First Law of Motion

You will find out
- how friction affects motion;
- the first law of motion;
- what is meant by equilibrium in motion.

Figure 3.12 A hockey puck travels fast and far on smooth ice because friction is reduced.

Until about 350 years ago it was thought that the natural state of an object was that of rest. People believed that if a force were used to set an object in motion the object would come to rest when the force was removed. If you look around, your common sense seems to agree with this. A book pushed across the floor comes to rest after you stop pushing it. A ball thrown through the air takes longer to come to rest, but eventually it does.

Experiments by scientists such as Galileo showed that our common sense is wrong in many cases. Motion is, in fact, as natural a state as rest. Objects do not come to rest on their own. **Friction** is one force that slows objects down and stops them. Friction acts on a moving object in a direction opposite to the motion of the object. The more the friction can be reduced, the longer an object will stay in motion.

Newton gave a name to the tendency for objects to continue their state of motion or rest. He called this tendency **inertia** [ihn-UR-shuh]. Newton's **first law of motion,** or the law of inertia, states that every object stays in its equilibrium state unless it is acted on by outside forces. This equilibrium can exist when the object is at rest or as it moves in a straight line.

Objects will not change their motion if nothing acts on them to cause a change. For objects at rest, this is easy to understand. A book, for example, does not fly

Figure 3.13 The motion of an object in space does not change unless a force acts on it.

Figure 3.14 The law of inertia explains why you lurch forward when the car you are riding in stops suddenly.

across a room unless some outside force acts on it. What is sometimes difficult to understand is that motion with a constant velocity is also a state of equilibrium.

Consider, for example, a car moving along a straight, level road at a constant velocity. The car and its passengers are in a state of equilibrium. Now suppose that the driver of the car suddenly applies the brakes. Because of inertia, the passengers will keep moving at a constant velocity until some outside force acts to slow them down. If they are wearing seat belts, the seat belts will exert a force to cause the passengers to slow down to the same velocity as the car. If not, the dashboard or the windshield will slow them down, perhaps not so gently. Seat belts, then, protect people from the effects of the law of inertia.

According to the law of inertia, a car will have a tendency to keep moving in a straight line even if the road curves. However, friction between the tires and the road will cause the car to move in a curve along the road. As the car rounds the curve, the passengers that are not buckled in will keep moving in a straight line until they bump into the sides of the car. Next time you are riding in a car notice the ways in which inertia pulls on you as you round a curve, slow down, or speed up.

Do You Know?
The frictional force at any given joint in your body is less than a third of that encountered by the steel blade of a skate gliding on ice.

Study Questions for 3.4

1. What happens to motion when friction is reduced?
2. State the first law of motion.
3. Under what condition can a moving object be in a state of equilibrium?

3.5 The Second Law of Motion

You will find out
- what happens when an object is not in a state of equilibrium;
- the equation for Newton's second law of motion.

The law of inertia explains what happens when an object is in a state of equilibrium. When an object is not in a state of equilibrium, the object will accelerate. How will it accelerate? Newton's **second law of motion** answers this question. The second law of motion states that an object acted on by a constant force will move with a constant acceleration in the direction that the force is acting. This law can be written very simply in equation form.

Force = mass × acceleration

The second law of motion is one of the most important laws in physical science. If you know the mass of an object and the forces acting on it, you can use this law to tell exactly how an object will accelerate.

Figure 3.15 Rapid acceleration is important in a bicycle race.

The first part of the law is obvious. Objects accelerate in the direction that you push them. To get a feeling for the other parts of the law, imagine two vehicles at a stoplight. One is a subcompact car; the other, a dump truck.

Mass

Force

The mass of the truck is ten times the mass of the car. The drivers of the two vehicles want to accelerate away from the stoplight at the same rate. This means that the truck will need an engine that applies ten times more force than the subcompact car's engine. In other words, the greater the mass of an object the more force is needed to give that object the same acceleration.

Now imagine that two subcompact cars of the same mass are at the stoplight. One car has a normal four-cylinder engine. The other car has a high-powered turbocharged engine that can supply twice as much force as a normal engine. The car with the turbocharged engine will be able to move away from the stoplight with twice the acceleration as the car with the normal engine. The acceleration increases directly with the increased force.

Newton's second law applies to decelerations as well as accelerations. For example, it takes ten times as much force to stop a ten-ton dump truck traveling 80 km per hour as it takes to stop a one-ton car traveling the same distance at the same speed.

Figure 3.16 The truck has greater mass so it requires a greater force to accelerate.

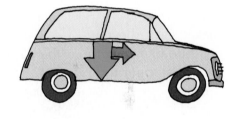

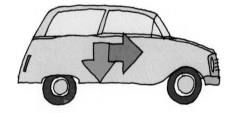

Figure 3.17 The car with the more forceful engine accelerates faster.

Study Questions for 3.5

1. What happens when the net force on an object is not zero?
2. Write Newton's second law in equation form. What happens to the force when either mass or acceleration is increased?

3.6 The Third Law of Motion

You will find out
- Newton's third law of motion;
- some examples of Newton's third law of motion.

Suppose you were to run into a tree. It would probably hurt. But it wouldn't hurt because you hit the tree. It would hurt because the tree hit you back. This observation is explained by Newton's **third law of motion.** This law states that for every action by one object there must be an equal and opposite reaction on the other object.

ACTIVITY

Materials
graduated cylinder
12 plastic straws, dowels, or round pencils
petroleum jelly
plastic gas collecting bottle or 1-L bottle
rubber stopper to fit bottle
100 mL vinegar
2 spoonfuls of baking soda
safety glasses
paper towels
apron

What Is Newton's Third Law?

Procedure

1. Put on the safety glasses and apron.

2. Place the straws about 5 cm apart side by side on the table.

3. Pour 100 mL of vinegar into the gas collecting bottle.

4. Tilt the bottle on its side. Do not let the vinegar flow into the neck of the bottle.

5. Coat the rubber stopper with petroleum jelly.

6. Place the bottle horizontally on the straws.

7. Place the baking soda in the neck of the bottle.

8. Quickly push the stopper loosely into the bottle. As you do this, make sure that the baking soda is pushed into contact with the vinegar. CAUTION: Do not stand near the bottle.

9. Observe what happens.

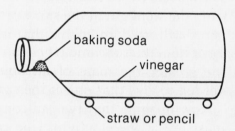

Questions

1. What happens when you mix vinegar and baking soda?

2. What does the foaming action indicate?

3. What happens to the stopper? The bottle?

4. How do the motions of the bottle and the stopper differ?

5. What caused the stopper to leave the bottle?

6. How can this experiment be used to illustrate Newton's third law of motion?

7. Did the stopper and the bottle move equal distances? Why or why not?

8. Why was the bottle put on straws?

Figure 3.18 According to Newton's third law, the oars push on the water and the water pushes on the oars.

The third law of motion completes the description of an object's motion. The first law describes how an object moves when there is no net force on it. The second law describes how an object moves when a force is applied. The third law tells what the effects are on the object that applied the force. For example, the third law explains why if you jump from a rowboat onto a dock, the boat will move backward as you move forward. When you jump, you push the boat backward, and the boat pushes you forward. In a similar way, a ship's propeller pushes on the water. The water pushes back on the ship's propeller which causes the ship to move forward.

A far more familiar example of the third law is walking. You push back on the ground with your feet and the ground pushes you forward. If the ground is icy, then you cannot push on it with enough force. The ground's push on you is therefore equally weak and you move forward slowly, if at all.

This law of action equals reaction is used in the design of jet engines and rockets for spacecraft. The rocket fuel burns producing hot gases. The gases are forced out of the rocket. This action produces an equal and opposite reaction that pushes the rocket up into space.

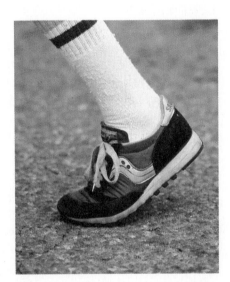

Figure 3.19 When you walk, you push on the ground and the ground pushes on you.

Study Questions for 3.6

1. What do scientists mean when they say that action equals reaction?
2. Give three examples of Newton's third law.

What Did You Learn?

- A force is a push or a pull that is applied to an object.
- The amount of gravitational force that one object exerts on another depends on the masses of the objects and how far apart their centers are.
- The universal law of gravitation states that the force of gravitation exists between any two objects in the universe.
- The measure of gravitational pull on an object is the object's weight in newtons.
- When gravitational force changes, mass remains the same but weight changes.
- Electric forces are the forces between electric charges.
- Electrically neutral objects have equal numbers of positive and negative charges.
- Two objects with like charges repel each other. Two objects with unlike charges attract each other.
- The sum of the forces acting on an object is the net force.
- A state of equilibrium is one in which the net force on an object is zero in all directions.
- The center of gravity is the point on an object where all the gravitational forces act.
- Friction is a force that slows down an object by acting in a direction opposite to the motion of the object.
- Inertia is the tendency for objects to continue their state of motion.
- Newton's first law, the law of inertia, states that every object stays in its equilibrium state unless acted on by an outside force.
- Newton's second law of motion states that force is equal to mass times acceleration.
- Newton's third law of motion states that for every force (action) there is an equal and opposite force (reaction).

Key Terms

force
gravitational force
universal law of gravitation
weight
newton
electric forces
electric charge
electrically neutral objects
attract
repel
net force
equilibrium
center of gravity
friction
inertia
first law of motion
second law of motion
third law of motion

Biography

Isaac Newton (1642–1727)

When Newton was 24, the bubonic plague struck London. In one summer 31,000 people died. Since schools had to close, Newton, who had been teaching mathematics at Cambridge University, went back to the family farm for two years. During those years, he set down the three laws of objects in motion. He also figured out the universal law of gravitation, which explains the conditions under which apples fall to the ground and the planets move around the sun.

Isaac Newton's discoveries changed the way people would look at the world forever after. Because Newton was so secretive, however, it would be almost 20 years before more than a very few people knew about his work. How was he able to do so much scientific work? "By thinking about it night and day," Newton himself said.

When thinking about a problem, Newton would forget to eat. Or if he did come to the table, he might wander off and forget to come back. According to one story, Newton got up soon after dinner was served and wandered off, leaving his food untouched. His companion took his plate, ate the food, and returned the empty plate to Newton's place. When Newton returned, he said, "I don't remember eating, but I see from my plate that I must have finished already."

Isaac Newton, a giant of science, was so small when he was born that it was said he could fit in a quart mug. Isaac was born only a few months after his father died. When Isaac was three, his mother remarried, leaving Isaac to be raised by his grandmother. Although he considered himself a poor student at the grammar school he attended, Isaac showed a natural ability for making and inventing things. He invented a small windmill to grind wheat and corn, and he even created a sundial on the wall of his grandmother's house.

TO THINK ABOUT AND DO

Number your paper from 1 to 10. Write T beside the numbers of sentences that are true and F beside the numbers of sentences that are false. If you decide a sentence is false, change the word or words in italics to make the sentence true.

1. *Gravitation* is any push or pull that affects matter.
2. Motion is caused by *balanced* forces.
3. The quantity or amount of an object is the object's *weight*.
4. *Newton* is the unit used to measure force in the metric system.
5. A state of equilibrium is one in which the net force on an object is zero in *two* directions.
6. The attraction between two objects of opposite charges is caused by *electric* forces.
7. The point where all gravitational forces act on an object is the *center of gravity*.
8. *Inertia* causes all things at rest to remain at rest until an outside force moves them.
9. Force equals mass times *acceleration*, according to Newton's second law of motion.
10. For every action there is an *unequal* and opposite reaction.

What Do You Remember?

1. What is inertia?
2. What two factors affect gravitational force?
3. What is weight? Why does weight change as you move about the earth or the solar system?
4. What force slows down moving objects?
5. Give an example to illustrate each of Newton's laws of motion.
6. Explain how you would find the force of an object if you were given its mass and acceleration.

Applying What You Have Learned

1. If you double the net force on an object, how will its acceleration be affected?
2. What will happen to the acceleration if the mass of an object is tripled but the force is kept the same?
3. What must be done to overcome the inertia of an object?

Research and Investigation

Friction affects all moving objects. Design and perform experiments to answer these questions. Before you do the experiments, have your teacher check your procedures.

1. Is there more friction between two rough objects or two smooth objects?
2. Will ball bearings or oil reduce friction more?
3. How does an increase in mass affect the amount of friction?

Work, Machines, and Power

4

Henry Ford was a man who became famous and very wealthy by using machines to make automobiles. Very likely, the machines that help people today were beyond Ford's imagination. Since Ford's time, machines have helped change the face of the earth. They have even made it possible for people to leave the earth and travel into space.

Machines and the work they do are a vital part of your everyday life. You may think most machines are big, expensive, and complicated to operate. A crane certainly is. How many people on your block own a crane? If your neighbor did own one, would you know how to run it? You and your neighbors do own and use many kinds of machines, however. Some of them require fuel or electricity to operate. Most of the machines you use have no fuel tanks or plugs. They are very inexpensive to buy and easy to use. Yet without these simple machines you could not easily turn a faucet, open a door, or even swat a fly.

4.1 Work

You will find out
- what a physical scientist means by the word *work*;
- how to find the amount of work done by a force.

Figure 4.2 No work is being done.

Many of the words used in physical science are familiar words that you use in your everyday life. Sometimes this causes a problem because physical scientists use the words in a slightly different way. Scientists don't use words differently just to be difficult. They are simply trying to communicate their observations as accurately and precisely as possible. The word *work* is a good example of this. Imagine that you spend two hours studying for a science test. Or suppose that you are a guard standing absolutely still at Buckingham Palace. In either case, there would be no doubt in your mind that you were working. But a physical scientist would say, "No. As far as physical science is concerned, you have done no work."

In physical science, **work** is done only when a force *moves* an object. The amount of work done in moving the object is equal to the strength of the force that you use times the distance the object moves.

Work = force × distance

Figure 4.3 Work is being done.

The unit of work is equal to the unit of force (newton) times the unit of distance (meter), or a newton-meter. In the metric system, the newton-meter is usually called the **joule,** abbreviated J. Therefore, one joule is the amount of work needed to maintain a force of one newton over a distance of one meter. The following example should help you understand how to find the number of joules of work that must be done.

EXAMPLE   A student lifts a book that weighs 10 newtons a distance of 50 centimeters off the floor. How much work does the student do?

SOLUTION   Here the force used to lift the book up must be equal to the gravitational force acting down on the book. Therefore an upward force of 10 newtons is needed. The distance moved is 50 centimeters, or 0.5 meters.

Work = force × distance
Work = 10 N × 0.5 m
Work = 5 N.m, or 5 J

Study Questions for 4.1

1. According to the physical scientist, what must happen in order for work to be done?
2. Tom uses 20 newtons of force to push a baby carriage a distance of 5 meters. How much work does he do?

4.2 Machines and Work

You will find out
- how machines help you to do work;
- the work principle on which all machines operate;
- how to compute the mechanical advantage of a machine.

A **machine** is a device that helps you to do work. If you remember that work is equal to force times distance, a machine helps you by changing the force or the distance or both. All machines are made up of one or more **simple machines.** Simple machines are devices that increase forces. In this way simple machines make it easier for you to do work.

No one would want a machine that makes work harder. There must be an advantage in using machines, or nobody would buy or use them. The advantage in using a machine is called a **mechanical advantage.** This mechanical advantage measures how much force you gain by using a machine rather than doing the work yourself. The bigger the mechanical advantage, the less effort you must supply.

Figure 4.4 How many of these simple machines have you used?

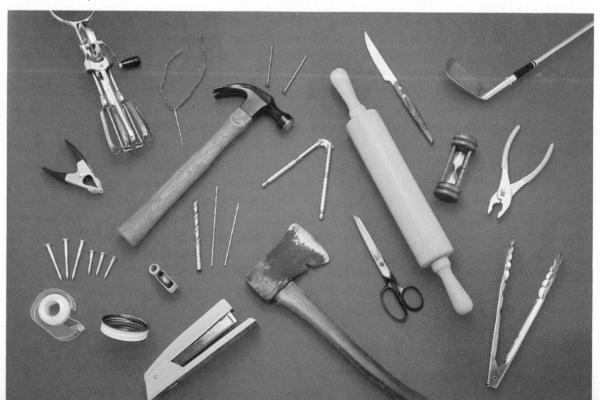

In using a machine to do any work (force times distance), there are really two forces involved. One force acts on the machine. It is called the **effort force.** When you use a machine, you provide this effort force. The second force is the force you and your machine are working against. This force is called the **resistance force.** Often the resistance force is the weight of the object to be moved.

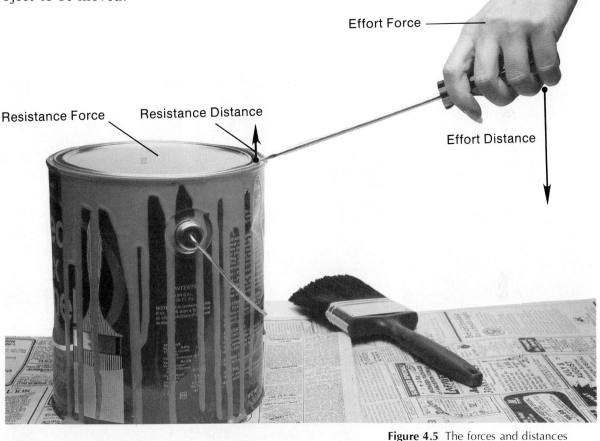

Figure 4.5 The forces and distances involved in doing work

There are also two distances involved in doing work. The distance over which your effort force acts is called the **effort distance.** The **resistance distance** is the distance the object you are doing work on is moved. Sometimes effort distance and resistance distance are the same.

All machines, no matter how simple or complex, operate on this one basic principle:

Work or energy in = work out + energy losses

Keep in mind that the work that comes out of a machine can never exceed the work that goes in. For simple machines the energy losses are usually so small that there is no need to worry about them. For this reason the principle can be written in a simple form:

Work in = work out

Since work is equal to force times distance, this principle can also be written this way:

Force × distance (effort) = force × distance (resistance)

Figure 4.6 Doing work without the help of a machine

Figure 4.7 Work finished

Figure 4.8 Doing work with the mechanical advantage of a machine

The mechanical advantage (M.A.) of any work can be calculated using either the two kinds of force mentioned or the two kinds of distance described. If you choose to use forces, you must divide the effort force (F_E) into the resistance force (F_R).

$$\text{M.A.} = \frac{F_R}{F_E}$$

Sometimes it is easier to measure the distances involved than it is to measure the forces. When that is the case, you can calculate the mechanical advantage using distances instead of forces. You divide the resistance distance (D_R) into the effort distance (D_E).

$$\text{M.A.} = \frac{D_E}{D_R}$$

Whichever way it is calculated, the mechanical advantage tells you the same thing. It tells you how much effort force was gained in using a specific machine to do a specific amount of work. Cartoon and movie superheroes don't have to worry about machines and mechanical advantages. They are strong enough to do anything without the help of machines. However, you are not! Some relatively easy work would be almost impossible for you to accomplish without the mechanical advantage of machines.

ACTIVITY

Materials

smooth board
5 books
string and scissors
spring scale

How Does a Ramp Help Do Work?

Procedure

1. Arrange 4 books and the board to form a ramp as shown in the diagram. Measure the length and height of your ramp.

2. Attach a string to the fifth book and use the spring scale to measure the effort force needed to lift the book straight up to a height equal to the height of your ramp.

3. Place the book on the very end of the ramp and use the spring scale to measure the effort force needed to pull the book up the ramp.

Questions

1. How much effort force was required to lift the book straight up? This amount equals the weight of the book.

2. How much effort force was required to pull the book up the ramp?

3. What is the mechanical advantage when you divide the weight of the book (resistance force) by the effort force needed to lift it straight up?
(Hint: $\dfrac{F_R}{F_E}$ = M.A.)

4. What is the mechanical advantage when you divide the length of the board by the height to which you lifted the book? (Hint: $\dfrac{D_E}{D_R}$ = M.A.)

5. Were your two mechanical advantages the same? If not, can you think of a reason why?

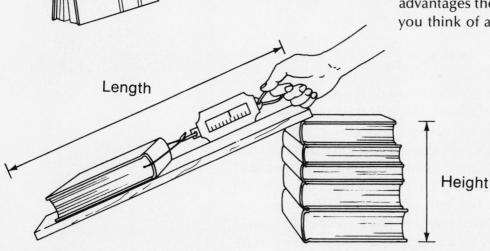

Length

Height

Figure 4.9 When you use a jack, the amount of effort force you must apply to lift a car is reduced.

Imagine that you have to change a flat tire. You have to do work. You have to use a force to lift an object, the car, up a distance off the road. You need the mechanical advantage of a machine to get this work done. A jack is a simple machine. It gives you a mechanical advantage by reducing the amount of effort force you must supply. It requires much less effort to operate a jack than it does to lock your hands under the bumper of a car and lift it up. Thus simple machines allow you to do the same amount of work with less effort.

Maybe you have never changed a tire. You are still an experienced simple machine operator. You're never out of practice. You use some types of simple machines nearly every day. You use them to open a bottle, open a door, or open a can. You use them to raise a flag, raise a sail, or raise a window shade. Simple machines help you land a fish, hit a home run, or split a log. You use them to shovel snow, rake leaves, and hammer nails. Without these simple machines many small tasks would become more difficult and time-consuming.

Figure 4.10 A simple machine you probably use often

Study Questions for 4.2

1. How do machines help you to do work?
2. What is the work principle on which all machines operate?
3. If a 100-newton force (F_E) is used to lift a 500-newton weight (F_R), what is the mechanical advantage?

4.3 The Six Simple Machines

You will find out
- how simple machines change the force;
- the names and uses of the six simple machines.

It is important to remember that simple machines operate on a single principle: apply a small force over a large distance to get a large force working over a small distance. There are six kinds of simple machines: the inclined plane, the wedge, the screw, the lever, the wheel and axle, and the pulley.

1. The **inclined plane,** or ramp, is the simplest of all machines. It increases the effort distance through which you move an object and decreases the effort force necessary to move it. An inclined plane allows you to lift heavy objects that would otherwise be very difficult to move. You can calculate the mechanical advantage of the inclined plane by dividing the length of the inclined plane (D_E) by its height (D_R). Imagine you use an inclined plane 5 meters long to lift a heavy box 3 meters up onto a platform.

$$\text{M.A.} = \frac{D_E}{D_R}$$

$$\text{M.A.} = \frac{5 \text{ m}}{3 \text{ m}} = 1.77$$

Figure 4.11 Using an inclined plane

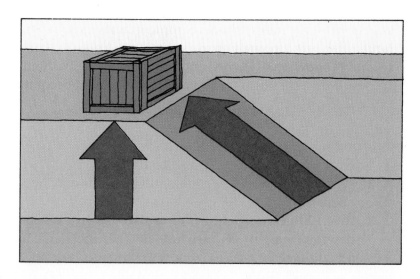

Figure 4.12 An inclined plane increases the effort distance while decreasing the effort force required.

2. The **wedge** is an inclined plane that moves. Most wedges—a woodcutter's wedge, an ax, and a nail—are made of two inclined planes. You move material *up* an inclined plane; you move a wedge *through* material. In both cases, material is moved across a sloping surface. In the case of the inclined plane, the sloping surface is held fixed and the material is pushed along it. In the case of the wedge, the material is held fixed and the sloping surface is pushed through it. For example, imagine a nail being hammered into a board. The board doesn't move. The nail, acting as a wedge, moves through it.

Figure 4.13 Using a wedge

3. The **screw** is just a combination of an inclined plane and a cylinder. Each time the screw makes a full turn, it is moved a definite distance up or down. The distance it is moved up or down in one turn depends on the distance between two threads, as shown in the diagram of the screw. In a finely threaded screw, the distance between the threads is quite small. If the distance between threads is small, you must turn the screw more times to move it into place. The more turns you use, the greater your effort distance will be. Thus the M.A., or $\dfrac{D_E}{D_R}$, of finely threaded screws is greater than that of coarsely threaded screws.

Figure 4.14 The finely threaded screw involves a greater effort distance but also requires less effort force.

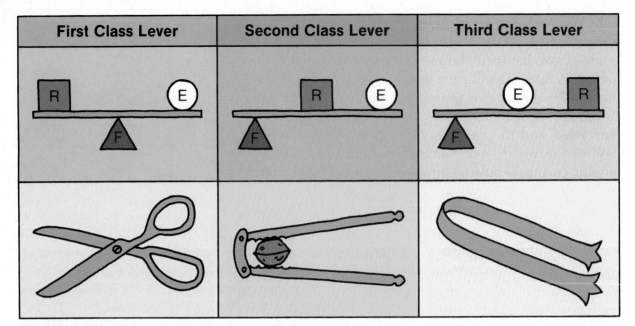

First Class Lever	Second Class Lever	Third Class Lever

Figure 4.15 Notice the relative locations of the fulcrum, the effort force, and the resistance force.

4. The **lever** is probably the simple machine that you are most familiar with. Many household gadgets and tools are forms of levers. A lever is a bar or board that is free to pivot about a fixed point. The fixed point is called a **fulcrum.**

Levers are divided into three groups: first-class, second-class, and third-class. The classes are based on the relative locations of the fulcrum, the effort force, and the resistance force. Scissors and shovels are examples of first-class levers. Bottle openers and nutcrackers are second-class levers. Tweezers and fishing rods are third-class levers.

The mechanical advantage for any lever can be quite large. To calculate the mechanical advantage for a first-class lever, you divide the distance from the effort to the fulcrum (D_E) by the distance from the resistance to the fulcrum (D_R). Imagine you use a crowbar as a lever to lift up a window. The fulcrum is located very close to the bottom of the window. If the effort distance is 50 cm and the resistance distance is 5 cm, what is the mechanical advantage?

$$\text{M.A.} = \frac{D_E}{D_R} = \frac{50 \text{ cm}}{5 \text{ cm}} = 10$$

If you have a fixed point and a long and rigid enough lever, you can lift any weight. The great Greek scientist Archimedes said it best: "Give me a fixed point, and I will move the earth."

5. The wheel is often used much like a roller as a means to reduce friction. When used as an axle, on the other hand, it is considered to be a machine. The **wheel and axle** is a simple machine that is made up of two circles. The axle is the smaller circle. The wheel is the larger one. A screwdriver or a steering wheel is a wheel and axle. So is the crank shown in Figure 4.17.

From these examples you can see that the wheel and axle is really just a lever that can move around in a circle. Since the wheel has a larger radius than the axle, the distance over which the force is applied, or effort distance, is greater than the distance over which the weight is lifted, or resistance distance.

The mechanical advantage is calculated by dividing the radius of the wheel (D_E) by the radius of the axle (D_R). Imagine you are making ice cream in an ice-cream machine. The crank you are turning is the wheel part of your wheel and axle ice-cream machine. The radius of your wheel (length of the crank) is 25 cm. The radius of the axle is 5 cm. What is the mechanical advantage of using this ice-cream machine?

$$\text{M.A.} = \frac{D_E}{D_R} = \frac{25 \text{ cm}}{5 \text{ cm}} = 5$$

Figure 4.16 Using wheels and axles

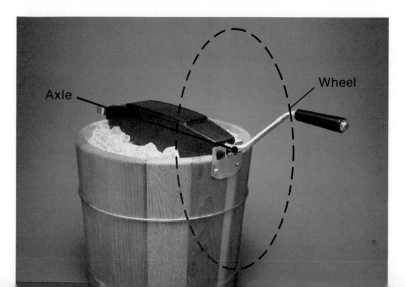

Figure 4.17 The crank is the wheel part of this wheel and axle machine.

Axle

Wheel

6. A pulley is a lever that rotates around a fixed point. It has two functions: to change the direction of the force and to provide a mechanical advantage. For the first function a simple pulley such as the one shown on the left will do. To achieve a mechanical advantage, you need a movable pulley such as the block and tackle shown on the right.

Figure 4.18 *left:* A simple pulley; *right:* A block and tackle

The rule for pulleys is the same as for the other machines. If you want to lift a heavy weight with a smaller force, then you must apply the smaller force over a larger distance than the weight is to be lifted. Suppose, for example, you must lift a car engine that weighs 1,000 newtons a distance of 1 meter. With a block and tackle, you can do this by exerting a smaller force over a greater distance. If, for instance, you exert enough force to lift only 100 newtons, then you must pull the cable over the greater distance of 10 meters. The important thing to keep in mind is that the total work done must remain the same.

ACTIVITY

Materials

pulleys
ring stand and ring
string
scissors
meterstick
book
spring scale

How Do Pulleys Help Do Work?

Procedure

1. Tie a string around the book and weigh it using the spring scale.

2. Attach the ring halfway up the ring stand.

3. Attach a pulley to the ring.

4. Tie a longer piece of string to the book and thread it through the pulley.

5. Place the book on the table and attach the spring scale to the free end of the string.

6. Have a friend hold the ring stand while you pull the spring scale and note the reading on the scale when the book is lifted off the table.

Questions

1. What was the weight of the book?

2. How much force was needed to lift the book?

3. Draw a diagram of the setup and label the fulcrum.

4. How is a pulley like a lever?

5. How do pulleys help do work?

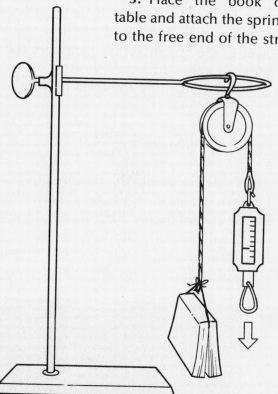

Study Questions for 4.3

1. How do simple machines change the force?
2. List the names of the simple machines and briefly describe how each is used.

4.4 Power and Efficiency

You will find out
- how to compute the rate at which work is done;
- what is meant by efficiency.

In many cases it is necessary to know more than the amount of work to be done. You must also know how long it takes to do the work. Suppose, for example, that you want to move a thousand books onto the storeroom shelves. You can use a forklift to raise all the books onto the shelves. Or you can place the books onto the shelves one at a time. In either case, the amount of work done against gravity will be the same. But the time it takes to do the work in the two cases will be greatly different. You need a quantity that measures how fast work is done. **Power** is the quantity that measures the rate at which work is done. In other words, power is the amount of work divided by the time it takes to do the work.

$$\textbf{Power} = \frac{\textbf{work}}{\textbf{time}}$$

The unit of power commonly used by physical scientists is the **watt,** named after the Scot, James Watt, who improved the steam engine. One watt is one joule of work done in one second. The watt is usually used in connection with electric power, as in a 60-watt light bulb, but a watt can describe any kind of power.

Figure 4.19 The electric mixer is more powerful than the spoon because the mixer can do the same amount of work in less time.

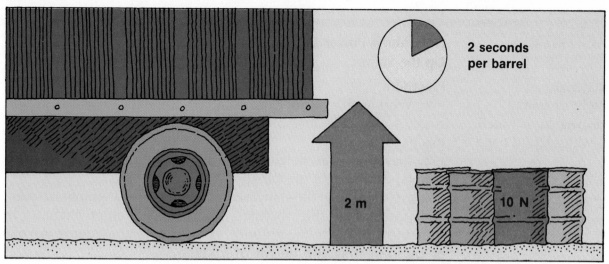

Figure 4.20 Calculating power

EXAMPLE   One hundred barrels weighing 10 newtons each are lifted 2 meters onto a truck at a rate of 1 barrel every 2 seconds. How much power is involved in doing this work?

SOLUTION   Since power $= \dfrac{\text{work}}{\text{time}}$, and you are not given the amount of work in the problem, you must first find the work in joules by using the formula, work $=$ force $\times$ distance. Therefore, work $= 10 \text{ N} \times 2 \text{ m} = 20 \text{ N.m}$, or 20 J for each barrel lifted. For 100 barrels, 20 J/barrel $\times$ 100 barrels, or 2,000 J, are needed. The total time for all 100 barrels is 2 seconds per barrel times 100 barrels, or 200 seconds.

$$\text{Power} = \frac{2{,}000 \text{ J}}{200 \text{ s}} = 10 \frac{\text{J}}{\text{s}}, \text{ or } 10 \text{ watts}$$

How much power would be used if all the barrels are lifted onto the truck in 4 seconds? Since the work to lift 100 barrels remains the same, you use the 2,000 joules of work that you found above.

$$\text{Power} = \frac{2{,}000 \text{ J}}{4 \text{ s}} = 500 \frac{\text{J}}{\text{s}}, \text{ or } 500 \text{ watts}$$

(Since 1 kilowatt $=$ 1,000 watts,
        500 watts $=$ 0.5 kilowatt.)

Do You Know?
A sleeping adult uses energy at a rate of about 80 watts.

ACTIVITY

How Much Power Do You Use to Walk Up the Stairs?

Materials
flight of stairs
stopwatch or watch
    with second hand

Procedure

1. Work with a partner. Construct a chart like the one on this page.

2. Measure the height (in meters) of the flight of stairs by going to the side of the staircase and measuring the distance from the top step to the ground or by measuring the height of one step and multiplying it by the number of stairs. Convert the height to meters.

3. Stand at the bottom of the stairs. When your partner says go, walk up the stairs.

4. Have your partner record the time in seconds that it took you to walk the distance.

5. Now time your partner and record the time on your partner's chart.

Questions

1. Complete the chart. Find the power you used by finding the work you did going up the stairs and dividing it by your time in seconds.

2. Prepare a graph to compare the different amounts of power among students in your class.

Name	Weight *(newtons)*	Distance *(meters)*	Work = Force (*N*) × Distance *(joules)*	Time *(seconds)*	Power = $\dfrac{\text{work}}{\text{time}}$ *(watts)*

A machine that could do a lot of work in a short time would be considered very powerful. When people buy and use machines, they are interested in power. They are also interested in the **efficiency** of their machines. Efficiency is a measure of how much work a machine puts out compared to the amount of work put into that machine. No machine can put out more work, output, than the work put in, input. If a machine's output equals its input, it is a very efficient machine. This almost never happens. The reason most machines have less output than input is that some of the effort force put into a machine is lost due to friction. Machines with the least amount of friction are the most efficient. High efficiency and power together are a winning combination.

Figure 4.21 The photographs show two machines used for snow removal. The power and efficiency of each machine is different.

Do You Know?
It has been estimated that all the machines in the United States do the work equivalent of over a thousand workers for every man, woman, and child in the country.

Study Questions for 4.4

1. Find the power delivered by a force of 10 newtons that acts through a distance of 4 meters in 8 seconds.
2. Why is the output of a machine almost always less than the input?

What Did You Learn?

- The amount of work done in moving an object is equal to the strength of the force that is used times the distance the object is moved in the direction of the force.
- The unit of work is the joule.
- A machine is any device that helps people do work.
- Simple machines are machines that do work by increasing forces.
- All machines operate on the principle that work or energy in equals work out plus energy losses.
- The effort force is the force applied to an object in order to move it; the resistance force is the weight of the object being moved.
- The distance over which the effort force acts is the effort distance; the distance over which the resistance force acts is the resistance distance.
- The mechanical advantage of a machine is the amount by which a machine increases the effort applied.
- To increase force, simple machines apply a small force over a large distance.
- The six simple machines are the inclined plane, the wedge, the screw, the lever, the wheel and axle, and the pulley.
- There are three classes of levers.
- The rate at which work is done, or the power, is the amount of work divided by the time it takes to do the work.
- The unit of power is the watt.
- Efficiency measures how much work a machine puts out compared to the amount of work put in.

Key Terms
work
joule
machine
simple machines
mechanical advantage
effort force
resistance force
effort distance
resistance distance
inclined plane
wedge
screw
lever
fulcrum
wheel and axle
pulley
power
watt
efficiency

Biography
Archimedes (287–212 B.C.)

Archimedes was perhaps the greatest in a long line of great Greek scientists. He was known far and wide as the best mathematician of his day, and his understanding of simple machines made him the one man in the world that the Roman army feared the most.

In the course of writing about the use of pulleys and levers to do work, Archimedes once boasted, "Give me a fixed point, and I will move the earth."

The king of Syracuse didn't want to move the earth, but he did have something heavy he wanted moved. It seems that his navy had built a very large ship. This ship was so large, in fact, that the navy could not push it into the water. The king heard of Archimedes' boast about moving the earth and took him up on it. "Move that boat into the water," he challenged Archimedes.

"I will," said Archimedes, and he constructed a system of rope pulleys and wheels and axles to do the job.

When the system was ready, Archimedes hooked one end of the rope to the ship and handed the other end to the king. As the king pulled the rope, the ship moved steadily down the beach into the water.

The last time the king of Syracuse came to Archimedes for help was when the Romans were planning an invasion. Almost single-handedly, Archimedes held off the Romans. He did this by building huge cranes that could seize the Roman ships, raise them into the air, and smash them to pieces against the rocks. In addition, he designed huge levers that hurled great rocks over the walls.

The Romans retreated in panic, terrified by "this mathematician, who plays pitch and toss with our ships and hurls a multitude of missiles at us."

TO THINK ABOUT AND DO

Vocabulary

Number a piece of paper from 1 to 10. Each numbered phrase below describes a term used in the chapter. On your paper write the term next to the number of the phrase describing it. Unscrambling the words listed may help you.

1. force times distance
2. weight of object you apply work on
3. work divided by time
4. amount by which a machine increases your effort
5. machine made up of two circles of different sizes
6. fixed point about which a lever turns
7. unit used to measure work done
8. a lever rotating about a fixed point
9. unit used to measure power
10. any device that helps to do work

wpeor
atwt
orkw
uoelj
kwro utnip
clufmur
kowr tuuopt
lyuelp
rvele
rscwe
seristcean recof
gdwee
nilnicde nealp
eewhl nda xela
hicenam
ehnclmcaia avnaedatg

What Do You Remember?

1. What two conditions must be met for work to occur?
2. What is a machine?
3. How do machines help you work?
4. What is the basic work principle on which simple machines operate?
5. How do all simple machines help do work?
6. Name six simple machines. Describe each. Give an example of each.
7. How are effort force and resistance force related?
8. What is meant by mechanical advantage?
9. What is power? Why is it important?
10. How is the power of a machine calculated?

Applying What You Have Learned

1. How much work is done if a box is moved 80 meters with a force of 5 newtons?
2. How much work is done if Sally spends 2 hours pushing a refrigerator. She uses 45 newtons of force, but the refrigerator doesn't move.
3. Explain how wedges and screws are like inclined planes and how pulleys and wheels and axles are like levers.

4. One of two trucks allows you to do 560 joules of work in 40 seconds. The other truck lets you do 999 joules of work in 45 seconds. Which is more powerful?

Research and Investigation

1. Construct a working model of each of the simple machines. Display them in such a way that others can see how they help to do work.
2. Many science-fiction stories deal with a world that is dominated by machines. Read a few of these stories in the library. Then write a story of your own to share with your classmates or to publish in the school journal.

Forces in Liquids and Gases

5

Although you are probably not aware of it, the forces in liquids and gases affect you every day of your life. Air (a gas) and water (a liquid) are important parts of your world. You experience the forces in liquids and gases every time you take a breath, turn on a faucet, or feel a soft breeze across your face. These same forces allow you to drink from a straw, float in a swimming pool, and vacuum a carpet.

Why do some objects sink in water while others float? How is it possible for a submarine to do both? What keeps an airplane up? What keeps a hot-air balloon up? What brings it back down? Why do astronauts have to wear special pressurized suits? The answers to these questions are simple when you understand the forces in liquids and gases.

Figure 5.1 Forces in liquids and gases keep a sailboat afloat and moving.

5.1 Pressure in Liquids

You will find out
- how to find the pressure exerted by an object;
- how pressure varies with area;
- how pressure varies with depth.

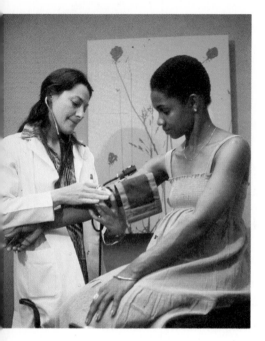

Figure 5.2 Measuring blood pressure

All of you have a rough idea of the meaning of the word *pressure*. Water pressure, air pressure, and blood pressure are three ways you may have heard the word used. To be precise, **pressure** is a force applied over a certain area. You can find pressure if you divide the force in newtons by the area in square centimeters.

$$\text{Pressure} = \frac{\text{force}}{\text{area}}$$

EXAMPLE Consider an aquarium which has a bottom surface area of 1,000 square centimeters. The weight of the aquarium and the water it contains will exert a force of 300 newtons on the table supporting the aquarium. What is the pressure exerted on the tabletop by the aquarium and the water?

SOLUTION The pressure will depend on the area, 1,000 square centimeters, over which the force acts.

$$\text{Pressure} = \frac{\text{force}}{\text{area}} = \frac{300 \text{ N}}{1,000 \text{ cm}^2} = 0.3 \text{ N/cm}^2$$

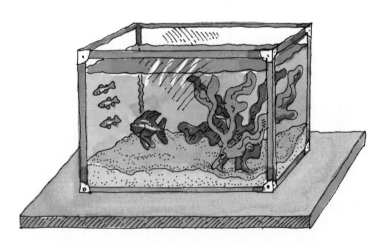

Figure 5.3 The force is concentrated over the entire area of the bottom of the aquarium.

On the other hand, if instead of a table the aquarium was supported by narrow legs having a total area of 10 square centimeters, the force would be concentrated over a much smaller area. Now the pressure would be a hundred times greater.

$$\text{Pressure} = \frac{300 \text{ N}}{10 \text{ cm}^2} = 30 \text{ N/cm}^2$$

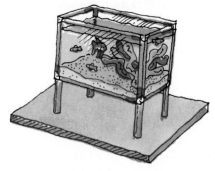

Figure 5.4 The force is concentrated over the relatively small area of the aquarium's narrow legs.

From the example you can see that the smaller the area to which a force is applied, the greater the resulting pressure. This explains why it is more comfortable to sleep on a mattress than on a bed of nails. On a mattress your weight is spread out evenly over a large area. On a bed of nails your weight is spread out over a small area—only the points of the nails.

Because a liquid has weight, it pushes down on the bottom of a swimming pool or an aquarium. In fact, the deeper the liquid the greater its pressure becomes. Consider, for example, two identical swimming pools, one full of water and the other only half full. The pressure at the bottom of the full pool is twice as great as the pressure at the bottom of the half-full pool.

Do You Know?
A person weighing 600 newtons in high-heeled shoes exerts a pressure on the floor of about 80 N/cm², more than three times that of a six-ton elephant.

Figure 5.5 The pressure at the water's surface in both pools is the same—zero. The pressure at the bottom of the half-full pool is only half as much as it is at the bottom of the filled pool.

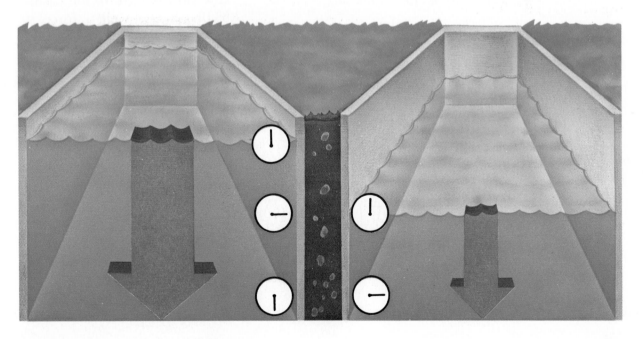

ACTIVITY

How Can You Measure Water Pressure?

Materials

ruler
milk carton
balance
plastic bottle
  or can with a
  vertical row of
  holes
adhesive tape
collection tin

Procedure

1. Copy the chart below.
2. Open the top of your milk carton so that it is a rectangular box.
3. Measure the length and width of the base of the carton and multiply these numbers to find the area.
4. Use the balance to find the mass of the milk carton. Record this mass on your chart.
5. Fill the carton to a depth of 5 cm and use the balance to find the mass of the carton plus the water. Record this mass on your chart.
6. Subtract the mass of the carton from the mass of the carton plus the water to find the mass of the water. Record the result on your chart.
7. Think about how depth effects pressure.
8. Cover the holes in your container with tape.
9. Fill the container with water.
10. Place the container over your collection tin and remove the tape from all the holes.
11. Observe the streams of water to see whether they all squirt the same distance.

Questions

1. What is the weight of the water? Hint: 1000 g = 9.8 N.
2. Recall that weight is a measure of the pull of gravitational force. Then calculate the pressure on the base of the carton by dividing the weight (force) of the water by the area of the carton's base.
3. Do all the streams of water squirt the same distance?
4. Which stream squirts the farthest?
5. From your observation of the streams of water how are pressure and depth related?

Length of carton bottom (cm)	
Width of carton bottom (cm)	
Area of carton bottom (cm²)	
Mass of carton (g)	
Mass of carton with water (g)	
Mass of water (g)	
Weight of water (N)	
Pressure (N/cm²)	

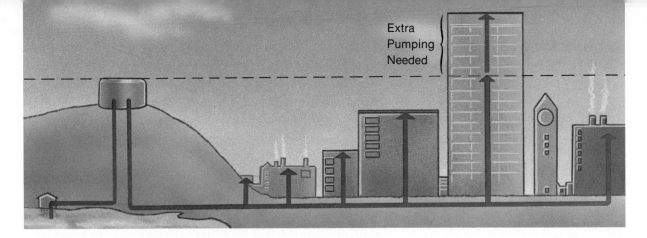

Extra
Pumping
Needed

One of the most important applications of the increase of pressure with depth is water towers. Water is pumped from a reservoir into a tower that is usually located on the highest hill in the area. The weight of the water in the tower produces a large amount of pressure at the bottom of the pipe. This pressure is used to drive the water through the pipes to houses and other buildings. In the case of houses on a hill higher than the water tower or in skyscrapers above the water tower, water pumps have to be used.

The increase of pressure with depth is true of all **fluids.** By fluids, scientists mean any substance that flows. Generally, liquids and gases are considered to be fluids, and solids are not. Even though liquids and gases flow readily, there is no perfectly fluid substance. All fluids do not flow at the same rate. Honey, water, and air, for example, flow at different rates.

Figure 5.6 The weight of the water in the tower produces the pressure to drive water through pipes and into buildings.

Study Questions for 5.1

1. A container that weighs 120 newtons is placed on a tabletop. If the base of the container has an area of 3,600 square centimeters, how much pressure does the container exert on the tabletop?

2. Two blocks each weighing 100 newtons are placed on a table. If the base of block A has an area of 50 square centimeters and the base of block B has an area of 10 square centimeters, which block exerts the greater pressure?

3. What effect does increasing water depth have on scuba divers?

5.2 Buoyancy

You will find out
- what is meant by the word *buoyancy;*
- what is stated in Archimedes' principle;
- how to find the density of an object;
- how to predict whether an object will float.

Have you ever noticed that it's easier to lift a person in water? This is due to the upward force, or **buoyancy** [BOY-uhn-see], of water. Buoyancy is the name given to the force that pushes an object up and makes it seem to lose weight in a fluid. In this case, the amount of weight a person seems to lose in the water is actually the weight of the water that the person moves aside by standing in it.

Why do some objects float in water while others sink? If you want to know which objects will float in water, you need to know more about the force exerted by the fluid. You need to know the strength of the buoyant force compared to the weight of an object.

Over 2,000 years ago the Greek scientist Archimedes figured out the strength of the buoyant force as he was taking a bath. Legend has it that Archimedes became so excited about having solved the buoyancy problem that he jumped out of the tub and ran naked down the main street of town, yelling "Eureka! Eureka!" which means "I have found it." What Archimedes discovered is that the buoyancy of any object is equal to the weight of the liquid that the object displaces, or pushes aside. This relationship between buoyancy and the weight of the fluid being displaced is known as **Archimedes' principle.**

Figure 5.7 The buoyant force of water allows you to float on it.

Since the buoyant force acts upward, it opposes the downward force of the weight of the object. If the buoyant force is equal to the weight of the object, then the object will float. For example, a piece of wood having a volume of 100 cubic centimeters weighs only half as much as 100 cubic centimeters of water, so it will float on water. In other words, an object will float if it weighs less than the weight of the water it displaces.

On the other hand, a piece of steel having a volume of ten cubic centimeters weighs about eight times as much as the same volume of water. You can see that steel will not float. Why then are ships made out of steel? The answer lies in the ship's design. The ship is constructed so that it is made mostly of air. That is, the inside of the ship is hollow. Since the combination of steel plus air weighs less than the water the ship displaces, the ship will float.

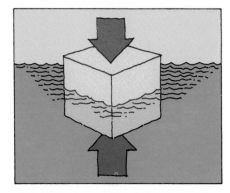

Figure 5.8 The weight of the water displaced by the block equals the weight of the block.

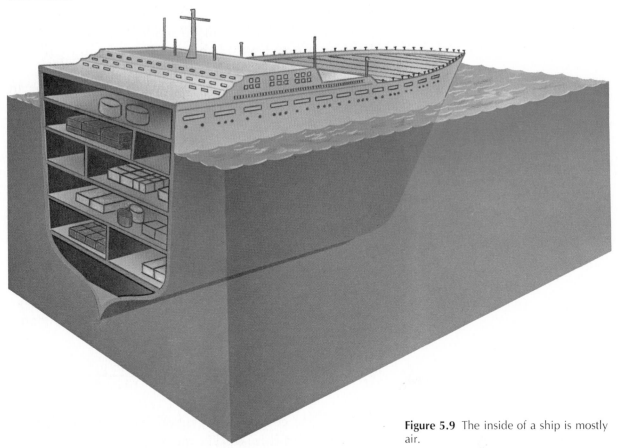

Figure 5.9 The inside of a ship is mostly air.

Figure 5.10 Like submarines, the oceanographic research vessel *Alvin* sinks below the water's surface by filling its hollow tanks with water.

If a ship is built so that it can take water into tanks in its hollow interior, it can be made to sink. When the water is pumped out of these tanks, the ship will rise again. This is the principle behind the submarine.

Another way to express Archimedes' principle is in terms of the **density** of a substance. Density is the mass of a substance in grams divided by its volume in cubic centimeters.

Do You Know?
Not all wood floats. Ironwood has a density of 1.07 times that of water, so it sinks when put in water.

$$\text{Density} = \frac{\text{mass}}{\text{volume}}$$

EXAMPLE The mass of 10 cubic centimeters of iron is 78 grams. The mass of the same volume of mercury is 136 grams. Which substance has the greater density?

SOLUTION

$$D(\text{iron}) = \frac{\text{mass (iron)}}{\text{volume (iron)}} = \frac{79 \text{ g}}{10 \text{ cm}^3} = 7.9 \text{ g/cm}^3$$

$$D(\text{mercury}) = \frac{\text{mass (mercury)}}{\text{volume (mercury)}} = \frac{136 \text{ g}}{10 \text{ cm}^3} = 13.6 \text{ g/cm}^3$$

Mercury, a liquid metal, has a greater density than iron, a solid metal.

Stated in terms of density, Archimedes' principle says that an object will float in a fluid if the density of that object is less then the density of the fluid. From Table 5–1, you can see that wood, ice, and gasoline will float in water, whereas most other substances will not.

Because it contains salt, sea water is more dense than fresh water. As a result, the same boat would float higher in sea water than in fresh water. The reason for this is that it takes a smaller amount of displaced salt water to equal the weight of the boat.

The water in the Great Salt Lake in Utah is very salty and much more dense than sea water. If you were to go swimming in the Great Salt Lake, you would immediately notice the amazing buoyancy of the very dense and salty water. In fact, you could almost float in a sitting position!

Table 5–1 Densities of Several Materials

Material	Density (g/cm³)
hydrogen*	0.00009
helium*	0.00018
air*	0.0013
white pine	0.5
gasoline	0.7
oak	0.7
ice	0.92
human fat	0.92
water	1.00
sea water	1.02
bone	1.8
aluminum	2.7
iron	7.9
lead	11.3
mercury	13.6
gold	19.3

*gas densities measured at room temperature at sea level

Figure 5.11 The salt water of the Dead Sea is so dense that you can float effortlessly.

You have seen how a solid can float in a liquid that is more dense. It is also possible for a liquid to float on another, more dense liquid. A very familiar example of this situation occurs with bottled salad dressing. What do you do to bottled dressing before pouring it on a salad? You shake the bottle to mix the dressing. Why won't the dressing stay mixed? Why must you shake the bottle every time you use it? Salad oil is less dense than vinegar. The oil floats in a layer on top of the vinegar.

ACTIVITY

How Do The Densities of Some Solids and Liquids Compare?

Materials

1 liter clear bottle
200 mL corn syrup
200 mL vinegar
200 mL cooking oil
red food coloring
blue food coloring
Styrofoam pieces
    about 1 cm × 1 cm
aluminum foil pellets
    the size of small
    pebbles
toothpick pieces
    2 cm long
2 safety matches
penny
graduated cylinder
Styrofoam cup ·
stirring rod
apron

Procedure

1. Put on your apron.
2. Pour 200 mL of vinegar into your bottle.
3. Add a few drops of red food coloring. Stir.
4. Pour 200 mL of corn syrup into a Styrofoam cup.
5. Add a few drops of blue food coloring. Stir.
6. Pour the corn syrup into the bottle of vinegar and observe.
7. Pour 200 mL of cooking oil into the bottle and observe.
8. Drop the matches into the bottle and observe.
9. Drop the Styrofoam pieces into the bottle and observe.
10. Drop the penny into the bottle and observe.
11. Drop the aluminum pellets into the jar and observe.
12. Drop the toothpick pieces into the jar and observe.

Questions

1. What happened when the corn syrup was added to the vinegar?
2. What happened when the cooking oil was added to the bottle?
3. Draw a picture with labels to show how the materials arranged themselves in the jar.
4. Which material is the most dense?
5. Which material is the least dense?
6. Name 2 materials more dense than vinegar.
7. Name 4 materials less dense than vinegar.
8. What determines whether a material will float or sink in a certain liquid?

Shaking the bottle mixes the oil and vinegar only temporarily. After a short while the two liquids return to their original layered positions.

Another example of a liquid floating on a liquid occurs with crude oil and sea water. When a supertanker accidentally spills its cargo of crude oil into the sea, what happens? Crude oil is less dense than sea water so the oil floats on top of the water creating an oil slick. Oil slicks can cause serious ecological problems. Sea birds become coated with the oil and die. The oil sometimes floats to shore and fouls beaches. Sea life under the oil layer is threatened. Scientists and engineers are currently studying ways to clean up such oil slicks.

Figure 5.12 Because it is less dense, oil floats on top of water.

Study Questions for 5.2

1. What is the name of the upward force on an object in a fluid?
2. What is stated in Archimedes' principle?
3. The volume of a 20-gram bar is 5 cubic centimeters. What is the density of the bar?
4. If the density of mercury is 13.6 grams per cubic centimeter, is it possible for lead, whose density is 11.3 grams per cubic centimeter, to float in mercury?

5.3 Atmospheric Pressure

You will find out
- what is meant by atmospheric pressure;
- why atmospheric pressure decreases with height;
- how you use atmospheric pressure.

Figure 5.13 As altitude increases, atmospheric pressure decreases.

0 N/cm²

1 N/cm²

10 N/cm²

So far you have only seen examples of increasing pressure in liquids. This same effect also occurs in air, a gas. To be sure, it takes a huge column of air to produce a noticeable pressure. Keep in mind, however, that you are living at the bottom of a rather deep ocean of air. The weight of several kilometers of air produces what is known as the **atmospheric pressure,** or air pressure. Atmospheric pressure is therefore the pressure exerted by the weight of the earth's atmosphere.

At the earth's surface, the atmospheric pressure is equal to a little more than ten newtons per square centimeter. This pressure does not crush you because it is balanced by other pressures from inside your body.

As you go upward from sea level, the atmospheric pressure decreases. This happens because you're not as deep in the atmosphere. Therefore, the weight of the overlying layers of the atmosphere is less. In outer space there is little or no atmosphere. The pressure is zero. What would happen to an astronaut in space who did not have a pressurized suit? The astronaut would explode, since pressure inside the body would be greater than pressure outside the body.

Jets fly at heights of ten kilometers above sea level. There the atmospheric pressure is less than a third the pressure at sea level. Jet cabins must be pressurized for the comfort and safety of the passengers and crew.

Figure 5.14 Astronauts must wear pressurized suits.

Figure 5.15 The hot air in a hot-air balloon is less dense and, thus, weighs less than an equal volume of cooler air. This situation explains why hot-air balloons float in air.

The air exerts a buoyant force on objects, just as liquids do. According to Archimedes' principle, an object will float in air if it weighs less then the air it displaces. Thus, objects whose density is less than the density of air will float. Since air has such a low density, not many objects can float in it. But large balloons filled with hot air or helium are less dense than air and rise to great heights.

Back on the earth, you continually use the air pressure all around you to your advantage. For example, by expanding your lungs, you create a low-pressure region inside the lungs. The higher pressure outside your body will force air into your lungs. You do this thousands of times every day, each time you take a breath.

You also use air pressure to force liquids into your body. When you suck on a straw, for example, you lower the air pressure inside your mouth. This lowered pressure causes the outside air pressure to push the liquid in a glass up through the straw and into your mouth. This same principle of suction that causes a liquid to be forced into a straw is used in pumps to raise water from wells and in vacuum cleaners.

Do You Know?
To fill its lungs for the first time, a new baby must create a suction 50 times greater than a healthy adult creates to take an average breath.

Study Questions for 5.3

1. What is atmospheric pressure?
2. Where is atmospheric pressure greater, at sea level or on a mountaintop?
3. Describe two ways in which you use air pressure.

5.4 Objects Moving in Air

You will find out
- what is meant by the term *drag;*
- how the shape of an object affects drag;
- what is meant by the term *lift;*
- how the velocity of a fluid affects pressure.

Can a substance as light as air exert a force? Any time the wind blows, the force of air in motion becomes evident. It causes blades of grass and branches of trees to bend. It pushes kites up in the air. It can move a boat across a lake or even an ocean. By standing in front of a fan, you can get an idea of the strength of the forces of moving air.

Air, whether moving or still, causes friction with any object moving in it. Friction, you remember, is a force that acts on a moving object in a direction opposite to the motion of that object. Friction generally acts to decrease the speed of a moving object. When you are walking through calm air, you are not aware of the friction created between your moving body and the air. Even so, the force is there. When you throw or hit a baseball, friction is created between the moving ball and the air. A moving car or airplane also experiences friction with air. Engineers often refer to friction created when objects move in air as **drag**.

Figure 5.16 The force of air in motion is often evident during bad weather.

The amount of drag depends on the shape of the moving object. If the air has to make too sharp a turn in flowing around the wings of a plane, for example, the flow pattern becomes highly disordered. The flight becomes turbulent. In this case, there is too much drag. Engineers get around this by designing planes with streamlined bodies that have long tapered shapes. The air can then flow smoothly around the tapered bodies, and the drag is reduced.

The best shape for reducing drag depends on the speed of the object. For the low speeds of propeller-driven planes, the teardrop shape is the best. For supersonic aircraft, a slender body with a pointed nose is best.

Because of the increasing cost of fuel, engineers and scientists are doing a great deal of research on ways to reduce the drag of automobiles and trucks. They have found that changing the shape can change the air flow pattern and reduce the drag. Reducing the drag saves fuel.

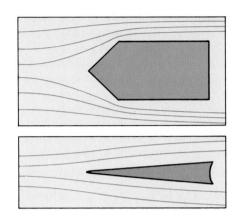

Figure 5.17 Air flows more smoothly around the tapered shape.

Figure 5.18 In this specially designed speed bicycle, the cyclists are positioned to minimize drag.

Buoyant forces can lift objects into the air only if the objects are less dense than air. How do objects that are denser than air, such as airplanes, get off the ground and fly? **Lift** is used. Lift is the upward force of air moving around an object. In the case of an airplane, the lift is produced by a difference in air pressure on the top and bottom sides of the wing.

ACTIVITY

Materials

2 pieces of string
(30 cm long)
2 Ping-Pong balls
straw
ring stand and
clamp
dowel
scotch tape
index card

How Can You Demonstrate Differences in Air Pressure?

Procedure—Part I

1. Place the dowel in the clamp so it is parallel to your desk.

2. Tape a piece of string to each Ping-Pong ball.

3. Suspend the balls from the dowel so they are the same distance above the desk and about 2 cm apart.

4. Use the straw to blow a stream of air between the balls. Observe.

Part II

1. Fold the ends of the index card on the imaginary lines shown in the diagram.

2. Place the index card on your desk so it is standing on the folded edges as shown in the diagram.

3. Use the straw to blow a stream of air under the index card. Observe.

4. Use the straw to blow a stream of air over the top of the index card. Observe.

Questions

1. How did the Ping-Pong balls act when you blew a stream of air between them?

2. Explain why they acted as they did.

3. When did the index card flip over?

4. Explain why it flipped over.

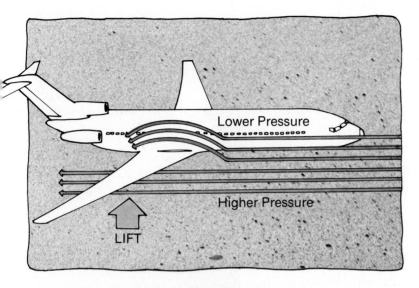

Figure 5.19 The lift of an airplane results from pressure differences below and above the wing.

Daniel Bernoulli, a Swiss scientist who lived in the eighteenth century, discovered that the faster a fluid moves the less pressure it exerts. You can see this effect by holding a thin slip of paper under your mouth and blowing across it. The pressure in the stream of air moving across the top of the paper will be less than the pressure in the still air underneath the paper. As a result, the force on the bottom side of the paper will be greater than that on the top, and the paper will be pushed upward, or lifted.

Airplane wings are designed so that the air will flow faster across the top of the wing than across the bottom. This makes the pressure lower on the top of the wing than on the bottom. The wing is pushed upward. The same principle lifts helicopters off the ground, except that in their case, the lift is produced by rotating wings.

Study Questions for 5.4

1. What is drag?
2. How can an object's shape reduce drag?
3. What is lift?
4. Why are airplane wings designed so that the airflow across the top of the wing is faster than the flow across the bottom?

What Did You Learn?

- Pressure is the force applied by an object divided by the area over which the force acts.
- The smaller the area to which a force is applied, the greater is the resulting pressure.
- Pressure increases as the depth of a fluid increases.
- Buoyancy is the upward force on an object in a fluid.
- Archimedes' principle states that the buoyancy of any object is equal to the weight of the fluid that the object pushes aside.
- Density is the mass of a substance divided by its volume.
- An object will float in a fluid if the density of that object is less than the density of the fluid.
- Atmospheric pressure is the pressure exerted by air as a result of the weight of the earth's atmosphere.
- Atmospheric pressure decreases as height increases because the weight of overlying air layers decreases with increasing altitude.
- Examples of the use of atmospheric pressure include forcing air into the lungs and liquids into the mouth, sucking dirt into a vacuum cleaner, and pumping water from wells.
- The friction that is created by an object moving in air is often called drag.
- The shape of an object can reduce drag by allowing air to flow smoothly around the object.
- Lift is the upward force of moving air on the the wings of an airplane.
- The faster a fluid moves the less pressure it exerts.

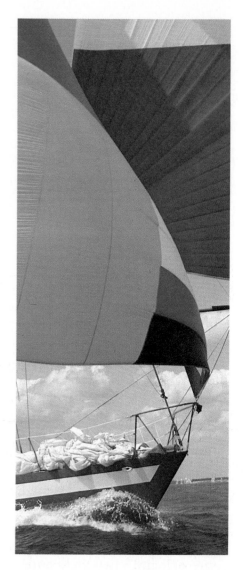

Key Terms

pressure
fluids
buoyancy
Archimedes' principle
density
atmospheric pressure
drag
lift

Career

Aerospace Careers

Aerospace engineers, scientists, and technicians work as a team to design and develop airplanes and spacecraft. For example, scientists will do research on the drag and lift expected on a certain shape of aircraft. Engineers and technicians will then build a scale model of this design and test it in wind and heat tunnels. If this testing is successful, then a full-sized experimental model, or prototype, is built and thoroughly tested on the ground and in the air. Before the aircraft is put into production, the design will be changed many times until the test results are completely satisfactory.

The aerospace industry employs thousands of workers in many different companies as scientists, engineers, technicians, production workers, or administrators. The largest concentration of aerospace jobs in this country is in California, but New York, Washington, Connecticut, Texas, Missouri, and Kansas also have a large number of aerospace companies.

TO THINK ABOUT AND DO

Vocabulary

Number a sheet of paper 1 through 9. Select the best answer to complete each of the following sentences. Record the letter of each answer next to the proper number.

1. The force applied by an object divided by the area over which the force acts is the (a) drag, (b) buoyancy, (c) pressure.
2. Pressure increases with an increase in a fluid's (a) depth, (b) altitude, (c) velocity.
3. Any substance that flows is called a (a) force, (b) fuel, (c) fluid.
4. The upward force on an object in a fluid is called (a) gravitation, (b) drag, (c) buoyancy.
5. The mass of a substance divided by its volume is the (a) density, (b) pressure, (c) lift.
6. The pressure exerted by air as a result of the weight of the earth's atmosphere is called (a) atmospheric pressure, (b) water pressure, (c) blood pressure.
7. The friction created when an object moves in air is often called (a) lift, (b) gravitation, (c) drag.
8. The upward force of moving air on the wing of an airplane is called (a) drag, (b) lift, (c) density.
9. The fact that the faster a fluid moves the less pressure it exerts was discovered by (a) Archimedes, (b) Bernoulli, (c) Newton.

What Do You Remember?

1. If you reduce the area to which you apply a force, what happens to the amount of pressure being exerted?
2. What is the name of the principle that describes the relationship between buoyancy and the weight of a displaced fluid? State the principle.
3. How can you predict whether an object will float?
4. Why must the cabins of jet planes be pressurized?
5. How does an object's shape affect the drag on the object?

Applying What You Have Learned

1. A block has an area of 55 square centimeters and a weight of 495 newtons. How much pressure can it exert?
2. Explain how an eyedropper is used. Use the term *air pressure* in your explanation.
3. How can density be used to determine whether objects float or sink in liquids?
4. Why does an object seem to lose weight when you put it in water?

Research and Investigation

Use the reference books in your library to answer these questions.
1. If you were a scuba diver, how would you protect yourself from increased water pressure at great depths?
2. How is specific gravity related to density?

Unit Two

The Structure of Matter

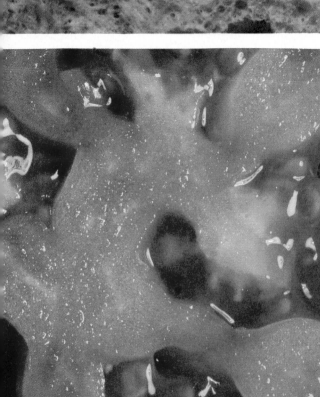

The Atom

6

As you study the structure of matter, the simplest question you might ask is "What is matter?" You have already learned that matter occupies space and is the substance that the universe is made of. In this chapter you will probe more deeply into matter, take it apart, and find out what it is made of.

In probing matter, you will follow in the footsteps of people who lived over two thousand years ago in Egypt and Greece. For the Egyptians of that day the chemistry of matter was strongly connected with the embalming of the dead and religious ritual. The Greeks, on the other hand, were more concerned with changing one substance to another. If wood could be changed to fire and ashes, why couldn't iron be turned to gold?

Today scientists study matter in chemical laboratories and in giant atom smashers that tear apart the cores of atoms. The goal is the same, however. The scientists are trying to understand matter and to see if they can take it apart and rearrange it in more useful ways.

Figure 6.1 Can you identify the four familiar items pictured? The photographs were taken at very close range. In this chapter you will examine matter at much closer range.

6.1 The Atomic Model of Matter

You will find out
- how the alchemists contributed to science;
- what elements are;
- what atoms are;
- what compounds are.

When you look at the world around you, you see that it is filled with an amazing variety of substances. You see all different shapes, sizes, and colors. Some substances are soft; others are hard. Some are solids, others are liquids, and still others are gases.

Figure 6.2 Your world is filled with different substances having different properties.

Long ago the people who sought to answer the question of what matter is made of were called **alchemists.** Alchemists believed that if they could find the basic unit of matter, or primary matter as they called it, they could do wonderful things. With primary matter they thought they could change ordinary metals into gold and ordinary water into a liquid that would stop the aging process. In the course of their search they tested all known substances. They burned them, boiled them, crushed them, strained them, filtered them, and mixed them. Some of the alchemists went crazy in the process. But none of them ever found the primary matter.

Figure 6.3 A painting of alchemists at work

What the alchemists did do was to establish the laboratory and an experimental approach of taking matter apart to analyze it. This set the stage for eighteenth and nineteenth century scientists who showed that all matter is composed of basic substances called **elements.** Elements are substances that cannot be chemically broken down into simpler basic substances.

The smallest particles of individual elements are called **atoms.** The element hydrogen is made only of hydrogen atoms, the element helium only of helium atoms, the element oxygen only of oxygen atoms, and so on. All hydrogen atoms are alike, but they are different from all helium and oxygen atoms. For example, one oxygen atom weighs sixteen times as much as one hydrogen atom.

Figure 6.4 *left:* All items made of the element gold contain only gold atoms. *right:* All items made of the element iron contain only iron atoms.

ACTIVITY

What Are the Properties of Some Elements?

Materials

copper wire
iron wire
magnesium ribbon
carbon pieces
iodine crystals
beaker
aluminum foil
Bunsen burner
battery
bell wire
light bulb in
  porcelain socket
2 jar lids
ring stand and
  small ring
forceps
safety glasses
apron

Procedure

1. Copy the chart and use it to record your observations.

2. Put on your safety glasses and apron.

3. Place each element in a beaker of water. If it is more dense than water, it will sink. If it is less dense than water, it will float.

4. Set up the conductivity apparatus as shown. Test each element. If it is a conductor, the bulb will light.

5. Test the effects of heat in the following ways:

a. Make a handle by wrapping aluminum foil around the end of the copper wire, iron wire, and the magnesium ribbon.

b. Light the Bunsen burner. One at a time, hold each element by its handle and heat. CAUTION: Do not look directly at the magnesium ribbon while heating it. Turn off the Bunsen burner.

c. To test carbon and iodine, use a clean jar lid for each. Set up the ring stand and ring so that the Bunsen burner can be placed under the ring. Place a lid on the ring.

d. Place a small amount of the element on the lid and heat.

e. What change do you immediately notice in iodine? Remove the flame. Use forceps to handle the heated lid.

f. Heat the carbon for only three minutes.

Questions

1. Complete the chart.

2. Based on your observations, place similar elements together in groups.

Element	Color, Shape	Denser Than Water?	Conductor of Electricity?	Changes When Heated
copper				
iron				

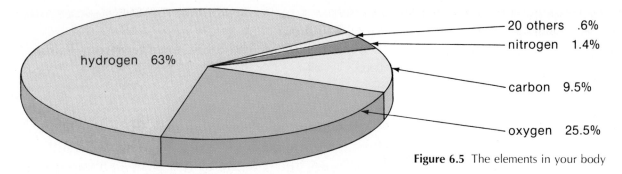

Figure 6.5 The elements in your body

More than a hundred different elements have been discovered so far. Most of these elements last a very long time—no one knows for sure just how long. Many have been around for at least as long as the earth. These elements are called **natural elements.** Natural elements are found in nature and do not have to be made in the laboratory. Other elements have been observed only in the laboratory where they were made. Some of these do not last long. The element einsteinium, for example, lasts for only a fraction of a second.

Everything in the world around you is made of one or more elements. Some familiar substances such as silver and gold are elements. Other substances are combinations of elements. For example, water is a combination of hydrogen and oxygen. By itself hydrogen is a colorless, tasteless gas. Oxygen is a colorless, odorless gas that must be present for burning to occur. In the right combination, however, hydrogen and oxygen form water, a liquid whose properties are completely different from either hydrogen or oxygen. Carbon dioxide is another combination of elements. It is made of carbon and oxygen. These combinations of two or more elements are called **compounds.**

Study Questions for 6.1

1. How did the alchemists contribute to the progress of science?
2. What are the basic substances of which all matter is composed?
3. What are atoms?
4. What are compounds? Give two examples.

6.2 The Structure of Atoms

You will find out
- what ideas about the atom emerged from Rutherford's work.

What are atoms made of? What makes one type of atom different from another? It is not the atom's size. Almost all atoms are about the same tiny size. About a million atoms stacked end to end would have a thickness equal to the thickness of only five pages in this book!

The clue to differences among atoms was found in 1911 in England by Ernest Rutherford and his co-workers. Rutherford was known to students as the alligator because of his ferocious personality. A short time before, it had been discovered that radium and certain other elements were **radioactive.** That is, certain elements give off high-energy particles. Rutherford saw that these high-energy particles could be used to probe the structure of atoms.

To understand how atomic structure was investigated, imagine you are an inspector at a secret physical science laboratory that is making a special metal. This metal is so strong that a sheet of it, no thicker than a page of this book, could cause bullets to bounce off it. A man shows up at the gate. He wants to take a truckload of old books and reports out of the laboratory to the dump. You suspect that he may be smuggling a sheet of this metal out of the laboratory in one of the books, but there is no way you can look through all the pages of all the books. What do you do?

After some thought you come upon a plan. You will shoot a bullet through each book. If the bullet passes through the book, it has none of the metal in it. If the bullet bounces off the book, it contains the metal. In this way you catch the smuggler and become a hero.

This is basically what Rutherford's group did. They shot high-energy particles into atoms and watched to see what happened. Some of the particles bounced back. A careful study of how the particles bounced back showed that the atom has a small but dense core called

Figure 6.6 The atoms in an enormous elephant are no bigger than the atoms in a tiny fly.

Figure 6.7 Like a spider web, an atom is mostly open space.

the **nucleus.** At each point where a particle hit a nucleus, the particle bounced back. If the particle didn't strike a nucleus, it just kept going. The nucleus, which has a positive electric charge, is surrounded by negatively charged particles called **electrons.** The electrons have a much smaller mass than the nucleus has. Yet the actual size of the nucleus is very small. Its diameter is a hundred thousand times smaller than that of the whole atom. Nevertheless, the tiny nucleus has 99.9 percent of the mass of the atom.

A new idea of the atom emerged from these studies. In the center is the massive nucleus, with a positive charge. Orbiting around the nucleus at great distances from it are the negatively charged electrons.

The structure of the nucleus of an atom determines what kind of element you have. In the next lesson, you will see why.

Do You Know?
It takes about 300,000 atoms stacked end to end to get a thickness equal to a hair.

Study Question for 6.2

How did Rutherford's work contribute to knowledge of atomic structure?

6.3   The Atomic Nucleus

You will find out
- what types of particles make up the nucleus;
- what is meant by atomic number and atomic mass number;
- what is meant by isotopes;
- what quarks are.

You have seen that most of the mass of an atom is concentrated in a very small region called the nucleus. Can the nucleus be made of smaller units, just as elements are made up of atoms? If the nucleus is hit with particles of high enough energy, it can actually be split apart. The answer then is yes; the nucleus is made of smaller units.

As a result of studies by Rutherford and others, it was learned that every nucleus consists of two types of particles. One type, the **proton,** has a positive charge of one unit. This is just the opposite charge of an electron, which has a negative charge of one unit. The other type of particle, the **neutron,** has no charge. It is electrically neutral as its name suggests. Neutrons have a mass that is about the same as that of the proton. Both neutrons and protons have a mass about 1,800 times larger than the electrons. This explains why most of the mass of an atom is concentrated in the nucleus.

Figure 6.8 The locations of the proton, the neutron, and the electron in an atom

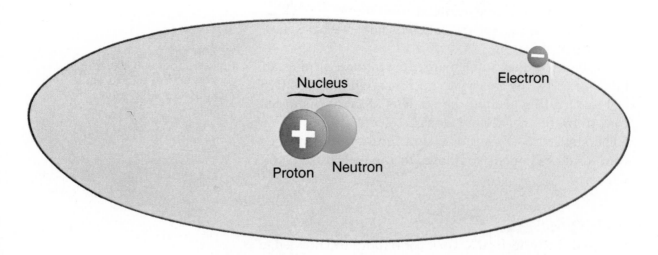

ACTIVITY

Materials
gumdrops
index cards
wire coat
   hanger
thread and
   blunt needle
clay
glue

How Can You Build a Model of the Atom?

Procedure

1. To create a model of helium, select three gumdrops of one color, three gumdrops of a second color, and three gumdrops of a third color.

2. Use the needle and thread to sew together two gumdrops of one color and two gumdrops of another color. This will be the nucleus.

3. Stretch out your coat hanger until it is as circular as possible. Then glue two gumdrops of a third color on the hanger.

4. Stand the hanger up in a lump of clay.

5. Use a piece of thread to suspend your nucleus in the center of the atom.

6. Glue a gumdrop of each color on an index card you have labeled Key to Helium Atom and write which particle of the atom each represents.

Questions

1. Why is the nucleus made up of two different colors of gumdrops?

2. Given a key for lithium with three protons and four neutrons in the nucleus, how would you create an atomic model of lithium?

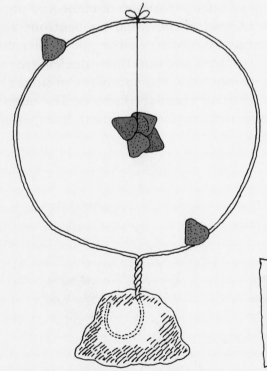

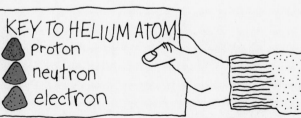

KEY TO HELIUM ATOM
proton
neutron
electron

The total number of protons in a given nucleus determines the type of element you have. This number, which is also called the **atomic number** of the element, is different for each element. For example, hydrogen has one proton in its nucleus, or an atomic number of one. Helium has two, and lithium three.

In most nuclei, the number of neutrons is equal to or slightly greater than the number of protons. Most helium nuclei have two protons and two neutrons. Most carbon nuclei have six protons and six neutrons; most oxygen nuclei have eight protons and eight neutrons. As the elements get more massive, they tend to have an excess number of neutrons. For example, the nucleus of uranium, the heaviest natural element, has 146 neutrons but only 92 protons.

The sum of protons and neutrons in a nucleus is called the **atomic mass number** of that element. It is possible for different nuclei of the same type of element to have different atomic mass numbers. For example, rare carbon atoms have nuclei made up of eight neutrons and six protons, instead of the usual six neutrons and six protons. Atoms of the same element that differ only in the number of neutrons in their nuclei are called **isotopes.** Remember that the number of protons always determines which element the atom is. The number of neutrons may vary to form different isotopes of the same element.

Figure 6.9 The isotopes of hydrogen

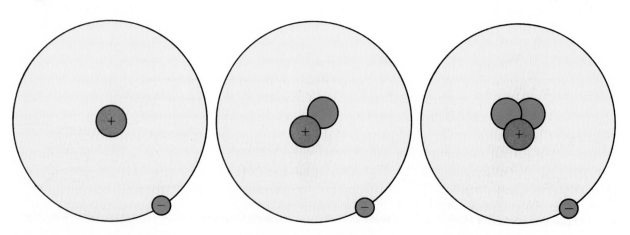

(+) Proton

◯ Neutron

(−) Electron

From what you have read, you may think that all matter is made up of only three particles—electrons, protons, and neutrons. It is true that different combinations of these particles result in all the matter known. Yet experiments with beams of very high-energy particles have shown that protons and neutrons may be made of even smaller particles called **quarks.** The evidence found so far seems to show that protons and neutrons are made of three quarks. There also seem to be several different types of quarks. These quarks combine in different ways to make protons and neutrons as well as short-lived particles that have been seen in high-energy experiments.

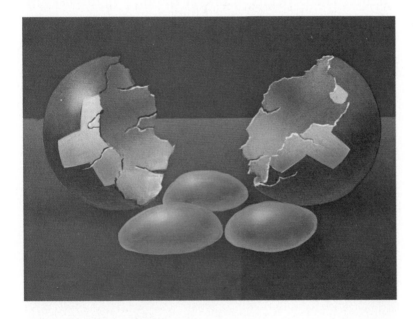

Figure 6.10 Recent studies suggest that protons are made of three quarks.

Study Questions for 6.3

1. What types of particles make up the nucleus?
2. What is the difference between the atomic number and atomic mass number?
3. What is the name of atoms of the same element that differ only in the number of neutrons in their nuclei?
4. Of what smaller particles are protons and neutrons composed?

6.4 Electron Structure of the Atom

You will find out
- why the solar system model doesn't accurately explain atomic structure;
- what is meant by electron shells;
- what forces hold atoms together.

The model of the atom that was developed during the time of Rutherford is similar to a model of the solar system. In the solar system model the planets orbit the massive sun. Atoms are often shown as electrons orbiting a nucleus. This picture can give you some idea of the structure of an atom, but it is not a completely accurate picture. Theoretically, a planet could be in almost any orbit around the sun. Electrons can only be in certain areas, or energy states, around the nucleus. Also, the electrons move in spherical rather than flat orbits.

The specific energy levels around the nucleus where electrons can be found are called **shells.** Each shell is at a different distance from the atom's nucleus. Because an electron is moving very fast, it is impossible to know its exact location at any one time. You can, however, be sure that it is somewhere in the spherical area of its shell. Together the shells form a three-dimensional **electron cloud** around the nucleus of an atom.

Figure 6.11 Like an electron in its shell, the exact location of a car in this photograph is unknown. However, you can be sure that the car is somewhere along the highway.

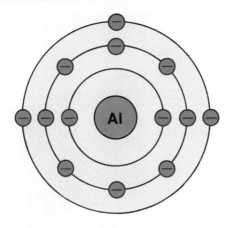

Figure 6.12 The electrons in an aluminum atom

Each kind of atom has a certain number of electrons in its electron cloud. In general, the electrons fill the shell closest to the nucleus first. When that shell has all the electrons it can hold, the second shell begins to fill. When that shell is full, the third shell fills. As the number of electrons in an atom increases, more shells are used.

Each shell can hold only a limited number of electrons. The shell closest to the nucleus, the first shell, holds two electrons. The next shells are considered full when they have eight electrons. Shells farther out from the nucleus can take up to thirty-two electrons.

What holds the electrons in their shells? Electrons are held in an atom by electric forces. Electric forces act between the negatively charged electrons and the positively charged protons in the nucleus. This attraction between the electrons and the protons keeps the atom from flying apart.

Another kind of force, **nuclear force,** holds the neutrons and protons together in the nucleus. The nuclear force keeps the nucleus from flying apart.

Study Questions for 6.4
1. Why can't the solar system be used to explain atomic structure?
2. What are electron shells?
3. Name the two forces that hold the atom together.

What Did You Learn?

- The alchemists contributed to science by establishing the laboratory and the method of taking matter apart to analyze it.
- Elements are the basic substances of which all matter is composed.
- Atoms are the smallest particles of individual elements.
- Compounds are combinations of two or more elements.
- The atom is kept from flying apart by electric forces between the negative electrons and the positive protons.
- The positively charged proton and the electrically neutral neutron are the two types of particles that make up the nucleus.
- The type of element is determined by its atomic number, or the number of protons in an atom of that element.
- Most of the atomic mass is in the nucleus because neutrons and protons have a mass about 1,800 times larger than the electrons, which are outside the nucleus.
- The atomic mass number is the total number of protons and neutrons in the nucleus of an atom.
- Isotopes are forms of the same element whose atoms differ only in the number of neutrons in their nuclei.
- Quarks are the particles that make up protons and neutrons.
- Electrons orbit the nucleus at high speed within the spherical areas of their shells.
- Together all the electron shells of an atom form its electron cloud.
- Electric forces hold the electrons in their shells.
- Nuclear force holds the neutrons and protons together in the nucleus, thereby keeping the nucleus from flying apart.

Key Terms

alchemists
elements
atoms
natural elements
compounds
radioactive
nucleus
electrons
proton
neutron
atomic number
atomic mass number
isotopes
quarks
shells
electron cloud
nuclear force

Biography

Vera Kistiakowsky   (1928–   )

Vera Kistiakowsky is a professor of nuclear physics at Massachusetts Institute of Technology (M.I.T.). With a group of 30 other scientists, technicians, and engineers she studied the structure of the proton. By accelerating protons to very high energies and banging them together, the M.I.T. group and other groups of scientists around the world have shown that the proton is probably made up of three quarks.

When she is not busy probing the deepest structures of matter, Kistiakowsky works with students. She teaches them and directs their research projects. Since Kistiakowsky would like to see more women in science, she spends a large amount of her spare time giving talks to encourage young women to become scientists. Why does Kistiakowsky encourage women to enter the sciences? She does this because she herself likes science and she thinks other women would like it too.

"I like doing calculations; I like building equipment and making it work; I like thinking about explanations of the results. I enjoy being on the edge where you can really see things people haven't seen before and maybe contribute something to the knowledge of the universe."

TO THINK ABOUT AND DO

Vocabulary

Number your paper from 1 to 9. Match the term in column A to the phrase that describes it in column B. Write the letter of the phrase next to the appropriate number.

A	B
1. compound	**a.** positive particle in the nucleus
2. nucleus	**b.** small but dense core of the atom
3. neutron	**c.** number of protons in the nucleus
4. proton	**d.** negatively charged particle outside the nucleus of an atom
5. shells	**e.** certain energy states in which the electrons of an atom can exist
6. quarks	**f.** combination of two or more elements
7. atomic number	**g.** particles of which protons and neutrons may be made
8. isotopes	**h.** particle in nucleus with no charge
9. electron	**i.** forms of the same element that differ only in the number of neutrons in their nuclei

What Do You Remember?

1. What is an element?
2. What is a compound?
3. How many different elements compose all matter?
4. Compare protons, electrons, and neutrons by making a chart with the electrical charge, location, and mass of each.
5. Distinguish between the atomic number and the atomic mass number.
6. What two forces exist in an atom? What is the function of each?

Applying What You Have Learned

1. Describe how an atom of chlorine and an atom of fluorine differ.
2. How would you determine how many neutrons an atom has?
3. Why are atoms electrically neutral?

Use the following chart to answer questions 4–6.

Symbol	Atomic Number	Atomic Mass Number
N	7	14
Al	13	27
Ge	32	73
Os	76	190
Mg	12	24
Be	4	9
K	19	39
Fe	26	56
Pb	82	207

4. How many protons are in an atom of each of the following: N, Al, Ge, and Os?
5. How many neutrons are in an atom of each of the following: Mg, Be, Os, and N?
6. How many electrons are in an atom of each of the following: Fe, K, Pb, and Ge?

Research and Investigation

1. Describe the contributions of the physicists J. J. Thomson and H. G. J. Moseley to modern chemistry.
2. Select one element. Write a report describing its properties and its uses. Then make a collage to illustrate its uses.

The Elements

7

The element cadmium makes paint yellow. Cobalt makes porcelain and tile blue. Chromium makes rubies red. Other elements have familiar properties or uses. Uranium is radioactive. Mercury is a liquid metal. Barium produces green colors in fireworks. Strontium gives red colors to fireworks. Sulfur is a bright yellow solid. Chlorine is a yellowish-green poisonous gas. Osmium is very heavy. Lithium is explosive and very light.

In all there are 106 known elements on the earth. Are any of the elements similar? Is there some way they could be grouped? How could they be organized into groups? Heavy and light elements? Solids, liquids, and gases? Color groupings? Through observation and experimentation, scientists have agreed on a way to group the elements. Elements are grouped according to their properties.

7.1 The Periodic Table of the Elements

You will find out
- how the elements are organized on the periodic table;
- what is meant by the term *valence electron;*
- what determines families of elements.

For many years scientists tried to organize elements with similar properties into groups. The first person to sensibly group elements showing similar properties was a Russian scientist, Dimitri Mendeleev. In 1869 Mendeleev published a table of the elements arranged according to properties. An updated version of his table called the **periodic table** is shown on pages 138–139. The elements are arranged in order of increasing atomic number in horizontal rows called **periods.** Elements with similar properties appear lined up in vertical columns called **families.** For convenience, two subfamilies are separated out and displayed below the main body of the table.

If you look at the periodic table, you will see a key that explains the information in the boxes of the table. The dark line that looks like steps down the right side of the chart divides **metals** and **nonmetals.** Metals are on the left of the line, and nonmetals are on the right. Metals are good conductors of heat and electricity, are shiny, can be pounded into different shapes, and can be

Figure 7.2 In the periodic table, elements are grouped according to properties. In a band, players are grouped according to the instrument and part played.

Figure 7.3 Copper is a metal.

drawn out into wires. Nonmetals are poor conductors of heat and electricity, are dull, and break instead of bend. The division between metals and nonmetals is not so sharp as the dark line would show. The elements near the boundary line have properties of both metals and nonmetals.

Of the 106 known elements 85 are metals. However, this does not mean that the nonmetals are unimportant or even rare. In fact, 75 percent of the material in the earth's outer layer and atmosphere is made of nonmetals.

Each of the 106 known elements is made up of its own kind of atom. What is it about these atoms that causes elements to have similar properties? The answer lies with the tiny electrons.

Figure 7.4 Sulfur is a nonmetal.

Periodic Table

Families

I A

H 1	
Hydrogen	
1 (1)	

II A

3 **Li** Lithium 7 (1)	4 **Be** Beryllium 9 (2)
11 **Na** Sodium 23 (1)	12 **Mg** Magnesium 24 (2)

Key:

solid | **Si** |
liquid | **Hg** |
gas | **H** |

| 14 ← atomic number |
| **Si** ← symbol |
| ← name |
| Silicon ← atomic mass number |
| 28 (4) ← valence electrons |

Transition

19 **K** Potassium 39 (1)	20 **Ca** Calcium 40 (2)	21 **Sc** Scandium 45 (2)	22 **Ti** Titanium 48 (2)	23 **V** Vanadium 51 (2)	24 **Cr** Chromium 52 (1)	25 **Mn** Manganese 55 (2)	26 **Fe** Iron 56 (2)	27 **Co** Cobalt 59 (2)
37 **Rb** Rubidium 85 (1)	38 **Sr** Strontium 88 (2)	39 **Y** Yttrium 89 (2)	40 **Zr** Zirconium 91 (2)	41 **Nb** Niobium 93 (1)	42 **Mo** Molybdenum 96 (1)	43 **Tc** Technetium 97 (1)	44 **Ru** Ruthenium 101 (1)	45 **Rh** Rhodium 103 (1)
55 **Cs** Cesium 133 (1)	56 **Ba** Barium 137 (2)	57 to 71 Lanthanides	72 **Hf** Hafnium 178 (2)	73 **Ta** Tantalum 181 (2)	74 **W** Tungsten 184 (2)	75 **Re** Rhenium 186 (2)	76 **Os** Osmium 190 (2)	77 **Ir** Iridium 192 (2)
87 **Fr** Francium 223 (1)	88 **Ra** Radium 226 (2)	89 to 103 Actinides	104 **Unq** Unnilquadium 257 (2)	105 **Unp** Unnilpentium 260 (2)	106 **Unh** Unnilhexium 263 (2)			

57 **La** Lanthanum 139 (2)	58 **Ce** Cerium 140 (2)	59 **Pr** Praseodymium 141 (2)	60 **Nd** Neodymium 144 (2)	61 **Pm** Promethium 145 (2)	62 **Sm** Samarium 150 (2)
89 **Ac** Actinium 227 (2)	90 **Th** Thorium 232 (2)	91 **Pa** Protactinium 231 (2)	92 **U** Uranium 238 (2)	93 **Np** Neptunium 237 (2)	94 **Pu** Plutonium 244 (2)

of the Elements

Families

VIII A

III A	IV A	V A	VI A	VII A	

2
He
Helium
4 (2)

5 **B** Boron 11 (3)	6 **C** Carbon 12 (4)	7 **N** Nitrogen 14 (5)	8 **O** Oxygen 16 (6)	9 **F** Fluorine 19 (7)	10 **Ne** Neon 20 (8)

Metals

13 **Al** Aluminum 27 (3)	14 **Si** Silicon 28 (4)	15 **P** Phosphorus 31 (5)	16 **S** Sulfur 32 (6)	17 **Cl** Chlorine 35 (7)	18 **Ar** Argon 40 (8)

28 **Ni** Nickel 59 (2)	29 **Cu** Copper 64 (1)	30 **Zn** Zinc 65 (2)	31 **Ga** Gallium 70 (3)	32 **Ge** Germanium 73 (4)	33 **As** Arsenic 75 (5)	34 **Se** Selenium 79 (6)	35 **Br** Bromine 80 (7)	36 **Kr** Krypton 84 (8)
46 **Pd** Palladium 106 (18)	47 **Ag** Silver 108 (1)	48 **Cd** Cadmium 112 (2)	49 **In** Indium 115 (3)	50 **Sn** Tin 119 (4)	51 **Sb** Antimony 122 (5)	52 **Te** Tellurium 128 (6)	53 **I** Iodine 127 (7)	54 **Xe** Xenon 131 (8)
78 **Pt** Platinum 195 (1)	79 **Au** Gold 197 (1)	80 **Hg** Mercury 201 (2)	81 **Tl** Thallium 204 (3)	82 **Pb** Lead 207 (4)	83 **Bi** Bismuth 209 (5)	84 **Po** Polonium 209 (6)	85 **At** Astatine 210 (7)	86 **Rn** Radon 222 (8)

Metals   **Nonmetals**

63 **Eu** Europium 152 (2)	64 **Gd** Gadolinium 157 (2)	65 **Tb** Terbium 159 (2)	66 **Dy** Dysprosium 163 (2)	67 **Ho** Holmium 165 (2)	68 **Er** Erbium 167 (2)	69 **Tm** Thulium 169 (2)	70 **Yb** Ytterbium 173 (2)	71 **Lu** Lutetium 175 (2)
95 **Am** Americium 243 (2)	96 **Cm** Curium 247 (2)	97 **Bk** Berkelium 247 (2)	98 **Cf** Californium 251 (2)	99 **Es** Einsteinium 254 (2)	100 **Fm** Fermium 257 (2)	101 **Md** Mendelevium 258 (2)	102 **No** Nobelium 255 (2)	103 **Lr** Lawrencium 256 (2)

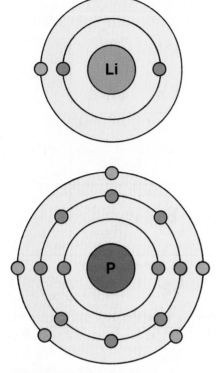

Figure 7.5 The valence electrons are in the shell farthest from the nucleus.

Do You Know?
The oceans of the earth contain 20 million billion tons of sodium in the form of salt.

In Chapter 6 you learned that all electrons can be thought of as moving in different shells around the nucleus of an atom. The electrons in the shell farthest from the nucleus are called **valence** [VAY-luhns] **electrons.** It is the number of valence electrons that tells which family an element is in. For example, all the elements in family IA on the periodic table have one valence electron. All those in family IIA have two valence electrons, and so on. Elements with the same number of valence electrons have similar properties. It is important to remember that the number of valence electrons an element has is the key to its placement on the periodic table.

The periodic table has withstood the test of time and proved to be an accurate and useful way to group the elements. What is most amazing is that when Mendeleev first set up the periodic table there were only 66 known elements. Yet his arrangement still works today when 106 elements are known!

The idea behind Mendeleev's table was so accurate that he was able to predict correctly the existence of certain elements before they were discovered. He did this by describing the properties these elements would have. Mendeleev was so sure the elements germanium, gallium, and scandium existed that he left spaces for them on his periodic table. They were later discovered and proved that he was right!

Figure 7.6 In this section of Medeleev's periodic table, you can see the spaces he left for elements that were later discovered.

			Ti = 50	Zr = 90	? = 180.
			V = 51	Nb = 94	Ta = 182
			Cr = 52	Mo = 96	W = 186.
			Mn = 55	Rh = 104,4	Pt = 197,4
			Fe = 56	Ru = 104,4	Ir = 198.
		Ni = Co = 59		Pl = 106,6	Os = 199.
H = 1			Cu = 63,4	Ag = 108	Hg = 200.
	Be = 9,4	Mg = 24	Zn = 65,2	Cd = 112	
	B = 11	Al = 27,4	? = 68	Ur = 116	Au = 197?
	C = 12	Si = 28	? = 70	Sn = 118	
	N = 14	P = 31	As = 75	Sb = 122	Bi = 210
	O = 16	S = 32	Se = 79,4	Te = 128?	
	F = 19	Cl = 35,5	Br = 80	I = 127	
Li = 7	Na = 23	K = 39	Rb = 85,4	Cs = 133	Tl = 204
		Ca = 40	Sr = 87,6	Ba = 137	Pb = 207.
		? = 45	Ce = 92		

ACTIVITY

Can You Describe the Missing Piece?

Materials

colored picture
glue
cardboard or
    oaktag
scissors
brown bag

Procedure

1. Take your picture and glue it onto a piece of cardboard. Trim the cardboard to the size of the picture.

2. Carefully cut up the picture into approximately 25 puzzle-shaped pieces. You can draw a jigsaw outline on the back of the cardboard and follow it with your scissors.

3. Put all the pieces into a bag except one. Then exchange bags with a classmate.

4. Assemble the puzzle in the bag you received.

Questions

1. What gives you clues about the look of the missing piece?

2. Predict the size, shape, and colors of the missing piece.

3. Describe what the picture on the missing piece looks like.

4. Get the missing piece from your classmate. How accurate were your predictions about its appearance?

5. How do you think Mendeleev made predictions about the characteristics of the missing elements from his original table?

6. One of the elements missing from Mendeleev's original table was germanium (Ge). Which elements might give you some clues about the properties of germanium? Explain your reasoning.

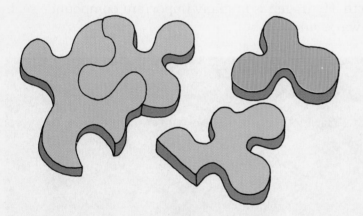

Study Questions for 7.1

1. What are the vertical columns on the periodic table called?
2. What are the horizontal rows on the periodic table called?
3. What are valence electrons?
4. What do all elements of the same family have in common?

7.2 Hydrogen and the Metals

You will find out

- what some characteristics of elements in families IA, IIA, and the transition metals are;
- how many valence electrons are in hydrogen, alkali metal, and alkaline earth metal atoms;
- what the transition metals are.

Alkali Metal Family

| **H** Hydrogen |
| **Li** Lithium |
| **Na** Sodium |
| **K** Potassium |
| **Rb** Rubidium |
| **Cs** Cesium |
| **Fr** Francium |

The atoms of elements in family IA of the periodic table have one valence electron. Hydrogen, although not a metal, is included in this family because it, too, has one valence electron. Hydrogen has a nucleus of one proton with a single electron around it. Although it is not the most common element on the earth, it is the most common element in the universe. The sun and the other stars are made mostly of hydrogen. Hydrogen is an essential part of many types of fuel. Petroleum and coal are compounds of hydrogen and carbon. Hydrogen is very reactive. It is almost never found alone on the earth. Hydrogen is in many important compounds such as water and alcohol.

Figure 7.7 Hydrogen is the most plentiful element in the universe.

The other elements in family IA are six very soft, silver-white metals. Family IA is called the **alkali** [AL-kuh-ly] **metal family.** All the alkali metals are very reactive. Even though they may be cool, they will burn your hand if you touch them. They will react quickly with oxygen. They are so reactive, in fact, that they are never found alone in nature.

Next to the very reactive alkali metals in the periodic table is a much calmer group of elements, IIA. These elements make up the **alkaline** [AL-kuh-lyn] **earth metal family.** Atoms of elements in this family have two valence electrons. The alkaline earth metals are slower than the alkali metals to react with other elements. The alkaline earth metal calcium is the fifth most common element in the earth's outer layer. It is found in limestone and gypsum. Your body has about one kilogram of calcium, which is found in your bones and teeth. Barium and magnesium, also in family IIA, have many different uses. Both elements are used in medicine and firecrackers.

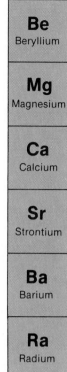

Alkaline Earth Metal Family

Be
Beryllium

Mg
Magnesium

Ca
Calcium

Sr
Strontium

Ba
Barium

Ra
Radium

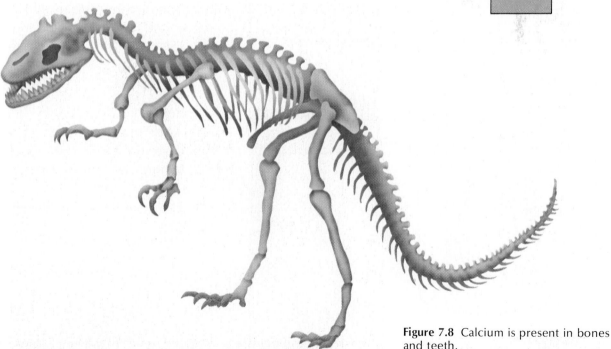

Figure 7.8 Calcium is present in bones and teeth.

Between families IIA and IIIA is a large group of elements that do not exactly fit in any family. These elements are the **transition metals.** Nearly all the transition metals have two valence electrons. In these elements the next to last shell of electrons is filled as the number of electrons increases. The transition metals have similar properties.

ACTIVITY

What Is Copper Plating?

Materials

copper sulfate
beaker
water
2 pieces of
   insulated copper
   wire
battery
iron bar
copper bar
steel wool
tweezers
safety glasses
apron

Procedure

1. Put on your safety glasses and apron. Get some copper sulfate in a beaker from your teacher. CAUTION: Do not touch the copper sulfate with your hands!

2. Rub a piece of copper and a piece of iron with steel wool until they shine.

3. Be sure the insulation has been removed from the wires near the ends.

4. Attach one end of each wire to the battery.

5. Look at the top of the battery. To the free end of the wire that is attached to the + pole, attach the copper bar. To the free end of the wire that is attached to the − pole, attach the iron bar.

6. Immerse the two strips in the copper sulfate solution but do not let them touch.

7. After one half hour remove the strips and examine them. CAUTION: Use a pair of tweezers. Do not touch the metals.

Questions

1. After one half hour what has happened to the iron bar?

2. Where did the copper on the bar come from?

3. How could you silver-plate a spoon?

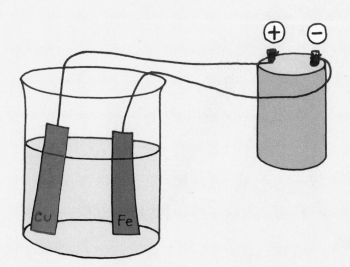

Transition Metals

Sc	Ti	V	Cr	Mn	Fe	Co	Ni	Cu	Zn
Scandium	Titanium	Vanadium	Chromium	Manganese	Iron	Cobalt	Nickel	Copper	Zinc
Y	Zr	Nb	Mo	Tc	Ru	Rh	Pd	Ag	Cd
Yttrium	Zirconium	Niobium	Molyb-denum	Technetium	Ruthenium	Rhodium	Palladium	Silver	Cadmium
	Hf	Ta	W	Re	Os	Ir	Pt	Au	Hg
	Hafnium	Tantalum	Tungsten	Rhenium	Osmium	Iridium	Platinum	Gold	Mercury

Most of the familiar metals—iron, nickel, copper, silver, and gold—are transition metals. Copper mixes with zinc to make brass. Copper and tin make bronze. Other less well-known transition metals have familiar uses. Chromium is used in stainless steel and chrome plate. Because it is almost perfectly rustproof, tantalum is used in skull plates and other surgical repairs to the human body. Yttrium is used in television tubes to make the color red.

Figure 7.9 The use of chrome plate was very popular in cars of the 1950's. Chromium is present in chrome plate.

Study Questions for 7.2

1. How many valence electrons are in hydrogen, alkali metal, and alkaline earth metal atoms?
2. What is different about the electron shell structure of transition metals?
3. What are some characteristics of elements in families IA and IIA?

7.3 From Metals to Nonmetals

You will find out
- how many valence electrons are in the atoms of elements in families IIIA through VIIA;
- what some elements in families IIIA through VIIA are.

After the transition metals is the boundary between metals and nonmetals. This boundary runs through families IIIA, IVA, VA, and VIA. These four families—boron, carbon, nitrogen, and oxygen—are named after the first element in each family. All of these families have both metallic and nonmetallic elements. Atoms of elements in the **boron family**, IIIA, have three valence electrons. The elements include boron, a nonmetal, and aluminum, which is the most common metal in the earth's outer layer.

After the boron family is one of the most important families, the **carbon family**, IVA. Atoms of the elements in this family have four valence electrons. Because of the four valence electrons, the carbon family is halfway between the highly reactive metals and the highly reactive nonmetals. The first element in this family, carbon, forms an almost unbelievable number of different compounds. Many of these are necessary for life. Carbon is found in oil, plastics, and nylon. More than 5 million carbon compounds are known.

Boron Family	Carbon Family
B Boron	**C** Carbon
Al Aluminum	**Si** Silicon
Ga Gallium	**Ge** Germanium
In Indium	**Sn** Tin
Tl Thallium	**Pb** Lead

Do You Know?
The symbol for lead, Pb, comes from the word *plumbum,* the Latin word for *lead.* The word *plumbing* also comes from this same Latin word.

Figure 7.10 Among the elements present in emeralds are aluminum from the boron family and silicon from the carbon family.

Next to oxygen, silicon is the most common element in the earth's outer layer. Silicon, a member of the carbon family, is found in sand and many rocks. It is used to make glass and cement. Silicon, together with another member of the carbon family, germanium, forms the backbone of one of the most important modern industries, computers.

The heavier elements in the carbon family, tin and lead, show definite metallic properties. Tin is used to coat steel to make rustproof cans.

Atoms of elements in the **nitrogen family,** VA, have five valence electrons. Their outer shell is over half full. The air you breathe is 78 percent nitrogen. Nitrogen forms many compounds. It combines with carbon, oxygen, and hydrogen to form explosives such as TNT. Nitrogen compounds are a very important part of most fertilizers.

The next member of the nitrogen family, phosphorus, is important for life. It is a basic part of your organs and bones. Arsenic, another member of this family, is best known as a deadly poison although arsenic can also be used as a medicine. The heavier elements in the family, antimony and bismuth, have metallic properties.

Nitrogen Family	Oxygen Family
N Nitrogen	**O** Oxygen
P Phosphorus	**S** Sulfur
As Arsenic	**Se** Selenium
Sb Antimony	**Te** Tellurium
Bi Bismuth	**Po** Polonium

Figure 7.11 Nitrogen compounds are present in fertilizers.

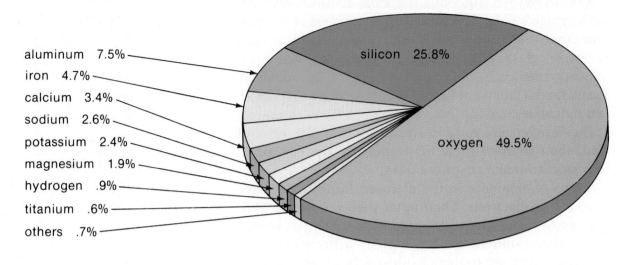

aluminum 7.5%
iron 4.7%
calcium 3.4%
sodium 2.6%
potassium 2.4%
magnesium 1.9%
hydrogen .9%
titanium .6%
others .7%

silicon 25.8%

oxygen 49.5%

Figure 7.12 Elements in the earth's outer layer

Atoms of the elements in the **oxygen family,** VIA, have six valence electrons. Oxygen is the most common element in the earth's outer layer. It makes up about 50 percent of the total material on the surface of the earth. It is basic for life. Oxygen is very reactive, forming compounds with practically every other element.

Sulfur, another element in this family, is also a very reactive element. The Latin word for *sulfur* means "brimstone," or "burning stone." Sulfur is used to make matches and rubber tires and is used in practically every branch of modern industry.

Figure 7.13 Sulfur is used in the production of rubber.

The heavier members of this family—selenium, tellurium, and polonium—show a combination of metallic and nonmetallic properties. Selenium becomes more metallic if it is exposed to light. This makes it extremely useful for solar cells and light meters. Polonium is the least common natural element. It is used mainly in laboratories.

The family of elements next to oxygen in the periodic table is called the **halogen** [HAL-oh-jehn] **family,** VIIA. Atoms of the elements in this family have seven valence electrons. They are extremely reactive. They react most readily with the alkali metals. Halogen compounds are commonly used in disinfectants and cleaning agents. Compounds containing bromine are used in drugs, in photographic film, and in gasoline to prevent engine knocking. Fluorine compounds are used in toothpastes, in insecticides, and in the preparation of some plastics.

Halogen
Family

F
Fluorine

Cl
Chlorine

Br
Bromine

I
Iodine

At
Astatine

Figure 7.14 Compounds containing bromine are used in photography.

Study Questions for 7.3

1. How many valence electrons are in atoms of elements in families IIIA, IVA, VA, VIA, and VIIA?
2. Name two elements in each of the following families: (a) boron family, (b) carbon family, (c) nitrogen family, (d) oxygen family, and (e) halogen family.

7.4 The Noble Gases

You will find out
- why the noble gases are different from other elements.

In the column on the far right of the periodic table are elements that are totally different from all the others. They are the members of the **noble gas family,** VIIIA. For years it was thought that the noble gases could not react with other elements. Just as the nobility in earlier times refused to mix with the common people, these elements were thought never to make compounds with other elements. That explains the name noble gases.

The noble gases mark the end of each period on the periodic table. They all have atoms with eight valence electrons except for helium. Helium atoms have two valence electrons. These electrons are in the shell closest to the nucleus, which holds only two electrons. The outer shells of all noble gas atoms are considered full. The noble gases are different from other elements because their electron shells are full.

Figure 7.15 *left:* The *Hindenburg* disaster occurred when the hydrogen used to inflate the blimp exploded and burned. *right:* Modern blimps use helium because it will not burn.

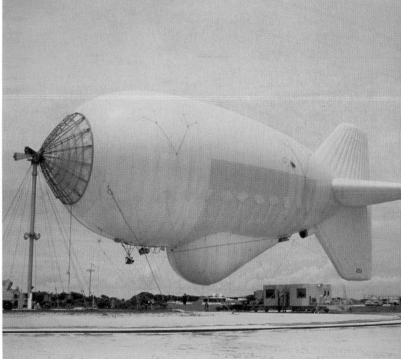

Helium is the lightest noble gas. Although it is the second most common element in the universe, helium is rare on the earth. It is found in natural gas wells. It is the lightest gas after hydrogen and does not burn. For these reasons, helium is used for inflating balloons and blimps.

The other noble gases are used in lighting and welding. In general, they do not react readily with other elements. Elements that burn are reacting with oxygen in the air. Because the noble gases will not react with oxygen and burn, they are much safer than other gases.

Noble Gas Family

Figure 7.16 Neon is often used in colorful signs.

Study Questions for 7.4

1. How many valence electrons are in a helium atom? A neon atom? An argon atom?
2. How are the noble gases different from the other elements?

7.5 The Lanthanides and the Actinides

You will find out
- why elements within the lanthanide and actinide families are so similar;
- how new elements are made in the laboratory.

The **lanthanide** [LAN-thuh-nyd] **family** begins with the element lanthanium. The **actinide** [AK-tih-nyd] **family** begins with actinium. These are the families displayed below the main body of the periodic table. These families include elements with atoms in which the outer two shells of electrons are similar. The third shell from the outside is different. Since the third shell from the outside of an atom does not change the properties of the element much, it is not surprising that all the elements within these families are very similar.

The lanthanides are almost always found together. They are used in the production of steel and glass.

All the actinides are radioactive. The best-known actinide is uranium, the heaviest natural element. Uranium is the source of energy for nuclear power plants.

Any element heavier than uranium is made in nuclear laboratories. Samples of uranium are bombarded with neutrons or nuclei of light elements. This bombarding can change uranium into heavier elements that are called **synthetic** [sihn-THEHT-ihk]. The word *synthetic* means that the elements are produced in the laboratory.

Figure 7.17 Synthetic elements 93 through 105 were discovered here at the Lawrence Berkeley Laboratory in Berkeley, California.

La	Ce	Pr	Nd	Pm	Sm	Eu	Gd	Tb	Dy	Ho	Er	Tm	Yb	Lu
Ac	Th	Pa	U	Np	Pu	Am	Cm	Bk	Cf	Es	Fm	Md	No	Lr

The search for new synthetic elements continues. When elements 104 and 105 were discovered, they were placed in the periodic table without names. This happened because there were disagreements over who discovered them first. Normally the discoverer has the privilege of naming the new element. An international group of scientists approves the naming of all new elements. In this case, the chairperson of this group has met with all the scientists involved in the disagreement over elements 104 and 105. However, the disagreement is still not fully settled.

Element	Familiar Name or Place
Californium	California
Einsteinium	Albert Einstein
Nobelium	Alfred Nobel (Nobel prizes)
Neptunium	Neptune
Plutonium	Pluto
Americium	America
Berkelium	Berkeley, California
Curium	Marie and Pierre Curie
Francium	France
Scandium	Scandinavia
Polonium	Poland

Figure 7.18 Many elements were named after familiar people or places.

Study Questions for 7.5

1. Why are elements within the lanthanide and the actinide families so similar?
2. How can new elements be made in the laboratory?

What Did You Learn?

- Elements are arranged on the periodic table in rows called periods.
- Elements with similar properties are lined up on the periodic table in columns called families.
- Valence electrons are in the electron shell farthest out from the nucleus of an atom.
- Atoms of elements in the same family have the same number of valence electrons.
- Hydrogen and the alkali metals, family IA, have one valence electron.
- The alkaline earth metals, family IIA, have two valence electrons.
- Nearly all the transition metal atoms have two valence electrons. The next to last electron shell is filling up.
- Some families of elements are very reactive.
- Atoms of elements in the boron family, IIIA, have three valence electrons.
- Atoms of elements in the carbon family, IVA, have four valence electrons.
- Atoms of elements in the nitrogen family, VA, have five valence electrons.
- Atoms of elements in the oxygen family, VIA, have six valence electrons.
- Atoms of elements in the halogen family, VIIA, have seven valence electrons.
- The noble gases mark the end of each period and all have eight valence electrons except for helium, which has two.
- The noble gases are different from other elements because their electron shells are considered full.
- Elements within the lanthanide and actinide families are very similar because their outer two electron shells are similar.
- Synthetic elements can be made in the laboratory by bombarding uranium atoms with neutrons or nuclei of light elements.

Key Terms

periodic table
periods
families
metals
nonmetals
valence electrons
alkali metal family
alkaline earth metal family
transition metals
boron family
carbon family
nitrogen family
oxygen family
halogen family
noble gas family
lanthanide family
actinide family
synthetic

Career

Metallurgical Engineer

Metallurgical engineers, or metallurgists, specialize in the study of metals. They probe metallic structure.

Some metallurgists work with ores, rocks containing metals that come out of mines. New and more efficient ways of getting metals from these ores are always needed. These new techniques are especially important because the supply of high-grade ores is being used up. Physical metallurgists study the physical properties of metals. They develop new types of metals to meet specific demands. For example, metals for spacecraft need to be heat resistant and very strong. Metals used in computers must be very pure. Mechanical metallurgists work on new ways to shape and form metals.

Many of the metal materials you encounter every day are the products of metallurgical research. These materials include tin cans, aluminum pots and pans, jewelry, braces and fillings for your teeth, fences, tools, and metals used in cars, bicycles, and other forms of transportation.

The iron and steel industries employ over half the metallurgical engineers. Metallurgical engineers also work in the aerospace, mining, and manufacturing industries. As technology increases and new types of materials are needed to meet new demands, more and more metallurgical engineers will be needed.

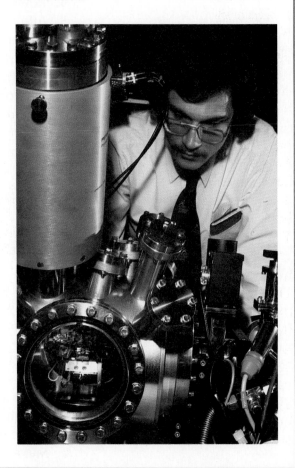

TO THINK ABOUT AND DO

Vocabulary

Number your paper from 1 to 10. Read each of the following sentences. If the sentence is true, write *true* beside the appropriate number. If it is false, make it true by changing the underlined expression.

1. In a family of elements all the atoms have the same number of <u>valence electrons.</u>
2. The <u>noble gases</u> combine readily with other elements.
3. Elements that are made in the laboratory are called <u>synthetic</u> elements.
4. <u>Rows</u> on the periodic table are called <u>periods.</u>
5. All elements in the <u>halogen family</u> are <u>nonmetals.</u>
6. All the <u>transition metals</u> are radioactive.
7. According to the periodic table, the atomic number for <u>chromium</u> is 35.
8. All atoms in the <u>alkali metal family</u> have one valence electron.
9. <u>Nonmetals</u> are shiny and are good conductors of heat and electricity.
10. New elements are made in the laboratory from <u>oxygen</u> atoms.

What Do You Remember?

1. Look at this square. Tell at least three things about the atoms of the element sulfur.
2. Name the scientist who first developed the periodic table.
3. How are the elements in a period related?
4. How are the elements in a family similar?
5. What are valence electrons?
6. List the atomic numbers and symbols of five synthetic elements.
7. Make a list of properties of metals and a second list of properties of nonmetals.

8. Name the eight families of elements —IA, IIA, IIIA, IVA, VA, VIA, VIIA, VIIIA—and tell the number of valence electrons in each.
9. Name one element from each family in question 8 and explain why it is important.
10. Name three transition metals and explain why they are important.

Applying What You Have Learned

Give the letter from the diagram of the periodic table that corresponds to the family or elements described.

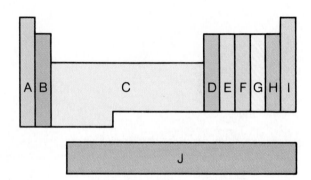

1. the alkali metals
2. the halogens
3. the alkaline earth metals
4. the lanthanides and the actinides
5. the noble gases
6. the transition metals
7. elements with atoms with one valence electron
8. elements with atoms with three valence electrons
9. elements with atoms with six valence electrons
10. elements with atoms with eight valence electrons

Research and Investigation

1. Silicon compounds are durable and hard. They are used in bone restructuring and grinding. Nitrogen has a low boiling point of 196°C. This makes it very useful in providing cold temperatures. Selenium, bromine, and cobalt are elements you do not often hear of. They have important uses. Find out what some of these uses are.
2. Fertilizers are labeled with three numbers. What element does each number refer to? How is each element important to plant growth?
3. Certain plants called legumes are important for their nitrogen-fixing ability. How do these plants make nitrogen available for people's use?

Combining the Elements

8

Suppose someone sprinkled a combination of two very dangerous chemicals on some food and ate it. Would you think that that person was crazy? Well, people do it every time they salt their food. Table salt is made of two dangerous chemicals, the elements sodium and chlorine. Yet when these elements are combined, they form a compound that is the most commonly used food seasoning.

Salt is just one example of a compound that looks and behaves very differently from the elements it is made of. A relatively small number of elements can make a world full of millions of different kinds of substances by forming compounds.

Why do some elements form compounds while others do not? How can compounds look and act so differently from the elements they are made of? Why do some materials break easily while others can be hammered into thin sheets? By understanding more about how elements combine, you will understand more about why the matter around you looks and acts the way it does.

Figure 8.1 Salt formations at Mono Lake in California

8.1 Compounds and Mixtures

You will find out
- how compounds and mixtures are different;
- what is meant by a solution.

Substances made of two or more elements chemically combined are called compounds. A compound is always made of the same elements combined in the same proportions. For example, pure water is always 11.19 percent hydrogen and 88.81 percent oxygen.

A compound looks and acts very differently from the elements it is made of. Liquid water looks nothing at all like hydrogen gas or oxygen gas. Water freezes at 0°C. Both hydrogen and oxygen must be cooled to more than 200°C below zero before they turn into solids. Hydrogen will explode. Oxygen must be present for a fire to burn. Water puts a fire out. The properties of a compound are different from those of the elements that make it.

Figure 8.2 The element hydrogen burns. The element oxygen supports burning. Water, a compound of hydrogen and oxygen, is used to put out fires.

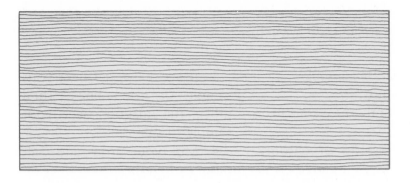

Figure 8.3 When you look at this mixture of colors from a distance, you see a new color. The original colors, however, remain unchanged.

Seawater, on the other hand, is not a compound. The amount of salt mixed in with the water can change. Seawater is an example of a **mixture.** Air, ice cream, brass, mayonnaise, orange juice, fog, and smog are also examples of mixtures. Mixtures are made of two or more elements or compounds that are not chemically combined. The amounts of each substance in a mixture are not fixed. For example, you can make a mixture of cereal and milk that has a little milk and a lot of cereal or a lot of milk and a little cereal or anything in between. This is an important difference between mixtures and compounds. The elements that form a compound are always combined in the same proportions. The proportions in a mixture can vary.

Do You Know?
Water tastes salty if there are 5 molecules of salt for every 10,000 molecules of water.

Figure 8.4 The proportions in a mixture of paint can vary.

ACTIVITY

Materials

test-tube rack
chromatography
  paper strip
iron filings
salt
4 test tubes
magnet

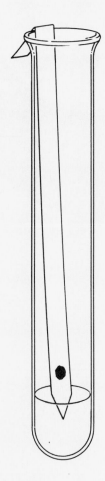

How Can You Separate a Mixture?

Procedure

Part I—Separating an Ink Mixture

1. Put 5 mL of water in a test tube.

2. Place a strip of chromatography paper stained with black ink into the test tube. The point of the paper should be in the water. Do not let the black spot touch the water. Fold the end of the strip over the test tube to hold it in place.

3. Allow the water to travel up the paper and observe what happens to the black spot.

4. Set your test tube in the test-tube rack. Check it periodically while you perform Part II. When the water has traveled to within 1 cm of the top of the test tube, remove the strip and allow it to dry.

Part II—Separating a Mixture of Iron and Salt

1. Place a sample of iron filings on a piece of paper. Place a sample of salt on a second piece of paper.

2. Fill two test tubes halfway with water. Add a small amount of iron to one and a small amount of salt to the other.

3. Move a magnet over your sample of iron filings. Then move the magnet over your sample of salt.

4. Mix your iron and salt samples together on a piece of paper. Divide the mixture into two parts. Place each part on a separate piece of paper.

5. Use a magnet to separate one sample of the mixture.

6. To separate the mixture by a different method, place a small amount of your second sample in a test tube and add 10 mL of water.

Questions

1. Describe what happens to the black spot as the water moves up the chromatography paper.

2. Can you use a magnet to separate a mixture of iron and salt? Explain your answer.

3. Can you use solubility to separate a mixture of iron and salt? Explain your answer.

4. Describe a mixture.

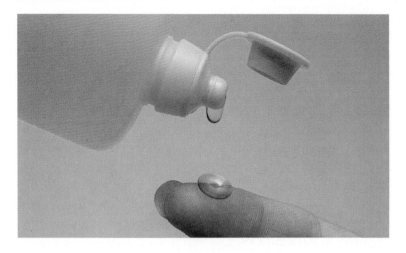

Figure 8.5 Many people are familiar with a liquid solution for contact lenses.

Some mixtures are called **solutions.** The substances in a solution are uniformly mixed. Sugar dissolved in water is a good example. If you stir sugar into water allowing enough time for all the sugar to dissolve, the resulting liquid will be the same throughout. One sample of the liquid would taste no sweeter or less sweet than any other sample. The sugar and water are uniformly mixed, forming a solution. The word *solution* is most often used with liquids. However, solids, such as brass, and gases, such as air, can also be solutions.

Figure 8.6 A liquid solution is being used to clean brass, a solid solution.

Study Questions for 8.1
1. How are compounds different from mixtures?
2. What is a solution?

8.2 Forming Molecules

You will find out
• what is meant by the term *molecule;*
• how chemical bonds join atoms to form molecules.

Sometimes the atoms of an element are found alone. At other times they are found joined together. Compounds are never made of single atoms. The different atoms in a compound are always found joined together. When two or more atoms, whether the same or different, combine, they form a **molecule** [MAHL-uh-kyool]. A hydrogen gas molecule is an example. Two hydrogen atoms combine to form a molecule of hydrogen gas. Just as elements can be represented by symbols, molecules can be represented by **molecular formulas.**

Figure 8.7 The air you breathe contains diatomic molecules.

The molecular formula for a hydrogen molecule is H_2. The H is the symbol for hydrogen. The number 2 beside and below the H, called a subscript, tells you that there are two hydrogen atoms in the molecule. This is an example of a **diatomic** [dy-uh-TAHM-ihk] **molecule.** Diatomic molecules are ones in which only two atoms join together. Another example of a diatomic molecule is O_2. Two oxygen atoms form an oxygen molecule.

Atoms	Molecules	Element or Compound?
I + I	I_2	element
O + O	O_2	element
C + O	CO	compound
C + O + O	CO_2	compound
H + H + O + O	H_2O_2	compound
H + H + S + O + O + O + O	H_2SO_4	compound
N + N	N_2	element

Figure 8.8 Elements are made of only one kind of atom. Compounds are made of two or more kinds of atoms.

Substances made of diatomic molecules such as H_2 and O_2 are considered elements, since they are made of only one kind of atom. In the molecules of compounds, atoms of two or more different kinds of elements join together. For example, a water molecule is a combination of hydrogen and oxygen atoms. The formula for the water molecule is H_2O. It contains two atoms of hydrogen and one atom of oxygen. Molecules are considered the basic units of compounds just as atoms are considered the basic units of elements.

The fitting together of atoms to form molecules can be compared to the fitting together of pieces in a jigsaw puzzle. If two atoms fit well together as pieces of a jigsaw puzzle do, a molecule is formed. When atoms fit together making a molecule, a **chemical bond** is formed.

Some atoms bond very readily with other atoms. Other atoms rarely form chemical bonds. The noble gases hardly ever form a bond with themselves or with any other kind of atom. On the other hand, hydrogen will very readily form bonds with many other kinds of atoms. So will fluorine. Some atoms readily form bonds, making molecules, while others do not.

ACTIVITY

What Does a Molecular Formula Tell You About a Compound?

Materials
pencil
paper

Procedure

1. Read the following rules for interpreting molecular formulas and study all the examples.

2. Interpret the formulas by telling how many atoms of each element are in a molecule of the compounds.

Formulas for you to interpret

1. ZnO
2. SO_2
3. $PbSO_4$
4. $NaOH$
5. $C_3H_5(OH)_3$
6. C_2H_5ONa
7. $Fe(OH)_3$
8. $CaSiO_3$
9. H_3BO_3
10. $KMnO_4$

Rule	Examples	
Rule 1: The element symbol stands for one atom of that element in the molecule.	**CaO**	1 atom of calcium 1 atom of oxygen
	NaOH	1 atom of sodium 1 atom of oxygen 1 atom of hydrogen
Rule 2: If a subscript is after the symbol, there is more than one atom of that element in the molecule. The subscript tells you how many atoms of that element are present in the molecule.	**MgCl₂**	1 atom of magnesium 2 atoms of chlorine
	H₂CO₃	2 atoms of hydrogen 1 atom of carbon 3 atoms of oxygen
Rule 3: If a symbol or group of symbols is surrounded by parentheses with a subscript outside the parentheses, multiply the number of each of the atoms inside the parentheses by the subscript.	**Ca(NO₃)₂**	1 atom of calcium 2 atoms of nitrogen 6 atoms of oxygen
	Mn(OH)₂	1 atom of manganese 1 atom of oxygen 2 atoms of hydrogen

Why do some atoms readily form bonds while others do not? The answer to this question can be found by looking at the valence electrons of an atom. Valence electrons are those found in the electron shell farthest out from the nucleus. An atom having eight valence electrons is considered very stable. The noble gases have eight valence electrons. They do not react readily with other elements and are considered very stable. Their outer electron shells are already stable.

In general, atoms will form chemical bonds with other atoms if the bonding will cause all atoms involved to have a stable outer electron shell of eight electrons. This rule is called the **octet** [ahk-TEHT] **rule.** Hydrogen and helium are exceptions. They each have only one electron shell. That shell is the one closest to the nucleus and is full and stable with two electrons instead of eight.

The octet rule states that atoms form chemical bonds to reach a more stable condition. That condition calls for complete electron shells. The complete shells are achieved in two general ways. One way is to shift electrons from one atom to another. The second way is to share electrons between atoms.

Figure 8.9 Which of these atoms would be most likely to form a chemical bond?

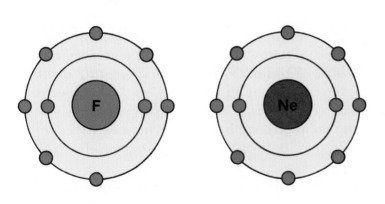

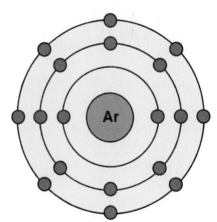

Study Questions for 8.2
1. What is a diatomic molecule?
2. What holds atoms together in a molecule?
3. What does the octet rule say?

8.3 The Ionic Bond: Shifting Electrons

You will find out
- how an ionic bond is formed;
- what positive ions and negative ions are;
- what crystals are.

An **ionic** [eye-AHN-ihk] **bond** is formed when one atom shifts an electron to another atom. This happens commonly when atoms with one valence electron, the alkali metals, are combined with atoms with seven valence electrons, the halogens. A good example is table salt, sodium chloride, which is formed by combining sodium and chlorine.

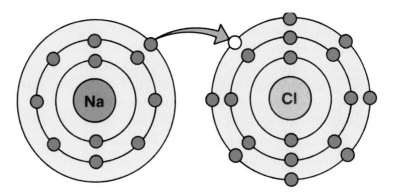

Figure 8.10 Forming an ionic bond

When an alkali metal atom such as sodium loses its one valence electron, a stable shell of eight electrons is left behind. If sodium's electron is taken by a chlorine atom, the chlorine atom will have 7 + 1, or 8, electrons in its outer shell. This gives it a stable outer shell. In forming an ionic bond both atoms have achieved a stable condition. Both have outer electron shells of eight electrons.

When the sodium atom loses an electron, the atom has one less electron than protons. The electrons each have a negative charge of one unit, and the protons each have a positive charge of one unit. The resulting atom has a net positive charge. Such an atom is called a **positive ion.** On the other hand, the chlorine atom has taken another electron. The chlorine now has an extra electron. As a result it has a net negative charge. Such an atom is called a **negative ion.**

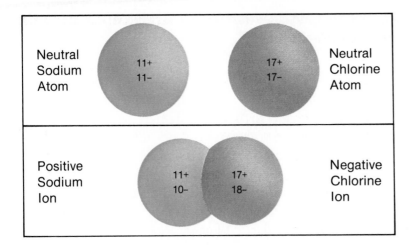

Figure 8.11 All atoms are neutral. All ions are charged.

Other members of the alkali metal family form positive ions in the same manner that sodium does. Similarly, other members of the halogen family form negative ions in the same manner that chlorine does. For example, the alkali metal potassium forms an ionic bond with the halogen bromine. Potassium shifts its one valence electron to bromine. Potassium becomes a positive ion. Bromine becomes a negative ion. The result is the ionic crystal potassium bromide.

Figure 8.12 The alkali metals form ionic bonds easily with the halogens.

ACTIVITY

Materials

beakers
copper wire
batteries
light bulbs in sockets
salt
distilled water
sugar
baking soda
alcohol
spoon
safety glasses
apron

Which Solutions Contain Ions?

Procedure

1. Make a chart like the one begun at the bottom of the page. Use this chart to record your observations.

2. Put on your safety glasses and apron.

3. Set up the battery, wires, and bulb as shown. To test each material for conductivity, place the free ends of the wires into the material. The wires should NEVER touch each other during the tests.

4. Fill a beaker about halfway with distilled water.

5. Test the distilled water for conductivity.

6. Put a spoonful of salt on a piece of paper. Test.

7. Dissolve a small amount of salt in the beaker of water. Test.

8. Add the rest of your salt sample to the salt solution. Test. Is the bulb brighter than before?

9. Empty and rinse the beaker. Repeat steps 4 and 6-8 with sugar and again with baking soda.

10. Pour a small amount of alcohol in the beaker. Test.

Questions

1. Solutions that allow electricity to pass through them contain ions. Complete the chart to show which contain ions.

2. Why do you think the bulb was brighter for the stronger solutions?

3. Why do you think solutions that contain ions are conductors while solutions that have molecules with covalent bonds are not?

4. Explain how you would determine whether or not a solution is a conductor of electricity.

Test Material	Bulb Lights?	Ions Present?
water		
salt		
salt water		
sugar		
sugar water		

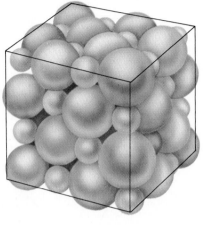

Figure 8.13 *left:* Crystals of sodium chloride; *right:* The crystalline structure of sodium chloride

The strong electrical attraction between the oppositely charged ions will pull them together in an ionic bond. Ionic bonds are strong. It takes a fairly large amount of energy to pull apart two ions of opposite charges. Because of this strong attraction, ionic bonds form materials called **crystals.** A crystal is a solid in which the atoms are arranged in a regular pattern. As a result, crystals tend to have flat surfaces. For example, salt (NaCl) forms crystals in which the positive sodium ions always have negative chlorine ions for neighbors. These salt crystals are cubes. Other crystals may have different shapes.

Study Questions for 8.3
1. How is an ionic bond formed?
2. What are negative and positive ions?
3. What is a crystal?

8.4 The Covalent Bond: Sharing Electrons

You will find out
- how a covalent bond is formed;
- how electron dot diagrams illustrate covalent bonds;
- how a diamond is formed.

Sometimes atoms form bonds in which they share two electrons. This is called a **covalent** [koh-VAY-luhnt] **bond.** The simplest kind of covalent bond is formed when two hydrogen atoms combine to form a hydrogen molecule, H_2. Two electrons, one from each atom, merge into one pattern, or shell, about the two hydrogen nuclei. The two shared electrons fill each hydrogen atom's electron shell. The strength of the covalent bond comes from the attraction of the positively charged nuclei for the negative electrons.

Figure 8.14 Atoms of hydrogen joined by a covalent bond

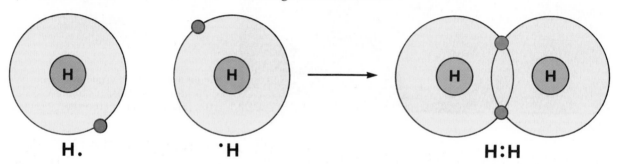

H.   **·H**   **H:H**

The hydrogen molecule is shown above using an **electron dot diagram.** In this kind of diagram the valence electrons of the atoms involved in the covalent bond are shown as dots. The pairs of dots placed between the element symbols represent shared electrons.

One atom can form more than one covalent bond. That is, it can share more than one pair of electrons. For example, a nitrogen atom shares three pairs of electrons with three hydrogen atoms to make a covalent ammonia molecule, NH_3. Ammonia is a strong-smelling compound used in cleaning solutions. Since the nitrogen atom has five valence electrons, sharing electrons with three hydrogen atoms gives it 5 + 3, or 8, electrons in its outer shell. At the same time, the sharing of electrons gives each hydrogen atom 1 + 1, or 2, electrons in its only electron shell.

H:N:H
 ̈
 H

Figure 8.15 Ammonia, a covalent compound, is used in window-washing solutions.

Another example of a covalent molecule is carbon dioxide, CO_2. Carbon has four valence electrons. It can complete its outer shell by sharing two pairs of electrons with one oxygen atom and two pairs with another one. Notice that in this case two pairs of electrons are shared between two atoms. In covalent bonding more than one pair of electrons can be shared between two atoms.

Carbon atoms also form covalent bonds with other carbon atoms. The results can be very beautiful. Diamonds are made of carbon atoms. In a diamond, each valence electron in the carbon atom is shared with another carbon atom. As a result, each atom is bonded to four other atoms. A diamond has a very high melting point, around 3,600°C, and is extremely hard. A large number of covalent bonds would have to be broken to destroy the crystal structure.

Do You Know?
Scientists have even produced diamonds from peanut butter! Unfortunately, to get gem-quality stones, it costs more to do this than to dig up the diamonds.

Figure 8.16 A diamond crystal

Study Questions for 8.4

1. How is a covalent bond formed?
2. Draw the electron dot diagram for ammonia.
3. How is a diamond formed?

8.5 The Metallic Bond: Wandering Electrons

You will find out
- how metallic bonds are formed;
- what explains many properties of metals.

There is another kind of chemical bond that involves sharing electrons. In a **metallic** [muh-TAL-ihk] **bond** many electrons are shared between many metal atoms. This sharing of electrons is different from covalent bonds. In covalent bonds electrons are shared between two specific atoms.

In the atoms that make up metals, the valence electrons are very loosely bound to the nucleus. When metal atoms are close together, the valence electrons break free, leaving behind positive metal ions. These ions are much heavier than the tiny electrons. The ions stay put, forming a crystal structure. The electrons, being lighter, wander through the crystal. The electrons are not attracted to any one, or even two ions, but to many metal ions.

The freely moving electrons of metallic crystals explain many familiar properties of metals. When you add heat to one part of a metal, the freely moving electrons will quickly carry heat to all parts of the metal. If you touch the metal handle of a heated pan without using a pot holder, you may burn your hand. Even though the handle of the pan is not directly over the burner, the electrons in the metal will very quickly transfer the heat from the stove to the handle and to your hand. This is the reason many pans and kitchen and barbecue utensils have wooden or plastic handles. Wood and plastic do not transfer heat as metals do.

In diamonds and salt crystals, all the electrons are bound to atoms or ions and cannot be easily moved. This makes these crystals hard but easy to break. If you hammer the crystal, the electrons cannot move to adjust. The crystal breaks into pieces. In metallic crystals, on the other hand, the electrons move easily. It is possible to change the shape of metals without breaking them. If a hammer pounds one layer of atoms over

Figure 8.17 Metallic bonds are present in this suit of armor.

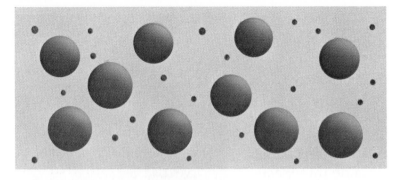

Positive
Metal Ion

Wandering
Electron

Figure 8.18 In metallic bonds, the wandering electrons are attracted to many metal ions.

another, the electrons move quickly and adjust to the new position. This makes it possible to hammer and stretch metals into many different shapes.

The properties that metals exhibit as a result of their bond structure make them very useful. Copper, tin, aluminum, and iron are used in cooking utensils. These metals conduct heat quickly and evenly. Copper is also used in pipes and electrical wiring. Gold and silver are pressed and pounded into many shapes to form jewelry and coins. Aluminum in aluminum foil can be folded and pressed tightly to cover and protect foods.

Figure 8.19 Metallic bonds make it possible to pound metals into different shapes.

Do You Know?
Only 28.4 g of gold can be drawn into a thin wire over 60 km long.

Study Questions for 8.5
1. How is a metallic bond formed?
2. What explains many of the familiar properties of metals?

What Did You Learn?

- The amounts of substances chemically combined in a compound are fixed.
- Compounds have different properties from the elements that form them.
- Mixtures are made of two or more elements or compounds that are not chemically combined.
- The amounts of substances in a mixture can change.
- A solution is a mixture that is the same throughout.
- Molecules are formed when two or more atoms join together.
- In diatomic molecules two atoms are combined.
- Molecules are the basic units of compounds.
- Chemical bonds join atoms together in molecules.
- Most atoms form bonds to achieve a stable outer shell of eight electrons.
- In ionic bonds electrons are shifted from one atom to another.
- Ions have unequal numbers of protons and electrons.
- A crystal is a solid in which the atoms or ions are arranged in a regular pattern.
- In covalent bonds pairs of electrons are shared between atoms.
- Electron dot diagrams illustrate covalent molecules.
- Diamonds are made of carbon atoms joined by covalent bonds.
- In metallic bonds electrons are shared by many metal atoms.
- The freely moving electrons of metallic crystals explain many familiar properties of metals.

Key Terms

mixture
solutions
molecule
molecular formulas
diatomic molecule
chemical bond
octet rule
ionic bond
positive ion
negative ion
crystals
covalent bond
electron dot diagram
metallic bond

Biography

Shirley Ann Jackson (1946–)

Shirley Ann Jackson is a physical scientist who specializes in the study of matter in the solid state. She works at the research and development branch of Bell Laboratories. Dr. Jackson seeks to describe and explain what happens to a solid, such as a metal, when outside conditions are changed. Two outside conditions she is concentrating on are temperature and pressure. Dr. Jackson hopes to explain at the level of atoms and molecules the effects of changes in temperature and pressure on solids. To do this, she uses computers, mathematics, physical laws, and imagination. The results of her work are useful in electronics, communications, and the development of new materials.

Dr. Jackson graduated valedictorian of her class at Roosevelt High School in Washington, D.C. From there she went to the Massachusetts Institute of Technology, M.I.T. After receiving a bachelor's degree in physics, she remained at M.I.T. and continued to study physics. She later received a doctor's degree in theoretical high-energy physics. Dr. Jackson was the first American black woman to receive a doctorate from M.I.T.

Dr. Jackson's involvement with M.I.T. goes beyond her degrees. She has worked successfully to encourage the enrollment of black students there. She is also a member of the M.I.T. Corporation, the school's board of trustees.

TO THINK ABOUT AND DO

Vocabulary

Unscramble the following words and then use them to complete the sentences.

1. In a salt _____ sodium and chloride ions are arranged in a definite pattern.
2. A charged atom is a(n) _____.
3. Seawater is a(n) _____ because the proportions of salt and water are not fixed.
4. The bond formed when electrons are shared by many atoms is a(n) _____ bond.
5. The rule that says atoms are stable when their valence shell has eight electrons is the _____.
6. A mixture that is the same throughout is called a(n) _____.
7. A bond in which the electrons are shared between two atoms is a(n) _____ bond.
8. When two or more atoms are joined together by a chemical bond, they form a(n) _____.
9. H_2 and O_2 are examples of _____ molecules.
10. Carbon atoms can bond together to form a very hard and very beautiful _____ crystal.

lecmoule
catmiido
ctote erlu
tasylrcs
niico
vatcnoel
xuemrit
middoan
tlmlicea
nio
ntlsouio
erehenoegusto

What Do You Remember?

1. What is the relationship between a molecule and a compound?
2. When atoms join to form molecules, what part of the atoms is involved?
3. How is water different from the hydrogen and oxygen that compose it?
4. Explain how a positive ion is formed.
5. Explain how a negative ion is formed.
6. Tell how ionic, covalent, and metallic bonds differ.
7. Draw electron dot formulas for H_2 and NH_3.
8. How do mixtures and compounds differ?
9. Explain why metals can be pounded into shapes and why they are good conductors of heat.

Applying What You Have Learned

1. Rubidium chloride is an ionic compound. Explain how it is formed.
2. How would potassium become an ion?
3. How would fluorine become an ion?
4. Describe, in terms of electrons, how copper and oxygen join to form copper oxide (Cu_2O).
5. For each of the following elements tell whether you would expect it to form an ionic bond, a covalent bond, a metallic bond, or to remain stable: Li, Kr, I, Si, Au, Cs, S, Cr, At, He.

Research and Investigation

1. Oxidation is a process that we see all around us. It results in the formation of compounds that are useful, but it also results in the formation of compounds we would rather not have. Oxidation is useful when food is broken down to release energy. It is not useful when rust is the result. What is oxidation? How does it occur?
2. Some covalent bonds are said to be polar. What does this mean?

Carbon Compounds

9

Every morning you wake up, climb from between the sheets, and dress for the day. The sheets you sleep on and the clothes you wear contain carbon compounds. After washing your face with a carbon compound, you sit down to breakfast. Your chair contains carbon compounds. You eat carbon compounds. After breakfast you brush your teeth with a toothbrush made of carbon compounds. The bus you take to school has rubber tires made of carbon compounds. The fuel the bus runs on is a carbon compound.

Carbon compounds are absolutely necessary for you to survive. Your body contains carbon compounds. Other living things, plants and animals, contain carbon compounds. Your food contains carbon compounds. So do the fuels that heat your home and power the cars, buses, trains, and planes you ride in. This book you are reading contains carbon compounds. By now you should be getting the idea. Carbon compounds are everywhere!

Figure 9.1 Look for items in the photograph that contain carbon compounds.

9.1　Organic Compounds

You will find out
- why carbon makes so many compounds;
- what organic compounds are.

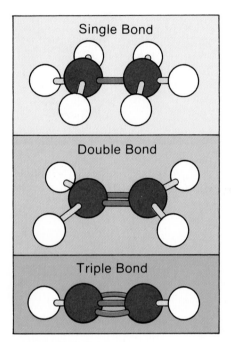

Single Bond

Double Bond

Triple Bond

Figure 9.2 Carbon atoms form single, double, and triple bonds with other carbon atoms.

The element carbon is the world champion when it comes to forming compounds. Carbon is unique because its atomic structure allows it to form many different molecules. A carbon atom has four valence electrons. It can form four single covalent bonds with other atoms to make a full, stable outer shell. It can also form double and triple bonds. In **double bonds,** two pairs of electrons are shared. Similarly, in **triple bonds,** three pairs of electrons are shared. A carbon atom can form single, double, and triple bonds with other carbon atoms as well as with other kinds of atoms. As a result, there are over five million different molecules that can be formed with carbon atoms.

You might think that other members of the carbon family would also form millions of different compounds. These other elements also have four valence electrons. However, atoms of other elements in the carbon family all have more shells of electrons than carbon atoms. These extra shells make it more difficult for the atoms to form bonds. Carbon, therefore, is truly unique.

Figure 9.3 Most of the substances in this picture contain carbon.

Figure 9.4 Seawater, rocks, and sand contain inorganic compounds.

Compounds that contain carbon are called **organic** [ohr-GAN-ihk] **compounds.** The study of organic compounds is called organic chemistry. The word *organic* was first used many years ago. At that time it was believed that all matter could be divided into three categories; animal, vegetable, and mineral. The animal and vegetable, or living part of the world, was called organic. Because organic material came from living things, it was thought to be made of substances different from those in nonliving, mineral material. The nonliving material was called inorganic.

Scientists no longer use the word *organic* to describe only living matter. It is now known that living things are made of the same substances as nonliving things. Both living and nonliving things are made of elements. Today, the word *organic* is used to describe any carbon compound whether or not it is found in living matter. Therefore, things such as toothbrushes, which contain carbon, are said to be made of organic compounds, even though toothbrushes are not alive, never have been alive, and never will be alive.

Study Questions for 9.1
1. What kinds of bond do carbon atoms form?
2. What is an organic compound?

9.2 Hydrocarbons

You will find out
- what hydrocarbons are;
- what isomers are;
- how crude oil is distilled.

Hydrocarbons [hy-droh-KAHR-buhnz] are compounds made of only carbon and hydrogen. Hydrocarbons are the basic parts of all organic compounds. The simplest hydrocarbon is methane. Methane, CH_4, is made of one carbon atom and four hydrogen atoms. The hydrogen atoms are joined to the carbon atom by single covalent bonds.

Covalent molecules can be illustrated by using electron dot diagrams. Two dots represent a single covalent bond. When dashes are used in place of the pairs of dots, the result is called a **structural formula.** Figure 9.5 shows the electron dot diagram and the structural formula for a methane molecule. Structural formulas are a little neater way to represent molecules with many atoms. For this reason they are used to illustrate hydrocarbons.

Figure 9.5 *left:* A model of methane; *right:* Formulas for methane

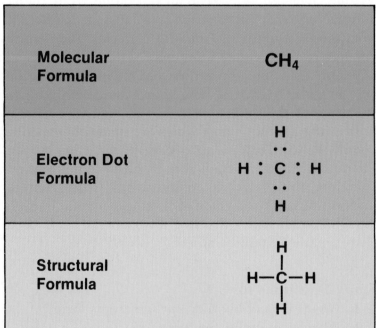

Molecular Formula	CH_4
Electron Dot Formula	H $\cdot\cdot$ H : C : H $\cdot\cdot$ H
Structural Formula	H | H—C—H | H

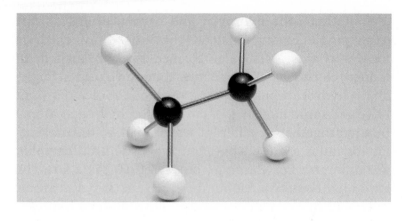

Figure 9.6 A model of ethane

Structural formulas give an idea of the structure of the molecule. However, you should always remember that they do not give the exact structure. They are drawn on a flat sheet of paper, and the molecules are three-dimensional. For example, the actual shape of a methane molecule is a pyramid with four faces. The carbon atom is in the center, and the hydrogen atoms are on the points of the pyramid.

Other hydrocarbon molecules similar to methane are made by linking together one or more carbon atoms in a chain. For example, in the ethane molecule, C_2H_6, two carbon atoms are bonded together and surrounded by hydrogen atoms. In propane, C_3H_8, three carbon atoms are bonded together. Each time another carbon atom is added to the chain, a new molecule is formed. These compounds are called **straight chain hydrocarbons.** The carbon atoms are bonded together in a single line.

Figure 9.7 Gasoline contains the hydrocarbon octane C_8H_{18}.

Sometimes the hydrogen and carbon atoms do not form single chains. Instead they form branched or looped chains. Molecules formed with branched or looped chains have properties different from straight chain hydrocarbons. Two hydrocarbon molecules may have the same numbers of carbon and hydrogen atoms bonded together in different ways. That is, the molecular formulas are the same, but the structural formulas are different. For example, butane, C_4H_{10}, is a straight chain hydrocarbon. Isobutane, C_4H_{10}, is a hydrocarbon with a branched chain. Butane and isobutane have the same molecular formulas but different structural formulas and different properties. Two compounds with the same molecular formulas but different structural formulas are called **isomers** [EYE-suh-muhrz].

Figure 9.8 The carbon atoms in butane form a straight chain. In isobutane, they form a branched chain.

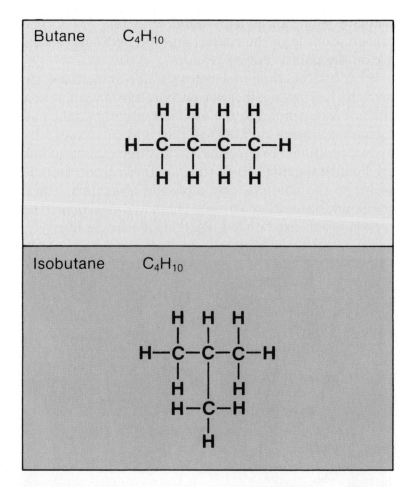

Do You Know?
It has been calculated that a hydrocarbon molecule with the formula $C_{30}H_{62}$ would have about 40 billion possible isomers.

Figure 9.9 A common ingredient in automotive antifreeze is ethylene glycol. Ethylene glycol contains carbon atoms joined by double bonds.

Sometimes the carbon atoms of a hydrocarbon are joined by double and triple bonds. Hydrocarbon compounds having double or triple bonds are grouped together. One of the more familiar members of this group is acetylene, C_2H_2. The two carbon atoms in the acetylene molecule are joined by a triple bond. The triple bond causes acetylene to burn with a very hot flame. For this reason, acetylene is used in welding torches.

Figure 9.10 Using an acetylene torch

Figure 9.11 Cooking gas is a short chain hydrocarbon.

Figure 9.12 Candles contain long chain hydrocarbons.

Hydrocarbon chains of different lengths have different properties and uses. In general, the shorter the chain is, the lighter the molecule is, and the lower the boiling point is. Because short chain hydrocarbons evaporate and burn easily, they are used as fuels. Cooking gas and gasoline are short chain hydrocarbons. The heavier long chain hydrocarbons are used as lubricating oils, as waxes, and as asphalt. They do not evaporate easily and are liquids or solids at room temperature.

Because they have different boiling points, hydrocarbons in crude oil from wells can be separated in a process called **distillation.** In distillation a liquid is changed to the gas state, and then the gas is collected and cooled, returning it to the liquid state. You start with a liquid and end up with a liquid. How does this process separate the hydrocarbons in crude oil? The different hydrocarbons boil and change to a gas at different temperatures. As the temperature rises, each hydrocarbon evaporates to the gas state and separates from the liquid crude oil. The hydrocarbon gas is then cooled and returned to the liquid state. After the hydrocarbons are separated, they are put through other chemical processes. Many useful products such as gasoline, kerosene, diesel fuel, asphalt, lubricating oil, wax, and petroleum jelly are produced in this way. Because the distillation of crude oil separates the oil into many parts, or fractions, it is often called **fractional distillation.**

Figure 9.13 This refinery separates the hydrocarbons in crude oil by fractional distillation.

Study Questions for 9.2

1. What are hydrocarbons?
2. Draw the structural formula for ethane.
3. What are isomers?
4. How is crude oil distilled?

9.3 Adding Other Atoms to Hydrocarbons

You will find out
- how alcohols are formed;
- how organic acids are formed;
- how some organic compounds are important to living things.

It is possible to replace one or more of the hydrogen atoms in a hydrocarbon with other atoms or groups of atoms. In this way new types of molecules are formed. These new molecules form new organic compounds. Many of these compounds are important in your life.

Three chlorine atoms can replace three hydrogen atoms in a methane molecule. This replacement changes methane, CH_4, into chloroform, $CHCl_3$. Before safer and more effective drugs were found, chloroform was commonly used to put surgical patients to sleep.

Figure 9.14 Replacing atoms in methane

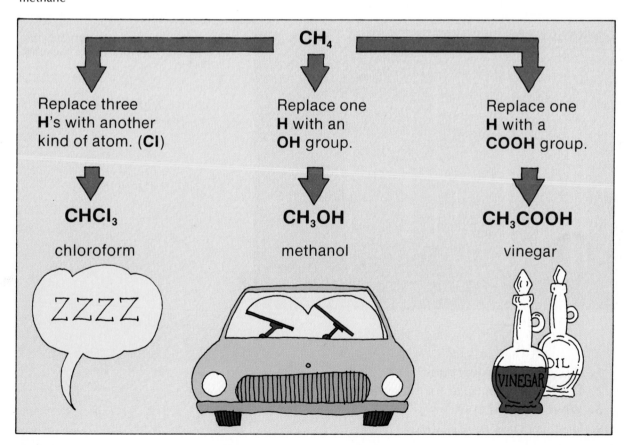

When an oxygen atom and a hydrogen atom, called the OH group, replace a single hydrogen atom in a hydrocarbon, an **alcohol** is formed. For example, if one of the hydrogen atoms in methane, CH_4, is replaced with an OH group, you get methanol, CH_3OH. Methanol, also known as methyl alcohol or wood alcohol, can be made from wood. It is a clear, poisonous liquid. Methanol freezes at $-93.9°C$. Because it freezes at a very low temperature, it is used in windshield washer fluid. Another alcohol, ethanol, can be used as a fuel. There are cars today running on ethanol instead of gasoline. Another gasoline substitute in current use is gasohol. Gasohol is a mixture of gasoline and alcohol. Most cars produced today have engines designed to burn gasoline. Those engines have to be modified to run on pure ethanol. Gasohol, however, can be used in gasoline-burning engines.

A carbon atom, two oxygen atoms, and a hydrogen atom, called the COOH group, form another group of atoms that can be added to hydrocarbons. Hydrocarbon chains with a COOH group are called **organic acids.** For example, when one of the hydrogen atoms in methane is replaced with a COOH group, the organic acid formed is acetic acid, CH_3COOH. Acetic acid is what gives vinegar its sour taste.

Figure 9.15 These citrus fruits contain the organic acid, citric acid.

ACTIVITY

How Can You Prepare an Organic Molecule?

Materials

test tube
250-mL beaker
hot plate
graduated cylinder
eyedropper
salicylic acid
(an organic acid)
methyl alcohol
(methanol)
concentrated sulfuric
acid
test-tube holder
test-tube stand
safety glasses
apron

Procedure

1. Put on your safety glasses and apron.

2. Prepare a hot-water bath by placing the beaker, half filled with water on the hot plate. Turn the hot plate on medium.

3. Measure 1 g of salicylic acid and put it in the test tube.

4. Add 5 mL of methyl alcohol to the test tube.

5. Holding the test tube with the test-tube holder, carefully add 3 drops of sulfuric acid to the test tube.

6. Carefully place the test tube in the hot-water bath for 15 minutes. Be sure that the test tube is not pointed toward anyone.

7. After 15 minutes, use the test-tube holder to remove the test tube from the hot-water bath.

8. Hold the test tube about 12 cm in front of your nose and use your hand to fan some of the vapors toward your nose.

Questions

1. What odor did you detect from the test tube?

2. The material you made is an ester, methyl salicylate. Do library research to determine what an ester is. How is the ester methyl salicylate (oil of wintergreen) used?

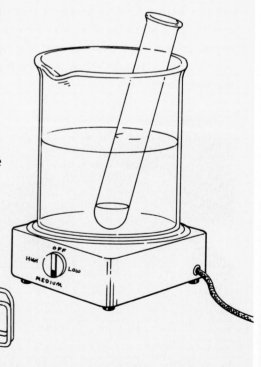

Figure 9.16 The human body contains proteins, fats, and carbohydrates.

An important group of organic acids are the **amino acids.** Amino acids are organic acids that contain nitrogen. The nitrogen atoms are present in NH_2 groups. Amino acids can join together to form long amino acid chains. These chains are called **proteins.** Proteins are a necessary part of living things. Thousands of different kinds of proteins are found in the human body. They are important parts of muscles, hair, bones, skin, blood, and other body organs.

Many organic compounds are made from different combinations of carbon, oxygen, and hydrogen atoms. Two categories of such compounds are fats and carbohydrates. Both fats and carbohydrates are found in living things. Plant carbohydrates provide animals with food energy and long chains of carbon atoms that are used to make other large molecules.

Study Questions for 9.3

1. How is methanol formed?
2. How is acetic acid formed?
3. How does your body use carbohydrates and proteins?

9.4   Synthetic Materials

You will find out
- what a polymer is;
- how synthetic materials are made.

Scientists have made progress in understanding the structure of matter. They can change and rearrange molecules in new and useful ways. One of the best examples of this progress is the manufacture of synthetic materials from hydrocarbons.

Organic molecules containing a large number of atoms are called **polymers** [PAHL-uh-muhrs]. Some polymers are natural, like some of the proteins in your body. Many other polymers are synthetic. In order to make a polymer in the laboratory, smaller molecules must be linked together to form the long chains of polymers.

Figure 9.17 The clothing these people are wearing and the raft they are riding on are made of synthetic materials. Over 33 percent of the fiber and over 70 percent of the rubber used in the world today are synthetic.

Figure 9.18 The grass in this stadium is synthetic turf.

Consider, for example, the making of polyethylene, a tough, waxy solid used in plastics. Polyethylene is a synthetic material made by linking together smaller ethylene molecules. Ethylene, C_2H_4, is a very small molecule of six atoms compared to the polymer polyethylene. A polyethylene molecule can have thousands of atoms.

Polymers can be formed into almost any shape. These shapes become familiar objects such as combs, bowls, pipes, and bathtubs Some polymers can be made into coatings for packages. Other polymers are formed into thin threads that are woven into cloth. In this way synthetic fabrics such as nylon and polyester are made.

In the hydrocarbon benzene, C_6H_6, six carbon atoms are bonded in a ring structure. Molecules made with benzene are used in making rubber, plastics, acrylic fibers, varnish, and detergents.

Do You Know?
Many compounds made with the benzene ring structure have a noticeable smell. They are called aromatic compounds.

ACTIVITY

How Do Three Substances Compare?

Materials

3 test tubes
salt
 (natural, inorganic)
sugar
 (natural, organic)
saccharin
 (synthetic, organic)
isopropyl alcohol
fingernail polish
 remover
3 can lids
ring stand and ring
Bunsen burner
matches
tongs
safety glasses
apron
marking pencil
test-tube rack
magnifying glass

Procedure

1. Put on your apron and safety glasses.

2. Copy the chart and use it to record your observations.

3. Obtain a sample of salt, sugar, and saccharin.

4. Examine each substance with a magnifying glass.

5. Describe and diagram the crystals of each.

6. Label 3 clean test tubes *A, B,* and *C.*

7. Fill each test tube halfway with water.

8. Put 20 grains of salt in A; put 20 grains of sugar in B; put 20 grains of saccharin in C. Gently shake each test tube and observe.

9. Repeat steps 7 and 8 once with isopropyl alcohol and once with fingernail polish remover. Be sure the test tubes are clean between trials.

10. Set up the ring stand, ring, Bunsen burner, and can lid as shown in the diagram.

11. Place a small sample of sugar on the can lid.

12. Light the Bunsen burner and observe the sugar.

13. Turn off the burner. Let the can lid cool and remove it with tongs.

14. Put a clean can lid on the ring.

15. Repeat steps 11–14 once with saccharin and once with salt.

Questions

1. What comparison can you make between organic and inorganic substances?

2. How are sugar and saccharin alike? How are they different?

Material	Describe Crystals	Dissolves in Water?	Dissolves in Alcohol?	Dissolves in Remover?	Reaction When Heated
salt (natural, inorganic)					
sugar (natural, organic)					
saccharin (synthetic, organic)					

Chapter 9 / Carbon Compounds

You use synthetic materials every day. They are in your home, in everything from furniture to kitchen utensils to sports equipment. In some ways synthetic materials may have advantages over comparable natural products because synthetics are produced under scientifically-controlled conditions. Synthetic materials can be made to have properties not found in natural products. Plastics, for example, are lightweight, can easily be shaped into different forms, and can be very strong.

Figure 9.19 Can you find all the plastic items in this photograph?

Study Questions for 9.4

1. What is a polymer?
2. How are synthetic polymers made?

What Did You Learn?

- Carbon atoms can form single, double, and triple covalent bonds.
- Compounds that contain carbon are called organic compounds.
- Hydrocarbons are compounds made of only carbon and hydrogen.
- Structural formulas are used to illustrate organic compounds.
- In straight chain hydrocarbons, the carbon atoms are bonded together in a single line.
- Isomers are compounds with the same molecular formulas but different structural formulas.
- Hydrocarbon chains of different lengths have different properties and uses.
- The hydrocarbons in crude oil can be separated by distillation.
- An alcohol is formed when an OH group replaces a hydrogen atom in a hydrocarbon.
- An organic acid is formed when a COOH group replaces a hydrogen atom in a hydrocarbon.
- Amino acids are organic acids with nitrogen atoms present in NH_2 groups.
- Proteins, fats, and carbohydrates are important organic compounds that are found in the human body.
- Polymers are organic molecules containing a large number of atoms.
- Synthetic polymers are made by linking together smaller molecules.

Key Terms

double bonds
triple bonds
organic compounds
hydrocarbons
structural formula
straight chain hydrocarbons
isomers
distillation
fractional distillation
alcohol
organic acids
amino acids
proteins
polymers

Biography
Wallace Hume Carothers (1896–1937)

synthetic rubber. In the 1930's, he began joining together molecules in long chains similar to the chains found in silk. Eventually he found one which was stronger than silk. He had discovered nylon.

The discovery of nylon began the new industry of synthetic fibers. Today the nylon industry is one of the most important industries in the world. Unfortunately, Carothers did not live to see what became of his discovery. He died two days after his forty-first birthday.

Wallace Carothers began his higher education wanting to be an accountant. After only a year at business college, he changed schools to study science. He must have been a very good science student because he was soon given the job of teaching chemistry to his fellow students. The only chemistry teacher at the school had left during World War I, and it was impossible to get another.

After graduate school at the University of Illinois, Carothers taught there and at Harvard University. He later went to work at DuPont, a chemical company. At DuPont he developed synthetic materials, such as neoprene, a

TO THINK ABOUT AND DO

Vocabulary

Number a piece of paper from 1 through 10. Beside the appropriate number write the letter for the term that is described.

1. groups of these form proteins
2. compounds containing only carbon and hydrogen
3. example of a straight chain hydrocarbon
4. compounds containing carbon
5. process for separating the hydrocarbons in crude oil
6. large organic molecules made of many atoms
7. forms when OH replaces a hydrogen atom in a hydrocarbon
8. compounds with the same molecular formulas but different structural formulas
9. example of an alcohol
10. represents a hydrocarbon molecule

a. alcohol
b. distillation
c. organic compounds
d. polymers
e. structural formula
f. amino acids
g. isomers
h. ethane
i. hydrocarbons
j. methanol

What Do You Remember?

1. What element is in all organic compounds?
2. What two elements are in all hydrocarbons?
3. Write the structural formula for methane.
4. What type of bond is used to join carbon atoms?
5. How can a hydrocarbon be converted to an alcohol?
6. How does an organic acid differ from a hydrocarbon?
7. Why are carbohydrates important?
8. How does an amino acid differ from an organic acid?
9. Name a synthetic polymer and tell how it is formed.
10. What property of hydrocarbons is used in the distillation of crude oil?

Applying What You Have Learned

1. Name four types of compounds an organic chemist might study.
2. Why do the hydrocarbons butane and isobutane have different properties?
3. The molecular formula for octane is C_8H_{18}. Draw its structural formula.
4. For each of the following formulas tell whether it represents a hydrocarbon, an alcohol, an organic acid, or an amino acid.

   (a) H_2CNH_2COOH
   (b) C_6H_6
   (c) C_2H_5OH
   (d) C_5H_{12}
   (e) CH_3COOH
   (f) CH_3OH

Research and Investigation

Soap is a product that people use in their daily lives. Find out how soap is made. Is soap made today using the same method that the pioneers used? How does soap work to remove dirt from clothes?

Unit Three

Matter, Energy, and Change

Chemical Reactions 10

The world you live in is constantly changing. Nothing is ever quite the same. Changes are a good thing. Without them you could not live.

Some changes take place very rapidly. Think of the burning of gasoline in a car engine or the explosion of gunpowder. Other changes like the making and baking of bread take minutes or hours to occur. Still other changes such as the decay of wood or the yellowing of paper take days or even years.

Think about the many different kinds of changes in matter that are going on around you. Some changes are useful to people. Others are not. Some changes are even harmful. By understanding how changes happen and why, scientists can learn how to make useful changes work even better. Scientists can also learn how to prevent or slow down harmful changes.

Figure 10.1 Colorful changes occur in autumn leaves.

10.1 Chemical Changes

You will find out
- how physical and chemical changes are different;
- how to read chemical equations;
- what the four main groups of chemical reactions are.

When an artist takes a block of marble and chips and polishes it to make a beautiful statue, the marble has changed shape. Some of the marble remains in the statue. The rest of it is left on the ground. But all of it is still marble. Only the size and shape of the marble have changed. An ice cube changes in size and shape when it melts. It also changes from the solid to the liquid state. But it is still the same chemical substance H_2O. Changes which affect the size, shape, or physical state of a substance but not its chemical properties and formula are called **physical changes.**

Figure 10.2 The faces on Mount Rushmore are the result of physical changes.

Figure 10.3 A chemical change occurs when iron rusts.

In changes such as burning, rusting, baking, and explosions chemical properties are changed. New substances are formed. Changes which affect the chemical properties of one or more substances are called **chemical changes.** For example, when wood burns, carbon in the wood combines with oxygen from the air to produce carbon dioxide.

The carbon dioxide is a new chemical substance. The properties of carbon dioxide are different from those of carbon and oxygen. When an iron nail is exposed to oxygen in the air, the oxygen combines with the iron to form rust. Note that chemical changes, like physical changes, can affect the size, shape, and state of substances. However, only chemical changes affect the chemical properties of substances.

People have been making use of chemical changes for thousands of years. They have burned wood and used the heat energy released to keep warm. The heat energy released has also been used to bring about other chemical changes such as those in cooking.

A chemical change is the result of a process called **chemical reaction.** Three different things can happen in chemical reactions. In some reactions, molecules break apart into atoms. In other reactions, atoms come together to form molecules. In a third type of reaction, atoms change places with other atoms to form new molecules.

Figure 10.4 A chemical reaction

A **chemical equation** [ih-KWAY-shuhn] uses formulas and symbols to show what happens in a chemical reaction. For example, the chemical equation for the reaction that occurs when the carbon in coal burns to form carbon dioxide is the following:

$$C + O_2 \rightarrow CO_2$$

This equation tells you that one atom of carbon plus two atoms of oxygen produce one molecule of carbon dioxide. The arrow is read as *produces*.

In chemical equations, the substance or substances you start with are called the **reactants** [ree-AK-tuhntz]. They are put on the left side of the arrow. The results of the reaction, the **products,** are put on the right side. Thus, a chemical equation has this general form:

$$\text{reactants} \rightarrow \text{products}$$

There are four main groups of chemical reactions. In *synthesis reactions,* two or more elements or compounds unite to form one compound. The formation of salt from the elements sodium and chlorine is an example of a synthesis reaction.

$$Na + Cl \rightarrow NaCl$$

In *decomposition reactions,* one compound breaks down into two or more other substances. An example is the breakdown of zinc chloride into zinc and chlorine.

$$ZnCl_2 \rightarrow Zn + Cl_2$$

Figure 10.5 *left:* A compound is formed. *right:* A compound is broken down.

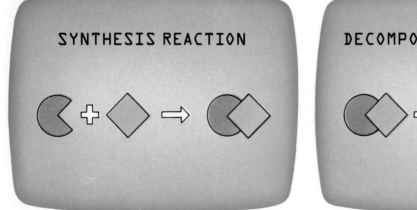

SYNTHESIS REACTION

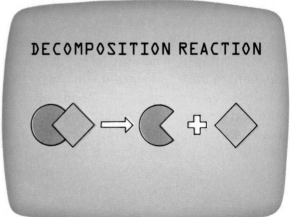

DECOMPOSITION REACTION

In a *single displacement reaction,* one element replaces another one in a compound. For example, magnesium can replace the beryllium in the compound beryllium fluoride. This reaction forms magnesium fluoride and beryllium.

$$BeF_2 + Mg \rightarrow MgF_2 + Be$$

In a *double displacement reaction,* two compounds react to produce two new compounds. For example, silver nitrate reacts with sodium chloride. Silver chloride and sodium nitrate are produced. As you can see, the sodium Na and the silver Ag change places. This results in two new compounds being formed.

$$AgNO_3 + NaCl \rightarrow AgCl + NaNO_3$$

Figure 10.6 *left:* One compound is changed. *right:* Two compounds are changed.

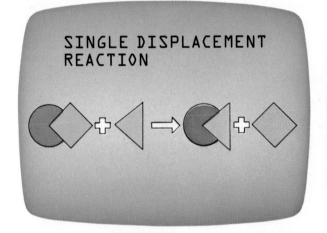

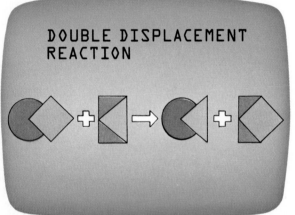

Study Questions for 10.1

1. Give an example of a physical change and an example of a chemical change.
2. Identify the reactants and products in the following equation:
$$BeF_2 + Mg \rightarrow MgF_2 + Be$$
3. Name the four main groups of chemical reactions.

10.2 Balancing Chemical Equations

You will find out
• how to balance chemical equations.

In a chemical reaction, no atoms ever just disappear and no new atoms are formed. In other words, the number of atoms of each element does not change. This fact is called the **law of conservation of mass.** Mass is the amount of matter present in a substance. You can keep track of mass in chemical equations by counting the numbers of atoms on both sides of the equation.

Figure 10.7 The law of conservation of mass applies to all chemical reactions.

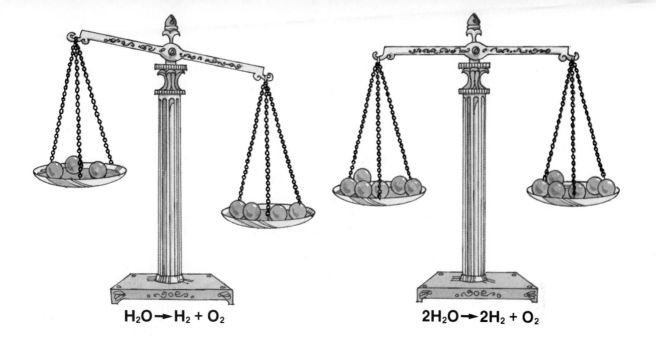

$$H_2O \rightarrow H_2 + O_2 \qquad 2H_2O \rightarrow 2H_2 + O_2$$

Because chemical reactions follow the law of conservation of mass, a chemical equation must show the same number of atoms of each element on both sides. In other words, the equation must be balanced. Consider, for example, the equation for the decomposition reaction in which water breaks up into hydrogen and oxygen molecules.

$$H_2O \rightarrow H_2 + O_2 \qquad \text{(not balanced)}$$

The equation is not balanced because there is only one oxygen atom on the reactant side and there are two on the product side. The balanced form of this equation is this:

$$2H_2O \rightarrow 2H_2 + O_2 \qquad \text{(balanced)}$$

The number 2 that you see in front of H_2O and H_2 is called a **coefficient** [koh-uh-FIHSH-uhnt]. A coefficient is a number placed in front of a formula or symbol that tells you how many atoms or molecules of that substance are present. If no coefficient appears in front of a symbol or formula, you know there is only one atom or molecule of that substance. To balance a chemical equation, you can change the coefficients but never the formulas or symbols.

Figure 10.8 In a balanced equation, the same number of atoms appears on both sides.

EXAMPLE Balance the chemical equation for the single displacement reaction in which fluorine replaces the chlorine in sodium chloride to produce sodium fluoride.

$$F_2 + NaCl \rightarrow NaF + Cl_2 \quad \text{(not balanced)}$$

1. Check the number of atoms of each element on both sides of the equation.

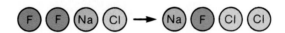

Reactants: 2 F atoms, 1 Na atom, 1 Cl atom
Products: 1 F atom, 1 Na atom, 2 Cl atoms

The equation is not balanced. The number of atoms of each element is not the same on both sides of the equation.

2. Balance the equation by changing the coefficients. First put 2 NaF molecules on the right. This balances F but puts Na out of balance. Balance Na by putting 2 NaCl molecules on the left. This balances both Na and Cl, and so you now have a balanced equation.

$$F_2 + 2NaCl \rightarrow 2NaF + Cl_2 \quad \text{(balanced)}$$

3. Recheck the number of atoms of each element on both sides of the equation to be sure you have balanced it correctly.

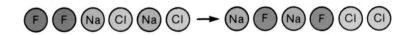

Reactants: 2 F atoms, 2 Na atoms, 2 Cl atoms
Products: 2 F atoms, 2 Na atoms, 2 Cl atoms

In changing coefficients to balance equations, you should always use the smallest coefficient possible. As in this example, a change in a coefficient sometimes puts one element that was in balance out of balance. To account for this possibility, you should recheck the number of atoms of each element when you have finished balancing the equation.

ACTIVITY

Is Mass Conserved in a Chemical Reaction?

Materials

lead nitrate solution
sodium iodide
  solution
2 test tubes
test-tube rack
balance
safety glasses
apron

Procedure

1. Copy the chart and use it to record your observations.

2. Put on your safety glasses and apron.

3. Fill one test tube ⅓ full with lead nitrate solution.

4. Fill the other test tube ⅓ full with sodium iodide solution.

5. Put both test tubes in the test-tube rack.

6. Measure the total mass of the rack, both test tubes, and solutions.

7. Pour the lead nitrate into the sodium iodide. Be careful to avoid spilling.

8. Put the empty test tube back in the rack.

9. Measure the mass of the rack, of the test tubes, and of the solution.

10. Find the difference in the mass before and after mixing.

11. Share your results with those of friends and add those results to your chart.

Questions

1. Do you think the change you observed was a chemical or a physical change?

2. How do you know a new substance was formed?

3. Why was it necessary to put the empty test tube back in the rack?

4. How does this experiment illustrate the law of conservation of mass?

	Mass Before Mixing	Mass After Mixing	Difference In Mass
Results			
Results of Friend			

Study Questions for 10.2

1. What does the law of conservation of mass tell you about chemical reactions?

2. Balance the following equation:

$$KClO_3 \rightarrow KCl + O_2$$

10.3 The Rate of Chemical Reactions

You will find out
- how the temperature affects the rate of chemical reactions;
- how the concentration of reactants affects the rate of chemical reactions;
- what is meant by the term *catalyst*.

It is important to know what the products will be in a chemical reaction. It is also important to know the rate of reaction. The rate of reaction is how fast the reaction occurs. For example, the rusting of iron releases heat energy. However, the reaction goes on so slowly at room temperature that no one would think of using a pile of rusting nails to keep warm. Other reactions proceed very quickly. Think of the explosion of dynamite. Knowing how fast a reaction will occur can be a life-or-death matter.

Figure 10.9 Some reactions proceed very quickly.

The rate at which a reaction occurs depends on many different things. Two very important considerations are the temperature and the concentration of the reactants. To understand why temperature and concentration are important, you must first understand what happens to the reactants in a chemical reaction.

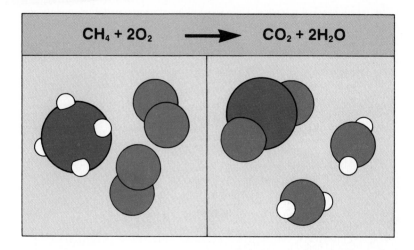

$$CH_4 + 2O_2 \longrightarrow CO_2 + 2H_2O$$

Figure 10.10 In the burning of methane, carbon dioxide and water are formed.

In chemical reactions, the reactants form new substances, the products. Reactant atoms and molecules must come in close contact with each other for this change to occur. When the reactants are molecules, the chemical bonds in those molecules must be broken so that the atoms involved can form new substances.

How are the bonds in reactant molecules broken? They are broken by collisions with other reactant molecules. If the reactant molecules are moving slowly, they will probably just bump into each other gently without breaking any bonds. Fast-moving molecules will collide with more force. These forceful collisions are more likely to break apart the molecules. So the faster the molecules are moving, the more likely it is that a collision will be strong enough to break one or both of them apart. Also, when the reactant molecules move faster, they collide more often. The rate of a reaction, then, depends on the force and frequency of collisions between reactants.

It is a general rule that reactions go faster when the temperature is raised. At higher temperatures the reactant molecules move faster. Thus, their chemical bonds are broken more quickly and easily than at lower temperatures. For example, most fires are started by raising the temperature of the material to be burned. You use a burning match to light a candle. The match raises the temperature of the reactants, the candle and the oxygen in the air around it.

Figure 10.11 Low temperatures slow down the chemical reactions that spoil food.

Figure 10.12 The same principle that applies to the concentration of reactants in a chemical reaction applies to cars on a highway. The greater the concentration of cars, the greater the chance of collisions.

Figure 10.13 Coal miners must be careful because coal dust has a large surface area and will ignite very easily.

When many reactant atoms and molecules are crowded into a given space, the concentration of reactants is high. In general, the higher the concentration of reactants, the faster the reaction will proceed. It will proceed faster because contact and collisions among reactants are increased.

If one or more of the reactants is a solid, contact between reactants is increased when the surface area of the solid is increased. Reactant contact and collisions are increased and the reaction proceeds more quickly. Imagine you are making a fire in a fireplace. Would it be easier to start one large log burning or to start a pile of small kindling? The surface area is increased when you use kindling so the fire starts and burns more quickly.

Another way to increase the rate of reaction is to use **catalysts** [KAT-uh-lihstz]. A catalyst is a substance that affects the rate of a chemical reaction without itself being changed or used up in the reaction. Catalysts are like go-betweens. A catalyst can speed up a reaction or cause one to occur by increasing the contact between reactants. Some catalysts are widely used in the chemical industry to speed up reactions.

Catalysts that promote chemical reactions in living things are called **enzymes** [EHN-zymz]. The enzymes in your body are made of proteins. Enzymes make it possible for the complicated chemical reactions necessary for life to occur at body temperature. Thousands of enzymes are known. Each serves a specific purpose by promoting a specific reaction. Some enzymes help your body digest food. Others help in getting energy for your body. Research into the nature of enzymes can lead to a better understanding of the causes and cures of some diseases. This knowledge should lead to a better chance for good health for everyone.

Do You Know?
A recently synthesized form of sugar has a differently shaped molecule that your enzymes can't digest. It tastes sweet but releases no calories.

Figure 10.14 The functions of thousands of enzymes contribute to a healthy body.

Study Questions for 10.3

1. Name two factors that affect the rate of a chemical reaction.
2. What is a catalyst?
3. What is an enzyme?

10.4 Energy and Chemical Reactions

You will find out
- what is meant by activation energy;
- how exothermic and endothermic reactions are different.

For many reactions to get started, energy must be added. This energy is necessary to begin breaking the bonds in the reactant molecules. The energy that must be supplied to start a chemical reaction is called **activation energy.** For example, to start a charcoal fire for a barbecue, you can supply the activation energy with a lighted match.

An important result of some chemical reactions is the release of heat energy. The heat energy comes from the formation of bonds in product molecules. In some reactions such as the burning of oil, the energy released in the formation of the product molecules is greater than the activation energy required. Such reactions produce a net release of energy.

A chemical reaction that releases energy is called an **exothermic** [ehk-soh-THUHR-mihk] **reaction.** All exothermic reactions do not produce large, noticeable amounts of energy in a short time as the burning of oil does. The rusting of iron, for example, is also an exothermic reaction. A rusting iron railing does not feel hot or even warm when you touch it. In this case, the energy is being released very slowly.

Do You Know?
Your body burns carbohydrates for fuel so why can't cars burn carbohydrates for fuel? Scientists are now working on methods to use beer and soybean oil as sources of fuel for cars.

Figure 10.15 Burning is an exothermic reaction.

In some chemical reactions, energy is absorbed instead of released. These reactions are called **endothermic** [ehn-doh-THUHR-mihk] **reactions.** The baking of a cake is an endothermic reaction. Heat energy is absorbed. The breakdown of water into hydrogen and oxygen is also an endothermic reaction. Electric energy is absorbed in this reaction.

While it is true that energy can be released or absorbed in a chemical reaction, energy is not being created or destroyed. It is just being changed from one form to another. The energy stored in the chemical bonds of reactant molecules may be released when the molecules break up and form product molecules. When energy is absorbed in a reaction, that energy is stored in the chemical bonds of the product molecules. Neither mass (matter) nor energy is created or destroyed in a chemical reaction.

Figure 10.16 Baking is an endothermic reaction.

Study Questions for 10.4

1. What is activation energy?
2. Describe and give an example of an exothermic reaction.
3. Describe and give an example of an endothermic reaction.

10.5 Acids, Bases, and Salts

You will find out

- what acids and bases are;
- what happens when an acid and a base react;
- how the strength of acids and bases is measured.

An interesting and important kind of chemical reaction involves two familiar and useful groups of compounds. Some of these compounds can be found in your home. To find them at home, you would look in the refrigerator, the kitchen cabinets, the cleaning closet, and the medicine cabinet. What are these groups of compounds? They are **acids** and **bases.** An acid is a substance that produces positive hydrogen ions, H^+, in liquid solution. A base is a substance that produces a negative ion in liquid solution, usually the OH^- ion. An ion is an atom or a group of atoms that has different numbers of positive protons and negative electrons. Acids and bases can be weak or strong depending on the concentration of H^+ and OH^- ions. The higher the concentration of H^+ and OH^- ions, the stronger the acid or base.

Almost all acids are combinations of hydrogen and one or more nonmetals. Acids react strongly with metals and are widely used in industry to process metals. Some acids are dangerous because they are poisonous and damage human skin.

Do You Know?
The acids in your stomach are strong enough to dissolve zinc and blister the skin.

Figure 10.17 Hydrangeas growing in basic soil produce pink flowers. The same plants produce blue flowers when growing in acidic soil.

Figure 10.18 Some familiar acids

You are personally familiar with many acids. You even eat and drink some of them! Obviously, the acids you eat and drink are not poisonous and do not damage human skin. Many foods contain some form of relatively weak acid. In general, the more acidic a substance, the more sour it tastes. For example, which is more sour-tasting: limes, tomatoes, or milk? Limes are very acidic, tomatoes less, and milk less still. Other foods and drinks that are acidic are oranges, lemons, vinegar, pickles, carbonated drinks, and tea.

Almost all bases are made of a metal, of hydrogen, and of oxygen. The primary exception is ammonia, NH_3. Substances that have a high concentration of a base in them have a bitter taste. Bases are slippery to touch. However, because many bases can damage human skin, you should always be careful when handling them. Relatively weak bases are widely used in cleaners and soaps. Weak bases are also used in medicines for upset stomachs. Stronger bases are used in products that unclog household drains.

Figure 10.19 Some familiar bases

When an acid and a base combine, they react in a **neutralization** [nu-truh-luh-ZAY-shuhn] **reaction.** The positive H^+ ion from the acid is neutralized by the negative OH^- ion from the base. An example of a neutralization reaction is the reaction of sodium hydroxide, NaOH, and hydrochloric acid, HCl.

$$\text{HCl} + \text{NaOH} \rightarrow \text{NaCl} + \text{H}_2\text{O}$$
$$\text{acid} \quad \text{base} \quad \text{salt} \quad \text{water}$$

The products of a neutralization reaction are always water and a salt. A **salt** is the compound produced in a neutralization reaction when the hydrogen in the acid is replaced with another element from the base. Usually a salt is a compound made of a metal and a nonmetal. You may have thought that there was only one kind of salt, table salt (sodium chloride). Although sodium chloride is the most common and familiar salt, it is not the only salt. Other familiar and useful salts are sodium bicarbonate, or baking soda, $NaHCO_3$ and silver nitrate, $AgNO_3$, which is used in photography.

Figure 10.20 Silver nitrate, a salt, is used in photography.

The strength of an acid or a base in a liquid solution is measured on the **pH scale.** The pH scale is a series of whole numbers from 0 to 14. The lower the pH number, the greater the concentration of H^+ ions. A neutral substance, such as pure water, has a pH of 7. A neutral substance is considered neither an acid nor a base. Any pH number over 7 indicates a base. The higher the number, the stronger the base. Similarly, any pH value under 7 indicates an acid. The lower the pH number, the stronger the acid.

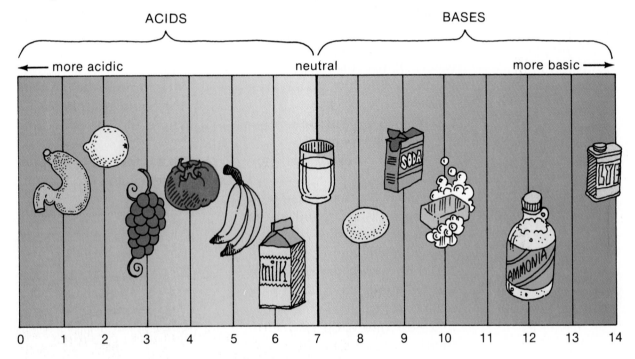

Figure 10.21 The pH scale

One way to tell whether a solution is an acid or a base is to use an **indicator.** An indicator is a special type of organic compound that changes color as the pH of a solution changes. A commonly used indicator is litmus paper. Litmus paper comes in both red and blue. Red litmus paper stays red in an acid or in a neutral solution but turns blue in a base. Blue litmus paper stays blue in a base or in a neutral solution but turns red in an acid. As you can see, litmus paper only tells you if a solution is acidic, basic, or neutral. It does not indicate a specific pH value.

ACTIVITY

Materials

dilute hydrochloric
  acid
dilute sodium
  hydroxide
phenolphthalein
tin pie plate
graduated cylinder
2 beakers
eyedropper
magnifying glass
apron
safety glasses

How Can You Form a Salt?

Procedure

1. Put on your safety glasses and apron.

2. CAUTION: Do not let any of the liquids touch your skin. If they do, run cold water over the area immediately and tell your teacher. Immediately wipe up any spills. Never put your eyedropper down on the desk; always put it in a beaker of water. Rinse the eyedropper thoroughly in the water after each use.

3. Pour 5 mL of sodium hydroxide into a beaker.

4. Add a drop of phenolphthalein.

5. Add hydrochloric acid drop by drop until the liquid in the beaker turns clear.

6. After the liquid clears, add one drop of sodium hydroxide and the liquid should turn pink again.

7. Add one drop of hydrochloric acid to reclear the liquid.

8. Pour the liquid into the pie plate and allow the liquid to evaporate.

9. After the liquid has evaporated, use a magnifying glass to compare the crystals that remain with those of table salt. CAUTION: Do not taste any salt.

Questions

1. What happens when phenolphthalein is added to sodium hydroxide?

2. What forms in the pie plate when the liquid evaporates?

3. Where did the salt come from?

4. What is the role of the phenolphthalein in the experiment?

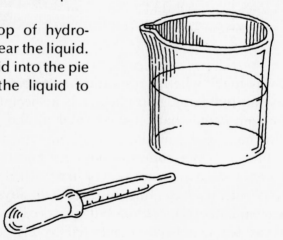

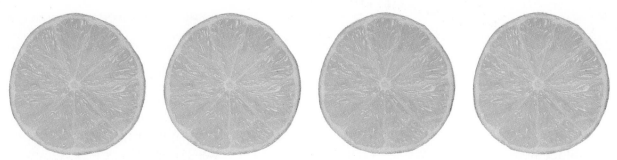

Another indicator is a liquid solution of phenolphthalein [fee-nahl-THAY-leen]. Phenolphthalein is colorless in an acidic solution. However, phenolphthalein turns bright pink in a basic solution. Like litmus paper, phenolphthalein does not indicate pH values, only whether a solution is acidic or basic.

Other indicators go through a range of colors as the pH of a solution changes. By comparing the color of the indicator with a special color chart, you can tell what the pH value of the solution is.

Figure 10.22 Limes contain citric acid. What would happen if you dipped a strip of red litmus paper and a strip of blue litmus paper into some lime juice?

Figure 10.23 Phenolphthalein has just been added to this base. After a few moments the entire liquid will be pink.

Study Questions for 10.5
1. Give a definition and an example of an acid.
2. Give a definition and an example of a base.
3. What happens in a neutralization reaction?
4. What does the pH scale measure?
5. What does an indicator tell you?

What Did You Learn?

- Physical changes affect the physical size, shape, or state of a substance.
- Chemical changes affect the chemical properties of a substance.
- The four types of chemical reactions are synthesis, decomposition, single displacement, and double displacement.
- The law of conservation of mass states that no atoms disappear and no new atoms are formed in a chemical reaction.
- The general form for a chemical equation is the following: reactants → products.
- To balance an equation, you can change the coefficents but not the formulas or symbols.
- The rate of reaction increases as the temperature and concentration of the reactants increase.
- A catalyst is a substance that affects the rate of reaction without being changed or used up in the reaction.
- Enzymes are catalysts in living things.
- Activation energy is the energy needed to start a chemical reaction.
- In exothermic reactions heat energy is released.
- In endothermic reactions heat energy is absorbed.
- An acid produces H^+ ions in liquid solution.
- A base produces negative ions, usually the OH^- ion, in liquid solution.
- In neutralization reaction, an acid and a base combine to produce water and a salt.
- The pH scale measures the strength of acids and bases.
- Indicators tell whether a solution is acidic or basic.

Key Terms

physical changes
chemical changes
chemical reaction
chemical equation
reactants
products
law of conservation of mass
coefficient
catalysts
enzymes
activation energy
exothermic reaction
endothermic reactions
acids
bases
neutralization reaction
salt
pH scale
indicator

Career

Chemist

Chemists search for new knowledge about substances and put this knowledge to practical use. About one half of today's chemists are engaged in research and development. Most of these chemists work to improve and create new products. Wonder drugs, synthetic materials such as nylon and polyester fabrics, and fuels for space travel are only a few examples of the many useful products that chemists have helped to develop.

Research chemists also work on research projects that extend scientific knowledge. Basic research often has practical uses. For example, synthetic rubber and plastics have resulted from research on polymers. Making polymers involves putting small molecules together to form larger ones.

Many other chemists work in analyzing and testing materials. In industry, tests must be made at practically every stage in the manufacture of a product. Industrial chemists also work in inspection and sales.

A chemist should be able to talk to and get along with others. This skill is important because chemists often work as teams on problems that require close cooperation. They must also be able to communicate clearly the results of their research. A chemist must have patience and the ability to stick to a job because many delays and problems come up during experiments.

Some of the specialties within chemistry include agricultural chemistry, paint chemistry, nutritional chemistry, petroleum chemistry, physical chemistry, and biochemistry.

TO THINK ABOUT AND DO

Vocabulary

Number a separate piece of paper from 1 through 10. Find the term in the second column that best describes the phrase in the first column. Write the letter for that term beside the appropriate number.

1. reaction that releases energy
2. substance to distinguish between acids and bases
3. change that affects the chemical properties of a substance
4. a substance that produces H^+ ions in solution
5. energy needed to start a reaction
6. reaction that absorbs energy
7. product of a neutralization reaction
8. number used to indicate how many molecules of a particular compound are present in a chemical equation
9. substance that produces OH^- ions in solution
10. substances formed in a chemical reaction

a. reactants
b. activation energy
c. exothermic reaction
d. physical change
e. acid
f. products
g. salt
h. indicator
i. chemical change
j. endothermic reaction
k. coefficient
l. base

What Do You Remember?

1. What is a chemical reaction? Give an example.
2. How do chemical changes differ from physical changes?
3. Balance these equations:

$$Na + H_2O \rightarrow NaOH + H_2$$
$$Mg + HCl \rightarrow H_2 + MgCl_2$$

4. How does a balanced equation illustrate the law of conservation of mass?
5. How do synthesis and decomposition reactions differ? Give an example of each.
6. What is activation energy?
7. How do exothermic and endothermic reactions differ? Give an example of each.
8. List three ways to increase the rate of a reaction.
9. What is a catalyst?
10. What is a neutralization reaction?

Applying What You Have Learned

1. How could you demonstrate the law of conservation of mass?
2. How could you determine if a substance is an acid or a base?
3. How could you determine the relative strength of an acid or a base?
4. Name two physical changes that happen in your home.
5. Name two chemical changes that happen in your home.

Research and Investigation

1. Throughout the ages, table salt has been a very valuable product. The term *salary* is derived from the word *salt* because at one time salt was so valuable it was used to pay debts. Look up the history of salt and find out some of the ways salt has been used.
2. Find out how acids are used in glass etching.

Nuclear Reactions

11

Energy from the sun is essential to life on the earth. Without it, green plants could not produce the foods you and other animals must eat to live. Without the sun's energy, temperatures and weather patterns would change drastically. The earth would be cold, dark, and barren.

The sun produces enormous amounts of energy day after day, year after year, century after century. How is all this energy produced? Is there an exothermic chemical reaction going on in the sun? Scientists know of no chemical reaction that could produce enough energy to equal the amount produced by the sun. The sun's energy must come from changes other than chemical changes. The sun's energy comes from changes in the nucleus of the atom.

Since life on the earth could not exist without energy from the sun, nuclear changes are clearly very important. Nuclear changes occur on the earth as well as on the sun. Here they have been put to use in science, medicine, and industry.

11.1 Nuclear Changes

You will find out
- what happens in a nuclear reaction;
- what holds the nucleus of an atom together.

Chemical reactions involve the breaking and forming of chemical bonds. Chemical bonds between atoms involve electrons. Chemical reactions, therefore, affect the electrons of the reactant and product atoms. These reactions do not affect the nuclei of the atoms. However, it is possible for the nucleus of an atom to change. The nucleus of one kind of atom is changed into the nucleus of a different kind of atom in a **nuclear reaction.** Nuclear reactions can release enormous amounts of energy.

To understand how the nucleus of an atom can change, you must keep in mind some basic facts about the nucleus. Positive protons and neutral neutrons make up the nucleus of an atom. The number of protons, the atomic number, determines the kind of atom. If the number of protons changes, the kind of atom changes. The number of neutrons can change without changing the kind of atom. Atoms with the same number of protons but different numbers of neutrons are called isotopes.

Figure 11.2 Energy from nuclear reactions was used to power the *Voyager* spacecraft.

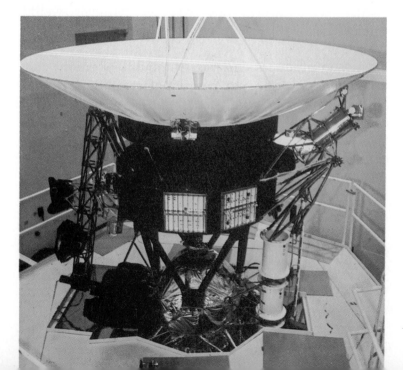

The nuclear force holds the protons and neutrons tightly in the tiny area of the nucleus. Since like electric charges repel, the positive protons tend to move apart from each other. The nuclear force must be very strong to counteract the electric forces that act to split the nucleus apart. The neutrons contribute to the binding strength of the nuclear force. Since the nuclear force is very strong, nuclear reactions can be a powerful energy source.

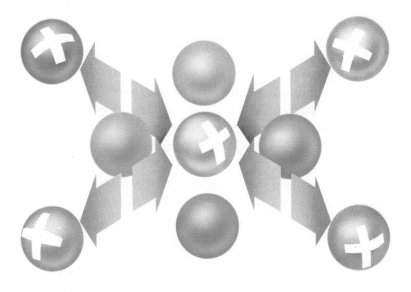

Figure 11.3 *left:* Electric forces act to split the nucleus apart. *right:* The nuclear force counteracts the electric forces and holds the nucleus together.

There are different kinds of nuclear reactions. In some, a single nucleus spontaneously releases particles of matter and energy. Other nuclear reactions involve the splitting apart of atomic nuclei in response to an outside influence. In a third kind of nuclear reaction, nuclei join together. No matter what kind of nuclear change occurs, one result is always the same. One kind of atom is changed into another kind of atom.

Study Questions for 11.1
1. What happens in a nuclear reaction?
2. Why don't the positive protons in the nucleus separate, splitting the nucleus apart?

11.2 Radioactivity and Radioactive Decay

You will find out
- how radioactivity was discovered;
- what happens in radioactive decay.

The energy given off when a nuclear change occurs is called **radioactivity.** Radioactivity was discovered because it rained one day in Paris in 1896. Because of the clouds and rain, Antoine Henri Becquerel could not do his experiment on the effects of sunlight on uranium. So he wrapped the uranium in black paper and put it inside a cardboard box. He stored the box in his desk drawer on top of some photographic plates. When Becquerel returned to his desk sometime later, he found that the photographic plates had been exposed. Since the plates had not been outside his desk drawer, the only thing that could have affected the plates was the uranium. But how could a rock give off energy that could go through a cardboard box and a sheet of black paper?

Becquerel called in two other scientists to investigate. They were Pierre Curie and his wife, Marie. The three scientists did many tests on uranium. The three found that the amount of energy given off by the uranium depended only on how much uranium was present. It didn't matter if the uranium was in a solid, liquid, or gas state. Nor did it matter if it was combined with

Figure 11.4 *left:* Antoine Henri Becquerel wearing his uniform as a member of the French Academy of Sciences; *right:* The exposed photographic plates that Becquerel discovered

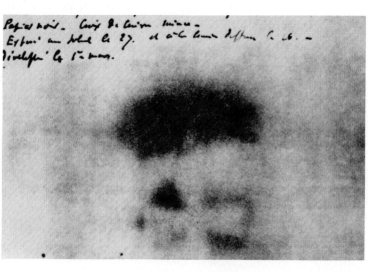

other elements. The mysterious release of energy had to be a property of the innermost part of the element. Scientists now call this innermost part the nucleus of the atom. Marie Curie gave this property the name *radioactivity*. In the years that followed, the Curies discovered two other radioactive elements, radium and polonium.

The radioactive elements the Curies discovered were undergoing a kind of nuclear reaction called **radioactive decay.** In radioactive decay, the nucleus of one kind of atom spontaneously changes into the nucleus of another kind of atom. For example, uranium nuclei can undergo radioactive decay and change into lead nuclei.

Radioactive decay produces **nuclear radiation.** Nuclear radiation can be in one of three forms: **alpha particles, beta particles,** or **gamma radiation.** An alpha particle, like a helium nucleus, has two protons and two neutrons. Beta particles are high-speed electrons. Gamma radiation is not in the form of particles. It is a form of energy without mass.

Do You Know?
Less than a thimbleful of radium gives off as much energy as the burning of 9 metric tons of gasoline.

Figure 11.5 Alpha particles (α), beta particles (β), and gamma radiation (γ) have different penetrating abilities. Which form of radiation could be stopped by a page from this book?

ACTIVITY

Materials

glass jar with lid
black cloth
blotting paper
wire
dry ice
small baking pan
alcohol
luminous watch dial
flashlight
apron
tongs

Can You See Nuclear Radiation?

Procedure

1. Put on your apron.

2. Cut the cloth so it fits inside the jar lid.

3. Cut the blotting paper so it fits in the bottom of the jar. Wet the blotting paper thoroughly with alcohol. Place the paper in the bottom of the jar and turn the jar upside down. If the paper does not stay on the bottom of the jar, make a wire ring that will fit inside the bottom of the jar and use it to hold the paper in place.

4. Using tongs, place the dry ice in the small pan. CAUTION: Do not touch the dry ice with your bare hands.

5. Remove the luminous watch dial from its case and place it on top of the black cloth.

6. Rewet the blotting paper with alcohol. Place the black cloth inside the lid. Holding the jar upside down, screw on the lid.

7. Place the jar upside down on the dry ice. Wait five minutes.

8. Your teacher will turn off the lights and make the room as dark as possible. Shine the flashlight through the side of the jar as you look down at the cloth. You should see vapor

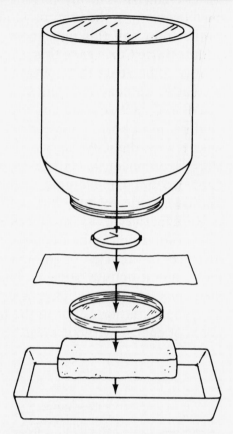

trails through the alcohol mist. The heavy trails are those of alpha particles. The weaker, wavy trails are made by beta particles.

Questions

1. Describe or draw the vapor trails that you see and identify them as those of alpha particles or beta particles.

2. Did all students see the same number of vapor trails? How can you account for this?

Many methods are used to detect nuclear radiation. One of the most commonly used devices is a Geiger counter. This device operates using a tube filled with a noble gas such as argon. Radiation passing through a thin window on the end of the tube knocks electrons off the argon atoms in its path. Electric forces are used to pull the electrons to a wire in the center of the tube. This creates a momentary electric charge that can be used to make a popping noise.

Too much nuclear radiation can be very harmful to living things. The radiation can cause sickness, suffering, and even death. For this reason, radioactive materials must always be handled with great care. Heavy shielding and protective material must be used. Unfortunately, the Curies did not know this. Marie and her daughter and son-in-law, who both worked with her, all died from overexposure to nuclear radiation.

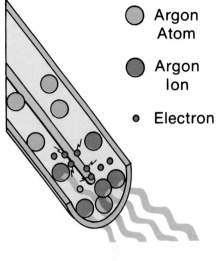

Argon Atom

Argon Ion

Electron

Figure 11.6 The tube of a Geiger counter

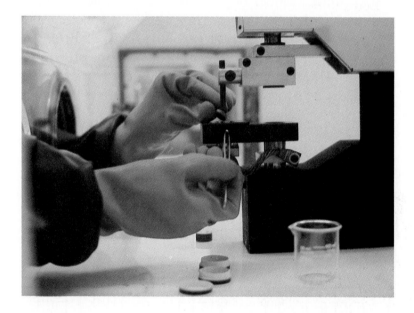

Figure 11.7 Using protective shielding to handle radioactive material

Study Questions for 11.2

1. Who were the discoverers of radioactivity?
2. What happens when a nucleus undergoes radioactive decay?
3. What are the three forms of nuclear radiation?

11.3 Radioactive Isotopes and Half-Life

You will find out

• what makes some isotopes radioactive;
• what is meant by the term *half-life*;
• how radioactive isotopes are useful.

In the years since the Curies, scientists have learned that all isotopes of elements heavier than bismuth (element 83 on the periodic table) are radioactive. Many of the lighter elements also have isotopes that are radioactive.

Why are some isotopes radioactive while others are not? Radioactivity is the result of an unbalanced, or unstable, nucleus. Nuclear balance depends upon the number of neutrons compared to the number of protons. For atoms with less than 20 protons, a balanced nucleus means that the number of neutrons is equal or almost equal to the number of protons. For example, the most common carbon isotope, carbon 12, has six protons and six neutrons. This form of carbon has a balanced nucleus and is not radioactive. Another isotope of carbon, carbon 14, has an unbalanced nucleus. It has six protons and eight neutrons. Carbon 14 is radioactive.

Figure 11.8 The number of neutrons associated with stable and radioactive isotopes of elements 1 through 18

○ Radioactive Isotope
● Stable Isotope

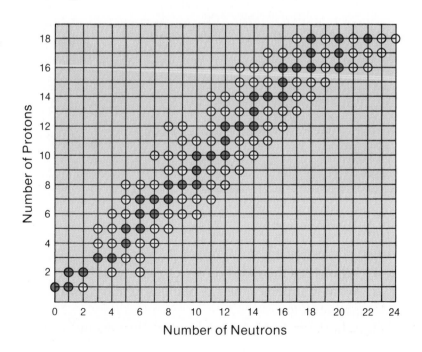

The nuclei of atoms with 20 or more protons can have many more neutrons than protons and still be balanced. For example, the most common lead isotope has 82 protons and 125 neutrons. This isotope is a stable form of lead. It is not radioactive.

The nucleus of a radioactive isotope will undergo one or more nuclear changes in the form of radioactive decay. This radioactive decay will continue until the unbalanced nucleus has become balanced. As a result, a radioactive isotope of one element becomes a stable isotope of another element. In the process, energy is released. For example, consider the radioactive decay of an isotope of uranium. The uranium 238 nucleus goes through a series of 14 nuclear changes, or decays. As a result, the unstable uranium 238 becomes lead 206, a stable isotope.

It is impossible to say exactly when the radioactive decay of any one unstable nucleus will take place. That is like trying to say when a specific kernel of popcorn will pop. You can't be completely sure exactly when it will happen.

Figure 11.9 The radioactive decay of uranium 238

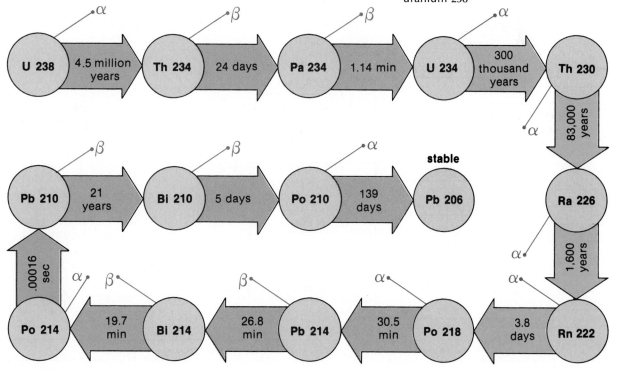

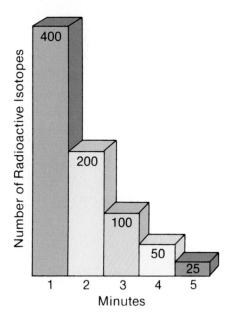

Number of Radioactive Isotopes

| 400 | 200 | 100 | 50 | 25 |

Minutes: 1 2 3 4 5

Figure 11.10 The half-life in this example is one minute.

Figure 11.11 The half-life in this tennis tournament is one round. After each round, half of the players are eliminated.

You can, however, make a generalization about all the nuclei in a sample of a radioactive isotope. For example, suppose you have a large number of unstable carbon 14 nuclei. You can be sure that in about 5,700 years, half of those carbon 14 nuclei will have changed into stable nitrogen 14 nuclei. After another 5,700 years, half of the remaining carbon 14 nuclei will have changed into nitrogen 14 nuclei, and so on.

The time it takes for half the nuclei in a sample of a radioactive isotope to undergo radioactive decay is called the **half-life** of that isotope. The half-life of a particular isotope is a property of that isotope. This property does not depend on whether the isotope is in the solid, liquid, or gas state. An isotope's half-life is the same whether the isotope is by itself or in a compound.

The half-life of carbon 14 is 5,700 years. Some radioactive isotopes have half-lives of only a few seconds. Others have half-lives of billions of years. These isotopes were produced long ago when the material that later formed the earth was bombarded by neutrons in an explosion inside a star. Other radioactive isotopes, such as carbon 14, are produced continually by the bombardment of the top of the atmosphere with high-energy particles from space.

Steve McCann				
Sherri Kane	Sherri Kane			
Ann Rahimi	Chris Behrens	Chris Behrens		
Chris Behrens			Kate Brown	
Kate Brown	Kate Brown			
Lori Wong		Kate Brown		
Dierdre Cline	Matt Keleshian			
Matt Keleshian				Kate Brown
Sandra Pinney	Dawn Perez			
Dawn Perez		Dawn Perez		
Rob Stevens	Caroline Davis			
Caroline Davis			Stan Casimo	
Stan Casimo	Stan Casimo			
Sara Boynton		Stan Casimo		
Larry Palmer	Larry Palmer			
Jim Hamilton				

| First Round | Second Round | Third Round | Fourth Round | Winner |

ACTIVITY

How Can You Demonstrate Half-Life?

Materials

100 blocks, each having one side painted
graph paper
pencil
large paper bag

Procedure

1. Copy the chart twice. Use one copy to record your group's results and the other copy for the total class's results.

2. Place the blocks in the bag. They represent a sample of a radioactive isotope.

3. Shake the bag. Dump the blocks out of the bag.

4. The blocks that fall with the painted side up represent nuclei that have undergone radioactive decay and are now stable. Count them and complete the information for trial 1 on your chart.

5. Do not put the stable blocks back into the bag. Put them aside. Put all the other blocks back in the bag. They represent nuclei that are still radioactive.

6. Repeat steps 3–5 until you have completed ten trials. Each time there should be fewer blocks to return to the bag.

7. Under your teacher's direction, share your group's results with those of the class. Record the total class's results on your class copy of the chart.

8. Make a graph of the class's results. Label the vertical axis *number of radioactive nuclei*. Label the horizontal axis *trials*.

Questions

1. Why wasn't the line on your graph straight?

2. What does your graph tell you about the number of radioactive nuclei left after each trial?

3. To what can you compare the number of trials?

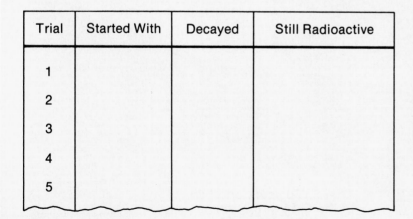

Trial	Started With	Decayed	Still Radioactive
1			
2			
3			
4			
5			

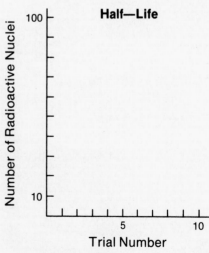

Many uses have been found for radioactive isotopes. In medicine, they are used to diagnose and treat illnesses. Radiation from radioactive isotopes of cobalt and radium is used to kill cancer cells. Radioactive iodine is used to study and treat problems with the thyroid gland. A number of different radioactive isotopes are used as tracers of chemical activity in the body. When a small amount of radioactive material is injected into the bloodstream, the flow of blood to various organs can be followed by observing the movement of the radioactive material.

Radioactivity is also used to study the process by which plants absorb carbon from the atmosphere. A fraction of the carbon in the carbon dioxide molecules in the atmosphere is in the form of radioactive carbon 14. By observing the radioactivity from carbon 14, scientists have been able to trace the absorption of carbon by plants.

Figure 11.12 The absorption and decay of carbon 14

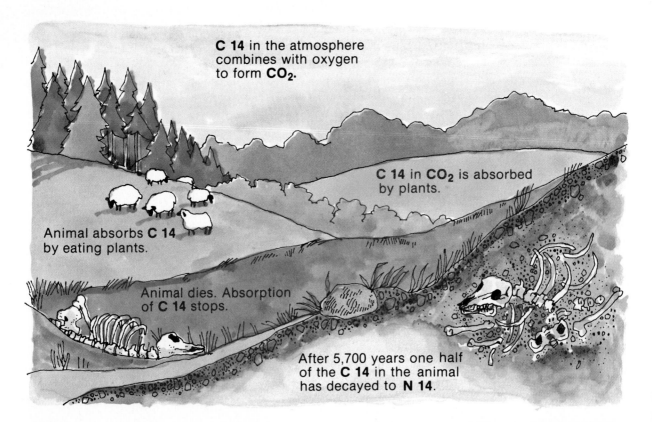

C 14 in the atmosphere combines with oxygen to form CO_2.

C 14 in CO_2 is absorbed by plants.

Animal absorbs C 14 by eating plants.

Animal dies. Absorption of C 14 stops.

After 5,700 years one half of the C 14 in the animal has decayed to N 14.

Figure 11.13 Scientists study the level of carbon 14 radioactivity in ancient artifacts to determine their ages. This Egyptian sarcophagus dates back to 600 BC.

Radioactive carbon 14 is also used to estimate the age of old material that was once living. When a plant dies, it stops absorbing carbon dioxide from the atmosphere. When an animal dies, it stops absorbing carbon from its food. The carbon 14 in the dead organic matter slowly changes into nitrogen 14 through radioactive decay. The decreasing number of carbon 14 nuclei will show up as decreased radioactivity. By studying the level of carbon 14 radioactivity in dead organic matter, scientists can tell how much time has passed since the plant or animal died. This same method has been used to date bones, wood from coffins in the Egyptian pyramids, and paper in old manuscripts. Radioactive dating using carbon 14 and other isotopes is helping to answer many questions about the history of life on the earth and the history of the earth itself.

Do You Know?
Radioactive rubidium isotopes have been used to show that some rocks in Greenland are 3.9 billion years old.

Study Questions for 11.3

1. How is a radioactive isotope different from a stable isotope?
2. What is the half-life of a radioactive isotope?
3. Give three ways that radioactive isotopes are useful.

11.4 Nuclear Fission

You will find out
- what is meant by the term *nuclear fission;*
- how a nuclear chain reaction proceeds.

An important kind of nuclear reaction is **nuclear fission** [FIHSH-uhn]. Nuclear fission is a reaction in which a heavy nucleus is split apart into nuclei of lighter elements and neutrons. Fission reactions are usually caused by the shooting of a beam of neutrons into a material containing a heavy radioactive isotope. Because they have no charge, neutrons are not repelled by the positive electric charge of the protons in the nucleus. So neutrons can enter the nucleus fairly easily. When a neutron enters a heavy nucleus, it upsets the nuclear balance, producing a fission reaction. For example, when a uranium 235 nucleus gains a neutron, the nucleus can split, or fission, into two lighter nuclei such as krypton 93 and barium 140 and three neutrons. The same nucleus could also split differently, producing different lighter nuclei and different numbers of neutrons.

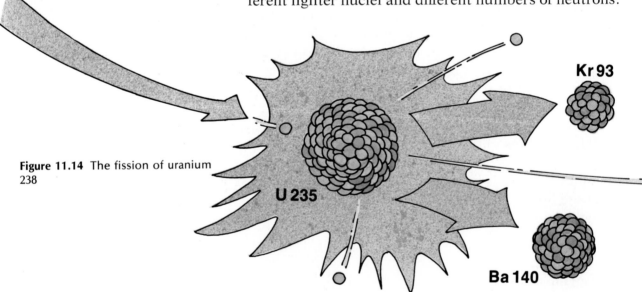

Figure 11.14 The fission of uranium 238

The energy released in fission is about 100 times greater than the energy released in radioactive decay. Therefore, nuclear fission can be a very powerful source of energy.

The energy of nuclear fission can be multiplied in a **nuclear chain reaction.** In a nuclear chain reaction, each fission reaction causes another fission reaction. For example, the neutrons released when a uranium 235 nucleus fissions can enter other uranium 235 nuclei, causing them to fission. Think about pushing over a long row of dominoes. As each domino falls, it knocks over the next domino, which falls and knocks over the next domino, and so on.

Once a chain reaction is started, it will keep going. The chain reaction can get out of hand very quickly. The first reaction may cause two more reactions. Each of these will cause another two reactions, making four. Each of these four will cause two more reactions, making eight, and so on. In a very short time most of the original nuclei will have fissioned. A very large amount of energy is released. This is what happens in an atomic bomb.

Figure 11.15 A nuclear chain reaction

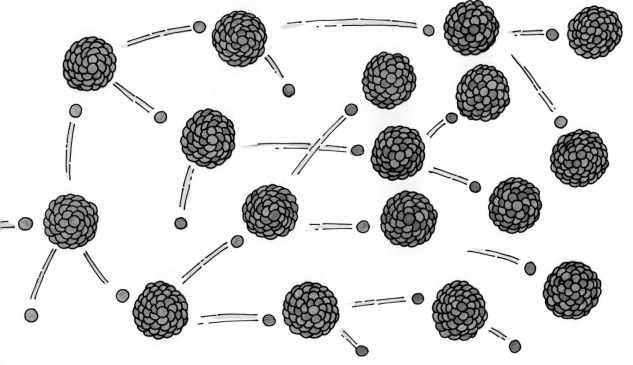

Study Questions for 11.4

1. What is nuclear fission?
2. Describe a nuclear chain reaction.

11.5 Nuclear Fusion

You will find out
- what is meant by the term *nuclear fusion*.

A third kind of nuclear reaction is **nuclear fusion** [FYOO-zhuhn]. In fusion reactions, nuclei of very light atoms such as hydrogen join together, forming a heavier nucleus. The energy released in nuclear fusion can be enormous. The words *fusion* and *fission* sound similar, but they are really opposites. In fusion, light nuclei join, or fuse, together. In fission, one heavy nucleus splits apart.

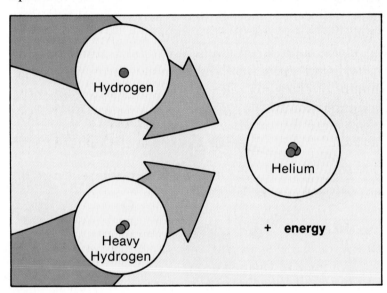

Figure 11.16 The fusion of hydrogen to form helium

It is much more difficult to start a fusion reaction than it is to start a fission reaction. The light nuclei must be moving very fast for the fusion reaction to proceed. Temperatures of 10,000,000°C or higher are needed. Such high temperatures exist deep in the centers of stars. The sun, a star, can be thought of as a giant nuclear furnace that is producing energy in nuclear fusion reactions.

In the sun, hydrogen nuclei join together, forming helium nuclei. Some of the hydrogen nuclei involved in this reaction are formed in another fusion reaction. In this other fusion reaction two light hydrogen nuclei combine to form a heavier hydrogen nucleus. Scientists

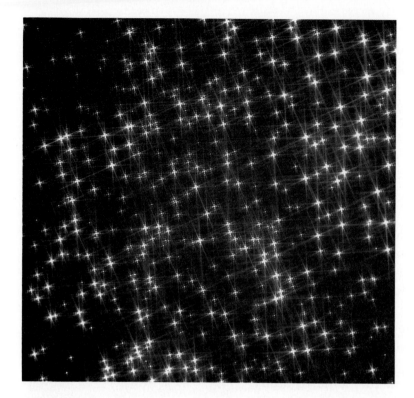

Figure 11.17 Fusion reactions in stars cause them to shine.

estimate that in the sun hundreds of millions of metric tons of hydrogen undergo fusion every second! As you might imagine, the amount of energy released every second is tremendous. The sun and all the other stars you see in the sky are shining due to the energy produced in nuclear fusion reactions.

On the earth the large amounts of energy released in fusion reactions could become an important source of energy. But first, scientists have to learn how to deal with the high temperatures required.

Fusion reactions have been used to provide the energy for hydrogen bombs. These weapons are triggered by a smaller fission bomb that heats the fusion material to very high temperatures. These temperatures start the fusion reaction.

Study Questions for 11.5
1. What is nuclear fusion?
2. How does the sun produce energy?

What Did You Learn?

- In a nuclear reaction, the nucleus of one kind of atom changes into the nucleus of another kind of atom.
- The nuclear force counteracts the repelling electric forces and holds the nucleus together.
- Antoine Henri Becquerel, Pierre Curie, and Marie Curie discovered radioactivity while working with uranium.
- In radioactive decay, the nucleus of one kind of atom spontaneously changes into the nucleus of another kind of atom.
- Nuclear radiation is produced in radioactive decay.
- The three forms of nuclear radiation are alpha particles, beta particles, and gamma radiation.
- Radioactive isotopes are the result of an unbalanced nucleus.
- The half-life of an isotope is the time it takes for half the nuclei in a sample of that isotope to undergo radioactive decay.
- Radioactive isotopes are used in medicine to study and treat illnesses.
- The age of an organic object can be estimated by measuring the level of radioactive carbon 14 in that object.
- In nuclear fission, a heavy nucleus is split apart into lighter nuclei and neutrons.
- In a nuclear chain reaction, one fission reaction triggers other fission reactions.
- In nuclear fusion, light nuclei join together, forming heavier nuclei.
- The sun and other stars produce energy from nuclear fusion.

Key Terms

nuclear reaction
radioactivity
radioactive decay
nuclear radiation
alpha particles
beta particles
gamma radiation
half-life
nuclear fission
nuclear chain reaction
nuclear fusion

Biography

Marie Curie (1867–1934)

Marie Curie was the first person ever to be awarded the Nobel prize twice. In 1903 she shared the prize with her husband and Antoine Henri Becquerel. The prize was awarded in recognition of their work with radioactivity. In 1911 Marie Curie received her second Nobel prize for work in chemistry. Her studies led the way to the modern theory of the atom and to the many practical uses of nuclear physics and chemistry.

Marie Sklodowska was born in Warsaw, Poland. Because of political troubles in Poland, she moved to Paris in 1891 to attend the university there. Two years later she graduated at the top of her class in physics. In 1895 she married Pierre Curie, a French chemist. Shortly afterward, she and Pierre began working with Becquerel on radioactivity. It was Marie who gave the name *radioactivity* to the process by which uranium gave off radiation.

Working with what their daughter called terrible patience, in a small wooden shed with a dirt floor and a leaky roof, Pierre and Marie Curie discovered radium and polonium. They had to go through several thousand kilograms of uranium ore to get a tenth of a gram of pure radium!

In 1906, Pierre was run over by a horse-drawn wagon and killed. Marie was heartbroken but continued their work alone. She was given Pierre's professorship at the University of Sorbonne in Paris. She was the first woman to teach there.

During World War I, Marie Curie pioneered the use of X rays to find foreign objects such as bullets. She took her X-ray devices to the battle zone. When she had trouble getting someone to drive her, she got a driver's license and drove herself.

After the war, she set up institutes for the treatment of illnesses, using radium, in France and Poland. In 1934, she died of overexposure to nuclear radiation.

TO THINK ABOUT AND DO

Vocabulary

Number your paper from 1 to 8. Select the one best term that completes each of the following sentences. Write the letter of the term next to the appropriate number.

1. The change of the nucleus of one element into the nucleus of another is called (a) physical change, (b) chemical reaction, (c) nuclear reaction.
2. Atoms of the same element with different numbers of neutrons are called (a) isotopes, (b) ions, (c) neutrons.
3. An isotope that can be used to determine the age of the organic matter in which that isotope is found is (a) uranium 235, (b) carbon 14, (c) lead 207.
4. The amount of time it takes for half the total amount of a radioactive isotope to decay is its (a) decay time, (b) half-life, (c) stability time.
5. The splitting of heavy nucleus into lighter nuclei and neutrons is (a) fission, (b) fusion, (c) decay.
6. A form of nuclear radiation with two protons and two neutrons is the _____ particle.
   (a) alpha (b) beta (c) gamma
7. Half-life is associated with (a) radioactive decay, (b) fusion, (c) fission.
8. The joining together of light nuclei with the release of energy is a reaction called (a) fission, (b) meltdown, (c) fusion.

What Do You Remember?

1. Describe how Becquerel and the Curies discovered radioactivity.
2. What is a nuclear reaction?
3. Distinguish among alpha particles, beta particles, and gamma radiation.
4. Name three radioactive elements.
5. How are isotopes of the same element different?

6. Why are some isotopes radioactive?
7. What is meant by the term *half-life?*
8. Describe carbon 14 dating.
9. What is nuclear fission?
10. What is a nuclear chain reaction?
11. What is nuclear fusion?
12. How do stars produce energy?

Applying What You Have Learned

1. Suppose that you must transport radioactive materials to a location 100 kilometers away from where you are. What safety measures would you take?
2. Pretend that you have found an ancient bone. What procedure would you use to determine its age?
3. How could radioactive phosphorus be used to determine the role of phosphorus in plant growth?
4. How is the sun a nuclear power plant?
5. You have 150 g of Fe 59, which has a half-life of 46 days. How many grams of Fe 59 will you have left at the end of 184 days?

Research and Investigation

1. If you want to use a radioactive isotope to trace the path of Ca in the human body, what characteristics should it have?
2. Robert W. Houghton and Richard G. Fairbanks of Lamont Doherty Geological Observatory have found that they can identify the source of water samples taken from the North American continental shelf by using isotopes. Each of the rivers that empty into the North Atlantic possesses a unique ratio of the stable oxygen isotopes oxygen 16 and oxygen 18. Why is it important for scientists to be able to identify the specific source of waters in the oceans? How could they use isotopes?

Heat 12

Suppose your hands are cold and you want to warm them. What do you do? Rub them together? Hold them in the warm sunlight? Hold them over a fire? Hold them near an electric heater? Touch something warmer than your hands such as a mug of soup? Heat can be produced in many different ways. It has many different uses. Heat keeps you warm, cooks your food, and runs the cars, buses, planes, and trains you ride in.

You see and feel the effects of changes in heat all around you. Steam rises from a whistling teakettle. A windshield on a car or bus fogs up on a cold morning. A sea breeze begins to blow on a warm afternoon. Frost covers the landscape during a cold night and disappears in the sun.

Heat is absolutely necessary for you to survive. Without it, there would be no motion, no chemical reactions, no life.

Figure 12.1 Pouring molten metal

12.1 Heat Energy

You will find out
- what the kinetic theory states;
- how heat energy and kinetic energy are related.

For a long time it was thought that heat was an invisible, weightless substance called caloric. This mysterious caloric passed from hot to cold objects. Then in 1798 an inventive scientist named Benjamin Thompson got a clue to what heat really is. Thompson, known as Count Rumford, was directing the drilling of a brass cannon in Germany. The brass became very hot as the drill ground through it. When the drilling stopped, the brass cooled. Rumford figured that the heat must be connected somehow to the energy of the drill in motion. Heat must be a form of energy.

To understand how heat can be a form of energy, you must keep in mind some facts about the basic particles of matter. Remember that matter is made of atoms and molecules. The **kinetic theory** states that these particles are always moving and that they often bump into each other. This random motion is present in varying degrees in solids, liquids, and gases. The particles in a solid are very close together. They do not move from one place to another. Instead they vibrate back and forth. In liquids, the particles move very small distances but still remain close together. In gases, the particles are quite far apart and move freely about. No matter what the state, all atoms and molecules are in motion. Energy of motion is called kinetic energy.

Figure 12.2 The heat in a desert, like all heat, is a form of energy.

Figure 12.3 The people in these photographs represent particles in matter. *left:* Particles in a solid are very close together and move very little. *center:* Particles in a liquid are farther apart and move more. *right:* Particles in a gas are very far apart and move freely.

The **heat energy** of a substance is the total kinetic energy of all the molecules or atoms of that substance. When a substance is heated, the atoms or molecules move faster. Faster-moving particles have more kinetic energy. The more kinetic energy the particles have, the greater the heat energy of that substance.

In the case of Rumford's cannon drill, the grinding motion of the drill against the brass cannon added energy to the particles of the brass. The particles moved faster. Their kinetic energy increased. This increase showed up as an increase in heat energy. Thus, the brass became hotter.

It is important to remember that the law of conservation of energy applies to heat energy. When energy changes forms, that energy may appear to have been created or destroyed. This is not the case. For example, the heat energy produced when Rumford's cannon drill was working was not newly created energy. The kinetic energy of the drill was changed into the heat energy of the brass.

Do You Know?
The water at the bottom of Niagara Falls is about 0.12°C warmer than the water at the top of the falls because the kinetic energy of the falling water is changed to heat energy when the water hits the bottom of the falls.

Study Questions for 12.1

1. State the kinetic theory.
2. What is heat energy?

12.2 Temperature and Specific Heat

You will find out
- how temperature and heat energy are different;
- what is meant by specific heat.

Figure 12.4 Measuring temperature in degrees Celsius and degrees Fahrenheit

The **temperature** of a substance is a measure of the average kinetic energy of the atoms or molecules that make up that substance. Temperature is measured in degrees Celsius. As the atoms or molecules of a substance move faster, the temperature of the substance increases. Similarly, when the atoms or molecules of a substance slow down, the temperature decreases.

On a hot day (30°C) the average speed of the molecules in air is about 440 m/s. On a very cold day (−20°C) the molecules average about 400 m/s. At a low enough temperature, (−273°C) the average speed would be almost 0 m/s. There would be only slight vibrational motion. Since −273°C is the lowest possible temperature, it is called **absolute zero.** Scientists have been able to create temperatures close to absolute zero.

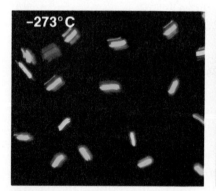
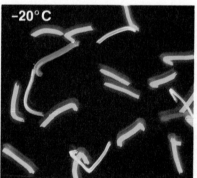
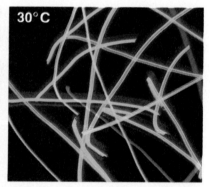

Figure 12.5 The lights in these photographs represent the movement of molecules in air. The higher the temperature, the faster the molecules are moving.

Do You Know?
Scientists have produced temperatures as low as one twenty-millionth of a degree C above absolute zero.

Suppose a large rock and a small pebble have the same temperature. Do they have the same amount of heat energy? No. The larger rock has more heat energy. Remember that heat energy is the total kinetic energy of all the particles in an object. The rock has more mass than the pebble. So the rock has more moving particles and therefore more kinetic energy than the pebble. Thus, the rock has more heat energy. It is important to remember that substances can have the same temperature but different amounts of heat energy. Temperature

Figure 12.6 All the soup is the same temperature. However, the soup in the pot has more heat energy because it has more mass.

refers to average kinetic energy. Heat energy refers to total kinetic energy.

Since heat is a form of energy, the unit for measuring heat is the same unit used for measuring any other type of energy or for measuring work. This unit is the joule. Another unit often used to measure heat is the **calorie.** A calorie is the amount of heat required to raise the temperature of one gram of water one degree Celsius. One calorie equals 4.186 joules. A calorie, then, is a larger unit of heat energy than a joule. Calories are measured using a device called a calorimeter.

You may have noticed that it is easier to raise the temperature of some substances than it is to raise the temperature of others. The amount of heat needed to raise the temperature of one gram of a substance one degree Celsius is called the **specific heat** of the substance. Specific heat is a property of matter. Iron has a specific heat only one tenth as large as that of water. This means that it takes about one tenth as much heat to raise the temperature of 1 kg of iron as it does to raise the temperature of 1 kg of water by one degree Celsius. The specific heat of nearly all gases, liquids, and solids is less than that of water.

Table 12-1   Specific Heat of Several Substances

Substance	Specific Heat (J/g)
water	4.18
alcohol	2.43
wood	1.75
sugar	1.15
marble	0.88
copper	0.39
silver	0.23

Study Questions for 12.2

1. What is temperature?
2. How can two substances have the same temperature but different amounts of heat energy?
3. What is specific heat?

12.3 The Effects of Heat Energy on Matter

You will find out
- how substances are affected by temperature changes;
- what happens when substances change state.

You have seen some of the effects of heat on matter. Puddles evaporate and disappear. Snow melts. Water boils. Lakes freeze and later melt. Both the physical state and the volume of substances are affected by the amount of heat energy present. If you keep the kinetic theory in mind, it will be easy to see how heat energy affects matter. Since all matter is made of particles that are moving, the effects of heat on matter can be understood in terms of how fast and how far those particles move.

Suppose you heat the air in a balloon. The kinetic energy of the molecules in that air increases. The air in the balloon expands. The increase in kinetic energy causes the molecules to bump into the walls of the balloon harder and more often. The result is an increased pressure on the walls of the balloon. This increased pressure causes the balloon to expand.

Most solids, liquids, and gases expand when heated. The atoms or molecules gain kinetic energy. They move farther apart. As you might guess, when most substances are cooled, the opposite changes occur. The particles lose kinetic energy. They move closer together. The volume of the substance gets smaller, or contracts.

Figure 12.7 The air inside a balloon expands when heated and contracts when cooled.

Heated

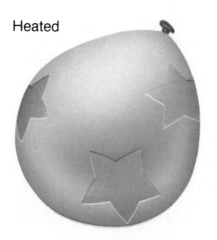

Cooled

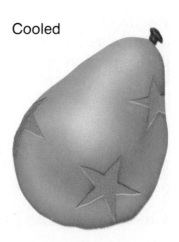

The mercury thermometer makes use of the expansion of liquid mercury to measure temperature. As the temperature around the thermometer increases, the mercury atoms gain kinetic energy and move apart. The mercury expands in a thin column up the thermometer. As the temperature decreases, the mercury atoms lose kinetic energy and move closer together. The liquid volume contracts. The column of mercury becomes shorter.

Different substances expand by different amounts when they are heated. An iron bar one meter long increases in length by about one millimeter when heated from 0°C to 100°C. Under the same conditions an aluminum bar increases in length by about two millimeters. A Pyrex glass rod expands by less than half a millimeter. The amount that a substance expands or contracts in response to changes in temperature is a property of that substance.

Construction engineers must consider the change in the volume of solids with temperature. For example, a 300-meter steel bridge will increase in length by about 6 centimeters when the temperature increases 20°C. Long steel bridges have special structures at the ends to allow for the expansion. Concrete also expands when heated. Concrete bridges are built with expansion joints between the concrete slabs. The expansion joints are needed to keep the bridge from buckling when the concrete expands.

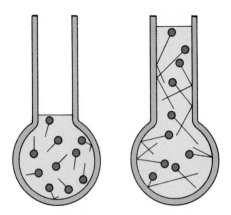

Figure 12.8 Atoms of mercury move more when they gain heat energy. As a result, the mercury expands.

Figure 12.9 Expansion joints

Figure 12.10 Unlike most substances, water does not contract when cooled. It expands.

Figure 12.11 This strip of two metals bends when heated because one metal expands more than the other.

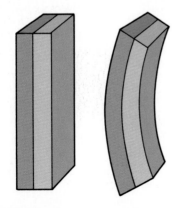

The different rates of expansion for different metals can be used to make a thermostat. Strips of iron and brass are welded together making a single strip. This strip will bend when heated. It bends because the brass side expands more than the iron side. This bending can be used to turn a pointer, to regulate a valve, or to turn a switch. In this way a thermostat can start and stop a heating system at whatever temperatures are desired.

Increases in heat energy account for the changes from solids to liquids and liquids to gases. Similarly, decreases in heat energy account for the opposite changes. As heat energy is added to a solid, the particles move farther apart. If enough heat is applied to the solid, the particles will move so much that they are no longer closely held in any particular arrangement. When this happens, the solid changes into a liquid. This process is called **melting.** The temperature at which a solid changes to a liquid is the **melting point** of that substance.

Once a solid reaches its melting point, its temperature does not change even as more heat is added. The temperature remains at the melting point as long as there is material to melt. The addition of heat only causes the substance to melt faster. The amount of heat energy used to melt a substance without changing its temperature is called the **heat of fusion** of that substance.

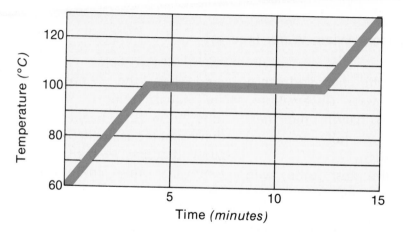

Figure 12.12 This graph shows the change in temperature of water as it boils and evaporates. The line remains level at the boiling point until all the water has evaporated.

You have observed the effects of the heat of fusion many times. When? You see the effects when you put ice cubes in a glass of water. The heat energy used to melt the ice cubes (heat of fusion) is taken from the water. The water cools as the ice cubes melt.

Once a solid has completely melted, the addition of more heat can change the liquid to a gas. As the temperature of a liquid increases, the particles move faster. Some of the particles will reach speeds so high that they can escape from the liquid into the air. The change from the liquid to the gas state is called **evaporation.**

Sometimes liquids boil when they evaporate. The temperature at which a liquid begins to boil is called the **boiling point** of that substance. Adding heat to a boiling liquid does not increase its temperature. The temperature remains at the boiling point until all the liquid has evaporated. Both the boiling and melting points of a substance are properties of that substance.

It is important to remember that liquids can evaporate without boiling. The puddles that remain after a rain shower eventually disappear. Have you ever seen a boiling puddle? Water does evaporate at temperatures below its boiling point. It does so more slowly, however.

Evaporation, like melting, is a cooling process. The fastest-moving liquid particles escape into the gas state. As these particles evaporate, they take energy with them. The heat energy used to evaporate a liquid is called the **heat of vaporization** [vay-puhr-ih-ZAY-shuhn] of that substance.

Figure 12.13 Puddles evaporate at temperatures below the boiling point of water.

ACTIVITY

What Happens When Water Freezes?

Materials

watch with a second
hand
600-mL beaker
test tube
ice
salt
2 thermometers

Procedure

1. Copy the chart and use it to record your observations. Be sure to handle the thermometers carefully to avoid breaking them.

2. Fill the test tube with water to a depth of about 2.5 cm.

3. Place one thermometer in the test tube. Record the water temperature on your chart beside *0 minutes.*

4. Set the test tube and your second thermometer in the beaker of ice as shown in the diagram. Immediately record the temperature of the ice on your chart beside *0 minutes.*

5. Pour salt over the ice. Record the temperature of both thermometers every minute until both show the same temperature.

6. When the temperatures are equal, remove the test tube from the beaker. If a thermometer is locked in ice, allow that ice to melt before removing the thermometer for cleanup.

Questions

1. Make a graph to show your results. Label the horizontal axis *time* and the vertical axis *temperature.* Use different colors to plot the water temperatures and the ice temperatures.

2. What happened to the water in the test tube?

3. Why was there no change in temperature while the water was freezing?

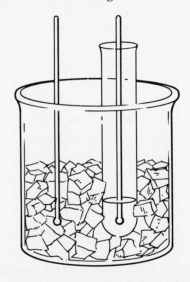

Time (minutes)	Temperature of Water (°C)	Temperature of Ice (°C)
0		
1		
2		
3		
4		

Figure 12.14 In cold weather, water vapor in the breath of people and animals often condenses forming a cloud you can see.

You have noticed the effects of the heat of vaporization many times. How often have you felt chilled when you stepped out from a shower or a swim dripping wet? Did you feel warmer after you dried off? The water on your skin was evaporating. The heat energy used to evaporate the water (heat of vaporization) was taken from you! When you perspire, your body is cooling itself following the same principles. As the perspiration evaporates from your skin, you feel cooler.

As you might guess, when temperatures decrease, the changes occur in reverse. A gas changes to a liquid. A liquid changes to a solid.

The change of a gas to a liquid is called **condensation** [kahn-duhn-SAY-shuhn]. Condensation is the opposite of evaporation. As the temperature drops, the particles in a gas move more slowly and cover shorter distances. They eventually come close together condensing into a liquid. Drops that form on the outside of a glass of cold water, fog, clouds, and dew are all examples of the condensation of water vapor.

The change of a liquid to a solid is called **freezing.** As the temperature of a liquid drops, the molecules in the liquid move more and more slowly. Finally, they come very close together, barely moving at all.

Do You Know?
On a brisk 5-km walk your body burns fuel, producing enough heat energy to raise the temperature of 10 kg of water by 21°C.

Study Questions for 12.3

1. How can heating cause a substance to expand?
2. What happens when a solid melts?
3. What happens when a liquid evaporates?

You will find out
- how heat energy is transferred in conduction, convection, and radiation.

When hot cocoa is poured into a mug, the mug itself gets warm. Heat is transferred from the cocoa to the mug by **conduction** [kuhn-DUHK-shuhn]. In heat conduction heat energy is transferred from a hot object to a cooler one by collisions between particles. The two objects must be touching for this transfer to occur. The faster-moving particles on the boundary of the hot object collide with the slower-moving particles on the boundary of the cooler object. The slower-moving particles gain energy. These particles move faster. They strike other particles inside the cooler object. In this way the heat energy is spread throughout the object. You feel the effects of heat conduction when you touch something hot. The heat is transferred from the surface of the hot object to your hand.

Figure 12.15 Only the bottom of this pan is touching the burner. However, you would still need a pot holder to grip the handle because heat is transferred from the burner to the bottom of the pan to the handle by conduction.

Some materials are better conductors of heat than others. Metals are very good conductors. Most gases are poor conductors of heat because the particles in a gas are far apart. They don't bump into each other very often, and so the heat is transferred slowly. Poor conductors of heat are called **insulators.** Gases such as air are good insulators. A knit sweater keeps you warm because the air trapped between the fibers slows down the flow of heat from your body to the cold air outside.

Figure 12.16 The air trapped between the fibers of a knitted hat acts as an insulator.

ACTIVITY

Which Material Is the Best Insulator?

Materials
2 beakers
tin can
hot plate
tongs
thermometer
insulating material,
    such as Styrofoam
    chips, cloth, news-
    paper
safety glasses

Procedure

1. Put on your safety glasses. Fill the can with insulating material. Place an empty beaker in the can and mold the insulation around it so the beaker fits snugly. Be sure that there is insulation under the beaker and all around it.

2. Use the hot plate to heat 100 mL of water in a beaker to 75°C.

3. Carefully pour the water into your insulated beaker. Use tongs to lift the beaker of hot water.

4. Immediately measure and record the temperature of the water and the time.

5. Watch the temperature of the water and determine how long it takes to cool to 40°C.

6. Copy the chart. Write your name, the kind of insulating material, and the time it took for the water to cool to 40°C on the chart. Share your information with your classmates and add their information to your chart.

Name	Insulating Material	Time Until Cooled to 40° C

Questions

1. Make a bar graph to compare the time it took for each group's water to cool to 40°C.

2. The best insulating material is the one that required the most time for the water to cool to 40°C. List the materials in order from the best insulator to the worst insulator.

Figure 12.17 In this example of convection, hot air rises and is replaced by cool air.

Conduction is a good way to spread heat energy in solids. In liquids and gases, **convection** [kuhn-VEHK-shuhn] is usually more efficient. Convection is the spreading of heat energy by large movements of a liquid or a gas.

To understand how convection works, picture a fire in a fireplace. The chimney opening is much smaller than the opening of the fireplace into the room. Why does the smoke so conveniently go up the chimney instead of pouring out into the room? The fire heats the air around it, causing the air to expand. As the hot air takes up more space, it becomes less dense. The less dense hot air floats on, or rises above, the more dense cool air surrounding it. This hot air rises up the chimney, taking the smoke and ashes with it. Cool air from the room flows into the fire from all sides to take the place of the rising hot air. This cool air is soon heated and rises to be replaced by more cool air. A continuous circulation pattern of hot and cool air is set up in the room. Heat energy is moved around. This circulation of air is an example of convection.

For heat to flow by conduction or convection, matter must be present to carry the heat. Can heat flow in empty space, that is, in the absence of matter? The answer must be yes. When you stand in the sunshine, you feel warm. Heat from the sun has reached you. Most of the space between the earth and the sun is empty. The sun's energy travels through empty space on its way to you on the earth. This energy is often called radiant energy because it flows by means of **radiation** [ray-dee-AY-shuhn]. Radiation is a form of energy transfer that occurs through matter and through empty space.

The sun produces radiant energy. So does a fire, a radiator, or a pan of hot water. So do you! You may have noticed that a room full of people is much warmer than an empty room. Radiant energy from the people heats the room. Radiant energy travels in all directions. It can be transferred from one object to another without contact between the two objects. The sun's energy warms the earth even though the earth and the sun never touch.

Figure 12.18 This collared lizard is warmed by the radiant energy of the sun.

Study Questions for 12.4

1. What is heat conduction?
2. What is heat convection?
3. How is radiation different from conduction and convection?

What Did You Learn?

- Count Rumford discovered that heat is a form of energy.
- The kinetic theory states that the atoms and molecules that make up matter are always moving.
- The heat energy of a substance is the total kinetic energy of all the particles of that substance.
- Temperature is a measure of the average kinetic energy of the particles that make up a substance.
- At absolute zero, the lowest possible temperature, almost all motion of particles stops.
- Heat energy can be measured in joules or calories.
- The specific heat of a substance is the amount of heat needed to raise the temperature of one gram of that substance one degree Celsius.
- Most substances expand when heated and contract when cooled.
- When solids gain enough heat energy, they change to a liquid, or melt.
- The heat energy required to melt a substance without changing the temperature is the heat of fusion of that substance.
- When liquids gain enough heat energy, they change to a gas, or evaporate.
- The heat energy used to evaporate a liquid is the heat of vaporization of that substance.
- The change of a gas to a liquid is called condensation.
- The change of a liquid to a solid is called freezing.
- In conduction, heat energy is transferred from a hot object to a cooler one by collisions of particles.
- Poor conductors of heat are called insulators.
- In convection, heat energy is spread by large movements of a liquid or gas.
- Radiation is a form of energy transfer that occurs through matter and space.

Key Terms

kinetic theory
heat energy
temperature
absolute zero
calorie
specific heat
melting
melting point
heat of fusion
evaporation
boiling point
heat of vaporization
condensation
freezing
conduction
insulators
convection
radiation

Career

Mechanical Engineer

Mechanical engineers work on methods to produce and use power. They design and develop machines that produce power. Some examples of these machines are internal combustion engines, jet and rocket engines, steam turbines, and nuclear reactors. Mechanical engineers also design and develop machines that use power, such as automobiles, heaters, air conditioners, printing presses, and steel-rolling mills.

A mechanical engineer may work in any one of many specialized branches. He or she could be working on the testing and design of cars, locomotives, or jet engines. Mechanical engineers also build precision instruments and machines for highly specialized work. This equipment is used in many fields such as underwater prospecting and rocket engines for the space shuttle.

Some mechanical engineers figure out how to build machines. Others test the machines. Still others oversee the actual manufacture of the machines. Highly complicated or technical machines are also sold by mechanical engineers, since they are the ones who best understand how the machines work.

In the years to come, industrial machines and processes will get more

complicated. Mechanical engineers will be needed to build new and better machines. Mechanical engineers will also be needed to develop new energy systems and to help solve environmental pollution problems.

To prepare for a mechanical engineering career, you should take as much mathematics as possible in high school. Physics and chemistry also provide good background. English should not be overlooked, since a mechanical engineer must be able to communicate skillfully with others about his or her work. Most jobs in mechanical engineering require a college degree.

TO THINK ABOUT AND DO

Vocabulary

Number your paper from 1 to 10. Beside each number write the word or words from the list that best complete each sentence.

1. Energy of motion of particles is _____ energy.
2. _____ is the measure of the average kinetic energy of particles.
3. The amount of heat required to raise the temperature of 1 g of a substance 1°C is its _____.
4. A unit used to measure heat energy is the _____.
5. The energy used to melt a substance is the heat of _____.
6. The energy used to change a liquid to a gas is the heat of _____.
7. A liquid changes to a gas in the process of _____.
8. A gas changes to a liquid in the process of _____.
9. The method of heat transfer that involves the movement of a liquid or a gas is _____.
10. Heat energy travels through empty space in _____.

calorie
radiation
fusion
kinetic
evaporation
temperature
specific heat
condensation
boiling point
convection
vaporization
absolute zero

What Do You Remember?

1. Name the scientist who proposed that heat results from the motion of molecules. Why did he believe this?
2. What is heat energy?
3. What is temperature?
4. What units are used to measure heat?
5. What is a calorie?
6. What units are used to measure temperature?
7. Explain the kinetic theory of matter.
8. Why does ice melt when it is heated?
9. Why does water freeze when it is cooled?
10. What is heat of fusion?

11. What is heat of vaporization?
12. Explain how evaporation occurs.
13. Define conduction, convection, and radiation as methods of heat transfer.
14. Name three good conductors.
15. Name three good insulators.

Applying What You Have Learned

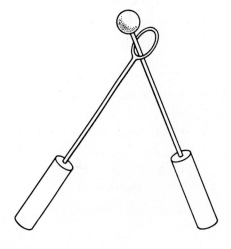

1. Study the drawing. If the ball is heated, will you be able to pull it through the ring? Explain your answer. How can you get the ball through the ring?
2. How can the way a thermos is constructed be used to illustrate convection, conduction, and radiation?
3. Why do railroad tracks have spaces between the rails at certain intervals?
4. If you pour hot water into a glass, it may break. But if there is a metal knife in the glass, it won't. Why?
5. Why do people put jars under hot water to help open them?
6. How does the motion of the molecules of a solid at 30°C compare to the motion of molecules in the same substance at 50°C?

Research and Investigation

1. Three temperature scales are used—Fahrenheit, Celsius, and Kelvin. Compare the boiling points and freezing points of water on each scale. Where or when is each scale used?
2. Cooling substances to near absolute zero often changes their properties. Give some examples of these changes.
3. What is sublimation? Give two examples.

Heat Energy in Your Life

13

Imagine for a moment what it would be like if all the machines and engines that depend on heat energy for their power suddenly stopped working. The first thing you might notice would be that the electricity would go off. Heat energy is a necessary part of most electrical power plants. You would have no lights, no television or radio, and none of the appliances that depend on electricity for their power.

Going outside, you would notice that all traffic had stopped. Automobiles, trucks, buses, and trains depend on heat energy for their power too. There would be no airplanes flying overhead and no subways running underground. The work in most factories would grind to a halt.

In short, the world as you know it would no longer exist. The modern industrial world of today has come about in large part because of the work heat energy has done and continues to do.

Figure 13.1 An early steam-powered tractor

13.1 Heat Engines

You will find out
- how heat engines do work;
- where the heat for heat engines comes from.

Figure 13.2 Trucks use heat engines.

Imagine that you are in charge of moving a piano to a place 400 kilometers away. You have to do work. To do work, a force must move an object a distance. You must supply a force to move the piano 400 kilometers. How will you do it? You can't carry it on your back. The distance is too far, and the piano is too heavy. You will probably use a truck. How is a truck able to do work? How does any truck or car operate? Many people know how to drive. They know how to turn the engine on and off and how to add fuel. But what makes a car or a truck move? If you look under the hood of a car or a truck, you will see a heat engine. Heat engines move cars and trucks.

A **heat engine** is a device that uses heat energy to do work. The engine does work by changing heat energy into energy of motion. How does this change occur? When a gas is heated, its pressure increases. The pressure increases because the gas molecules gain kinetic energy when heated. This increase in kinetic energy causes the molecules to move faster. The result is an increase in pressure.

If a container is elastic such as a balloon, that container will expand as the pressure increases. But what if the container is rigid and cannot expand? In that case, the pressure inside increases when heat is added.

Figure 13.3 Molecules are heated in an open, an expanding, and a sealed container. Inside which container is the pressure greatest?

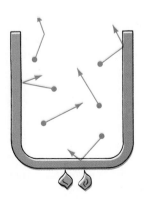
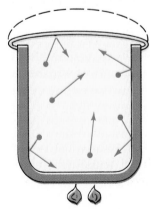
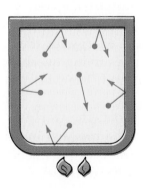

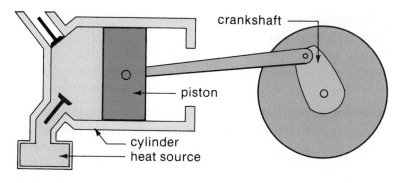

Figure 13.4 Parts of a heat engine

How does an increase in pressure produce energy of motion? You have probably observed the answer to this question. Suppose you boil water in a covered pan. The boiling water changes to steam, a gas. The pressure increases. Since the cover is not held tightly, the increased pressure forces it up. You can see the cover on a pan of boiling water move up.

Many heat engines work in a similar way. In a heat engine the container that confines the heated gas is a **cylinder.** The movable top of the cylinder, called a **piston,** corresponds to the cover on the pan. In these heat engines, the outward movement of the piston is used to turn a rod that turns a **crankshaft.** The turning crankshaft can be used to turn one or more wheels.

Where does the heat needed to increase the pressure inside the cylinder come from? It is released in the burning, or combustion [kuhm-BUHS-chuhn], of a fuel. If the burning takes place outside the cylinder, the engine is an **external combustion engine.** If the burning takes place inside the cylinder, it is an **internal combustion engine.** The fuel that burns can be wood, coal, gas, or oil.

In recent years the heat energy released in nuclear reactions has been used to supply the heat for some heat engines. Nuclear-powered submarines and aircraft carriers are in use today.

Do You Know?
A liter of water will boil into about 1,700 liters of steam if the pressure is constant.

Study Questions for 13.1

1. What causes the piston in a heat engine to move?
2. How are internal and external combustion engines different?

13.2 External Combustion Engines

You will find out
- how steam engines developed;
- how steam turbines work.

Some of the earliest heat engines were external combustion steam engines. The first external combustion steam engines were not very successful. The engines were large and inefficient. They worked so poorly that one observer complained that it took an iron mine to build the engine and a coal mine to run it. Finally in 1769, James Watt, a Scot, made a steam engine that was much more efficient. Soon Watt's steam engines were in use in factories all over Great Britain.

Figure 13.5 This painting illustrates a 21-kilometer race that took place in 1830 between a horse-drawn cart and the *Tom Thumb,* a locomotive powered by Watt's steam engine. The *Tom Thumb* was in the lead but broke down before the finish line.

The first locomotives were steam engines. These steam locomotives, nicknamed iron horses, quickly replaced boats and horses in moving goods and people. As you might guess, the early steam locomotives were not without problems. One of the first passenger trains in the United States was the *DeWitt Clinton.* It ran between Albany and Schenectady, New York. The *DeWitt Clinton* had a woodburning steam locomotive and open-air passenger cars. The train's jerk as it started knocked most of the passengers out of their seats. Sparks from the smokestack set fire to the umbrellas that passengers raised as shields from the smoke and wind. Through

Figure 13.6 The *De Witt Clinton*

trial and error the trains were improved. The trains in the United States were recognized as some of the best in the world.

The success of steam trains soon made other forms of land transportation in the United States out of date. The pony express, stagecoaches, and horse-drawn wagons all became part of history as the iron horses took over. The development of railroads was an important factor in the growth of industry and the westward expansion of the United States in the nineteenth century.

Figure 13.7 This modern plant uses steam in an external combustion engine to produce electricity.

ACTIVITY

Materials

turbine disks
eyedropper
ring stand and clamp
Bunsen burner
one-hole rubber
  stopper
test tube
long pencil with
  eraser
thimble
straight pin
safety glasses
apron

How Does a Steam Turbine Work?

Procedure

1. Put on your apron and safety glasses. Remove the rubber cap from the eyedropper, leaving only the glass tube. Wet the outside of the glass tube and carefully insert the wider end into the hole of the rubber stopper.

2. Fill the test tube 1/4 full with water. Carefully place the stopper in the test tube. The glass tube should extend out. CAUTION: The stopper should not be pushed into the test tube too tightly.

3. Set up the test tube, Bunsen burner, ring stand, and clamp as shown in the diagram.

4. Use the pin and thimble to mount the turbine disk on the pencil as shown in the diagram.

5. Light the Bunsen burner and wait for the water to boil. CAUTION: Do not stand or place your hand in front of the steam.

6. Holding the pencil, place the blades of the turbine disk in the direct path of the steam. Count how many times the red blade passes over your hand in one minute.

7. Repeat step 6 twice and find the average of the three trials.

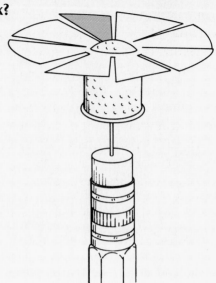

8. Replace your disk with a different disk. Repeat steps 6 and 7. If you need to add water to the test tube, turn off the burner and let the test tube cool before touching it. Never fill the test tube more than 1/4 full.

Questions

1. How was heat energy used to produce a rotational motion?

2. Why was the steam directed through the glass tube instead of just out the top of the test tube?

3. How did the size of the turbine disk affect the number of rotations per minute?

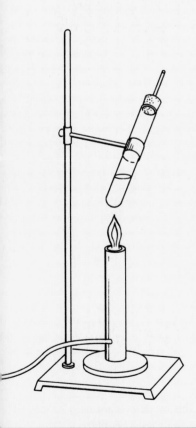

Today the steam engine is not used so much as another kind of external combustion engine, the **steam turbine** [TUHR-byn]. In a steam turbine, steam under pressure is used to produce a rotational motion. The steam is heated in a cylinder, creating a very high pressure. Then the hot steam is allowed to escape from the cylinder through a small opening. It rushes out in a forceful stream which is directed at blades mounted on a wheel. The steam hits the blades, causing the wheel to turn, or rotate.

You have seen the creation of rotational motion like the kind that occurs in a steam turbine. Falling water turns a water wheel in much the same way. Similarly, wind moves the blades of a windmill. Young children create a similar rotational motion when they blow on a pinwheel.

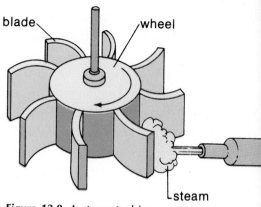

Figure 13.8 A steam turbine

Figure 13.9 When wind strikes the blades of a windmill, a rotating motion similar to the motion of a steam turbine is created.

Do You Know?
A large steam turbine can produce the power of a million horses.

Study Questions for 13.2
1. Describe the early trains.
2. How does a steam turbine work?

13.3 Internal Combustion Engines

You will find out
- how gasoline engines operate;
- how diesel engines operate;
- why heat engines cannot be perfectly efficient.

The idea of using a steam engine to power a carriage was first suggested many years before Watt perfected his steam engine. However, these early suggestions were not taken very seriously. In fact, one of the first men to propose a steam-driven carriage was considered so extreme he was certified as insane. Still, as years went by, the idea of a steam-powered carriage, or car, gained interest and support.

It is generally agreed that the first true car was a steam-driven vehicle invented in 1769. The inventor was a Frenchman, Nicolas-Joseph Cugnot. Cugnot's car had three wheels. A huge, heavy boiler placed out in front supplied the steam. Cugnot's car could run at a speed of 3.6 km/h. Later steam-driven cars were much better designed. In 1906, two Americans, the Stanley brothers, set the world speed record. Their Stanley steamer was clocked at 205.4 km/h.

Figure 13.10 This early car was powered by an internal combustion engine that used gasoline.

In the late 1800's cars using internal combustion engines had begun to draw attention. These cars soon became more popular than the external combustion steam cars. The internal combustion engines could be made smaller. They were also cheaper to operate than most external combustion engines.

Most gasoline engines have four basic parts: a carburetor, pistons, cylinders, and spark plugs. Gasoline evaporates and mixes with air in the **carburetor** [KAHR-buh-rayt-uhr]. The gasoline and air mixture is injected into a cylinder. The mixture is ignited by a spark from the **spark plug.** The burning releases heat. This heat increases the pressure inside the cylinder, causing the piston to move.

Most gasoline engines operate on a series of four **strokes,** or movements of the piston. The first stroke is the *intake stroke.* The piston moves out, allowing the air and gasoline mixture to enter the cylinder. Next comes the *compression stroke.* The piston moves in. This movement shrinks, or compresses, the space available to the mixture of air and gasoline. The *power stroke* follows. A spark ignites the compressed gasoline and air mixture. The explosion and heat released as the mixture burns forces the piston out. This downward movement turns the crankshaft. The fourth stroke is the *exhaust stroke.* The piston moves in. This movement pushes the waste products of the burning out of the cylinder. After the exhaust stroke, the cycle is complete and can be repeated. A typical gasoline engine has several cylinders. Each one goes through the four-stroke cycle thousands of times a minute.

Figure 13.11 The four basic parts of a gasoline engine

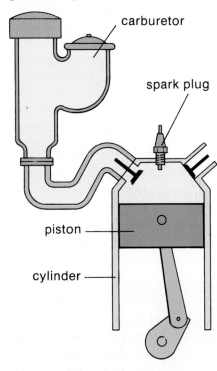

carburetor

spark plug

piston

cylinder

Figure 13.12 The four strokes of a gasoline engine

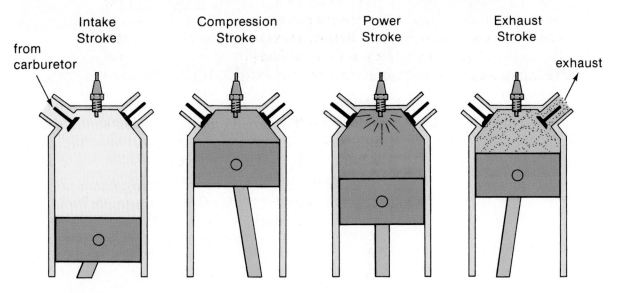

Intake Stroke

Compression Stroke

Power Stroke

Exhaust Stroke

from carburetor

exhaust

You may know someone who has a diesel car. Many trucks and some cars use diesel fuel instead of gasoline. Diesel engines operate without the carburetor and spark plugs necessary in gasoline engines. In diesel engines, air is drawn into the cylinder and compressed. This compression is greater than the compression that occurs in gasoline engines. It causes the temperature of the air to rise to about 800°C. Diesel fuel is then injected into the cylinder. Since the temperature is so high, no spark is needed to ignite the fuel. It burns almost instantly (0.01 second).

Because the compression and temperature are greater than in gasoline engines, diesel engines are more powerful. They use fuel more efficiently. They must also be built with very strong materials to withstand the high temperature and pressure.

Figure 13.13 A diesel truck

All the heat produced in a heat engine cannot be used to do work. The engine must be cooled so the heating and expansion cycle can start again. Also, the engine would become too hot if it were not cooled. Some heat is lost to the air around the engine. But a cooling system is also needed to carry away more heat. These heat losses, although necessary and unavoidable, limit the efficiency of heat engines. Thus, no engine is perfectly efficient. The most efficient heat engines are those that have the smallest amount of heat loss.

Figure 13.14 The ears of an elephant act like a radiator. Excess heat from the elephant's body is transferred to the air through the ears.

The cooling system in a car uses water or some other fluid to absorb heat. The fluid carries this heat to the radiator where it is quickly transferred to the air outside. If the cooling system fails, the four-stroke cycle will stop and the engine can become damaged. Most cars have a temperature gauge to alert drivers to a cooling system failure.

A car's exhaust system carries the waste products of burning to the outside. These waste products carry with them some of the heat released when gasoline is burned. The temperature of a car's exhaust can be 1,000°C or higher. If a gasoline engine were perfectly efficient, 100 percent of the heat energy produced would be used to do work. However, some of this heat must be lost to the cooling system. Additional heat is lost in exhaust. In the end, only about 25 percent of the heat energy produced is used to move the car. Cars are only about 25 percent efficient.

Study Questions for 13.3

1. What are the four basic parts of a gasoline engine?
2. What are the four strokes in the cycle of a gasoline engine?
3. How are gasoline and diesel engines different?
4. Why is no heat engine perfectly efficient?

13.4 Cooling and Heating Systems

You will find out

- how heat is transferred and moved in some cooling and heating systems.

You might think that an appliance that provides heat must be very different from one that cools. Surprisingly, these kinds of appliances can be very similar. In both cases the same process is occurring. Heat is being absorbed from one place, carried, and then released in another place. The heat energy is simply being moved from where it isn't wanted to where it is wanted.

Refrigerators and freezers produce low temperatures by moving heat from their food compartments to the air outside. To do this, these appliances make use of the special properties of certain compounds such as Freon. Freon both evaporates and condenses easily. When it evaporates, it absorbs heat. When it condenses, it releases heat. Freon is moved through a series of pipes that run both inside and outside the refrigerator. Freon evaporates in the pipes near the food compartment. As Freon evaporates, it absorbs heat from the compartment, causing it and the foods in it to cool. When Freon

Figure 13.15 In a refrigerator, Freon carries heat from one place to another.

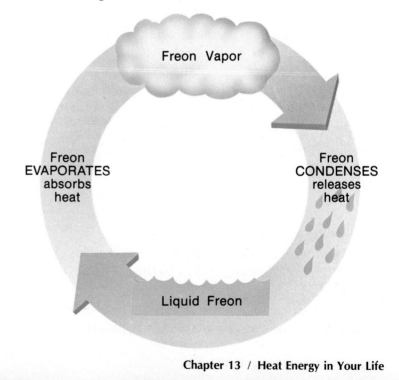

Freon Vapor

Freon
EVAPORATES
absorbs
heat

Freon
CONDENSES
releases
heat

Liquid Freon

flows in the pipes away from the compartment, it condenses, releasing that heat. In short, Freon acts as a heat carrier. It absorbs heat through evaporation from inside the refrigerator. Then it carries the heat to pipes outside the refrigerator and releases it through condensation. If you touch the back of a refrigerator that is running, you will feel the heat that is being released.

ACTIVITY   How Does Evaporation Affect Temperature?

Materials
thermometer
beaker
gauze
rubber band
alcohol
eyedropper
safety glasses

Procedure

1. Copy the chart and use it to record your observations. Put on your safety glasses.

2. Carefully wrap the bulb of the thermometer with gauze. Secure the gauze with a rubber band.

3. Place the thermometer in the beaker. Drop 10 drops of alcohol on the gauze. Record the temperature on your chart under *0 Minutes.* Continue to record the temperature every minute for 5 minutes.

4. Repeat steps 2 and 3 with water instead of alcohol. Use new gauze.

Questions

1. Make a graph of your results. The horizontal axis should show time. The vertical axis should show temperature. Use different colors to plot the results for alcohol and for water.

2. Which liquid required more heat to evaporate?

3. What do you call the amount of heat required to evaporate a liquid?

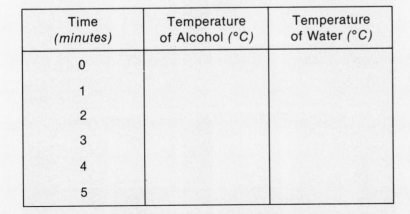

Time (minutes)	Temperature of Alcohol (°C)	Temperature of Water (°C)
0		
1		
2		
3		
4		
5		

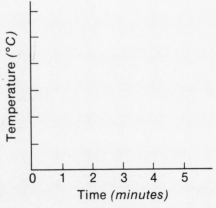

An air conditioner works on exactly the same principle as a refrigerator. In fact, an air-conditioned house could be thought of as a big refrigerator. The heat inside the house is absorbed through evaporation and released through condensation outside the house. Like a refrigerator, if you touch the part of a working air conditioner that is outside a house, the air conditioner will feel warm. You are feeling the heat that is being released from condensation.

It is possible to use the same principles that apply to refrigerators and air conditioners to take heat from outdoors and use it to heat a house. A machine that does this is called a **heat pump.** Although it is hard to imagine, even on very cold days the air outside does contain some heat. A heat pump absorbs that heat through evaporation and releases it through condensation inside the house. Most heat pumps can work in reverse in hot weather. Thus, the same machine can work both to heat and to cool a home.

Figure 13.16 Air conditioners carry heat from inside a building to the air outside.

Figure 13.17 Even on very cold days a heat pump absorbs heat from the outside air.

Heat pumps use less energy than other heating systems. A heat pump moves heat energy from one place to another. In other heating systems, energy is changed from one form to another to produce heat. For example, in many systems, heat is supplied by burning a fuel, such as natural gas, coal, or oil. Chemical energy in the bonds of the fuel molecules is being changed to heat energy. This heat is used to heat water, to boil water, which makes steam, or to heat air. The hot gas or water then moves to other parts of the building by convection or with the help of a fan. As the gas or water cools, it returns to the furnace where it is reheated.

Study Questions for 13.4

1. How are an air conditioner and a heat pump similar?
2. How is Freon used to cool the inside of a refrigerator?
3. How is a heat pump different from other home-heating systems?

What Did You Learn?

- Heat engines use heat energy to do work.
- Heat engines operate on the principle that when a gas is heated, its pressure increases.
- The pressure of a heated gas in a cylinder pushes out a piston.
- In external combustion engines fuel is burned outside the cylinder.
- In internal combustion engines fuel is burned inside the cylinder.
- James Watt made the steam engine more efficient.
- A steam turbine uses steam under pressure to produce a rotational motion.
- Nicolas-Joseph Cugnot invented the first true car in 1769.
- Cars and trucks use internal combustion engines.
- The four basic parts of a gasoline engine are a carburetor, pistons, cylinders, and spark plugs.
- The four strokes in most gasoline engines are intake, compression, power, and exhaust.
- Heat losses prevent heat engines from being perfectly efficient.
- Gasoline cars have a cooling system to prevent damage to the engine due to high temperatures.
- Refrigerators, freezers, air conditioners, and heat pumps all transport heat from one place to another.
- Heat can be absorbed, moved, and released by fluids such as Freon.
- Freon absorbs heat through evaporation.
- Freon releases heat through condensation.
- Most heat pumps can operate as both a heater and an air conditioner.

Key Terms

heat engine
cylinder
piston
crankshaft
external combustion engine
internal combustion engine
steam turbine
carburetor
spark plug
strokes
heat pump

Biography

Elijah McCoy (1843–1929)

Elijah McCoy was born in Ontario, Canada. He was the son of runaway slaves. His parents were very poor. They worked hard and sacrificed in order to send Elijah to Scotland. There he trained to become a mechanical engineer.

When McCoy finished his studies, he came to the United States. Because of his race, he could not find work as a mechanical engineer. Eventually he found a job with Michigan Central Railroad, oiling the moving parts on locomotives.

McCoy soon got bored with this work on the railroad. He began to think about ways to improve the oiling of locomotives. Working at night in his tiny workshop at home, he invented a lubricator cup. This device allowed small amounts of oil to drip continuously onto the moving parts of the engine. This invention would make locomotives run more efficiently. It would also eliminate the need to stop the train for oiling.

The buildup of heat caused by the friction of moving parts is a serious problem for all machines. It wasn't long before industries all over the world were using McCoy's lubricating cups. They were called "the real McCoy." The invention was a big money saver because the machines didn't have to be stopped to be oiled. Today, versions of McCoy's lubricating cup are widely used in locomotives, cars, buses, rockets, ships, and almost every other kind of modern machine.

TO THINK ABOUT AND DO

Vocabulary

Number your paper from 1 to 10. Match the phrase on the right with the description on the left. Write the letter of the phrase beside the appropriate number.

1. a device that changes heat energy into work
2. the burning of a fuel inside a cylinder
3. a device perfected by James Watt
4. the stroke in which the piston moves in to shrink the space available to the gasoline and air mixture
5. the stroke in which the piston moves out, allowing the gasoline and air mixture to enter the cylinder
6. that part of a gasoline engine where gasoline evaporates and mixes with air
7. fluid that absorbs, carries, and releases heat in a refrigerator
8. home-heating device that moves heat from one place to another
9. a device that ignites the gasoline and air mixture in the cylinder
10. that which prevents heat engines from being perfectly efficient

a. spark plug
b. heat pump
c. carburetor
d. heat loss
e. internal combustion
f. steam engine
g. intake
h. heat engine
i. external combustion
j. efficiency
k. Freon
l. compression

What Do You Remember?

1. What happens to the pressure of a gas when it is heated in a confined space?
2. Why don't diesel engines need spark plugs?
3. List and explain the four strokes of a gasoline engine.
4. Why aren't heat engines perfectly efficient?
5. What is an example of a substance that carries heat away from the food compartment of a refrigerator?
6. How is an air-conditioned house like a refrigerator?
7. How does Freon absorb and release heat?
8. Why do gasoline engines need a cooling system?
9. What are the functions of the piston, cylinder, and crankshaft in a heat engine?
10. Name the inventions credited to Watt and Cugnot.

Applying What You Have Learned

1. If a heat engine loses 38 percent of the heat it produces, how efficient is it?
2. If you were selecting a fluid to carry heat in a refrigerator, would you want one that required a lot of heat energy or a little heat energy to evaporate? Why?
3. What problems do you think the developers of gasoline cars faced?
4. Why do you think tune-ups are simpler for diesel engines than for gasoline engines?
5. What area in the food compartment of a refrigerator would you expect to be the coldest? Why?

Research and Investigation

1. Before they had refrigerators, people used iceboxes to keep food cold. Find out how iceboxes chilled food.
2. Visit one or more car dealerships. Ask for information on diesel cars and how they compare with gasoline cars. A salesperson may discuss this with you. There should also be pamphlets available detailing diesel and gasoline engines. Present the information you gather in a written report.

Unit Four

Magnetism and Electricity

Magnetic and Electric Forces

14

How important are magnets to you? Do you use them every day? Could you live without them? You could live without magnets. But your life would probably be changed much more than you realize. Magnets are an essential part of most appliances in your home. For example, hair dryers, tape recorders, televisions, and record players involve magnets. In many homes, even the electricity to run these appliances comes from power plants that use magnets.

Magnetic and electric forces are very closely related. In many ways the behavior of magnetic and electric forces is similar. Also the action of one force can affect the action of the other. For this reason, the study of magnetism is usually linked to the study of electricity. In this chapter you will learn about some of the basic properties of magnetized and electrified matter. In later chapters you will see how these properties affect your daily life.

Figure 14.1 A compass needle is a magnet. Rapid expansion of sea trade and exploration resulted from the development of the compass.

You will find out
- what magnetism is;
- how magnetism and electricity are alike;
- why some substances are magnetic.

Physical scientists have made hundreds of observations about matter. Many of these observations can be explained through the action of forces. You have already learned about some of these forces, such as nuclear force, gravitational force, and friction. Another very important force is magnetic force, or **magnetism.** Magnetism is a force produced by the motion of electric charges in a material. It shows up, for example, as the ability of a magnetized object, or **magnet,** to attract small pieces of iron.

Suppose you dip a magnet into a pile of iron filings. When you pull the magnet out, you see that the filings form a mossy covering on both ends. The rest of the magnet remains bare. The magnetic force is greatest at the ends of the magnet. The filings cling to the area of greatest magnetic force. The areas of greatest magnetic force are called **magnetic poles.** Every magnet has two poles. One is the north pole (N). The other is the south pole (S). It is easy to identify the two poles in a bar magnet. When the magnet is held by a thin wire, one end turns toward the north. This end is the north pole. The other end is the south pole.

In some ways magnetic force is similar to electric force. For example, if you bring the north poles of two magnets together, they repel each other. On the other hand, if the north pole of one magnet is brought near the south pole of another magnet, the magnets attract each other. It is a general rule that like poles of a magnet repel each other and unlike poles attract each other. This rule is very similar to one you learned earlier for electric charges. Opposite charges attract and like charges repel. Another similarity exists between magnetic and electric forces. Like the force between electric charges, the force between two magnets decreases as the magnets are moved farther apart.

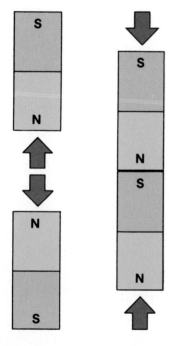

Figure 14.2 Like poles repel each other. Opposite poles attract.

A magnetic force acts between two magnets even though they may not be touching. Objects that experience the force of a magnet are said to be in the magnetic force field of that magnet. A magnetic force field, or **magnetic field,** is the area around a magnet where its magnetic force can be experienced. The magnetic field is strongest near the poles and weak farther away from the poles.

Figure 14.3 Iron filings are concentrated near the poles where the magnetic force is strongest.

An important difference between electricity and magnetism is that a single kind of electric charge can be put on an object. An object can be either positive or negative. This cannot happen with magnets. A single pole is never found on one magnet. The north and south poles cannot be separated. If you cut a magnet in half, each half instantly becomes a whole magnet. Both new magnets will have a north and a south pole. The poles cannot be separated because the basic units of matter—atoms and the particles they contain—have both a north and a south pole. No particles with a single magnetic pole are known to exist. Therefore, no form of matter with a single pole is known to exist.

Figure 14.4 No matter how you cut a magnet, the remaining pieces will always have both a north and a south pole.

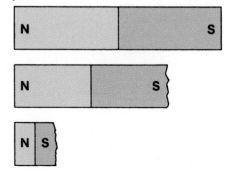

Most materials cannot be magnetized. Iron and a few other materials such as steel, nickel, and cobalt can be magnetized. These substances have regions called **magnetic domains** [doh-MAYNZ]. Magnetic domains, which are clusters of many atoms, can be thought of as tiny magnets. When the domains are randomly arranged, the material is not magnetic. However, if those domains are lined up, the material becomes a magnet. For example, when a steel bar is stroked in one direction with a magnet, the steel bar becomes magnetized. The magnetic domains in the steel are lined up by the action of the magnet. This magnetizing of a material by a magnet is called **induced** [ihn-DOOST] **magnetism.**

Figure 14.5 The magnetic domains in a magnetized object are lined up in the same direction.

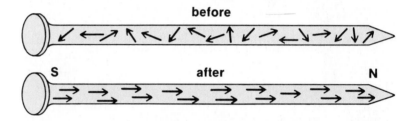

Nails, paper clips, and other objects made of iron can be temporarily magnetized. However, they keep their magnetism for only a short time. In a few materials, such as steel, and in some special mixtures of metals, the magnetism remains long after the inducing magnet is removed. These materials make permanent magnets. Some of the best permanent magnets are made of a mixture of iron, aluminum, nickel, and copper. These magnets are called alnico magnets. Can you guess where the name *alnico* comes from? Look at the first letters of the elements that form it.

If permanent magnets are heated to temperatures of from several hundred to a thousand degrees Celsius, they will lose their magnetism. Their magnetism is lost because the increased atomic motion produced by heating causes the magnetic domains to get out of line. Permanent magnets can also lose their magnetism if they are dropped too many times. The magnetic domains are bumped out of line when the dropped magnet strikes the floor.

Figure 14.6 A permanent magnet holds these paper clips at the top where they can be picked up easily.

Figure 14.7 In the outdoor sport of orienteering, compasses are used to determine location and direction.

The Greeks and the Chinese discovered more than 2,000 years ago that some rocks are natural magnets. These rocks are a form of iron ore called lodestone, or magnetite. The magnetic domains in lodestones are naturally lined up.

Lodestones were very important to sailors during the Middle Ages. A lodestone was used to magnetize the sailing ship's compass, keeping it in working order. Without a working compass, the sailors could become lost at sea. Because the ship's lodestone was so important, any sailor who tampered with it was tortured or put to death.

Study Questions for 14.1

1. What is magnetism?
2. How are magnetism and electricity alike?
3. How can a steel rod be magnetized?

14.2 The Magnetism of the Earth

You will find out
- how the earth acts like a magnet;
- how the north geographic pole and the north magnetic pole differ.

Have you ever wondered why a compass needle always lines up in the north-south direction? It does so because the earth has a magnetic field. The needle of a compass is magnetized. The earth's magnetic field acts to line up the compass needle. How can the earth have a magnetic field? The answer to this question is unclear. Scientists believe the earth's magnetism is somehow related to the rotation of the liquid iron center of the earth.

Because the earth has a magnetic field, the earth is acting as if there is a huge bar magnet stuck in it. This imaginary magnet does not lie perfectly straight up and down inside the earth. Instead the magnet is tilted. The **north magnetic pole** is the north pole of this imaginary magnet. A compass needle points to the north magnetic pole.

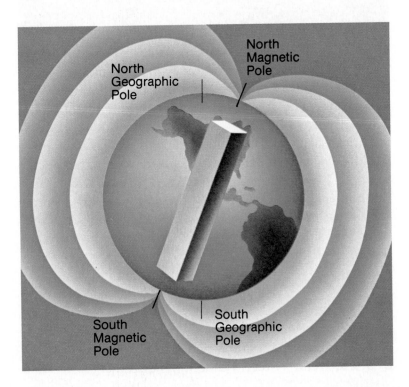

Figure 14.8 The earth acts as if there is an imaginary bar magnet stuck in it.

Figure 14.9 The magnetic needle of a compass always points to the north and south magnetic poles.

The north pole you are probably familiar with is the **north geographic pole.** The north geographic pole is on maps and globes at the very top, or northernmost point, of the earth. The north magnetic pole is near but not at the north geographic pole. The north magnetic pole is about 1,700 km south of the north geographic pole. On a map, this location is in northern Canada almost directly above the middle of the United States.

When compasses at different places point toward the north magnetic pole, they are not necessarily pointing in the same geographic direction. For example, a compass in Boston points between geographic northwest and north. But one in Los Angeles points between geographic northeast and north. Navigators must use special charts to allow for the difference between geographic and magnetic north. To make matters worse, the north magnetic pole of the earth moves. It slowly wanders around. For this reason navigation charts must be changed every ten years or so.

Do You Know?
Pigeons and dolphins have tiny particles of magnetite in their heads. Scientists think that these particles may act as compasses that help these animals navigate.

Study Questions for 14.2

1. How is the earth like a magnet?
2. Which north pole does a compass needle point to and why?

14.3 Static Electricity

You will find out
- how an object can build up a static electric charge;
- how static electricity can be detected;
- how an electric charge can be induced in an object.

Electric force, like magnetic force, can be traced to the atoms that make up matter. An atom has an equal number of positive protons and negative electrons. It has no overall electric charge. However, an atom can sometimes lose or gain electrons. If enough of the atoms in an object lose electrons, that object will have a noticeable positive electric charge. On the other hand, if the atoms in an object gain electrons, the object will become negatively charged.

The electric charge that builds up on an object is called **static electricity.** Static electricity is an electric charge that does not flow. You can produce static electricity with a plastic comb. When you comb your hair with a plastic comb, your hair loses electrons to the plastic. When this happens, your hair becomes positively charged. The comb becomes negatively charged. You can see the effects of these charges by holding the comb over your hair. Since opposite electric charges attract, the negative comb attracts the positive hair. Strands of your hair separate and move up toward the comb.

Figure 14.10 When you stroke a cat's fur, electrons move from the fur to your hand.

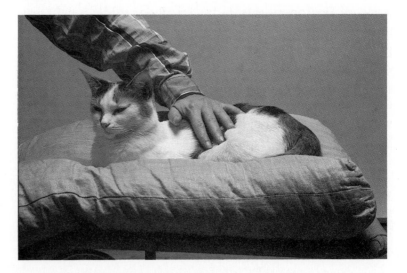

Another example of static electricity occurs in the laundry room. Clothes taken from a dryer often cling together. Why does this happen? The clothes rub against each other in the dryer. Electrons move from one piece of clothing to another. A positive charge builds up on the clothes that lose electrons. A negative charge builds up on the clothes that gain electrons. The oppositely charged clothing clings together.

ACTIVITY

How Do Electric Charges Act?

Materials
ring stand and ring
string
3 test tubes
silk
2 plastic combs
fur or flannel

Procedure

1. Use string to suspend a test tube from the ring of the ring stand.

2. Rub the test tube with silk for two minutes. Then let the test tube hang freely from the string.

3. Rub a second test tube with silk for two minutes. Now bring this test tube near the one hanging from the string. What happens? Put the test tube you are holding aside.

4. Again rub the hanging test tube with silk for two minutes.

5. Rub a comb for two minutes with fur or flannel. Bring it near the hanging test tube. What happens? Remove the test tube from the string.

6. Hang the plastic comb from the string. Rub it for two minutes with fur or flannel.

7. Rub a second comb for two minutes with fur or flannel. Bring this comb near the comb hanging from the string. What happens?

Questions

1. What happened when the two test tubes were brought together? Why?

2. What happened when the test tube and comb were brought together? Why?

3. What happened when the two combs were brought together? Why?

4. If the silk had a negative charge after it was rubbed on the test tube, what charge did the test tube have?

5. If the fur or flannel had a positive charge after it was rubbed on the comb, what charge did the comb have?

The presence of an electric charge on an object can be detected with an **electroscope** [ih-LEHK-truh-skohp]. An electroscope is a jar with a metal rod fitted into it. The top of the rod is in the form of a knob. Two metal leaves are attached to the bottom of the rod inside the jar. If you touch the knob with a negatively charged object, electrons will move from the object to the knob and down the rod into the metal leaves. The leaves will become negatively charged. Since like charges repel, the leaves will spread apart. If you touch a positively charged object to the knob, then electrons will move from the rod onto the object, leaving the metal leaves positively charged. Again the leaves move apart, since they have the same charge. If an uncharged object touches the knob, no electrons will move. The leaves will not become charged and will not separate. In this way an electroscope can tell you if the object you are testing has an electric charge. It cannot, however, tell you if the charge is negative or positive.

Figure 14.11 *left:* The leaves of the electroscope hang straight down. *right:* When a charged object touches the knob, the leaves separate.

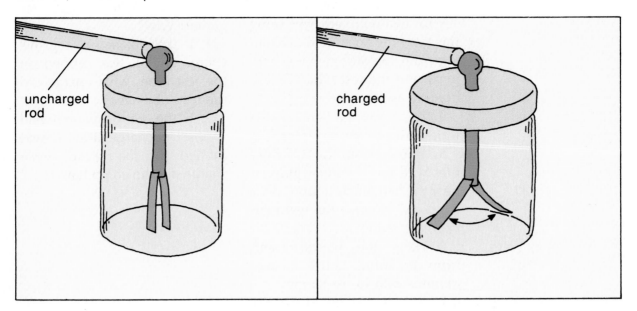

Electric forces can be described with electric fields in much the same way that magnetic fields describe magnetic forces. The electric field is strongest near the object carrying an electric charge. The field is weaker farther away from the object.

Figure 14.12 Balloons with a static charge produce an opposite charge on the wall through electrostatic induction.

Just as magnetism can be induced, an electric charge can be produced in an object if that object is brought near a charged object. This is called **electrostatic induction** [ih-lehk-truh-STAT-ihk in-DUHK-shuhn]. The electric field of the charged object will either attract or repel electrons in the neutral object. If the charged object is negative, it will repel electrons. If it is positive, it will attract electrons.

For example, suppose you bring a negatively charged plastic comb near an electrically neutral scrap of aluminum foil. The electrons in the foil will be repelled by the negatively charged comb. Some of them will move to the side of the foil away from the comb. This leaves the side of the foil nearer the comb with a positive charge. The electric forces will attract the foil toward the comb.

Study Questions for 14.3

1. Describe and explain an example of static electricity.
2. How does an electroscope detect an electric charge?
3. Give an example of electrostatic induction.

You will find out
- what moves an electric charge around;
- how electric discharges occur;
- how you can be protected from lightning.

Many objects, including your body, can have an electric charge. Sometimes this charge stays put as static electricity. What happens if the charge on an object does not stay put? The charge may quickly spread out over the entire object. Or the charge may flow from one object to another. Whether a charge will spread out, flow, or stay put depends on how easily the electrons in that object can move. It is the movement of electrons that moves a charge.

The same terms that apply to conduction of heat are used to describe the movement of electrons, or electric charges. Materials in which the electrons can move easily are called conductors. Ones in which electrons cannot move easily are called insulators. The best conductors are metals, such as silver, copper, and gold. Helium, argon, sulfur, rubber, and glass are examples of materials that are commonly used as insulators.

In conduction, a charge can flow from one part of an object to another part. A charge can also flow from one object to another when those objects are touching. It is also possible for a charge to flow from one object to another object even though the objects are not touching. For example, if you walk across a carpet, your body may

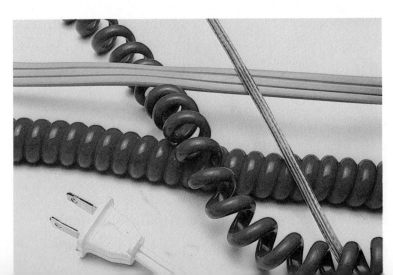

Figure 14.13 Colorful insulation covers these electric cords.

pick up electrons from the carpet. The air around you is an insulator. Therefore, the electrons you gained from the carpet do not move from your body to the air. You become a charged object. What happens if you now bring your hand near a metal object such as a doorknob? You see and feel a spark. The electric field between your charged fingers and the doorknob acts to produce a charge on the atoms in the air. The air now becomes a conductor and carries the electric charge from your body to the doorknob. The flow of an electric charge through a gas from a charged object to a conductor is called an **electric discharge.**

Figure 14.14 Particles of blowing sand or snow can cause a buildup of electric charges on a wire fence. Discharges from these fences can be powerful enough to knock people and cattle to the ground.

The electric discharges you experience from walking on a rug are harmless. However, not all electric discharges are harmless. For example, when the inside of a ship is washed, electric charges can build up on water drops as they rub against the inner sides of the ship. The buildup of charges on these drops can cause electric discharges. Sparks from these discharges have ignited fumes and caused explosions in oil tankers.

The movement of particles in the air by wind and rain can cause a buildup of charges in a cloud. If this charge gets too great, it will discharge to the ground or to another cloud. This discharge, or movement of electrons, appears as a bolt of lightning.

Lightning takes the easiest path to the ground. Thus it usually strikes the tallest object around. In flat regions, a tree may be the tallest object. You should, therefore, stay away from trees during a thunderstorm. Lightning may strike the tree. The electrons can move down the tree and discharge to your body. You should avoid standing near good conductors, such as metal fences, for the same reason.

Tall buildings also make good targets for lightning. The Empire State Building is usually struck dozens of times during a thunderstorm. Most tall buildings are protected by lightning rods. A lightning rod is a metal rod connected to conductors that lead to the earth. Electrons can move from a lightning bolt, to the metal lightning rod, down the conductor attached to it, and into the earth. A lightning rod does not prevent lightning strikes. It attracts them. The lightning rod makes a safe path for the electric charge to flow to the earth.

Lightning rods are examples of **grounded conductors.** A grounded conductor is one that is connected to another very large conductor such as the metal frame of a very large building or the earth. The very large conductor is called the **electrical ground.**

Figure 14.15 Lightning rods provide a safe path for electric charges to flow to the earth.

ACTIVITY

Which Materials Are Conductors?

Materials

light bulb and socket
3 pieces of insulated
   copper wire
battery

Procedure

1. Arrange your apparatus as shown in the diagram. Test the bulb to be sure it is working by bringing the free wires together. The bulb should light.

2. Use your apparatus to locate ten conductors and ten insulators in the room.

Questions

1. What similarities do you see among the materials that were conductors?

2. What similarities do you see among the materials that were insulators?

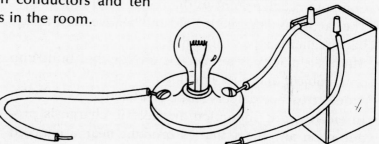

A grounded conductor cannot hold a charge. If the conductor is negatively charged, the extra electrons move from the conductor into the electrical ground. If the conductor is positively charged, then electrons move up from the electrical ground to cancel out the positive charge. The electrical ground acts as a very large storehouse of electric charge. Since it is so large, some electrons gained or lost do not have any overall effect. By grounding a conductor, you can prevent dangerous electric discharges from occurring. Electrical grounds are an important safety feature of many machines and appliances as well as buildings.

Do You Know?
The separation of charges in sandstorms can cause lightning.

Study Questions for 14.4

1. What makes some substances good conductors of electricity?
2. Describe and explain an example of an electric discharge.
3. Explain how a lightning rod works.

What Did You Learn?

- Magnetism is a force produced by electric charges in motion.
- Every magnet has a north and a south pole.
- The magnetic field is the area around a magnet where its magnetic force can be experienced.
- In magnets the magnetic domains are lined up.
- There are temporary magnets, permanent magnets, and natural magnets.
- Compass needles point to the north magnetic pole.
- The earth has a magnetic field and behaves as if a huge bar magnet is stuck through it.
- Static electricity is an electric charge that builds up on an object and does not flow.
- An electroscope detects static electricity.
- In electrostatic induction an electric charge is produced on an object that is brought near a charged object.
- The electrons in conductors can move around.
- The flow of electricity through a gas from a charged object to a conductor is an electric discharge.
- Lightning is an electric discharge.
- A grounded conductor cannot hold a charge because any charge that passes through it flows into the electrical ground.

Key Terms

magnetism
magnet
magnetic poles
magnetic field
magnetic domains
induced magnetism
north magnetic pole
north geographic pole
static electricity
electroscope
electrostatic induction
electric discharge
grounded conductors
electrical ground

Biography

Mildred Dresselhaus (1930–)

Mildred Dresselhaus is an electrical engineer and a physicist. Her work involves the study of how different types of materials conduct electricity under different conditions. The results of her studies could prove very useful in communications, computers, or other devices that involve magnetic and electric forces.

Dresselhaus was born in New York City. Her parents were immigrants who had come to the United States to find a new life. When Mildred was born, her parents were poor. She had to work even while in grade school at several dirty, dull jobs to help her family. Her parents taught her to have faith in herself, and they encouraged her to do well in school.

She did very well. She graduated near the top of her class from Hunter College High School. After that she graduated with highest honors from Hunter College and received a doctorate in physics from the University of Chicago.

As a result of her excellent original research, Mildred Dresselhaus is known and honored around the world. She is

now the director of the Center for Materials Science and Engineering at the Massachusetts Institute of Technology. She is also a member of the National Academy of Engineering. Dr. Dresselhaus advises the government on research and serves on several governmental committees.

TO THINK ABOUT AND DO

Vocabulary

Number your paper from 1 to 8. Beside each number write the letter of the word or words that best complete the sentence.

1. In a magnet the regions of greatest magnetic force are the (a) magnetic domains, (b) magnetic poles, (c) lodestones.
2. The attraction of scraps of aluminum foil to a negatively charged plastic comb is an example of (a) magnetism, (b) conduction, (c) electrostatic induction.
3. A lightning rod (a) attracts lightning, (b) repels lightning, (c) is an insulator.
4. A compass needle points to the _____ pole. (a) magnetic (b) geographic (c) closer
5. A device that detects the presence of an electric charge is (a) a conductor, (b) an electric field, (c) an electroscope.
6. Clusters of many atoms which can be thought of as tiny magnets are (a) insulators, (b) magnetic domains, (c) magnetic poles.
7. The electric charge that builds up on an object and does not flow is (a) an electroscope, (b) static electricity, (c) electrostatic induction.
8. An example of a grounded conductor is (a) a copper penny, (b) a negatively charged plastic comb, (c) a lightning rod.

What Do You Remember?

1. What is magnetism?
2. Why is some matter magnetic?
3. What happens when you bring the north poles of two magnets together? The south poles? The north pole of one magnet and the south pole of another magnet?
4. How is the earth like a magnet?

5. What are two ways that magnetism and electricity are alike?
6. How are magnetism and electricity different?
7. What is magnetic induction?
8. How does an electroscope detect an electric charge?
9. What is a grounded conductor?
10. Why do clothes sometimes cling together when they come out of the dryer?

Applying What You Have Learned

1. How can you magnetize an iron nail? Will the nail be a permanent or a temporary magnet?
2. If you rub a glass rod with a piece of silk, the silk will cling to the rod. Why does this happen?
3. Why are metals good conductors of both heat and electricity?
4. Why is it a good idea to keep strong magnets away from watches?

Research and Investigation

1. Benjamin Franklin used something called a Leyden (Leiden) jar in some of his experiments. What is a Leyden jar?
2. What is a Van de Graaff generator?
3. The earth has a magnetic field. Do any other planets have a magnetic field?

Electricity

Esto Photographics Inc.

Every now and then, because of a storm or an accident, the supply of electric power to your home may be cut off. Can you remember one of these power failures, or blackouts? What did you do? Did you use candles for light? For a while the blackout may have been fun because it was so different from your everyday life. However, you probably soon tired of it and were happy when things went back to normal. Certainly if you were in an elevator when the power went out, you were glad when the blackout was over!

The invisible flow of electric power is a basic part of your everyday life. You flip a switch, and the power is there to light your home and to power your radio and television, as well as practically every other appliance in your home. Electricity is important. Benjamin Franklin had no idea how important when he spoke about it over 200 years ago. He said, "Electrical fluid . . . may . . . be of use to mankind."

15.1 Electric Currents

You will find out
- what is meant by the term *electric current;*
- what causes electric current to flow;
- how a dry cell produces voltage.

It's very easy to use electricity. Almost anyone can flip a switch or turn a dial. You have probably had experience plugging in cords, replacing light bulbs, and changing batteries in a flashlight. But what are you really doing when you do these things? To understand how electricity acts to do all that it does in your life, you must first understand how electric charges move.

Electric charges can flow from one end of an object throughout that object. Charges can also flow from one object to another. The flow of electric charges from one point to another point is called **electric current.**

The flow of electric charges, or current, is similar to the flow of water in a hose. Water flows inside a hose because of differences in water pressure. When you turn on the faucet, the water pressure is higher at the faucet end of the hose than at the open end. Water flows from the area of high pressure to the area of low pressure. Similarly, current flows from a point of high electric potential, or pressure, to a point of low electric potential. This difference in electric potential that causes current to flow is called **voltage.** Voltage is measured in units called **volts.**

The currents in your home are created by voltages of 120 or 240 volts. By comparison, a flashlight battery has a voltage of about 1.5 volts. How does a flashlight battery produce a voltage? A flashlight battery is a device known as a **dry cell.** A dry cell produces voltage as a result of chemical reactions between a moist paste and a metal.

Figure 15.2 Differences in water pressure cause water to flow in a hose. Voltage causes current to flow in a conductor.

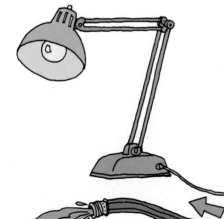

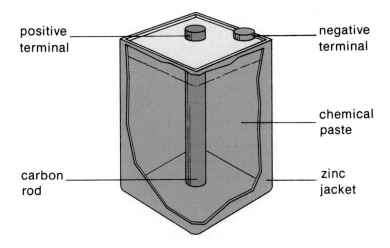

positive terminal

negative terminal

chemical paste

carbon rod

zinc jacket

Figure 15.3 The separation of charges in a dry cell produces a voltage.

A dry cell is made of a carbon rod surrounded by a mixture of chemicals that forms a paste. The paste is contained in a zinc jacket. Chemical reactions between the zinc, the carbon, and the paste cause a buildup of positive ions on the carbon rod. These positive ions give the carbon rod a positive charge. At the same time the zinc jacket is left with a negative charge. This separation of charges produces a voltage.

Since the carbon rod is positive, the place on it where contact is made with a conductor is called the **positive terminal.** Similarly, the place on the negative zinc jacket where contact is made is called the **negative terminal.** If the positive and negative terminals are connected with a conductor such as a metal wire, a current flows. Electrons move through the wire from the negative to the positive terminal.

Currents vary in strength. A current gets stronger as more charges flow through a conductor in the same amount of time. The amount of electric current, or number of charges, that passes a point in a conductor in one second is measured in **amperes** [AM-pihrz].

Do You Know?
A single bolt of lightning can carry 160,000 amperes of current through a voltage of 100 million volts.

Study Questions for 15.1

1. What is electric current?
2. What is voltage?
3. How does a dry cell produce a voltage?

15.2 Electric Circuits

You will find out
- how series and parallel circuits differ;
- how alternating and direct currents differ;
- what is meant by resistance.

When a voltage is created, charges do not automatically begin to flow. For example, a spare flashlight battery that is not being used has a voltage. But no current is flowing between the two terminals. No charges are flowing. For charges to flow there must be a path from the negative to the positive terminal. A conductor such as a metal wire can make this path. A path that connects the negative and positive terminals without any breaks is called a closed path. The path of an electric current is called an **electric circuit** [SUR-kiht].

You can build a simple electric circuit with a dry-cell battery, two wires, and a light bulb. You connect one of the wires to the light bulb and the positive terminal of the battery. You connect the other wire to the light bulb and the negative terminal of the battery. When these connections are made, the path for the current is closed. The circuit is closed, or complete. Current flows and the light bulb goes on. If a connection is broken anywhere along the current's path, that path is no longer closed. The circuit is open, or broken. Current cannot flow through an open circuit.

Figure 15.4 Current cannot flow through an open circuit.

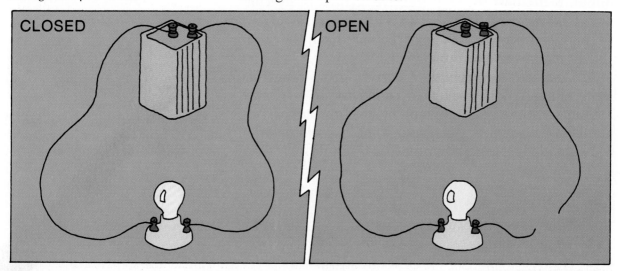

CLOSED   OPEN

A circuit made of a battery, two wires, and a light bulb is a very simple circuit. It has only a few parts. Most circuits are much more complicated. These circuits have many parts and may have several different paths for the current to flow through. Circuits can be grouped according to the kind of path the current takes.

If a circuit has only one path for the current, it is a **series circuit.** In a series circuit, all the current must go through each part of the circuit. A series circuit has the advantage of being easy to hook up and study. However, it has a major problem. If one part of the circuit—for example, a light bulb—goes out, the circuit is open and the current stops. The whole circuit goes dead. Some strings of decorating lights use series circuits. If one light goes out, all the lights go out.

Parallel circuits are more complicated than series circuits. In parallel circuits, the current divides and flows in two or more separate paths, or branches. If the current in one branch stops, the current still flows in the other branches. For example, many light fixtures have several light bulbs on a parallel circuit. When one bulb goes out, all the others stay lighted.

Figure 15.5 *left:* A parallel circuit offers more than one path. *right:* A series circuit offers only one path.

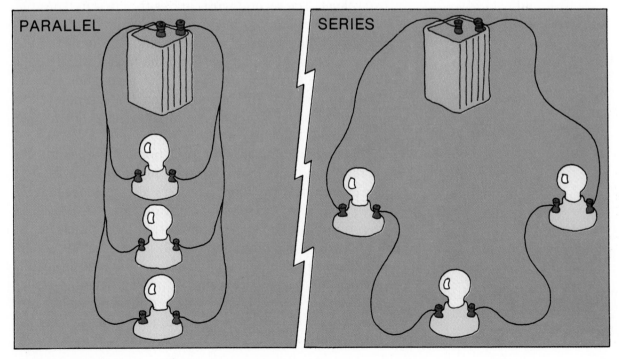

PARALLEL

SERIES

Figure 15.6 One branch of a parallel circuit

The electric wiring in your home is in the form of many parallel circuits. These circuits are designed so that new circuit parts such as lamps and appliances can be added by plugging them into wall outlets. The wall outlets work like the terminals of a battery.

Suppose you want to plug in and use a new record player. The record player has a cord made of two wires. The cord ends in a plug that has two prongs, one for each wire. You plug the record player into a wall outlet. When you turn on the record player, the current flows from the outlet into one prong of the plug. The wire connected to that prong carries the current into the record player. The second wire carries the current from the record player back to the outlet. The current flows into the outlet through the second prong. The path for the current from the outlet, through the record player, and back to the outlet is one branch of a parallel circuit. When you turn on the record player, that branch of the parallel circuit is complete, closed. Current flows. You hear music.

The current that flows in your home differs from the current that flows from batteries in an important way. The current flowing from a battery always moves in the same direction. Current that always flows in the same direction is called **direct current,** DC. The current in your home is not direct current. It is constantly switching directions. This kind of current is called **alternating** [awl-tur-NAY-tihng] **current,** AC. The alternating current in your home changes direction very quickly. It goes from forward to backward to forward again 60 times a second!

All circuits do not carry the same amount of current. What determines how much current flows in a circuit? This question was answered by the German scientist George S. Ohm in the early 1800's. Ohm found that voltage determines the amount of current that flows in a circuit. More current is produced by higher voltages. This is what you might expect. A higher voltage produces more current in much the same way that greater pressure differences produce more water flow in a hose.

You can make another useful comparison between a wire as a conductor of electricity and a hose as a conductor of water. The diameter of the hose affects the amount of water that can flow through it. A large-diameter hose carries more water than one with a small diameter. Ohm found that the amount of current that flows through a wire depends on the wire. A wire with a large diameter carries more current than a wire with a small diameter. Also, certain kinds of wire such as those made of copper, silver, or gold carry current more easily than wires made of other materials such as iron or lead.

Figure 15.7 Wires of different sizes and materials have different resistances.

Do You Know?
An electron in a circuit moves a distance of 1 mm per second.

ACTIVITY

How Can You Construct Electric Circuits?

Materials
3 batteries
7 sockets and
  light bulbs
small screwdriver
12 pieces of insulated
  copper wire
  (30 cm each)

Procedure
Follow the diagrams to construct three different circuits. You will need to refer to your circuits as you answer the following questions.

Questions
1. How does the brightness of the lights in the series circuit compare to the brightness of the light in the simple circuit?

2. How does the brightness of the lights in the parallel circuit compare to the brightness of the light in the simple circuit?

3. If you unscrew one light bulb in the series circuit, what happens to the others?

4. If you unscrew one light bulb in the parallel circuit, what happens to the others?

5. How can you explain the dimness in the series circuit?

6. How can you explain the fact that when one light bulb goes out, all the light bulbs in a series circuit go out?

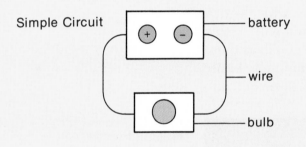

Simple Circuit — battery, wire, bulb

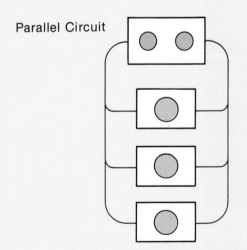

Parallel Circuit

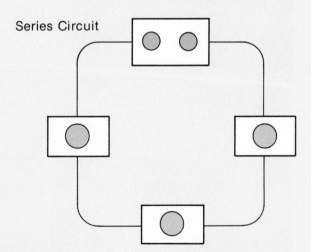

Series Circuit

The current-carrying properties of a material are summed up in the **resistance** [rih-ZIHS-tuhns] of that material. The resistance is the opposition a material offers to the flow of electric charges. All materials, even good conductors, offer some resistance. Therefore, all the parts of a circuit have some resistance. The wires used to carry current usually have a low resistance. Other parts of a circuit such as lamps and appliances have a high resistance. Resistance is measured in **ohms.**

Material	Resistance	Material	Resistance
silver	0.032 ohm	tin	0.22 ohm
copper	0.033 ohm	steel piano wire	0.23 ohm
gold	0.047 ohm	lead	0.42 ohm
aluminum	0.055 ohm	carbon	66 ohms

Table 15–1 Resistance of Several 20-Gauge Wires

The resistance in metals is related to voltage and current in a formula called **Ohm's law.** Ohm's law tells you that the greater the voltage, the higher the resistance. It also tells you that the more current, the lower the resistance. The formula for Ohm's law is the following:

$$\textbf{Resistance} = \frac{\textbf{voltage}}{\textbf{current}}$$

EXAMPLE Find the resistance of an automobile headlight that uses 4 amperes of current in a 12-volt circuit.

SOLUTION $\text{Resistance} = \dfrac{\text{voltage}}{\text{current}} = \dfrac{12 \text{ volts}}{4 \text{ amperes}} = 3 \text{ ohms}$

Study Questions for 15.2

1. How are series and parallel circuits different?
2. How are alternating and direct currents different?
3. What is resistance?
4. What does Ohm's law tell you?

15.3 Electric Power

You will find out
- what is meant by electric power;
- how electric companies measure and charge for electric energy.

Electric currents deliver electric energy to the parts of a circuit. This energy is then used in many different ways. For example, it can light lamps, run appliances, or produce heat. Different circuit parts operate on, or draw, different amounts of current when they are turned on. For example, an air conditioner draws more current than a blender. **Electric power** refers to the amount of electric energy that flows through a circuit at a given time. The electric power in an electric circuit depends on the voltage and the current.

Electric power = voltage × current

Electric power, like other kinds of power, is measured in watts. To measure large amounts of power, a larger unit, the **kilowatt,** is used. A kilowatt is 1,000 watts.

EXAMPLE A toaster in a 120-volt circuit draws 5 amperes of current. How much power does it use?

SOLUTION   voltage × current = Power
120 volts × 5 amperes = 600 watts

Table 15–2 Annual Energy Use of Several Appliances

Appliance	Average Wattage	Kilowatt–hour Use
dishwasher	1200	363
microwave oven	1450	190
toaster	1150	39
washing machine	500	103
clothes dryer	5000	933
vacuum cleaner	1000	46
blow dryer	1000	14
color television	200	440

Figure 15.8 How many of the electric appliances in this photograph have you used?

Electric companies bill according to how much energy is used. The basic unit they use to measure electric energy is the **kilowatt-hour.** A kilowatt-hour is the amount of energy produced by one kilowatt of power in one hour. Electric energy can be expressed in the following formula:

Electric energy = power × time

EXAMPLE   Suppose a utility company charges 10¢ per kilowatt-hour. How much does it cost to leave a 60-watt light bulb on for 100 hours?

SOLUTION   power × time = Energy
60 watts × 100 hours = 6,000 watt-hours
= 6 kilowatt-hours

Since 1 kilowatt-hour costs 10¢, 6 kilowatt-hours cost 60¢. It costs 60¢ to leave a 60-watt light bulb on for 100 hours.

Do You Know?
Scientists at Columbia University have reported that electric currents as small as 20 millionths of an ampere can help to heal broken bones.

Study Questions for 15.3
1. What is electric power?
2. What unit do electric companies use to measure energy use?

15.4 Electric Safety

You will find out
- why fuses and circuit breakers are important;
- what happens in a short circuit;
- how you can avoid accidents with electricity.

You use electricity every day in many ways. Even though electric power is familiar to you, you should always treat it with care and respect. When electric power is not used carefully, it can be very dangerous.

One danger involves the heat produced by electric currents. All electric wires have some resistance. This resistance causes some electric energy to be lost when current is flowing. Remember, energy never disappears. It only changes form. Therefore, the electric energy that is lost has really only changed form. It changes to heat energy. If too much current flows through a wire, too much electric energy may be changed to heat energy. The wire may become so hot that a fire starts.

A circuit can overheat if too many appliances are plugged in and used on it at the same time. This practice can cause too much current to flow and may start a fire. To prevent this from happening, all circuits should have a **fuse** or a **circuit breaker.** Fuses and circuit breakers are devices that break, or open, the circuit to stop the current. These devices do this automatically when there is a danger of overheating.

Figure 15.9 *left:* Circuit breakers; *right:* Too many appliances are plugged into this outlet.

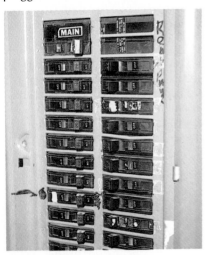

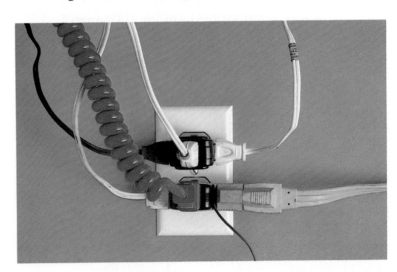

Most circuits in today's homes have circuit breakers that open the circuit when the current is greater than 15 or 20 amperes. Normally the currents drawn by lights or appliances are only a few amperes. However, some appliances such as electric heaters and hair dryers can draw 10 or more amperes. Care should be taken not to use more than one of these appliances on the same circuit at the same time.

ACTIVITY

How Can You Compare the Resistance of Different Wires?

Materials
ammeter
voltmeter
rheostat
switch
2 alligator clamps
7 pieces of insulated
    copper wire
    (30 cm each)
iron, aluminum, and
    copper wires of
    the same length
    and thickness
battery

Procedure

1. Set up the apparatus as shown in the diagram.

2. Set the rheostat so that the maximum resistance is in the circuit.

3. Place the aluminum wire between the alligator clamps.

4. Close the switch.

5. Adjust the rheostat so that the ammeter indicates a current is flowing. Record the ammeter and voltmeter readings.

6. Divide the voltage by the current to determine the resistance of the aluminum wire.

7. Repeat steps 3–7 with the copper wire and with the iron wire.

Questions

1. Create a bar graph to compare the resistance of the three wires.

2. Which wire had the highest resistance? Which wire had the lowest resistance?

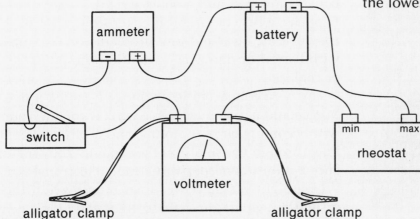

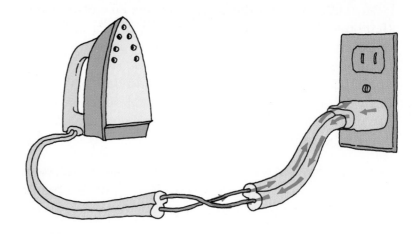

Figure 15.10 A short circuit

A circuit can also overheat if a **short circuit** occurs. In a short circuit, the current flows over an unintended path that has very low resistance. This could happen if the two wires in a cord accidentally touched. Then the current would not flow through whatever the cord was connected to at all. It would flow from the outlet to the point where the wires touched and back to the outlet. This circuit would have very low resistance. A large current would go through it. The result would be rapid overheating and possibly a fire.

Ordinarily, cords have a covering of insulation. The insulation keeps the wires from touching and creating a short circuit. Sometimes, however, the insulation becomes damaged and a short circuit occurs. When this happens, a fuse or circuit breaker should act to shut off the current. To avoid any problems or risk, any cord with frayed or damaged insulation should be repaired or replaced.

Any wire connected to a voltage is called a **live wire.** You should never touch a live wire. If you do, your body will become part of a circuit, and a large current will flow through you and into the ground. You will experience a painful and possibly deadly electric shock.

Live high-voltage power lines often have little or no insulation. Sometimes these lines fall to or near the ground as a result of a storm or an accident. If you ever see one of these lines down, do not touch it. Call the power company and your local authorities.

Figure 15.11 Power company employees must be very careful when working with live wires.

Figure 15.12 Birds can perch safely on power lines because no part of them offers the current a path to the ground.

Have you ever wondered why the same high-voltage power lines that are so dangerous to you make good, safe perches for birds? A bird on a wire is safe because no part of it offers the current a path to the ground. If, however, any part of the bird touches a pole or anything else that reaches the ground, then the bird will die of electric shock. It dies because its body now is providing the current with a path to the ground. The current takes that path going through the bird, through whatever it is touching, and into the ground. Sometimes birds and other animals, such as squirrels, are killed in this way.

There is a similar danger to you if you use an electric appliance while you are touching or standing in water. The water conducts electricity. Electric current from an appliance may take a path through you to the water you are touching. You could be seriously hurt or killed. It is for this reason that you are warned never to use electric appliances or touch sources of electricity such as light-bulb sockets and outlets while in contact with water.

Study Questions for 15.4

1. Why are fuses and circuit breakers necessary?
2. What is a short circuit?
3. Why is a bird safe sitting on a high-voltage line?
4. What can happen if you operate an electric appliance in water?

What Did You Learn?

- The flow of electric charges from one point to another is called electric current.
- Voltage causes charges to flow.
- A dry cell produces voltage as a result of chemical reactions between a moist paste and a metal.
- Current is measured in amperes.
- The path of an electric current is called an electric circuit.
- In a series circuit all the current follows one path.
- In a parallel circuit the current divides and flows in two or more separate paths.
- Direct current always flows in the same direction.
- Alternating current constantly switches direction.
- Resistance is the opposition a material offers to the flow of electric charges.
- Resistance is measured in ohms.
- Electric power refers to the amount of electric energy that flows through a circuit at a given time.
- Electric power is measured in watts and kilowatts.
- A kilowatt-hour is the amount of energy produced by one kilowatt of power in one hour.
- Resistance causes some electric energy to be changed into heat energy.
- Fuses and circuit breakers open a circuit when too much current is flowing and there is a danger of overheating.
- A short circuit is an unintended path of low resistance over which current may flow.
- Live wires that are not well insulated are dangerous and should never be touched.
- You should never use electricity while in contact with water.

Key Terms

electric current
voltage
volts
dry cell
positive terminal
negative terminal
amperes
electric circuit
series circuit
parallel circuits
direct current
alternating current
resistance
ohms
Ohm's law
electric power
kilowatt
kilowatt-hour
fuse
circuit breaker
short circuit
live wire

Biography

Thomas Alva Edison (1847–1931)

Thomas Alva Edison is a good example of someone with a good mind who became rich and famous through hard work. Edison used his mind to educate himself at home.

After reading a few science books, Edison wanted to do experiments of his own. He got a job as a newsboy on a train between Port Huron and Detroit, Michigan. Using the money he made, he soon set up a chemical laboratory in the baggage car of the train. Unfortunately, the laboratory caught fire and the railroad banned further experiments.

Accidents played a large role in young Edison's life. In one train accident he was pulled to safety by his ears. As a result Edison became permanently deaf. In another accident Edison rescued a small boy. The boy's father was so grateful that he offered to teach Thomas telegraphy. Edison's knowledge of the telegraph led him to several inventions. These inventions allowed him to set up his own business by the time he was 23 years old!

Before he was through, Edison had patented 1,100 inventions. In one four-year stretch he received 300 patents. This accomplishment is an average of one patent every five days! No other inventor has ever come close to Edison's

patent record. He improved the telephone, invented the phonograph and the first workable light bulb, and helped to create motion pictures.

How did Edison do so much? He worked almost continually. During his peak, he was working 20 hours a day and sleeping in catnaps. As Edison once said, "Genius is 1 percent inspiration and 99 percent perspiration."

TO THINK ABOUT AND DO

Vocabulary

Number your page from 1 to 10. Read each of the following sentences. If the sentence is true, write *true*. If it is false, make it true by changing the underlined term.

1. Moving electric charges produce <u>static electricity</u>.
2. The unit used to measure resistance is the <u>ohm</u>.
3. The carbon rod in a dry cell is the <u>negative terminal</u>.
4. The path of an electric current is called an <u>electric circuit</u>.
5. A <u>series circuit</u> occurs when current flows over an unintended path with low resistance.
6. When one part of a <u>parallel circuit</u> goes dead, the whole circuit goes dead.
7. <u>Energy</u> causes electric charges to flow.
8. <u>Direct current</u> constantly switches directions.
9. Electric power can be measured in <u>kilowatts</u>.
10. <u>Terminals</u> break, or open, a circuit, stopping the current.

What Do You Remember?

1. What is electric current?
2. What moves electric current?
3. What do the following units measure: ampere, volt, ohm, watt?
4. What is a circuit?
5. Why are short circuits dangerous?
6. How are series and parallel circuits different?
7. In what way is an electric outlet like the terminals of a battery?
8. What is Ohm's law?
9. How is voltage created in a flashlight battery?
10. How do direct current and alternating current differ?

Applying What You Have Learned

1. What is the resistance of a lamp that uses 2 amperes of current in a 120-volt circuit?
2. How many kilowatts of power are used by a heater that draws 10 amperes of current in a 120-volt circuit?
3. How much energy would you use if you ran the heater in question 2 for 100 hours?
4. Give at least three safety hints for using electricity in the home.

Research and Investigation

1. Contact the power company that provides electricity to your school. Request information about electric safety and what to do in electrical emergencies. Present this information in a report.
2. Wall switches control the flow of current through the rooms of many homes. Do research to find out how these switches work.

Electromagnetism

16

What did you do today? Did you listen to a tape recorder? Did you use the telephone? Did you see or hear a motor at work in a mixer, blender, refrigerator, washing machine, hair dryer, fan, vacuum cleaner, or elevator? Did you hear a doorbell or a buzzer sound?

If you saw or heard any of these devices or machines, you observed the combined effects of electricity and magnetism at work. In fact, if you used electric current in any way, you were using the combined effects of electricity and magnetism.

A little over a hundred years ago, scientists and inventors were discovering the relationship between electricity and magnetism. They learned how to use this relationship to produce electric currents and to make machines that would run on electricity. As you can see from the hundreds of electric devices and machines in use today, what those scientists and inventors did has made amazing changes in the way you live.

16.1 Magnetism from Electricity

You will find out
- how electric current and magnetism are related;
- how electromagnets are made;
- how electromagnets are used.

You know from experience that electric energy carried by electric currents does much useful work. But did you know that most electric devices involve not only electricity but magnetism as well? The branch of physical science that involves the combined effects of electricity and magnetism is called **electromagnetism** [ih-lehk-troh-MAG-nuh-tihz-uhm].

The relationship between electricity and magnetism was discovered in the early 1800's by Hans Christian Oersted, a Danish scientist. As part of a classroom experiment, Oersted placed a compass just above a wire carrying an electric current. To his surprise, the compass needle—a small magnet—moved from a position pointing north to a position at a right angle to the wire. When he reversed the direction of the current, the needle reversed direction. But it was still at a right angle to the wire. When the current was turned off, the needle pointed north again. Oersted had discovered that electric currents produce magnetic fields.

Figure 16.2 When current is flowing, the compass needle moves to a position at a right angle to the wire.

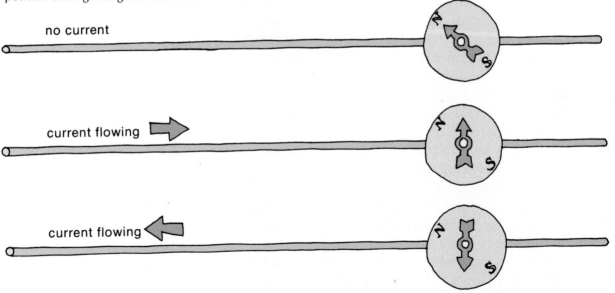

Oersted also discovered things that affect the magnetic field produced by an electric current. The direction of the magnetic field depends on the direction of the current. The magnetic field always acts in a direction at right angles to the direction of the current. When the current reverses direction, the direction of the magnetic field also reverses. The north magnetic pole becomes the south magnetic pole and vice versa. Oersted also found that the magnetic field is strongest near the wire. The strength of the field depends on the amount of current flowing through the wire.

A very strong magnetic field can be produced by a current in a wire that is wound into a tight coil. The magnetic field produced is directed along the center of the area inside the coil. What will happen if you put a bar made of a metal that can be permanently magnetized inside the coil? The bar will be magnetized by this magnetic field. When the current is turned off, the bar will remain magnetized. Most permanent magnets are made in this way.

Figure 16.3 The Japanese maglev train uses the magnetic forces of electromagnets on the train and on the track to attain speeds of up to 520 km/h.

Suppose the bar you put inside the coil is made of a metal like iron that loses its magnetism easily. When current flows through the coil, the bar will be magnetized. But the bar will lose its magnetism as soon as the current is turned off. If the direction of the current is reversed, the bar will be magnetized in the opposite direction. This behavior can be used to make a very useful magnet. It can make a magnet whose magnetism can be turned on and off by turning the current on and off. Also, the direction of the magnetic field can be reversed by reversing the direction of the current. Magnets in which magnetism is produced by an electric current are called **electromagnets.**

ACTIVITY

Materials
ring stand
ring clamp
fine iron filings
insulated copper
   wire (75 cm)
compass
6-volt battery
paper plate about 16
   cm in diameter

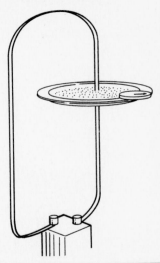

Can Electricity Produce Magnetism?

Procedure

1. Attach the ring clamp to the ring stand.

2. Use the point of a pencil to poke a tiny hole in the middle of the paper plate. Place the plate on the ring stand. Thread the wire through the hole in the plate.

3. Sprinkle some filings on the plate. Place a compass on the plate.

4. Attach the ends of the wire to the battery. The end coming from under the plate should be attached to the negative (−) terminal.

5. Observe the compass needle. Remove the compass and tap the plate gently. Observe the filings.

6. Reverse the attachment of the wire ends to the battery. The end coming from under the plate should now be attached to the positive (+) terminal.

7. Again place the compass on the plate.

8. Repeat step 5.

Questions

1. How did the filings and the compass needle change when the wire ends were first attached to the battery?

2. Did you notice any change in the filings or the compass needle when the battery attachments were reversed?

3. What caused the changes you observed?

Figure 16.4 Using an electromagnet

The magnetic force of electromagnets can be very strong. This force is often used to move very large masses. You can see electromagnets at work in junkyards, lifting tons of scrap metal onto railroad cars or trucks. A strong electromagnet the size of this book can lift a mass of 4,000 kg!

Because their magnetic force can be switched on and off, electromagnets are used as switches in telephones, doorbells, and hundreds of other devices. You are using the combined effects of electricity and magnetism when you use these devices.

Do You Know?
When you look at an object, the nerve cells in your brain generate electric currents that produce voltage changes of about a millionth of a volt.

Study Questions for 16.1
1. Describe Oersted's experiment and discoveries.
2. How are electromagnets made?
3. What are some uses of electromagnets?

16.2 Electricity from Magnetism

You will find out
- what is meant by electromagnetic induction;
- how electric generators produce electricity.

Electric currents can produce magnetic forces. Can the reverse happen? Can magnetic forces produce electric currents? Yes, they can.

Not long after Oersted's discovery, two men on opposite sides of the Atlantic Ocean made another important discovery at about the same time. Joseph Henry, an American, and Michael Faraday, an Englishman, found that a change in a magnetic field produces an electric current. When a magnet is moved into a coil of wire, a current starts to flow in the wire. The current stops flowing when the magnet stops moving. When the magnet is pulled out of the coil, a brief current flows again but in the opposite direction.

A current is produced in a coil of wire when a magnet is moved into or out of the coil. A current is also produced when the magnet is still and the coil is moved over it. As long as the magnetic field changes in relation to the coil, a current will flow. The creation of a current by a changing magnetic field is called **electromagnetic induction.**

Figure 16.5 *left:* The galvanometer indicates no current is flowing. *right:* The movement of the magnet produces a current in the coil.

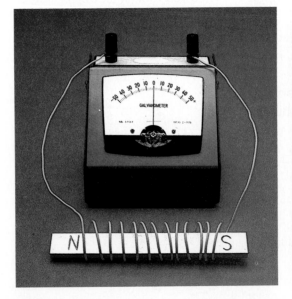
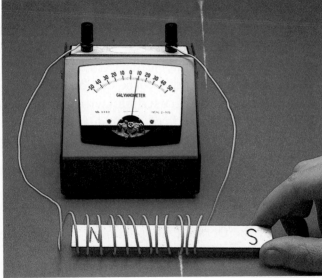

ACTIVITY

Materials

4 m of insulated
   copper wire
bar magnet
galvanometer
cardboard cylinder
   from a roll of
   paper towels
cellophane tape

Can Magnetism Produce Electricity?

Procedure

1. Wrap the wire around the cylinder 20 times. Wrap the coils close together.

2. Remove the insulation from the ends of the wire. Attach both ends to a galvanometer.

3. Observe the galvanometer as you insert the magnet and move it rapidly back and forth in the cylinder.

4. Detach the wires from the galvanometer. Wrap the wire around the cylinder 20 more times. Reattach the wires to the galvanometer.

5. Again insert the magnet in the cylinder and move it rapidly back and forth.

6. If a stronger magnet is available, repeat the experiment with it.

Questions

1. Why did you scrape the insulation off the wire?

2. What happened to the galvanometer needle when you moved the magnet back and forth in the cylinder?

3. Did the movement of the needle change when you used more coils of wire? Why?

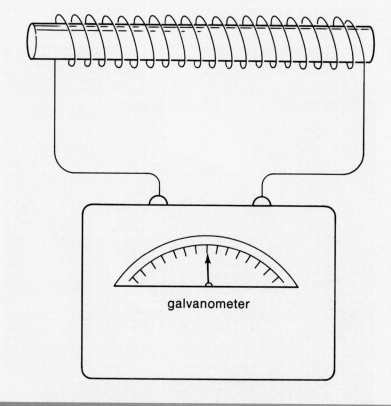

galvanometer

The discovery of electromagnetic induction was very important to science. It showed that a separation of charges, such as in a battery, is not the only way to produce electric current. In fact, most of the electric current you use comes from electromagnetic induction rather than batteries. The discovery of electromagnetic induction made it possible for practically everyone in the United States to have the benefit of electric power.

Electromagnetic induction is used in **electric generators.** An electric generator is a machine that changes kinetic energy into electric energy. To do this, a generator uses a permanent magnet or an electromagnet and metal wire to carry the current.

In a simple generator the magnet is fixed and the coil of wire moves. The coil revolves in the magnetic field between the north and south poles of the magnet. The result is the same as if the magnet were moving instead of the coil. The effect of the magnetic field on the coil changes as the coil moves. This change in the magnetic field causes a current to flow in the coil.

Figure 16.6 A simple generator

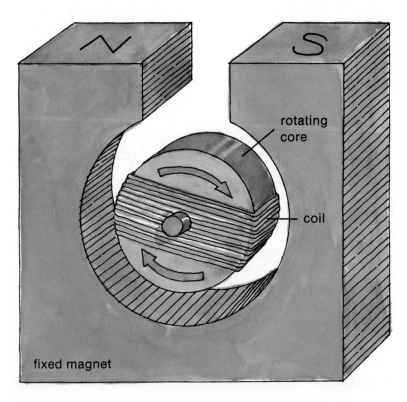

rotating core

coil

fixed magnet

Figure 16.7 Some bicycles have a small generator. When you pedal, the generator produces a current large enough to turn on a light.

Because the coil rotates, the direction of the magnetic field changes in relation to the coil. The changing direction of the magnetic field causes the current that flows in the coil to change direction as well. Thus, the current produced is alternating current. A generator that produces alternating current is often called an **alternator.**

In the simple generator the moving coil has kinetic energy. This kinetic energy is changed to electric energy because an electric current flows in the coil. The large generators that produce most of the electricity you use have more complicated parts and steps than the generator just described. But the same basic principle still applies. Electric energy is produced, or generated, from kinetic energy.

Do You Know?
Sharks have sensors that can detect induced voltages as weak as 5 billionths of a volt. They use these sensors to hunt for prey.

Study Questions for 16.2

1. How is electric current produced by electromagnetic induction?
2. How is electricity produced by an electric generator?

16.3 Electric Motors and Transformers

You will find out
- how an electric motor changes electric energy into kinetic energy;
- why transformers are important.

An **electric motor** is the reverse of a generator. A generator changes kinetic energy into electric energy. An electric motor changes electric energy into kinetic energy.

The heart of an electric motor is an electromagnet that rotates on an axle. The electromagnet rotates continuously between the two poles of a fixed permanent magnet. Like magnetic poles repel. So when the north pole of the electromagnet nears the north pole of the fixed magnet, the electromagnet is pushed away. It moves toward the south pole of the fixed magnet. Then, just as the north pole of the electromagnet reaches the south pole of the fixed magnet, the current is reversed. What was the north pole of the electromagnet becomes its south pole. So it is pushed away again. The continuous switching of the current causes the electromagnet to be continuously repelled by the fixed magnet. It spins around and around. The moving electromagnet has kinetic energy. This kinetic energy comes from the electric current flowing in the coil. The kinetic energy of the electromagnet can be used to do work.

Figure 16.8 The continuous repulsion of the electromagnet causes it to spin.

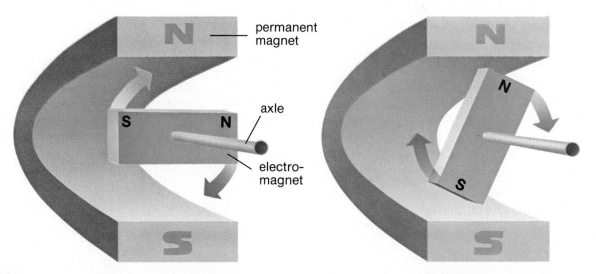

permanent magnet

axle

electro-magnet

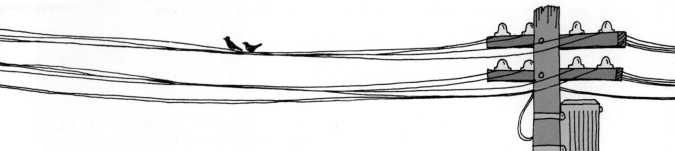

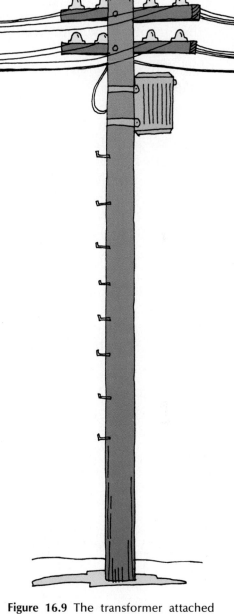

Electric motors of all sizes are constantly at work around you. They move subway cars and locomotives. They operate tape recorders, dishwashers, and hundreds of other machines. Most of the current used by electric motors comes from electric generators.

Electric current is carried along power lines from the electric generators where it is produced. Voltage causes the current to move along power lines. How much voltage is used to move electric current from a power station to your home? The amount of voltage changes. For example, a very large voltage is used to move current in long-distance power lines. A smaller voltage is used in the power lines running through cities and towns. Even less voltage is used in the lines running to and through individual homes. The voltage can change from hundreds of thousands of volts in long-distance power lines to 240 or 120 volts in your home.

How are voltages changed? Voltage is increased or decreased by a device called a **transformer** [trans-FAWR-muhr]. Some transformers increase voltage to move current over long distances. Other transformers decrease voltage to move current into towns and homes. You have probably seen transformers. They are often attached to the same poles that carry power lines. Transformers are also visible at ground level in fenced electrical yards. Since very high voltages are involved in transformers, they are very dangerous devices. You should never go near them.

Figure 16.9 The transformer attached to the pole changes voltage.

Study Questions for 16.3
1. How does an electric motor do work?
2. How are transformers used?

What Did You Learn?

- Electromagnetism is the branch of physical science that involves the combined effects of electricity and magnetism.
- Oersted discovered that electric currents produce magnetic fields.
- Electromagnets are magnets in which magnetism is produced by an electric current.
- Faraday and Henry discovered that a change in the magnetic field of a magnet produces an electric current.
- In electromagnetic induction, a current is created by a changing magnetic field.
- An electric generator uses electromagnetic induction to change kinetic energy into electric energy.
- An alternator is a generator that produces alternating current.
- An electric motor changes electric energy into kinetic energy.
- Voltage moves electric current along power lines.
- A transformer increases or decreases voltage.

Key Terms

electromagnetism
electromagnets
electromagnetic induction
electric generators
alternator
electric motor
transformer

Career

Electrical Engineer

An engineer uses scientific principles to solve practical problems. Electrical engineering is a large and rapidly growing branch of engineering. Electrical engineers help to design, develop, and produce electric equipment. They are also concerned with the generation and transmission of electric power.

Some electrical engineers help design electric appliances for people and businesses. Others work in the design and production of electric equipment for computers, aircraft, guided missiles, and spacecraft. Still other electrical engineers work in the planning and construction of power plants and power stations.

Good electrical engineers like to solve problems. They are able to carry out difficult calculations and do very careful work. They are also able to work well with others as part of a team.

To prepare for a career in electrical engineering, you should take as much mathematics as possible. Physics and chemistry are also important. English is important since engineers must be

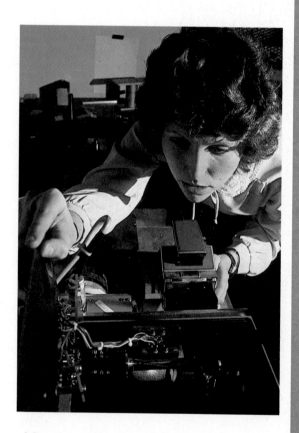

able to communicate well with others, both in conversation and in writing. Most electrical engineering positions require at least a college degree in engineering.

TO THINK ABOUT AND DO

Vocabulary

Number a piece of paper from 1 through 7. Beside the appropriate number write the letter for the term that is described.

1. The branch of physical science that involves the combined effects of electricity and magnetism
2. A magnet in which magnetism is produced by an electric current
3. The creation of a current by a changing magnetic field
4. A machine that changes kinetic energy into electric energy
5. A generator that produces alternating current
6. A machine that changes electric energy into kinetic energy
7. A device that increases or decreases voltage

a. electromagnetic induction
b. alternator
c. battery
d. electromagnetism
e. electric motor
f. electromagnet
g. electric generator
h. voltage
i. transformer

What Do You Remember?

1. How did Oersted discover that electricity could produce magnetism?
2. How are electromagnets used?
3. What did Henry and Faraday contribute to the study of electromagnetism?
4. How does an electric motor differ from an electric generator?
5. How does a generator produce electricity?
6. How does a motor use electric energy to do work?
7. What causes electric current to move along power lines?
8. How are transformers used?
9. What is electromagnetic induction?
10. What kind of current is produced by an alternator?

Applying What You Have Learned

1. How is an electromagnet different from a permanent magnet?
2. Why would alnico, which makes a strong permanent magnet, not be useful in making an electromagnet?
3. How could you vary the strength of an electric current produced by a magnet?
4. How could you prove an electromagnet is a magnet only while current is passing through it?

Research and Investigation

1. What are solenoid coils and how are they used?
2. How are electromagnets used in relays?

Electronics 17

Would you believe that thin squares smaller than postage stamps could change your life? Believe it or not, they already have. Pocket calculators, tape recorders, televisions, radios, telephones, home computers, and video games all work by using tiny squares, or chips of silicon. These chips can do things that a room full of equipment could not do 25 years ago.

What do silicon chips do? How do computers work? How does your television make a picture on the screen? How can complicated machines such as calculators, radios, and televisions be so small? You will be able to answer these questions when you have finished this chapter.

Figure 17.1 Electronic equipment in a jumbo jet

17.1 Electronic Devices

You will find out
- what electronic devices do;
- what vacuum tubes are;
- how a picture is made on a television screen;
- what semiconductors are.

Electronic [ih-lehk-TRAHN-ihk] **devices** have rapid and accurate control of the flow of electrons. Televisions, radios, record players, tape recorders, computers, cameras, and guidance systems for spacecraft are just a few of many different instruments, machines, and appliances that use one or more electronic devices.

Most electronic devices respond to short bursts of electric energy called **signals.** The signals may come from any one of many different sources such as television stations, the keyboard of a computer, or a microphone. An electronic device directs or strengthens these signals to get useful information from them. For example, your television has electronic devices that pick up very weak signals from many miles away. Those signals are strengthened so they can make an accurate copy of a picture and sound.

Figure 17.2 When you use a computer, you are using many electronic devices.

Machines that use electronic devices need a source of electric power in order to run. Often this power comes from the current in an electric outlet. Some electronic machines do not have a cord and a plug. Instead they operate on current produced by batteries. You have probably seen and used small calculators that operate on batteries.

The first electronic devices were glass tubes from which nearly all the air had been removed. These tubes are called **vacuum tubes.** A vacuum tube contains at least two metal parts. One part is a negatively charged metal wire. Another part is a positively charged metal plate. When a vacuum tube is put in an electric circuit, electrons are released from the wire and flow to the plate. The current in that circuit can be controlled by controlling the flow of electrons from the wire to the plate.

Until the 1950's vacuum tubes were the heart of the electronics industry. They were used in radios, televisions, and all other kinds of electronic equipment. However, vacuum tubes have limitations. Have you ever seen a very old radio or television? If you have, you were probably surprised at how big it is. It has to be big because the vacuum tubes inside it take up lots of space. Vacuum tubes also require a lot of electric power and give off lots of heat. Finally, they wear out after only a few thousand hours of use.

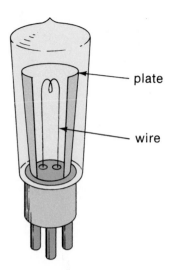

Figure 17.3 In a vacuum tube, electrons flow from the wire to the plate.

Figure 17.4 The radio in this photograph is big because the vacuum tubes inside it take up a lot of space.

One kind of vacuum tube is still in use and very familiar to you. It is the **cathode** [KATH-ohd] **ray tube.** The picture tube in your television is a cathode-ray tube. It is a vacuum tube in which a stream of electrons is directed onto a screen coated with a **fluorescent** [floo-REHS-ehnt] material. The word *fluorescent* describes a material that glows when struck by electrons. When the stream of electrons hits the fluorescent screen, a dot of light forms on the screen. A signal fed into the cathode-ray tube moves the stream of electrons around producing a pattern of dots. You see this pattern as a picture. Cathode-ray tubes are used to make pictures not only in televisions but also on computer display screens and other machines.

In a color television, the inside surface of the fluorescent screen is covered with tiny dots. These dots are arranged in three sets. One set of dots glows red when struck by electrons. Another set glows green. The third set glows blue. The cathode-ray tube sends out three streams of electrons, one for each set of dots. Together, the three sets of glowing dots form the color television picture you see.

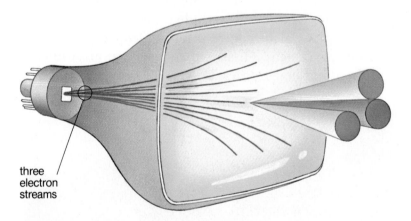

three electron streams

Figure 17.5 The cathode-ray tube of a color television

A television may be the only appliance or machine you are familiar with that still uses a kind of vacuum tube. Vacuum tubes have limitations, so scientists looked for and developed new and better ways to control the flow of electrons. Most electronic devices today use **semiconductors.** A semiconductor is a solid material

Figure 17.6 Assembling television sets

that has a conductivity in the range between that of an insulator and that of a good conductor. The most commonly used semiconductors involve crystals of germanium and silicon. When tiny amounts of other elements are added to a pure crystal of germanium or silicon, the conductivity of the crystal can be increased. The elements that are added are called **impurities.** The conductivity of a crystal is regulated by the kinds, amounts, and placement of impurities on it. Electronic devices that use semiconductors are smaller, require less power, produce less heat, and last much longer than vacuum tubes. Such electronic devices quickly replaced vacuum tubes in most electronic equipment.

The **transistor** [tran-ZIHS-tuhr] is the electronic device that replaced many kinds of vacuum tubes. In vacuum tubes electrons flow through a vacuum. A transistor uses semiconductors to control the flow of electrons. Semiconductors are solids. Because the electrons are flowing through a solid, transistors became known as **solid-state** devices. You may have seen or heard the term *solid-state* in reference to radios, televisions, or other electronic equipment.

Study Questions for 17.1
1. What is an electronic device?
2. What is a vacuum tube?
3. How is a picture made on a television screen?
4. What are semiconductors?

17.2 Functions of Electronic Devices

You will find out
- what rectifiers do;
- what oscillators do;
- what amplifiers do.

What would you do if you wanted to find out the latest weather report or who was leading in an election or a football game? You would probably turn on a radio or television. Someone in a broadcast studio far away from your home would answer your question. How did that answer reach you? Many different electronic devices were involved in bringing the answer to you.

Electronic devices control the flow of electrons. However, this does not mean that all electronic devices are the same. Different electronic devices control the flow of electrons to perform different functions. One function is to change the alternating current supplied to an appliance to direct current. The current produced by electric generators for homes and businesses is alternating current. However, many of the appliances and machines in homes and businesses require direct current. An electronic device called a **rectifier** [REHK-tuh-fy-uhr] changes alternating current to direct current. For example, when you turn on a radio, alternating current flows into the machine. A rectifier quickly changes that current to direct current. You hear the results. Most rectifiers today are solid-state devices.

Figure 17.7 Electric signals from distant broadcast studios are picked up by antennas.

The electronic signals that are picked up by machines such as radios and televisions are produced by an electronic device called an **oscillator** [AHS-uh-layt-uhr]. An oscillator produces electronic signals from direct current. Oscillators are used in radio and television broadcasting. They are also used to produce timing signals in watches and heart pacemakers.

As electronic signals travel, they become weaker. When a weak signal is picked up by a machine such as a radio, an electronic device is used to strengthen the signal. Such a device is an **amplifier** [AM-pluh-fy-uhr].

Did you watch television or listen to a radio or a tape recorder today? Did you hear someone talk over a microphone? If so, you made use of amplifiers. Most electronic equipment could not operate without fast and efficient amplification of weak signals. For example, without amplifiers the signals that reach your television are so weak that the cathode-ray tube could not make an accurate copy of the original picture.

Figure 17.8 The functions of a rectifier, an oscillator, and an amplifier

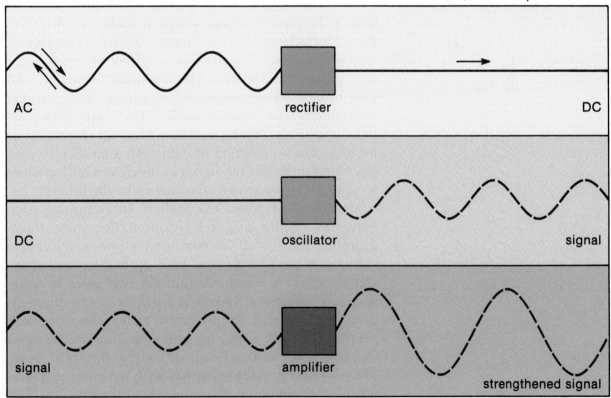

Figure 17.9 Many amplifiers are used to televise a baseball game.

Several amplifiers are used to make a picture on a television screen. Suppose you are watching a live broadcast of the World Series. When a television camera is pointed at the scene on the playing field, light from the scene enters the camera. The light is directed onto a fluorescent screen where it makes a pattern of dots. An electronic device changes these dots into a pattern of electronic signals. An amplifier in the camera strengthens these signals. The amplified signals are sent to a broadcasting station. An amplifier in the station strengthens the signals again. They are broadcast through the air. Your television picks up these signals by means of an antenna or cable. An amplifier in your television increases the signal as much as a billion times so that the cathode-ray tube can make the picture.

Amplifiers are used everywhere in communication networks. Radio and television stations use them. Amplifiers are used in communications satellites to strengthen the signals they pick up and to send those signals back to earth. Amplifiers are used in long-distance telephone lines and in the radar equipment used in navigation. Amplifiers in radio telescopes keep people in touch with the universe. Radio telescopes amplify very weak signals traveling through space. These signals provide scientists with information about what is happening in distant parts of the universe.

Materials

paper

pencil

How Do Shortwave-Radio Operators Communicate?

A ●■	B ■●●●	C ■●■●	D ■●●	E ●	F ●●■●
G ■■●	H ●●●●	I ●●	J ●■■■	K ■●■	L ●■●●
M ■■	N ■●	O ■■■	P ●■■●	Q ■■●■	R ●■●
S ●●●	T ■	U ●●■	V ●●●■	W ●■■	X ■●●■
Y ■●■■	Z ■■●●	1 ●■■■■	2 ●●■■■	3 ●●●■■	4 ●●●●■
5 ●●●●●	6 ■●●●●	7 ■■●●●	8 ■■■●●	9 ■■■■●	0 ■■■■■
. ●■●■●■	, ■■●●■■	? ●●■■●●	S.O.S. ●●●■■■●●●		Start ■●■
End of Message ●■●■●		Understand ●■●		Error ●●●●●●●●	

Procedure

Morse code signals are broadcast and amplified by electronic devices. Study the code and use it to write two messages. One message must be about electronics.

Questions

1. Trade messages with a friend. What do your friend's messages say?

2. What does the following message say?

Study Questions for 17.2

1. What is the function of a rectifier?

2. What is the function of an oscillator?

3. What is the function of an amplifier?

17.3 Integrated Circuits and Microelectronics

You will find out
- how an integrated circuit is made;
- what is meant by the term *microelectronics*.

The electrons that flow through electronic equipment follow a carefully laid-out path, or circuit. Each amplifier, rectifier, or other electronic device in the equipment must be connected to that circuit. In older electronic equipment such as early radios and televisions, all the parts of the circuit had to be wired together separately. This wiring took a long time to set up. It also resulted in a jumbled mess of wires in very complicated circuits. These problems disappeared with the use of **integrated** [ihn-tuh-GRAYT-ehd] **circuits.** An integrated circuit is a circuit that is put on a semiconductor chip by placing impurities in a very precise arrangement. The impurities are arranged in such a way that each different area of the chip conducts current differently. Each area on the chip becomes a different and specific electronic device that is part of the integrated circuit. Each circuit part has a specific function. Some parts are rectifiers. Other parts are amplifiers, oscillators, or switches.

Figure 17.10 This person is watching television! Advances in microelectronics have made it possible to produce a television so tiny that you must hold it up to your eye to see the picture.

Figure 17.11 This photograph illustrates the tiny size of a semiconductor chip.

When all the impurities have been added to a chip, all the electronic devices in that particular integrated circuit are in place. However, the circuit is still incomplete. The electrons that flow through each electronic device in the circuit must have a path to follow from one device to the next. A metal, usually aluminum, makes the desired connections between the different devices. A thin coating of aluminum is put over the entire chip. The aluminum is then carefully removed from some areas and left in place in others to complete the circuit. In this way it is possible to put an entire circuit containing over a thousand different electronic devices on a chip the size of a baby's thumbnail.

Integrated circuits form the basis of a new branch of electronics called **microelectronics.** Although integrated circuits are very tiny and complicated, they are easy to produce. They cost much less to make than other earlier kinds of circuits. Integrated circuits work faster, use less power, and are more reliable. Integrated circuits have made possible the amazing pocket calculators, electronic watches, computers, and other electronic machines that are in general use today.

Do You Know?
All the words in this book can be stored on a microchip this size:

Study Questions for 17.3
1. How is an integrated circuit made?
2. What is microelectronics?

17.4 Computers

You will find out
- what the three basic functions of computers are;
- what units are used to perform the three basic functions of computers;
- how computers are used.

Imagine that in 1960 someone chose one hundred people at random. Those one hundred people were asked one question, "Have you ever used a computer?" How many would have said yes? There is no way of knowing exactly how many. But you can be sure that if the same survey were made today, many more people would say yes.

The computers in use today are very different from the huge, expensive earlier computers that could be used only by highly trained experts. Today's computers are everywhere. They are in offices, government agencies, stores, banks, libraries, schools, and homes. They are operated by people like you. If you haven't seen or used a computer yet, the chances are very good that you will have that opportunity soon.

Figure 17.12 This early computer took up a whole room and could be used only by specially trained operators.

A **computer** is a machine that can carry out a detailed set of instructions to perform a task. The set of instructions is called a **computer program.** The computer program is written in a special language the computer understands. Computer language makes it possible to store and use large amounts of information in very small amounts of time. A computer programmer makes up the programs.

A computer is just a tool. It does not have a mind of its own. It can only follow instructions. Any computer, no matter how complicated, operates by performing three basic functions. It takes in information, does something with that information, and gives out new information. Different parts, or units, of a computer perform these three functions.

A computer uses an **input unit** to perform the first basic function. The input unit takes in information. This unit usually is a keyboard. Computer programmers use the keyboard to type programs into the computer. A computer operator also uses the keyboard to type in the information needed for the computer to perform a task. In the input unit, the information that is typed in is changed into the special computer language.

Do You Know?
Computers can process information so quickly that the speed of their operation is often measured in nanoseconds. One nanosecond is one billionth of a second.

Figure 17.13 Using a computer

The second basic function of a computer is to do something with the information that has been received by the input unit. This function is called **processing.** Three units are involved in the processing of information in a computer. The **memory unit** stores all the programs and information that have been put into the computer. The **control unit** regulates the flow of information in the computer. When information to be processed is received by the input unit, the control unit brings that information together with the appropriate program in the **processing unit.** The processing unit carries out the program by following its instructions.

Figure 17.14 The flow of information in a computer

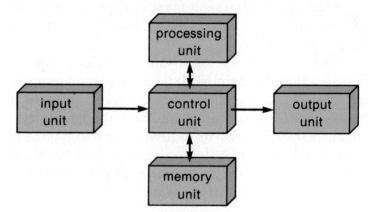

The third basic function of a computer is to give out new information. This function is carried out by the **output unit.** The output unit changes the results of the processing unit from computer language back into words, numbers, and symbols and prints this new information on a screen or a paper.

It is important to remember the three basic computer functions: input, processing, and output. Computers use electronic devices to perform these functions. Using electronic devices allows computers to solve problems millions of times faster than you could with a pencil and paper. Simple problems, such as finding the average of a list of numbers, can be solved so quickly that the output unit shows the answer almost as soon as the problem is typed in. Problems that require complicated programs, such as those used to interpret weather patterns, can take many minutes, even hours, to solve.

Figure 17.15 Computers are being used in sports and the arts. Ballet dancers use computers to design their dances.

Computers are used to solve scientific and engineering problems, to keep records, and to organize files. Even if you have never used a computer yourself, computers are involved in your life. For example, when you call the telephone operator for a number, a computer is used to search rapidly through the listings for the number. All new telephone numbers are entered into the computer system, keeping the lists up-to-date. At the end of the year the computer is hooked up to a machine that sets the type for the new telephone books. Computers are also used in the direct-dial system that almost instantly connects your telephone to others across the country.

The airlines use computers both in the air and on the ground. Suppose you live in Los Angeles and want to reserve a seat on a flight to New York City. You call a reservation agent in Los Angeles and explain what you want. The agent checks with a computer for the ticket price, the flight times, and whether or not seats are available. In a matter of seconds the computer displays the information. If you reserve a seat, the computer prints out a ticket, stores the information that another seat has been taken, and is ready for the next request.

Do You Know?
It would take half the people in the United States between the ages of 18 and 45 to run the nation's telephone system if it were not computerized.

ACTIVITY

How Can You Create a Flowchart?

Materials
paper
pencil
ruler

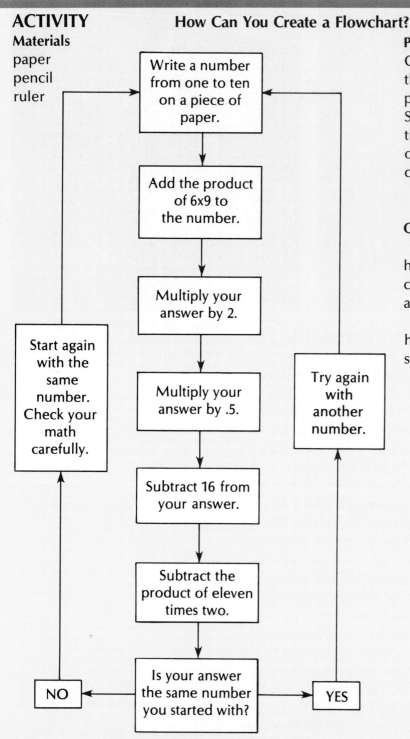

Procedure

Computer programmers write the directions they wish a computer to follow on a flowchart. Study the flowchart given. Notice that each box contains only one direction. Follow the flowchart's directions.

Questions

1. Make a flowchart telling how to construct a simple circuit with a battery, two wires, and a light bulb and socket.

2. Make a flowchart telling how to go from your home to school.

0 7

41280 03252

Figure 17.16 *left:* A computerized supermarket checkout; *above:* The supermarket product code

Airline pilots use computers, too. Just before take-off, the latest weather information is put into a computer on the ground. The computer uses this information to determine the best route, speed, and altitude for greatest safety and fuel economy. Computers on board the airplane help to guide the plane in flight.

Computers are used in supermarkets, too. Have you ever noticed the little rectangle filled with black lines on the items you buy at supermarkets? The lines are a coded message. The message tells the name, manufacturer, and size of the item. When the cashier slides the item over a small window set into the checkout counter, an electronic device picks up the code and relays the information to a computer. The computer reads the code and prints the information on a paper tape. The computer also notes in its memory unit that there is one less of that item on the shelf. The store manager can use that information to decide when to reorder.

Study Questions for 17.4

1. What are the three basic functions of a computer?
2. Name and define the units of a computer.
3. Give an example of a way that computers affect your life.

What Did You Learn?

- Electronic devices have rapid and accurate control of the flow of electrons.
- Most electronic devices respond to short bursts of electric energy called signals.
- The first electronic devices were vacuum tubes.
- The cathode-ray tube is a vacuum tube that directs a stream of electrons onto a fluorescent screen.
- Semiconductors have a conductivity in the range between that of an insulator and that of a good conductor.
- Transistors use semiconductors to control the flow of electrons.
- Rectifiers change alternating current to direct current. Oscillators produce electronic signals from direct current.
- Amplifiers strengthen electronic signals.
- An integrated circuit is a circuit that is put on a semiconductor chip by placing impurities in a very precise arrangement.
- Microelectronics is a branch of electronics which involves electronic devices connected in integrated circuits.
- A computer is a machine that can carry out a detailed set of instructions to perform a task.
- The three basic functions of a computer are to take in information, to process that information, and to give out new information.
- Computers have five units: the input unit, the memory unit, the control unit, the processing unit, and the output unit.
- Computers are used to do many things such as store and locate telephone numbers, make airline reservations, and analyze weather information.

Key Terms

electronic devices
signals
vacuum tubes
cathode-ray tube
fluorescent
semiconductors
impurities
transistor
solid-state
rectifier
oscillator
amplifier
integrated circuits
microelectronics
computer
computer program
input unit
processing
memory unit
control unit
processing unit
output unit

Career

Broadcast Technicians

Broadcast technicians operate and maintain the electronic equipment used to record and transmit radio and television programs. They work with microphones, sound recorders, television cameras, videotape recorders, and other equipment.

Broadcast technicians operate equipment in the control room that regulates the quality of sounds and pictures being recorded or broadcast. They also operate controls that switch broadcasts from one camera to another, from film to live programming, or from network to local programs. On occasion broadcast technicians may be required to go out and set up a remote broadcast in a football stadium, an airport, or wherever news is breaking.

In small studios, broadcast technicians perform a variety of duties that may range from giving technical direction to people in the studio to operating the record turntable as a disk jockey. In large studios, the work is more specialized. For example, a broadcast technician might be an audio–control specialist who operates the controls that regulate sound pickup, transmission, and switching. Audio–control technicians also find work at sound recording studios.

Jobs for broadcast technicians can be found wherever there are broadcasting stations or recording studios. This means most jobs are in large cities. About a third of the jobs are in towns having fewer than 10,000 people.

Students interested in becoming broadcast technicians should take physical science and mathematics courses in high school. After high school they should take electronics and communications courses in a technical school, college, or university.

TO THINK ABOUT AND DO

Vocabulary

Number your paper from 1 to 7. Select the one best term that completes each of the following sentences. Write the letter of the term next to the appropriate number.

1. Devices that have rapid and accurate control over the flow of electrons are (a) circuit parts, (b) electronic devices, (c) machines.
2. Short bursts of electric energy used by most electronic devices are called (a) signals, (b) beeps, (c) bits.
3. The first electronic devices were (a) radio tubes, (b) vacuum tubes, (c) cathode-ray tubes.
4. A material that has a conductivity in the range between that of an insulator and that of a good conductor is called (a) an amplifier, (b) an oscillator, (c) a semiconductor.
5. An electronic device that strengthens weak electronic signals is (a) a rectifier, (b) an amplifier, (c) an oscillator.
6. The part of a computer that receives information is the (a) output unit, (b) memory unit, (c) input unit.
7. The part of the computer that carries out a program is a (a) memory unit, (b) processing unit, (c) output unit.

What Do You Remember?

1. What is an electronic device? Give three examples of machines that use electronic devices.
2. Describe a vacuum tube.
3. List three limitations of vacuum tubes.
4. How is the picture on a television screen produced?
5. What is a fluorescent material?
6. Identify the function of each of the following: rectifier, amplifier, oscillator.

7. What is an integrated circuit?
8. What is a computer program?
9. What are the three basic functions of a computer?
10. Name the five basic parts of a computer and identify the function of each.

Applying What You Have Learned

1. Name at least two appliances or machines in your home that use amplifiers.
2. Why are rectifiers not found in battery-powered radios?
3. In what ways might a bank use a computer?
4. How do computers help people to deal with large amounts of information?

Research and Investigation

1. Electric eyes are often used to open doors, ring buzzers, or set off burglar alarms. How do they work?
2. By using remote control you can open a garage door while in a car or change channels on a television without touching the set. How does remote control work?

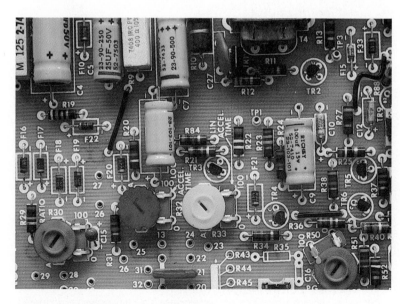

Unit Five

The Action of Waves

Waves 18

You may have thought that all waves occur in water. In fact, when you picture waves you probably think of an ocean. But you do not have to be near an ocean or any water at all to encounter waves. Every morning when you open your eyes, you encounter waves. Every sound you hear, from a whisper to a siren to a song, involves waves. You can make waves in a rope by tying one end to a doorknob and moving the other end up and down.

You can see waves in water and in a rope. Many waves, however, are invisible. These waves are in the air around you, in the earth under your feet, or in the empty space among the stars. In this chapter, you will learn how to describe waves and how the characteristics of waves can change.

Figure 18.1 Detail from a Japanese print called *The Wave* by Hokusai

18.1 The Nature of Waves

You will find out
- what a wave is;
- how waves are grouped;
- what some characteristics of waves are.

Have you ever tossed a stone into a pond and watched what happened? A pattern of ripples spreads away in circles from the point where the stone enters the water. These ripples are an example of a **wave.** A wave is a disturbance that travels through matter or space. A disturbance refers to anything that changes the situation of matter or space. Waves can travel through solids, liquids, or gases. Some waves travel through empty space. The matter or space through which a wave travels is called a **medium.** Often waves come in a series of disturbances, as in the ripples of a pond. This series is also called a wave.

Figure 18.2 An example of a wave

Waves can be divided into two groups. The groups are based on the direction of the wave motion and the direction of the wave disturbance. Imagine a bottle floating in the ocean. As waves move by the bottle, it bobs up and down. The up-and-down motion of the bottle indicates the direction of the disturbance. This bobbing up and down is at right angles to the direction of the waves which are moving in the water. Ocean waves are an example of **transverse** [trans-VURS] **waves.** In transverse waves, the disturbance occurs at right angles to the direction of the wave motion.

Now imagine a long, closely packed line of people waiting to get into a movie. Suppose someone in the back of the line gives the next person a shove. That person bumps into the next person and so on down the line. No one person moves very far, but the disturbance moves all along the line. As the wave goes by, the people move forward in the direction of the wave and then back again as they get their balance. This is an example of a **compressional** [kuhm-PRESH-uhn-uhl] **wave.** In compressional waves, the disturbance occurs back and forth along the direction of the wave motion. The medium—people in the example—is pushed together, or compressed, as the wave goes by.

Figure 18.3 The two kinds of waves

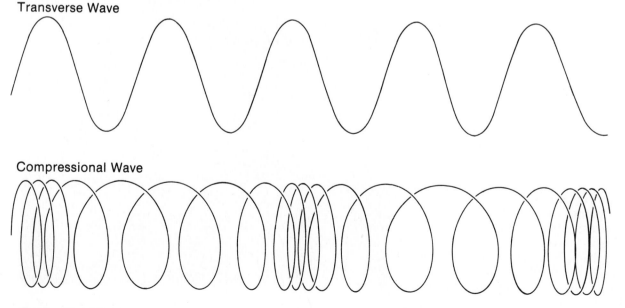

Transverse Wave

Compressional Wave

Two kinds of waves that are of special interest to physical scientists are sound waves and light waves. Light waves are transverse waves. Sound waves are compressional waves. Because light and sound are so important, each will be discussed in a separate chapter.

Waves have several characteristics that can be measured. It is easy to see how this can be done if you think of a wave as a series of hills and valleys. The highest point of a wave is called the **crest.** The crest corresponds to the top of a hill. The lowest point of a wave is called the **trough** [trawf]. The trough corresponds to the bottom of a valley. The height of a wave is called its **amplitude** [AM-pluh-tood]. The amplitude is the distance from a point halfway between the crest and the trough straight up to the crest. Amplitude is often measured in meters.

Figure 18.4 A wave with a large amplitude

Do You Know?
Sightings of unusually high ocean waves—up to 30 meters high—have been reported by sea captains. Such waves are thought to be the result of interference involving many ocean waves.

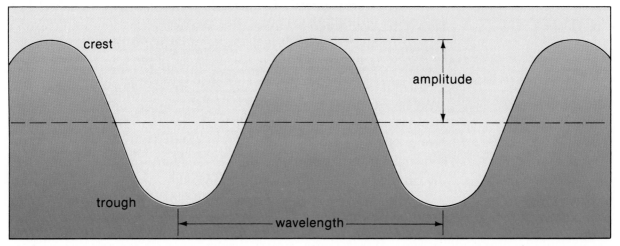

Figure 18.5 Characteristics of a transverse wave

Waves carry energy from one place to another. The amplitude of a wave can indicate how much energy it is carrying. The greater the amplitude, the more energy the wave has. Expert surfers enjoy riding on waves that have a large amplitude. The energy of such waves offers surfers long and exciting rides.

The distance from one crest of a wave to the next can be measured. This distance is called the **wavelength.** Wavelength varies greatly depending on the waves. For example, the wavelength of waves on the open ocean might be several meters. However, the ripples made when you toss a stone into a pond could have wavelengths of only a few centimeters.

Wavelength is directly related to another wave measurement called **frequency** [FREE-kwuhn-see]. The frequency of a wave is the number of crests that pass a point in a second. Frequency is measured in **hertz** [hurts]. One hertz (Hz) is one crest or trough past a point in a second.

Figure 18.6 These waves have equal amplitudes. What measurement is unequal?

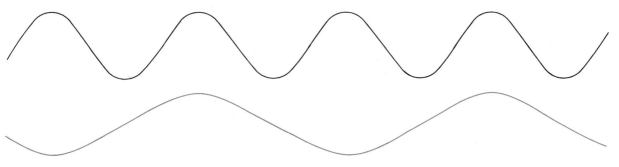

ACTIVITY

How Can You Make a Model of a Wave?

Materials
ring stand
clamp
straight pin
candle
matches
tuning fork
tuning fork hammer
carbon paper
safety glasses
ruler
tape

Procedure

1. Put on your safety glasses.

2. Light the candle. Use a drop of wax from the candle to fasten a straight pin to one prong of the tuning fork as shown in the diagram. Put out the candle.

3. Set up the clamp, ring stand, and tuning fork as shown in the diagram.

4. Place the carbon paper under the pin. Adjust the height of the tuning fork so the pin lightly touches the paper.

5. Use the hammer to strike the prong of the tuning fork that is not holding the pin. The tuning fork will vibrate.

6. With a slow, steady motion, pull the carbon paper under the pin to make a model of a wave. You may have to practice several times to make a satisfactory model.

7. Cut out your best wave model and tape it to your paper.

Questions

1. Label the crests and troughs on your wave model.

2. Use an arrow to indicate wavelength. How long is the wavelength in mm?

3. Draw a horizontal line through the center of your wave model. Use an arrow to indicate the amplitude. How large is the amplitude in mm?

4. Study your wave model. Does the wavelength change? Explain your answer.

5. Does the amplitude of the wave change? Explain your answer.

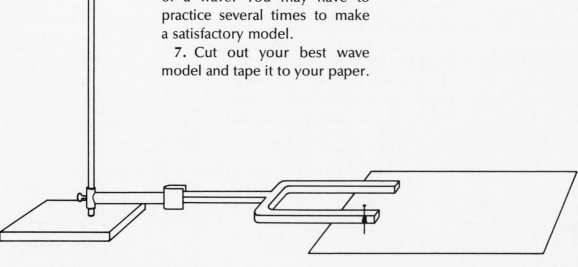

Figure 18.7 The waves are traveling. The water is not.

Wavelength and frequency are related to another characteristic of waves, speed. Wave speed is measured in meters per second. The speed of a wave can be calculated using this formula:

Speed = wavelength × frequency

EXAMPLE Find the speed of a wave with a wavelength of 0.5 m and a frequency of 20 Hz.

SOLUTION Speed = wavelength × frequency
= 0.5 m × 20 Hz = 10 m/s

The speed at which a wave travels depends on the properties of the medium it travels through. Remember, a wave may move through matter, but a wave itself is not matter. A wave is a disturbance in a medium. The medium is not traveling. The disturbance is traveling. Thus, the speed of a wave is the speed of a disturbance.

Do You Know?
Tidal waves caused by earthquakes can have speeds of up to 800 km/h.

Study Questions for 18.1

1. What is a wave?
2. How do transverse and compressional waves differ?
3. Name four characteristics of waves that can be measured.

18.2 Changes in Waves

You will find out

- how waves are changed by boundaries and barriers;
- how waves are changed when the medium changes;
- how waves are changed by other waves.

Waves can change. You have observed some of these changes. You observe them every time you use a mirror, hear an echo, see a rainbow, or watch water waves come together. Since a wave is a moving disturbance, anything that affects the wave motion changes the wave. Sometimes the changes are caused by a boundary or barrier that the waves encounter. Changes can also result from changes in the medium. A third way waves can change is by encountering other waves.

If you watch the waves in a swimming pool carefully, you will see that they bounce back when they hit the sides of the pool. The bouncing back of a wave when it hits a boundary is called **reflection** [rih-FLEHK-shuhn]. Waves bounce off the surface of a boundary in much the same way as a rubber ball bounces off a hard surface. If a wave hits a surface head on, it is reflected straight back. Similarly, a ball that is thrown straight at a wall bounces straight back. When a wave hits a surface at an angle, it is reflected back at the same angle to the other side. This behavior is similar to the behavior of a ball thrown against a surface at an angle. Basketball players know that a ball thrown against a backboard at an angle will rebound at the same angle to the other side.

Do You Know?

The structure of a cat's eyes allows them to reflect light waves very effectively. This is why cats' eyes seem to shine in the dark.

Figure 18.8 Reflection

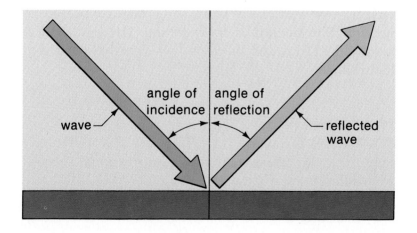

angle of incidence | angle of reflection

wave

reflected wave

How Can You Observe Wave Behavior?

Materials
Slinky
book

Procedure

1. Stretch out a Slinky between you and a partner so that there is a space of about 1 cm between each coil. As you perform the following steps, carefully observe the results.

2. Have your partner hold one end steady while you give your end a series of sharp, steady taps.

3. Have your partner hold one end of the Slinky against a book while you give your end one sharp tap.

4. Have your partner hold one end of the Slinky against his or her stomach while you give your end one sharp tap.

5. On the count of three you and your partner should give each end of the Slinky one sharp tap.

Questions

1. Describe the Slinky as a wave passed through it.

2. Was the wave transverse or compressional?

3. What happened when the wave hit the book?

4. What happened when the wave hit your partner's stomach?

5. Why do you think the wave behaved differently when it struck the book than it did when it struck your partner's stomach?

6. What happened when two waves met each other?

The angle at which a wave hits a surface is called the **angle of incidence** [IHN-sih-duhns]. The angle at which it is reflected is called the **angle of reflection.** The general rule for waves is that the angle of incidence equals the angle of reflection.

You are able to see yourself in a mirror because the mirror reflects light waves. Reflection of light waves also allows you to see yourself in a shiny plate, a smooth, shiny piece of metal, and the glassy surface of a calm pond. The reflection of sound waves causes the echoes that you hear when you call out in a large, empty room.

Figure 18.9 Diffraction

Waves sometimes bend around objects. For example, imagine water waves approaching a pier. When the waves arrive against the posts of the pier, the waves bend and move around them. The posts act as a barrier. The bending of waves around the sides of a barrier is called **diffraction** [dih-FRAK-shuhn].

The speed of a wave changes when the wave medium changes. This change in speed can cause the wave to bend. The bending of waves due to a change in the medium is called **refraction** [rih-FRAK-shuhn]. A rainbow is the result of the refraction of light waves.

A simple way to understand refraction is to compare the motion of a wave to the motion of a car traveling from one surface to another. Suppose a car is driven off a paved parking lot onto a soft, sandy beach. The sand will slow down the motion of the car. If the car approaches the beach at an angle, one front wheel will hit the sand sooner than the other front wheel. For a short time the wheel in the sand will move slower than the wheel still on the pavement. This difference in speed causes the car to make a slight turn. In the same way, a wave moving from one medium to another changes speed. The wave can bend, or refract. The amount of refraction depends on two things. First, it depends on

Figure 18.10 Waves bend, or refract, when their medium changes. A car may turn when the surface it is traveling on changes.

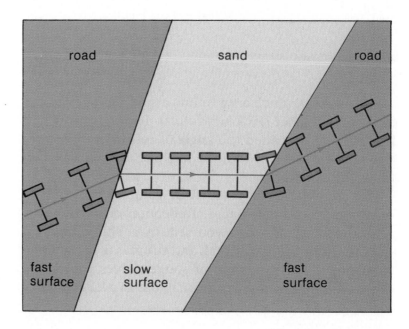

road   sand   road

fast
surface   slow
              surface   fast
                            surface

Chapter 18 / Waves

how much the speed of the wave changes when it enters the new medium. Second, it depends on the angle of incidence. Waves that hit a new medium almost head-on are refracted less than waves that hit at a large angle. The sharper the angle of incidence, the greater the refraction.

Waves can affect each other. What happens when two or more waves meet? Different things happen depending on the characteristics of the waves. The combined effects of two or more waves coming together is called **interference** [ihn-tuhr-FIHR-uhns]. The word *interference* may suggest to you that waves that meet must cancel or oppose each other. This sometimes happens. However, the energy of waves that meet is in some cases added together. For example, interference occurs when the crests of two waves meet. When this happens, the energy of the two waves is added together.

Figure 18.11 Interference

Study Questions for 18.2
1. What is reflection?
2. What happens when waves encounter a barrier?
3. What is refraction?
4. Give an example of interference.

18.3 The Doppler Effect

You will find out
- how the frequency of waves can appear to change;
- what the Doppler effect is;
- how the Doppler effect can be used.

Imagine you are sitting in a boat tied to a pier. Waves are moving directly toward you. You measure the frequency of those waves by counting the number of crests that pass the front of your boat. Now imagine that your boat starts moving directly into the oncoming waves. You again measure the frequency of the waves just as you did before. Nothing about the waves has changed. But this time you measure a higher frequency. More crests pass the front of your boat in the same amount of time because you are moving toward them. Remember, the actual frequency of the waves never changed. Your measurement of that frequency changed because you were moving. If you had not been moving, the frequency you measured would not have changed.

Figure 18.12 The observed frequency of sound waves from a moving car increases as the car approaches and decreases as it moves away.

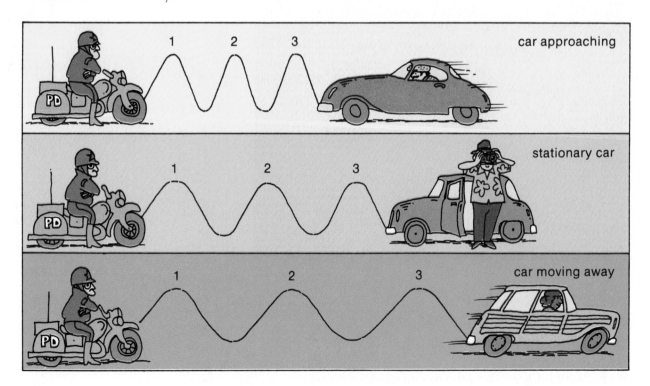

What would happen if your boat were moving in the same direction as the waves? If you again measure the frequency, you will find it to be lower than the frequency you measured when your boat was tied to the pier. Fewer crests pass the front of your boat now because you are moving with the waves.

The same changes in measured frequency occur when the observer is stationary and the source of the waves is moving. What do you hear when a fast moving truck approaches you, passes you, and speeds on away from you? The sound of the truck changes in loudness and in quality. The frequency of sound waves in relation to you changes because the source of those waves, the truck, is moving. You can't measure those changes in frequency by counting the crests of the sound waves because you can't see them. But you do observe the changes with your ears. You hear a higher sound as the truck approaches and a lower sound as it moves away. The frequency of the sound waves is greater as the truck approaches than it is as the truck moves away.

The change in the frequency of a wave as measured by an observer due to the motion of the wave source or of the observer is called the **Doppler effect.** The principle behind the Doppler effect can be used to determine whether a wave source is moving away from or toward an observer. If you know the actual frequency of a wave and its measured frequency is different, you can figure out the speed of the wave source.

Many drivers have been caught for speeding by radar equipment that uses the Doppler effect. The radar equipment sends out waves of a certain frequency in the direction of a moving car. When those waves reach the car, they are reflected back by the car. The car becomes a moving source of reflected waves. The change in measured frequency of those reflected waves as the car moves is used to calculate the car's speed.

Figure 18.13 Using the Doppler effect to detect speeding

Study Questions for 18.3
1. What is the Doppler effect?
2. Name a way the Doppler effect can be used.

What Did You Learn?

- A wave is a disturbance that travels through matter or space.
- The matter or space through which a wave travels is called a medium.
- In transverse waves, the disturbance occurs at right angles to the direction of the wave motion.
- In compressional waves, the disturbance occurs back and forth along the direction of the waves.
- The crest is the highest point of a wave.
- The trough is the lowest point of a wave.
- Amplitude is the distance from a point halfway between the crest and trough straight up to the crest.
- The larger the amplitude of a wave, the more energy it has.
- The wavelength is the distance from one crest to the next.
- Frequency, measured in hertz, is the number of crests that pass a point in a second.
- The speed of a wave equals wavelength times frequency.
- Reflection is the bouncing back of a wave when it hits a boundary.
- Diffraction is the bending of waves around the sides of a barrier.
- Refraction is the bending of waves due to a change in the medium.
- Interference is the combined effects of two or more waves coming together.
- The Doppler effect is the change in the frequency of a wave as measured by an observer due to the motion of the wave source or of the observer.
- The Doppler effect is used to measure the speed of cars.

Key Terms

wave
medium
transverse waves
compressional wave
crest
trough
amplitude
wavelength
frequency
hertz
reflection
angle of incidence
angle of reflection
diffraction
refraction
interference
Doppler effect

Career

Physical Oceanographer

Oceanography is the scientific study of the ocean. Different kinds of oceanographers study different aspects of oceans. Physical oceanographers study the motions of ocean waters and the exchange of energy between the land, the atmosphere, and the ocean. Some physical oceanographers specialize in the study of waves. For example, they may forecast the frequency and amplitude of the waves produced by storms and earthquakes. Or they may study the impact and effects of wave energy on shorelines.

Physical oceanographers can study the ocean in different ways. They often go to sea on research ships. In the laboratory, physical oceanographers use wave tanks to study the motion and behavior of waves. Physical oceanographers also use computers to carry out complicated calculations relating to wave motion.

A good educational background in physics is necessary to be a physical oceanographer. Generally, a college degree is required. If you are interested in becoming a physical oceanographer, you should take math and science courses in high school.

Although not all physical oceanographers spend time at sea, many do. For those who do, the adventurous life at sea is one of the main attractions of their career. These physical oceanographers are able to combine an exciting outdoor life with important and challenging work.

TO THINK ABOUT AND DO

Vocabulary

Number your paper from 1 to 10. Read each of the following sentences. If the sentence is true, write *true*. If the sentence is false, make it true by changing the underlined expression.

1. An ocean wave is an example of a <u>compressional</u> wave.
2. <u>Wavelength</u> is measured in hertz.
3. Waves with a large <u>amplitude</u> have a large amount of energy.
4. The change in the frequency of a wave as measured by an observer due to the motion of the wave source or the observer is called the <u>frequency shift</u>.
5. <u>Refraction</u> is the combined effects of two or more waves coming together.
6. The bouncing back of a wave when it hits a boundary is called <u>reflection</u>.
7. The highest point of a wave is the <u>crest</u>.
8. A <u>trough</u> is a disturbance that travels through matter or space.
9. The bending of waves due to a change in the medium is called <u>the Doppler effect</u>.
10. In <u>transverse</u> waves the disturbance occurs back and forth along the direction of the waves.

What Do You Remember?

1. What is a wave?
2. What units are used to measure frequency?
3. What is a medium?
4. What are the two groups of waves?
5. What two wave characteristics are related to speed?
6. What causes refraction?
7. What is the Doppler effect?
8. How is the Doppler effect used?
9. What is the distance from crest to crest called?
10. What is interference?

Applying What You Have Learned

1. What wave change is involved in each of the following situations?
   (a) You hear voices of people around the corner.
   (b) A dentist uses a small, round mirror to observe your teeth.
   (c) A person standing on a cliff shouts out a word and hears an echo.
2. Tell whether each of the following produces transverse or compressional waves.
   (a) a stone thrown in a pond
   (b) a ringing telephone
   (c) a glowing light
3. What is the frequency of a wave with a speed of 30 m/s and a wavelength of 0.5 m?

Research and Investigation

1. Earthquakes produce invisible waves that travel through the earth. Do research on earthquake waves.
2. What does absorption of waves mean? How does absorption of ocean waves affect shorelines?

Sound 19

Things that move usually make sounds. Many of those sounds can be heard. Think of things that move. What words are used to describe the sounds they make? Water trickles. Streams gurgle. Brooks babble. Waterfalls roar. You use moving vocal cords to make sounds. People whistle, sneeze, cry, yell, and whisper. Animals make many sounds. Dogs bark and wolves howl. Cats purr. Snakes rattle and hiss. Elephants trumpet and bellow.

Moving parts of machines make sounds as well. A dentist's drill whines. Jet engines rumble and roar. Wheels squeak. Typewriters clack.

This chapter will tell you how these and all sounds are produced. You'll learn about sounds you hear and sounds you don't hear. You will also find out what makes the sounds you hear loud and soft and high and low.

19.1 Sound Waves

You will find out
- how sound waves are produced;
- why sound waves must travel in matter;
- what affects the speed of sound waves.

Listen. What do you hear? Is a clock ticking? Can you hear traffic? Is someone talking? All the sounds you hear involve **sound waves.** A sound wave is a compressional wave produced by a back-and-forth motion. For example, when a bell rings, the sides of the bell move back and forth rapidly, making sound waves. The rapid back-and-forth motion is called a **vibration.** As the bell vibrates, it pushes together, or compresses, the air around it, making a compressional wave.

In Chapter 18, a compressional wave was compared to a disturbance that travels along a closely packed line of people. Someone in the back of the line gives the next person a push. People are then pushed together as the disturbance moves down the line. Just as the people bumped into each other as a result of a push, the molecules in matter bump into each other as the result of a vibration. In this way a sound wave is produced.

Sound waves move outward through matter from the source of the vibration. They cannot travel in empty

Figure 19.2 A vibrating bell produces sound waves.

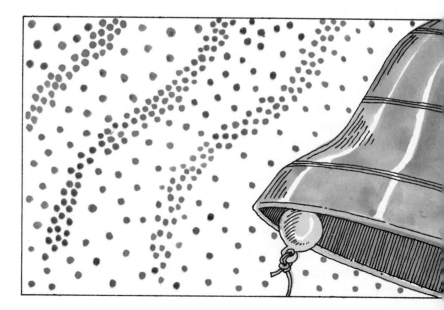

space. For sound waves to exist, molecules or atoms must be present to bump into each other.

All sound waves are compressional waves that travel through matter. However, all sound waves do not travel at the same speed. Two important factors affecting the speed of sound waves are the matter present and the temperature.

It is said that when hunters tracked buffalo, they put their ears to the ground and listened. In this way they could hear a herd of buffalo approaching. Why could a hunter with an ear to the ground hear the buffalo better and sooner than a hunter on a horse? The ground is a solid. The molecules in the ground are closer together than the molecules in air. Sound waves are able to move faster when molecules are closer together and can bump into each other more easily. The hunter on the horse would eventually hear the buffalo. But the hunter with an ear to the ground would hear them first. Sound waves travel faster through solid ground than they do through air. In general, sound waves travel fastest in solids, less fast in liquids, and slowest in gases.

The kind of matter present also affects the speed of sound waves. For example, iron and glass are both solids. But sound waves travel 5,103 m/s in iron and only 4,540 m/s in glass. Both the kind of matter present and the state of that matter affect the speed of sound waves.

Temperature also affects the speed of sound waves. For example, when the air temperature is higher, the molecules in the air move faster. They bump into one another more often. Thus, the speed of sound in air at 20°C is 343 m/s. But at 0°C, the speed is only about 331 m/s. In general, the higher the temperature, the faster sound waves travel.

Table 19-1 The Speed of Sound in Different Mediums

Medium	Speed (m/s)
granite	6,000
steel	5,200
iron	5,103
aluminum	5,000
glass	4,540
oak	3,850
seawater at 25°C	1,531
water at 25°C	1,498
cork	500

Study Questions for 19.1

1. What are sound waves?
2. Why can't sound travel in a vacuum?
3. What two factors affect the speed of sound?

19.2 The Sounds You Hear

You will find out
- what determines the loudness of a sound;
- what factors affect pitch;
- what ultrasonic sounds are;
- how sound waves can be used to locate objects.

You can make a loud noise by shouting. Or you can make a soft noise by whispering. Both sounds are produced by the same kind of vibration. Why is one sound louder than the other?

When you shout, your vocal cords vibrate with more energy than they do when you whisper. A vibration with more energy produces sound waves with more energy. The more energy a sound wave has, the greater its amplitude. The loudness, or **intensity** [ihn-TEHN-suh-tee], of a sound depends on the amplitude of the sound waves involved. The sound waves of a shout have greater amplitude than the sound waves of a whisper.

Intensity is measured in **decibels** [DEHS-uh-behlz]. The decibel (dB) is named after Alexander Graham Bell, the inventor of the telephone. You can barely hear sounds of less than 1 dB. Sounds of over 120 dB are so loud they can be painful.

Table 19–2 The Intensity of Some Familiar Sounds

Sound	Intensity (dB)
jet plane taking off	150
chain saw	115
power mower	100
noisy restaurant	80
vacuum cleaner	75
average home	50
purring cat	25
rustling leaves	20
whisper	15
faintest sound that can be heard	0

Figure 19.3 In which of the situations pictured would you be likely to speak in a voice of low intensity?

The intensity of any sound decreases as you move away from the source of that sound. For example, a thunderclap right over your head will sound louder to you than it will to a person 2 km away.

An important characteristic of sound waves is frequency. The frequency of a sound wave depends on how rapidly the source of the sound is vibrating. The faster the vibration, the higher the frequency.

Frequency is closely related to **pitch.** Pitch describes the highness or lowness of a sound that the ear hears. High-frequency sound waves produce high-pitched sounds. Low-frequency sound waves produce low-pitched sounds. Frequency is measured in hertz. Pitch cannot be measured. It can only be heard.

Figure 19.4 A bird's song is high-pitched.

Frequency is not the only characteristic of sound waves that affects pitch. Intensity can also affect pitch. A sound of high intensity may seem to have a slightly higher pitch. The frequency stays the same whether the intensity changes or not.

You use pitch to tell the difference between one sound and another. For example, one way to recognize the difference between a siren and a foghorn is by the difference in pitch. The siren has a high pitch while the foghorn has a low pitch.

Figure 19.5 A bullfrog's croak is low-pitched.

If you or someone you know has a dog, you may have noticed that dogs can hear sounds that you cannot. A pet dog may show signs that it hears a person or car approaching long before any person hears a thing. The human ear can hear sound waves of frequencies from about 20 to 20,000 Hz. Dogs and cats can hear frequencies as low as 15 Hz. They can also hear frequencies of over 50,000 Hz. Porpoises and bats can hear even higher frequencies, over 100,000 Hz.

People and other animals not only hear sounds of different frequencies, but they also produce sounds of different frequencies. It might surprise you to learn that you and other animals can hear more frequencies than you can produce. For example, you can hear frequencies of 20 to 20,000 Hz. But your vocal cords can only produce frequencies of 85 to 1,100 Hz.

Do You Know?
Sound waves with frequencies as high as several billion hertz have been produced.

Figure 19.6 The frequencies of sounds heard and produced by people and some other animals

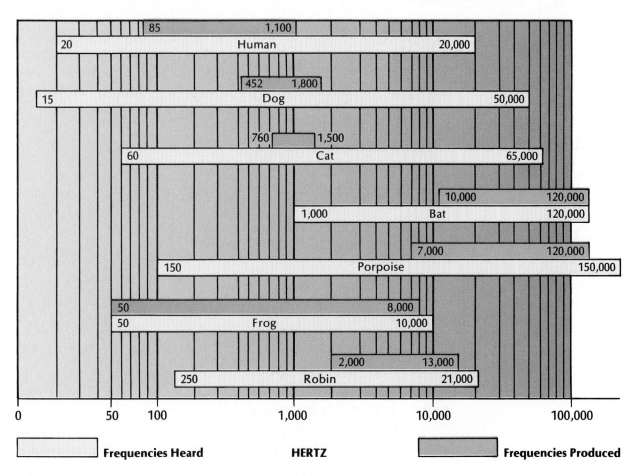

Sound waves above 20,000 Hz are called **ultrasonic.** Ultrasonic waves have a very short wavelength. Because of their short wavelength, ultrasonic waves are reflected by small objects. Bats are able to produce and hear ultrasonic sounds. While flying, bats produce ultrasonic squeaks with wavelengths of only a few millimeters. These squeaks are reflected by tree limbs, insects, and other things. Bats use the reflected sounds to find their way in total darkness.

ACTIVITY

What Do You Hear?

Materials

tuning forks of different frequencies

meterstick

Procedure

1. Work in groups of five. One person will be the noisemaker and recorder. The other four people will be listeners.

2. The listeners should stand 30 cm from the noisemaker with their eyes closed.

3. The noisemaker should then strike a tuning fork against the palm of his or her hand. All listeners who hear the sound should raise their hands. The noisemaker then records the number of listeners who hear the sound.

4. The noisemaker then moves back 1 m from the group and repeats step 3.

5. Keep repeating step 4 until none of the listeners can hear the sound.

6. Repeat the activity using tuning forks of different frequencies. A different group member should act as the noisemaker for each tuning fork used.

Questions

1. Why were the listeners told to close their eyes?

2. How far away was the noisemaker when no one heard the sound? Was the distance the same for all tuning forks used?

3. Were the listeners able to hear the high-frequency or low-frequency sounds at greater distances?

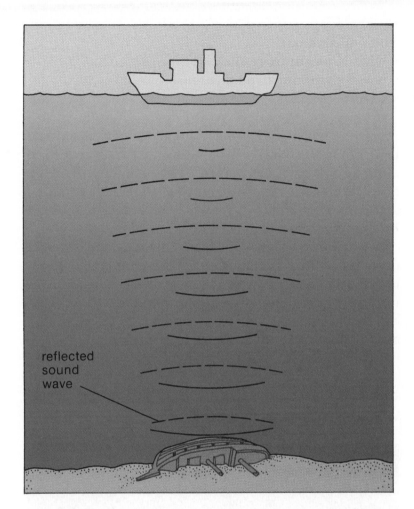

reflected
sound
wave

Figure 19.7 Sound waves sent down from a ship are reflected back to the ship by an object underwater. The use of reflected sound waves to gather information is called **sonar**—*so*und *n*avigation *a*nd *r*anging.

All sound waves, not only ultrasonic ones, can be reflected. You produce sound waves that are reflected when you shout into a canyon and hear an echo. Research ships send sound waves deep underwater and study the waves that are reflected back up. Such studies are done to locate objects underwater and to measure the depth of the ocean.

Do You Know?
Experiments with bats have been conducted in totally dark rooms having many piano strings stretched across them. Using reflected sound waves, the bats were able to detect the piano strings and fly around them.

Study Questions for 19.2
1. What affects the loudness of a sound?
2. What factors affect pitch?
3. What are ultrasonic waves?
4. How do bats find their way in darkness?

19.3 The Sound of Music

You will find out
- what is meant by resonance;
- how different instruments make music;
- what is meant by overtones.

Are you a musician? Have you ever played a musical instrument? You have if you've ever blown over the top of an empty bottle or tapped on the rim of a drinking glass to make it ring. An empty bottle and a drinking glass produce sounds in the same way that the musical instruments of an orchestra do.

Musical instruments produce musical sounds using a property called **resonance** [REHZ-uh-nuhns]. Resonance amplifies the sound that a musical instrument makes. For example, if you pluck a guitar string, it vibrates. The vibrating string causes the body of the guitar to vibrate, or resonate. This vibration amplifies the sound. If you were to stuff the body of the guitar with cloth, it would not vibrate. The guitar string would still vibrate when you plucked it. But the guitar would not produce the same sound. It would not resonate.

Figure 19.8 Piano strings of different lengths produce notes of different frequencies.

Musical instruments can produce notes of different pitch. For example, you can play different notes on a guitar by pressing your finger down at different places on a string and plucking it. When you press your finger on the string, you are shortening the part that will vibrate. A change in a string's vibrating length changes the frequency of the sound wave produced. The change in frequency produces a change in pitch. The shorter the vibrating part of the string, the higher the pitch of the note produced.

ACTIVITY

How Can You Change Pitch?

Materials

shoe box
scissors
three rubber bands
    of different
    thicknesses

Procedure

1. Cut three pairs of slits in each end of the shoe box. Each slit should be 1 cm long. The two slits in each pair should be 1 cm apart. Stretch the rubber bands over the length of the open side of the shoe box and fasten each to a pair of slits.

2. Pluck each rubber band and listen to the pitch.

3. Press the rubber band of medium thickness in the center to make a shorter vibrating part. Now pluck it again. Listen for a change in pitch.

4. Cut a pair of slits opposite each other across the width of the shoe box. Place your medium-thickness rubber band in these slits. Again, pluck the rubber band and listen to the pitch.

Questions

1. Which of the three rubber bands has the highest pitch?

2. Which of the three rubber bands has the lowest pitch?

3. How does the pitch change when the vibrating part of the rubber band is shortened?

4. How does the pitch change when the rubber band is not as tightly stretched?

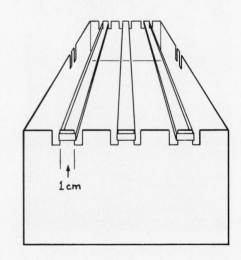

Figure 19.9 Different notes are produced on a clarinet by opening and closing holes in the instrument.

Figure 19.10 The valves in a French horn are used to change the frequency of notes produced.

In wind instruments, the body of the instrument contains a column of air which resonates. The simplest kind of wind instrument is an empty bottle. If you blow across the top of a bottle, you can cause the air in the bottle to vibrate. The length of the column of air in the bottle determines the frequency of the note you make. Short air columns produce high notes. Tall ones produce low notes. In instruments such as flutes or clarinets, musicians change the length of the column of air by opening and closing holes in the sides of the instruments. In this way the musicians produce different notes.

Brass wind instruments, such as trumpets and tubas, have tubes of different lengths through which the sound resonates. The musicians shift from one tube to another by opening and closing valves. In this way notes of different frequency are produced. With a trombone, it is possible to shift gradually from one frequency to another by sliding the tube in and out. Notes are made on drums, cymbals, and xylophones by hitting a surface and causing vibrations.

Most musical instruments produce more than simple notes of only one frequency. These instruments also produce notes of frequencies that are multiple frequencies of simple notes. Such notes are called **overtones.** Different musical instruments vibrate and resonate differently. They also produce different overtones. This is why the same note played on a piano and a flute sound different.

Figure 19.11 Notes are made on drums and cymbals by striking them.

Study Questions for 19.3

1. What is resonance?
2. How are sounds of different frequencies produced in a guitar, a clarinet, and a trumpet?
3. What are overtones?

19.4 Noise

You will find out
- what is meant by noise pollution;
- what can happen when sound waves are reflected;
- how echoes can be prevented.

People hear and appreciate sounds differently. The same sounds that are beautiful music to one person may be just unpleasant noise to someone else. There are, however, many sounds that are unpleasant to most people. High-pitched sounds, loud sounds, and disturbing echoes in a room are generally considered unpleasant. An excess of unpleasant sounds is called **noise pollution.**

Recent studies have found that noise pollution can do more than just keep people awake or bother them. It can actually make them sick. Constant exposure to sound levels over 100 dB can cause permanent hearing losses. These sound levels can also cause headaches, an upset stomach, and high blood pressure. To avoid these problems, workers in factories wear ear protection. So do workers who use noisy machines, such as chain saws and jack-hammers, and airport employees who work near loud jet engines.

Have you ever heard a speaker in a large ball park or stadium? If you listened and watched carefully, you probably noticed that the speaker's voice seemed to continue even after the speaker stopped. You were hearing **reverberations** [rih-vur-buh-RAY-shuhnz]. Reverberations are mixtures of reflected sounds. They can occur in any stadium, auditorium, or large hall.

A reflected sound that is heard more than 1/20 of a second after the original sound is called an **echo.** Echoes can be fun. When you yell into a canyon, you can hear yourself two, three, or maybe four times as the sound is reflected back to you. However, echoes in an auditorium can cause a speech or concert to sound jumbled and unpleasant.

Most large halls and auditoriums are built and decorated to prevent echoes. Materials are used that absorb sounds instead of reflecting them. Fabrics and special wall and ceiling tiles absorb sounds. Cloth-covered

Figure 19.12 Using ear protection

Figure 19.13 Which of these settings would reduce echoes and reverberations?

chairs, drapes, and curtains are used to reduce echoes as well as to provide comfort and decoration.

A good concert hall is designed not only to reduce echoes but to allow the music to reach everyone in the audience. This is done by a design that allows the musical sounds to reverberate in a certain way. Concert halls are designed for a specific use. For example, opera houses are designed differently than halls for orchestra concerts.

Proper design in factories and other workplaces can reduce noise pollution. The same principles that apply to the design of a quiet workplace also apply to the design of concert halls. However, in the workplace, the main goal is to absorb sound. No echoes or reverberations of any kind are desired.

Study Questions for 19.4

1. What is noise pollution?
2. Name two kinds of reflected sound waves you can hear.
3. How can echoes and reverberations in a hall be prevented?

Chapter 19 / Sound   407

What Did You Learn?

- A sound wave is a compressional wave produced by a back-and-forth motion.
- Matter must be present for sound waves to be produced and travel.
- The matter present and the temperature affect the speed of sound waves.
- The loudness, or intensity, of a sound depends on the amplitude of the sound waves involved.
- Intensity is measured in decibels.
  Pitch describes the highness or lowness of a sound that the ear hears.
- Frequency and intensity affect pitch.
- Sound waves above 20,000 hertz are called ultrasonic.
- Reflected sound waves can be used to locate objects.
- Musical instruments amplify sounds by resonating.
- Most musical instruments produce overtones.
- An excess of unpleasant sounds is called noise pollution.
- Reverberations are mixtures of reflected sounds.
- An echo is a reflected sound that is heard more than 1/20 of a second after the original sound was made.
- Concert halls are designed and furnished to prevent echoes and unwanted reverberations.

Key Terms

sound waves
vibration
intensity
decibels
pitch
ultrasonic
resonance
overtones
noise pollution
reverberations
echo

Career

Industrial Hygienist

Industrial hygienists are involved with health and safety concerns in the workplace. They do research on work-related health problems and inspect the workplace to see that conditions there promote good health and safety.

Some workers have become ill as a result of the jobs they do. Some jobs expose workers to high noise levels and other factors affecting health, such as dust, chemicals, and high heat. These jobs must be modified to protect the workers involved. Industrial hygienists study the ill effects of such jobs and help to develop ways to eliminate those effects.

In 1970 the federal government set health and safety standards for the workplace in the Occupational Safety and Health Act (OSHA). Studies and reports from industrial hygienists helped to determine those standards. One of the standards requires that the noise level of a workplace be no higher than 85 decibels. Noise pollution is not the only concern of OSHA. The quality of the air that workers must breathe and the dangers of equipment that workers must use are also concerns.

Some industrial hygienists work for private companies. Others are employed by governmental agencies. In many cases an industrial hygienist is required to have a college degree in engineering or in physical or biological science. As workers and employers become more aware of health and safety factors on the job, more industrial hygienists will be needed to inspect and evaluate conditions in the workplace.

TO THINK ABOUT AND DO

Vocabulary

Number a piece of paper from 1 through 10. Beside the appropriate number write the letter for the term that is described.

1. unit used to measure intensity
2. quality that describes the highness or lowness of a sound
3. property of a musical instrument that amplifies its sound
4. a reflected sound that is heard more than 1/20 of a second after the original sound was made
5. notes produced by most musical instruments
6. a mixture of reflected sounds
7. a compressional wave produced by a back-and-forth motion
8. an excess of unpleasant sounds
9. a rapid back-and-forth motion
10. loudness

a. vibration
b. intensity
c. pitch
d. decibel
e. frequency
f. echo
g. reverberation
h. resonance
i. ultrasonic
j. noise pollution
k. sound wave
l. overtones

What Do You Remember?

1. What two factors affect the speed of sound waves?
2. Why can't sound waves travel in empty space?
3. Why does a guitar sound different if its body is stuffed with cloth?
4. What happens when you press a finger on a guitar string and pluck it?
5. What can happen to people who are exposed to noise pollution?
6. How are auditoriums built to reduce echoes?
7. What quality of sound is affected by the amplitude of the sound waves involved?
8. How do bats find their way in darkness?
9. What kind of a sound is produced by a high-frequency sound wave?
10. What two factors affect pitch?

Applying What You Have Learned

1. Name two sounds you might encounter daily that have a low decibel rating. Name two that have a high decibel rating.
2. How could sound waves be used to locate a sunken ship?
3. How would you furnish a large room to prevent echoes?
4. How is a musical instrument such as a clarinet different from a bottle you blow on?
5. The word *ultrasonic* means "above sound." Why do you think the frequency of 20,000 Hz was chosen to mark the beginning of ultrasonic frequencies?

Research and Investigation

1. How can sound be recorded?
2. In 1975, scientists used a special sonar camera unit to try to photograph Nessie, the Loch Ness Monster. In 1981, the Goodyear blimp *Europa* flew over the waters of Loch Ness in search of Nessie. The blimp located an object moving underwater at a depth of 14 m to 18 m. *Europa* used sonar to track the object. Do research on the Loch Ness Monster and how sonar has been used to try to find Nessie.

Light 20

Lights! Camera! Action! In order to film a scene, you must first see it. To see it, you must have light. There are many sources of light. Of course, there is sunlight and starlight. Fireflies give off light. Volcanic eruptions can light the sky.

People have devised many methods to produce light. They have burned wood, whale oil, candle wax, kerosene, and natural gas. They have used electricity to produce light in flashlights, table lamps, spotlights, automobile headlights, traffic lights, decorating lights, neon lights, and lighthouses.

All the light you see, no matter what the source, is alike in many ways. In this chapter you will find out about the light waves you can see and about other, invisible waves that also affect your life.

20.1 The Electromagnetic Spectrum

You will find out
- what electromagnetic waves are;
- how sound waves and electromagnetic waves differ;
- how electromagnetic waves behave;
- how some kinds of electromagnetic waves are used.

Right now, as you sit reading this book, waves are traveling all around you. You have already learned about the sound waves around you. You can hear some sound waves. Others you cannot. Light waves are also all around you. As with sound waves, you can see only some light waves. The light waves you can see make up what is called **visible light.** What you cannot see are many other kinds of waves that, along with visible light waves, are called **electromagnetic** [ih-lehk-troh-mag-NEHT-ihk] **waves.** Electromagnetic waves are transverse waves that result from the action of electric and magnetic forces. The word *electromagnetic* comes from the names of these two forces. All the kinds of electromagnetic waves together make up the **electromagnetic spectrum** [SPEHK-truhm].

Figure 20.2 Visible light from the sun

Electromagnetic waves differ from sound waves in some important ways. Sound waves are compressional. Electromagnetic waves are transverse. Sound waves can only travel through matter. Electromagnetic waves can travel through empty space as well as through matter. This ability allows you to see stars on a clear night. Electromagnetic waves of light from distant stars travel through empty space, through the atmosphere, and to your eyes.

Electromagnetic waves travel much faster than sound waves. The speed of sound waves in air at 0°C is 331 meters per second. Electromagnetic waves can travel through that same air at 300,000,000 meters per second! This speed is often referred to as the speed of light. You have probably noticed the difference in the speeds of sound waves and electromagnetic waves during a thunderstorm. You see the lightning before you hear the thunder. The light from the lightning travels faster than the sound of the thunder.

The behavior of electromagnetic waves is much more difficult to describe than the behavior of sound waves. Sound waves always behave like waves. But electromagnetic waves behave in some ways like particles and in other ways like waves.

Do You Know?
Because electromagnetic waves behave in some ways like waves and in other ways like particles, some people have suggested calling them *wavicles*.

Figure 20.3 It is obvious to people watching a rocket launch from a distance that light waves travel faster than sound waves. They see the launch begin before they hear the roar of the engines.

Figure 20.4 A photon is released when an excited electron returns to its original energy level.

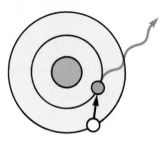

The particle nature of electromagnetic waves involves **photons.** Photons are tiny bundles of energy. Photons are not matter. But they come from matter. They are produced after atoms gain energy, usually in the form of heat or electricity. A particle that has gained energy is described as excited. When an atom is excited, the electrons in that atom are affected. In an unexcited atom, all the electrons are moving around the nucleus in certain specific energy levels. When the atom gains energy, some of the electrons become excited and move temporarily to higher energy levels. As those electrons return to their original energy levels, they release photons. Electromagnetic waves involve photons. Photons behave like particles.

Electromagnetic waves behave like waves by exhibiting reflection, refraction, diffraction, and interference. Also, like other waves, their frequency and wavelength can be measured. Frequency and wavelength are related. Electromagnetic waves with high frequencies have short wavelengths. Similarly, those with low frequencies have long wavelengths.

Figure 20.5 The electromagnetic spectrum

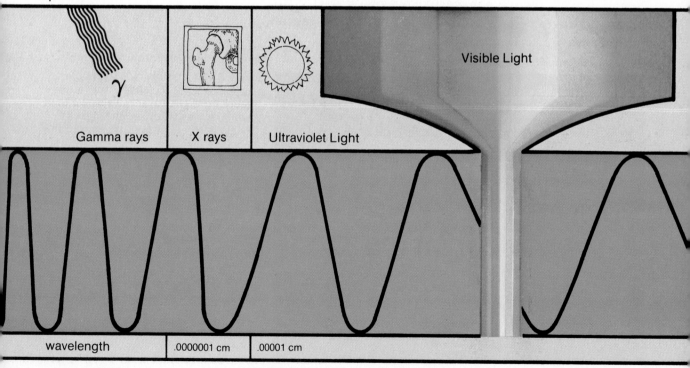

Gamma rays   X rays   Ultraviolet Light   Visible Light

wavelength   .0000001 cm   .00001 cm

Different kinds of electromagnetic waves are identified by their wavelengths. Figure 20.5 shows the different kinds of waves in the electromagnetic spectrum in order according to their wavelengths. They range from gamma rays, which have the shortest wavelengths, to radio waves, which have the longest.

Different kinds of electromagnetic waves affect you differently. Gamma rays are able to penetrate many substances. They can cause damage to the cells of your body. Doctors use gamma rays to kill cancer cells.

X rays can penetrate all but the very dense parts of your body. Doctors and dentists use X rays to examine your bones and teeth. X rays are also used to examine the contents of containers. Airport security guards use X rays to inspect luggage and other cargo.

Ultraviolet light can be used to sterilize objects. Hospitals use ultraviolet light to sterilize equipment. Some school science departments use it to sterilize safety glasses. Light from the sun and from sunlamps contains ultraviolet light. These waves can penetrate your skin, causing suntans and sunburns. Recently, scientists have

Do You Know?
Scientists have used X rays to determine the diseases present in Egyptian mummies at the time of their death.

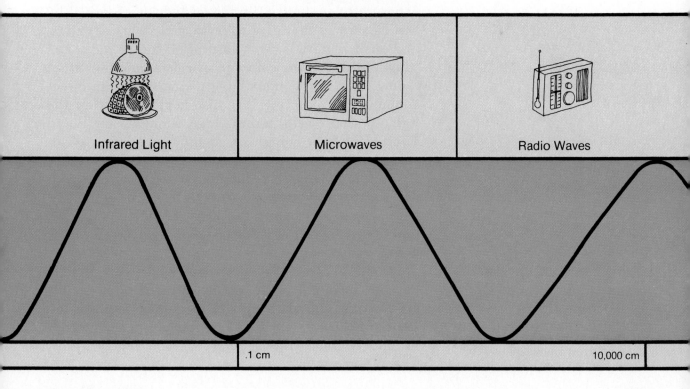

| Infrared Light | Microwaves | Radio Waves |

.1 cm   10,000 cm

discovered a link between the ultraviolet light in sunlight and skin cancer. To minimize this danger, people are advised to limit their exposure to sunlight.

Have you ever noticed that the colors of clothing, curtains, and upholstered furniture often fade after long exposure to sunlight? Ultraviolet light is absorbed by the substances that give color to some fabrics, paints, and other materials. This absorption causes the colors to fade. To keep the colors in priceless paintings from fading, museum workers hang them away from direct sunlight. The paintings are also kept away from the light of fluorescent lamps. Like sunlight, unfiltered fluorescent light contains a significant amount of ultraviolet light.

You cannot see infrared light, but you can feel it. You feel warmer as your body absorbs infrared light. Your body also gives off infrared light. Some animals that hunt at night can see the infrared light given off by warm bodies. This ability helps them to track their prey. Special cameras that can detect infrared light take heat, or infrared, photographs. Infrared photographs are in color. But the colors of the subject are not the same as the colors you see when you look at the subject. In infrared photographs, different colors represent different temperatures.

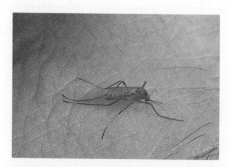

Figure 20.7 Female mosquitos have antennae that detect the infrared light given off by warm-blooded animals. These antennae can lead them to you!

Microwaves are very useful. In microwave ovens, microwaves are produced and are absorbed by food but not by the material that holds or contains that food. Foods cook quickly because they cook all at once instead of from the outside in, as happens with conventional ovens. Microwaves are also used in communications. Telephone and television signals can be carried by microwaves. Some telescopes also use microwaves.

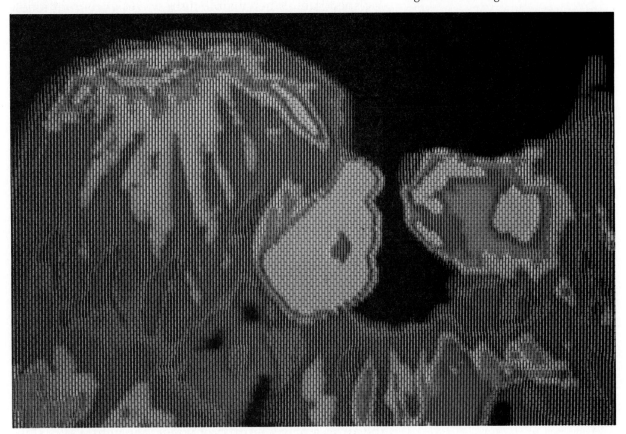

Figure 20.8 An infrared photograph of a girl and her dog

Study Questions for 20.1

1. What are electromagnetic waves?
2. How do sound waves and electromagnetic waves differ?
3. What are photons?
4. Name three kinds of electromagnetic waves and tell how each kind affects people.

You will find out
- what makes a rainbow;
- why objects have the colors they do;
- why the sky changes color.

The electromagnetic waves of visible light fall between ultraviolet light and infrared light in the electromagnetic spectrum. When visible light waves encounter a new or changed medium, they either pass through it or are refracted, reflected, or absorbed. This behavior of visible light waves accounts for everything you see.

An example of the refraction of visible light that you have probably seen many times is a rainbow. Did you know that you do not need rain to see a rainbow? You can make one by directing a fine spray of water from a hose into the sunlight. In fact, you do not even need water to make a rainbow. If you direct light through a triangular piece of glass called a **prism,** you will see a rainbow of colors.

Where do the colors of the rainbow come from? Visible light includes light waves of seven distinct colors: red, orange, yellow, green, blue, indigo, and violet. Each color is made up of electromagnetic waves of a different wavelength. Red has the longest wavelength. Violet has the shortest. When all the colors of visible light are mixed together, you see colorless or **white light.** When the colors are separated, as in a rainbow, you see each individual color.

Prisms and drops of water separate white light into its colors by refraction. When white light passes from the air to a prism or drop of water, the light waves slow down. This change in speed causes the waves to bend, or refract. Waves of different wavelengths are bent to different degrees. Since each color involves waves of a different wavelength, each color is bent to a different degree. Violet waves are bent the most. Red waves are bent the least. In this way the colors that make up white light are separated.

White light can pass through some materials, such as air. But many materials reflect the waves of all or some

Figure 20.9 You can remember the order of the seven distinct colors that appear when white light is separated by remembering the name *Roy G. Biv*.

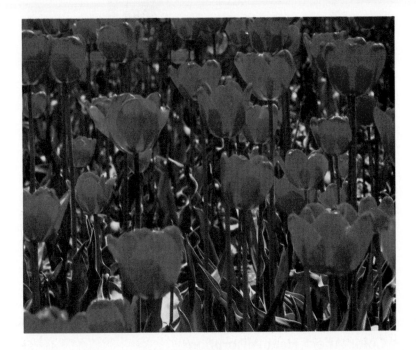

Figure 20.10 What color of light is reflected by these tulip blossoms?

of the colors in white light. The waves of colors that are not reflected are absorbed. The color of an object you see depends on which colors that object reflects and which colors it absorbs. A green leaf is green because it reflects mostly green light. It absorbs most of the waves of the other colors. A banana is yellow because it reflects mostly yellow light.

What do you see when an object absorbs all colors? You see black. A black cat's fur absorbs almost all the white light that strikes it. What if an object reflects all colors? You see white. A polar bear's fur reflects almost all the white light that strikes it.

Only a few colors have been mentioned. But scientists estimate that the human eye can see about 17,000 different colors. Where do all these colors come from? What makes mud brown, fish silver, and flowers pink? All the colors you see are mixtures of the colors in white light. When objects reflect a mixture of more than one of these colors, you see a new color. The 17,000 different colors you can see come from 17,000 different mixtures. All the colors you see in this book come from different mixtures of magenta (pinkish red), cyan (a shade of blue), yellow, and black.

Do You Know?
In an experiment, special lights shone on the food at a dinner party. Celery looked pink; steak, gray; and peas, black. Most of the guests could not eat at all. Those who did felt ill.

In white light, a red apple is always red. A black and orange tiger is always black and orange. But the same sky overhead is not always the same color. Around noontime, it is blue. At sunrise and sunset, it may show shades of pink, orange, and red. What causes these changes in color? The sky is lighted by white light from the sun. The sun's white light must travel through the atmosphere to reach your eyes. Two things about the atmosphere affect the color of the sky you see. First, the color of the sky depends on the amount of atmosphere the sun's light travels through to get to your eyes. Second, it depends on the groups of molecules and tiny particles that are present in the atmosphere.

The sky is blue when the sun is high in the sky. With the sun in this position, light waves from it pass through

ACTIVITY

How Does Color Affect Heat Absorption?

Materials

3 squares (12 cm by 12 cm) of one color of cellophane
3 rubber bands
3 ice cubes of the same size
3 clear plastic cups
clock or watch

Procedure

1. Place an ice cube in the center of a square of cellophane. Pull up the four corners and secure them with a rubber band so that the ice cube is in a sack.

2. Put the sack in a cup and place the cup in direct sunlight or in direct lamplight.

3. Measure the time it takes for the cube to melt completely.

4. Repeat steps 1–3 two more times.

5. Find the average time of your three trials. Share your results with your classmates. Collect the results of classmates who used colors of cellophane that were different from yours.

Questions

1. Make a bar graph to compare the melting times of the different colors.

2. If you wanted a house to warm up quickly in the sunshine, which color would you select for the roof?

3. Why do people who live in hot, desert climates wear light colors?

Figure 20.11 In colorful sunsets, you can see only the longer wavelengths of visible light.

fewer kilometers of atmosphere to reach your eyes than they do when the sun is low in the sky. Small groups of molecules and very tiny particles in the atmosphere are able to reflect in all directions, or scatter, only the shorter wavelengths contained in white light. The shorter wavelengths involve blue shades. The scattered blue light waves make the sky look blue.

A different situation exists at sunrise and at sunset. Where do you see the sun at sunset? It is very low in the sky. When you see the sun low in the sky, light waves from it travel through many more kilometers of atmosphere to reach your eyes. The shorter-wavelength blue waves are scattered many kilometers farther away from your eyes. Thus, you do not see them. You see only the longer wavelengths of reds and oranges. Forest fires, dust storms, and volcanoes release a lot of particles into the atmosphere, producing unusually brilliant red sunsets. The added particles scatter more of the longer wavelengths, allowing only the longest, red wavelengths to reach your eyes.

Study Questions for 20.2

1. How do raindrops make a rainbow?
2. Why does a green leaf look green?
3. What two things about the atmosphere affect the color of the sky you see?

20.3 Changing Visible Light Waves

You will find out
- how mirrors reflect light waves;
- how refraction of light waves can fool your eyes.

Why do some mirrors show you just as you are, while others make you look distorted? Why do you sometimes see puddles ahead on the highway when no water is present? The visible light waves that reach your eyes travel in straight lines until they encounter changes in their medium. These changes sometimes cause you to see things differently from what they really are.

Many surfaces reflect light. A rough surface may appear not to reflect light. It looks dull because it is reflecting light in many different directions. A smooth surface reflects most light in the same direction. A mirror has a smooth surface. Light waves that hit anywhere on the surface of a mirror are reflected in the same way. If you look at yourself in a mirror, your reflection looks just like you. The only difference is that, in the reflection, the right and left sides are reversed. You may not notice this difference when you see your own reflection. But

Figure 20.12 The water's glassy surface acts like a mirror.

Figure 20.13 The word *ambulance* is spelled backward on the hood of this emergency vehicle. When drivers see it in their rear-view mirrors, the word appears normally written and is easy to read.

the difference is obvious when you look at a word in a mirror. The word is spelled backwards. Also, the letters appear backwards. Dental students have to learn to allow for the backward reflection they see when using a mirror to examine a patient's teeth.

The reflection you see of yourself in a fun-house mirror looks nothing like the real you. Why? Although the mirror may look smooth, its surface is uneven. When you look into such a mirror, light waves from different parts of your body are reflected at different angles. The net result is a very distorted and funny view of your body.

Figure 20.14 The uneven surface of this mirror causes the distortion you see.

Figure 20.15 Light waves from the part of the pencil underwater are bent as they pass from the water to the air.

One way to get an inaccurate view of an object is to look at it in an uneven mirror. Another way is to look at an object underwater. If you look at an object that is in water, you may notice that its shape or location appears different from what is really the case. To understand how this happens, imagine a pencil in a glass half full of water. You see the pencil when light waves reflected from it reach your eyes. You see the part of the pencil out of the water exactly as it is. But the light waves from the part of the pencil underwater are bent, or refracted, as they pass from one medium—water—to a new medium—air. This refraction makes the part of the pencil that is underwater appear to be in the wrong place in relation to the part above water.

Light waves can be refracted when they travel from one medium to another. They can also be refracted

ACTIVITY

How Can You Produce a Mirage?

Materials

glass with straight
  sides
candle
matches
safety glasses

Procedure

1. Put on your safety glasses. Fill the glass with water until it is almost full. Place it near the edge of a table.

2. Place the candle behind the glass. Light the candle. The top of the flame should be just below the level of the water. CAUTION: Be sure the candle cannot tip over. Also be sure someone watches it all the time that it is lighted.

3. Look down on the surface of the water. Do you see the flame?

4. Kneel down so that you are lower than the glass of water. Look up through the water at the candle. Do you see the flame?

Questions

1. How many flames did you see when you looked down on the glass of water?

2. How many flames did you see when you looked up through the glass of water?

3. Where were the flames you saw when you looked up through the glass?

4. What caused you to see two flames?

5. What was the mirage that you saw?

Light waves from the sky bend

Mirage appears here

Figure 20.16 *left:* The water that appears on the road is a mirage. *right:* The mirage is produced when light waves are bent as they pass from denser, cooler air to less dense, warmer air.

within the same medium if the density of that medium changes. For example, the density of the air around you is affected by temperature. When the temperature increases, the density decreases. In hot weather, the air near the surface of a highway may become hotter and less dense than the air above. Imagine you are riding in a car on such a highway. Light waves traveling to your eyes from patches of blue sky will be refracted as they pass from the cooler, denser air above to the warmer, less dense air near the highway. As a result, you see what appear to be puddles of water on the road ahead. You are seeing an example of a **mirage.** A mirage is an illusion caused by the refraction of light waves, making objects that are far away appear to be nearby, floating in air, or upside down.

Study Questions for 20.3

1. How are fun-house mirrors different from ordinary mirrors?
2. Why does a pencil in a glass of water look broken at the water's surface?
3. What is a mirage?

20.4 Diffraction and Polarization

You will find out
- how a diffraction grating separates the colors in white light;
- how polarizing sunglasses reduce glare.

You have learned that refraction of white light can separate it into colors. Refraction is not the only way to separate the colors in white light. You can also separate them by interference.

Imagine a thin piece of glass with thousands of parallel slits close together. Such a device is called a **diffraction grating.** When white light passes through a diffraction grating, different wavelengths are diffracted, or bent, differently, causing them to spread out. As the light waves are spread out, they run into each other. Interference results. Where crests meet troughs, the waves are cancelled out and dark bands appear. Where crests meet crests or troughs meet troughs, bright bands in a rainbow of colors appear.

Figure 20.17 The path of light waves through a diffraction grating

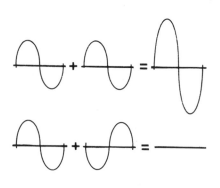

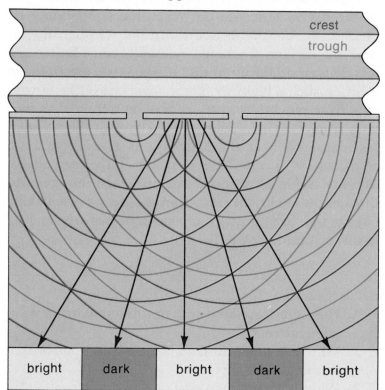

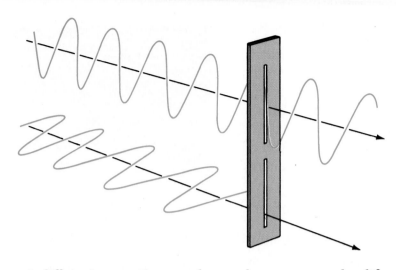

Figure 20.18 Polarizing light waves

A diffraction grating can be used to separate the different wavelengths of light given off by a substance. For example, neon gives off light when it is electrified. The light appears red. But when it is passed through a diffraction grating, other colors are apparent as well. A diffraction grating can be used to identify a substance by identifying the different wavelengths of light given off by that substance. The different wavelengths given off identify a substance as surely as fingerprints identify a person.

Although you probably enjoy bright sunny days, you may remember some days when the sun's light was so bright that your eyes were bothered. You may have used sunglasses or wished you had a pair. Have you ever heard of **polarizing** [POH-luh-ry-zing] sunglasses? A material that is polarizing allows only light waves with crests and troughs at a certain angle to pass through. All other light waves are reflected or absorbed. If very bright sunlight is shining in your eyes, polarizing sunglasses can be helpful. Since only some of the light waves will be able to pass through to your eyes, glare is reduced.

Figure 20.19 Some areas of the sky polarize sunlight. Honeybees are able to detect this polarization. This ability helps them to navigate.

Study Questions for 20.4

1. How does a diffraction grating separate the colors in white light?
2. How do polarizing sunglasses reduce glare?

What Did You Learn?

- The light waves you can see make up visible light.
- Electromagnetic waves are transverse waves that result from the action of electric and magnetic forces.
- The electromagnetic spectrum is made up of all the kinds of electromagnetic waves together.
- Photons are tiny bundles of energy that are given off when excited electrons return to their original energy levels.
- The photons of electromagnetic waves behave like particles.
- Electromagnetic waves behave like waves by exhibiting reflection, refraction, diffraction, and interference.
- Different kinds of electromagnetic waves are identified by their wavelengths.
- Raindrops and prisms separate the colors in white light by refraction.
- The color of an object depends on which colors that object reflects and which colors it absorbs.
- The color of the sky depends on the amount of atmosphere the sun's light travels through to get to your eyes and the groups of molecules and tiny particles that are present in the atmosphere.
- All light waves are reflected from the smooth surface of a mirror in the same way.
- An object underwater may appear to be in the wrong place because light waves from it are refracted as they pass from the water to the air.
- Light waves can be refracted if the density of their medium changes.
- A mirage is caused by the refraction of light waves making objects that are far away appear to be nearby, floating in air, or upside down.
- A diffraction grating separates the colors in white light by interference.
- Polarizing sunglasses reduce glare by allowing only light waves with crests and troughs at a certain angle to pass through.

Key Terms
visible light
electromagnetic waves
electromagnetic spectrum
photons
prism
white light
mirage
diffraction grating
polarizing

Career

X-ray Technician

X-ray technicians work in hospitals, clinics, and public-health agencies. They work with both doctors and patients. Following a doctor's order, an X-ray technician prepares and positions a patient for an X ray. The technician also operates the equipment used to take the X ray. It is the X-ray technician who is responsible for taking a picture at the correct exposure. Therefore, the technician must know about X-ray equipment as well as about the human body.

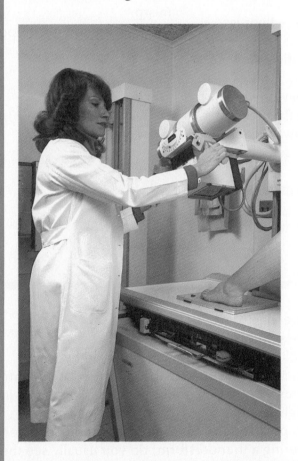

Many patients needing X rays are very ill or are experiencing pain. An X-ray technician must be understanding of a patient's condition and feelings. The technician must enjoy working closely with and helping people. He or she must also follow directions exactly and pay close attention to the operation of X-ray equipment. Doctors rely on proper X rays to help them diagnose conditions and prescribe treatments.

There is a great demand for qualified X-ray technicians. To become an X-ray technician, you must complete a two-year training program after high school. Such programs are offered by many hospitals, medical schools, colleges, junior colleges, and vocational schools and in the military services.

TO THINK ABOUT AND DO

Vocabulary

Number your paper from 1 to 10. Unscramble the words. Beside each number write the unscrambled word or words that best complete the sentence.

1. When excited electrons return to their original energy levels, they release bundles of energy called _____.
2. All the kinds of electromagnetic waves together make up the _____.
3. Your body absorbs _____ and you feel warmer.
4. When all the colors of visible light are mixed together, you see colorless or _____.
5. A triangular piece of glass that refracts white light is called a _____.
6. A banana is yellow because it _____mostly yellow light.
7. _____ sunglasses allow only light waves with crests and troughs at a certain angle to pass through.
8. When you see puddles ahead on a highway even though no water is present, you are seeing a _____.
9. A thin piece of glass with thousands of parallel slits close together is called a _____.
10. _____ are transverse waves that result from the action of electric and magnetic forces.

gearim
zipinalrog
mortteaelcecign sawev
shootnp
dreafrin gilth
thiew thilg
fatciifdrno aggritn
misrp
tteeeccgarmonil mustrepc
cleerstf

What Do You Remember?

1. What are electromagnetic waves?
2. How are photons produced?
3. What colors of white light are reflected by snow?
4. How does a prism separate the colors in white light?
5. How does a diffraction grating separate the colors in white light?
6. How do polarizing sunglasses help to reduce glare?
7. Why, during a thunderstorm, do you usually see the lightning before you hear the thunder?

8. How can the sky be different colors at different times of the day?
9. Why do you look strange in a fun-house mirror?
10. Give an example of a mirage.

Applying What You Have Learned

1. What part of the electromagnetic spectrum would be used for each of the following?
   (a) taking pictures of a person's lungs to look for evidence of lung disease
   (b) making a surface free of germs
   (c) keeping food warm in a cafeteria
2. Why do polar bears have black skin?
3. When you look at people standing in a swimming pool, often their legs look strange? Why?

Research and Investigation

1. Write a report on why electromagnetic waves are described as behaving both like particles and like waves. What makes gamma rays seem more particle-like and radio waves more wave-like?
2. What contribution did each of the following people make to the study of light: Michelson, Roemer, Einstein, Newton, and Huygens?

The Uses of Light

Before the 1600's, no one knew that germs caused diseases or that pond water was full of tiny plants and animals. People did not know about germs and tiny plants and animals because they could not see them. In the early 1600's, the microscope was invented. A whole new world opened up to people.

At about the same time that the microscope was being invented, the telescope was being developed. With the telescope, people could see distant stars and planets. Microscopes and telescopes direct light waves so people can see objects that are not visible to their eyes alone.

Recently, there has been a development that uses light in a way that has nothing to do with seeing. This special kind of light can be used to carry television signals and telephone messages. It is powerful enough to cut diamonds and precise enough to perform surgery.

In this chapter you will find out how microscopes, telescopes, and other devices help you to see. You will also find out about light that is used to carry messages and perform surgery.

Figure 21.1 A laser-light show from the Empire State Building

21.1 Lenses

You will find out
- what a lens is;
- what the two basic kinds of lenses are;
- how to find the focal length of a convex lens;
- how virtual images and real images differ.

Do you or does someone you know collect stamps, or coins, or butterflies? A collector of small objects usually uses a magnifying glass to examine his or her collection. Only with the help of a magnifying glass can the interesting and important details be seen on a stamp, a coin, or the wing of a butterfly. A magnifying glass is an example of a lens.

Lenses are curved pieces of glass or plastic that refract light waves. Lenses can bring light waves together or spread them apart. A lens does this by refracting, or bending, light waves. Light waves that pass through a lens often form a picture you can see. The picture is called an **image**.

Do You Know?
Most insects have compound eyes, each with hundreds of lenses.

Figure 21.2 Light waves are brought together by convex lenses and spread apart by concave lenses.

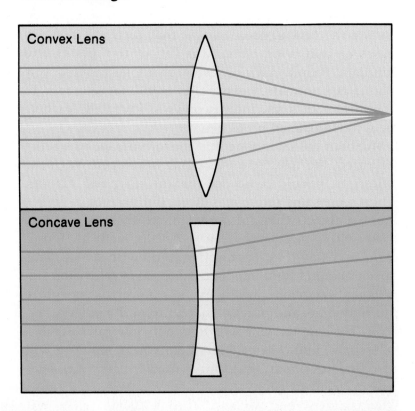

Convex Lens

Concave Lens

There are two basic kinds of lenses. A **convex** [kahn-VEHKS] **lens** has curved surfaces that bulge out in the middle. The lens is thicker at the middle and thinner at the edges. Convex lenses bring light waves together. A **concave** [kahn-KAYV] **lens** has curved surfaces that dip in at the middle. The lens is thinner in the middle and thicker at the edges. A concave lens spreads light waves apart.

Light waves that pass through a convex lens come together at a point. This point is called the **focal** [FOH-kuhl] **point** of the lens. The distance from the center of the lens to the focal point is called the **focal length** of the lens. The focal length and the thickness of a convex lens are related. The thicker the lens, the shorter the focal length.

A magnifying glass uses a convex lens. You can find the focal length of a magnifying glass by holding it between the sun and a flat surface. If you move the magnifying glass slowly back and forth, you will eventually see a sharp point of light. This point is the focal point. The distance between your magnifying glass and the focal point is the focal length.

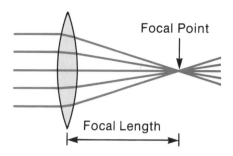

Figure 21.3 The focal point and focal length of a convex lens

Figure 21.4 *left:* To get the background in focus, the camera's lens was moved so that the film was at the focal point. *right:* To get the foreground in focus, the photographer increased the distance between the film and the lens.

Two kinds of images can be formed by lenses. You can see both kinds of images with a common magnifying glass. When you hold a magnifying glass over an object and move the lens up just a little, you see a **virtual** [VUR-choo-wuhl] **image** of the object. A virtual image is an image that appears right side up and cannot be focused on a screen. The virtual image appears magnified as long as you hold the magnifying glass a distance from the object that is close to but not equal to the focal length of the lens. When you move the magnifying glass a focal length away, you see a blur.

ACTIVITY

Material
magnifying glass

How Can You See Images?

Procedure

1. Place the magnifying glass over the number below.

2. Pick the glass up and slowly move it toward your eye. Observe the number as you do so.

3. Stand up. Hold the magnifying glass at arm's length over the number. Slowly move the magnifying glass up. You will see the same things you saw in step 2. Continue to move the magnifying glass up until you see another clear image.

Questions

1. What happens to the number as you raise the magnifying glass? Does its size change? Does the image remain clear?

2. What happens to the number as the magnifying glass is moved farther from it?

3. When the image became clear again, how did it differ from the first image?

4. What kind of image did you see in step 2?

5. What kind of image did you see in step 3?

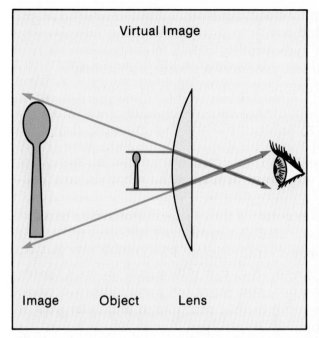

Virtual Image

Image   Object   Lens

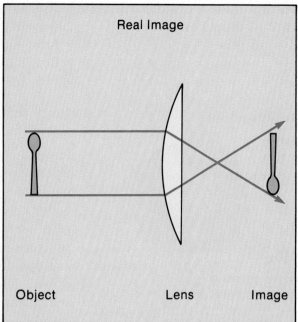

Real Image

Object   Lens   Image

Figure 21.5 *left:* Forming a virtual image; *right:* Forming a real image

You see the second kind of image formed by lenses when you hold a magnifying glass at arm's length over an object and slowly move it up. First, you see the virtual image of the object. Next, you see a blur. Finally, you see an image of the object again. But this time it appears upside down. You are seeing a **real image.** A real image is an image that appears upside down and can be focused on a screen. A real image is upside down because light waves from the object are bent sharply when they pass through the lens. Light waves from the top of the object pass through the lens and are bent down. Light waves from the bottom of the object pass through the lens and are bent up.

Study Questions for 21.1

1. Describe a convex lens and tell how it affects light waves.
2. Describe a concave lens and tell how it affects light waves.
3. How is the focal length of a lens related to the focal point of that lens?
4. How are virtual images and real images different?

21.2 Using Lenses

You will find out
- how your eyes see;
- how a camera produces a photographic image;
- how microscopes and telescopes use lenses.

Figure 21.6 The eye

Retina

Lens

Muscles

Nerve carrying image to the brain

What do cameras, microscopes, telescopes, and your eyes all have in common? They all have lenses. The lenses in your eyes, however, are unique because their thickness can change depending on what you are looking at.

Light waves entering the eye are directed by a lens onto a surface called the **retina** [REHT-uhn-uh]. A real image is formed on the retina. Remember, real images are upside down. Does everything you see look upside down? The world you see is not upside down because your brain receives that real image and interprets it right side up.

Each of your eyes has a clear, changeable lens. The lens is not rigid. Muscles in your eye change the thickness of the lens. This allows you to clearly see objects that are close and objects that are far away. When you look at this page, the muscles in your eyes cause the lenses to thicken. You see the printed page clearly. If you look up from this book and across the room to a poster on the wall, your eye muscles stretch out the lenses and they become thinner. You then see the poster clearly.

Figure 21.7 *left:* When you look at something distant, the lenses in your eyes stretch out. *right:* When you look at something close up, the lenses thicken.

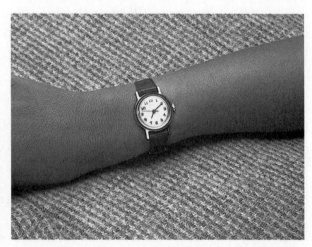

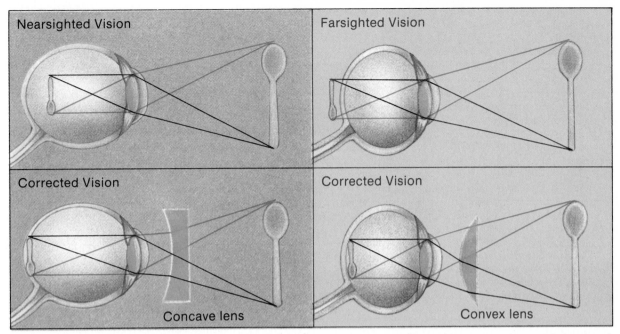

Nearsighted Vision

Farsighted Vision

Corrected Vision

Concave lens

Corrected Vision

Convex lens

Figure 21.8 Correcting nearsighted and farsighted vision

The distance between the lens and the retina is very important to good eyesight. If this distance is too short, a person is farsighted. The real image is formed behind the retina instead of on it. Farsighted people can clearly see faraway objects. But nearby objects are unclear. Farsightedness can be corrected by convex lenses. Convex lenses change the path of light waves entering the eye, causing them to form an image on the retina instead of behind it.

Many older people develop farsightedness even though the distance between the lens and the retina in their eyes may be normal. The muscles in the eyes in older people may become weak and unable to thicken the lens for clear vision of close objects. Corrective lenses can solve this problem.

If the distance between the lens and the retina is too long, a person is nearsighted. The real image is formed in front of the retina instead of on it. Nearsighted people can clearly see objects nearby. But faraway objects are unclear. Nearsightedness can be corrected by concave lenses. Concave lenses change the path of light waves entering the eye, causing them to form an image on the retina instead of in front of it.

Do You Know?
Many experts believe that the Chinese were the first to invent and develop eyeglasses.

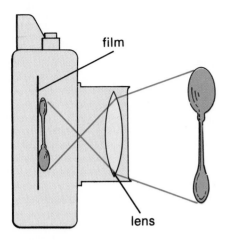

Figure 21.9 In a camera, light waves pass through a lens and form an image on photographic film.

A camera is similar to any eye. In an eye, a real image is formed on the retina. In a camera, a real image is formed on photographic film. The film contains chemicals that are affected by light. Light waves that strike the film cause chemical reactions to take place. These chemical reactions produce a photographic image.

A camera, like your eyes, has a lens. Your eyes focus on an object by changing the thickness of the lens. A photographer may focus a camera on an object by moving the lens back and forth.

Most microscopes use two or more convex lenses. Light waves from very tiny objects are refracted by the lenses so that a magnified image is formed. Many objects that were once mysterious and invisible to human eyes are now very familiar sights when seen through a microscope.

ACTIVITY

Why Do You See Motion in Movies?

Materials
pencil
cellophane tape
white card

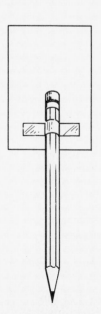

Procedure

1. Hold the card so the longer edge is parallel to the edge of your desk that is closest to you.

2. On one side of the card draw a tree. Make your lines heavy and dark.

3. On the other side of the card over the same area that has the tree, draw 10 small apples. Make your lines heavy and dark.

4. Tape the card to the top of your pencil as shown in the diagram.

5. Hold the pencil between the palms of your hands. Rub your hands together to spin the pencil. Observe the card.

Questions

1. What happened to the apples when you spun the card?

2. Persistence of vision means that an image remains on the retina of your eye. Can you explain why the apples seemed to be on the tree and falling from it?

3. In a movie there are hundreds of individual pictures. Each differs only slightly from the previous picture. When you watch a movie, why do the objects in the still pictures appear to be moving?

A microscope uses lenses to help you to see very tiny objects. The lenses in a telescope help you to see objects of enormous size. Your eyes need help in seeing these objects, not because they are small, but because they are so far away. Most **refracting telescopes** use two convex lenses to concentrate and bend light waves from distant objects. The light waves are bent so that they produce a magnified image of the object. **Reflecting telescopes** use a curved mirror and a convex lens. Thus, both reflection and refraction of light waves are involved in forming a magnified image.

Study Questions for 21.2

1. How is each of the following involved in seeing: lens, retina, muscles in the eye?
2. How do eyeglass lenses help farsighted and near-sighted people to see better?
3. How is a photographic image produced?
4. How do microscopes and telescopes help you to see tiny or distant objects?

21.3 Lasers and Optical Fibers

You will find out
- what laser light is;
- how lasers produce laser light;
- how lasers are used;
- what optical fibers are.

Most light sources produce light waves of different wavelengths and those light waves travel in many directions. It is possible to have light waves all of the same wavelength and all traveling in the same direction. Every crest is lined up with every other crest. Every trough is lined up with every other trough. The result is an intense, narrow beam of light called **laser light.** Since all the light waves in laser light have the same wavelength, they are all of the same color. A device that produces laser light is called a **laser.**

A laser must have three basic components to produce laser light. First, a substance, or medium, that can produce laser light must be present. Second, a form of energy must be available to excite the atoms of the medium. The atoms must be excited in order to produce the light waves of laser light. Third, the direction of the laser light produced must be controlled. The controlling is usually done with mirrors.

Do You Know?
The word, *laser,* comes from the words *l*ight *a*mplification by *s*timulated *e*mission of *r*adiation.

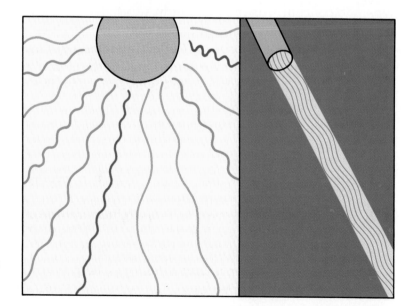

Figure 21.11 In laser light, all the waves are of the same wavelength and are traveling in the same direction.

The first laser developed was the ruby laser. In this laser, the substance that produces laser light is a solid ruby rod containing chromium atoms. Energy in the form of bursts of light is supplied to the ruby rod. A coating of silver on each end of the rod acts like a mirror to control the direction of the laser light produced.

One of the most commonly used lasers is the helium-neon laser. Helium and neon gases in a glass tube produce the laser light. An electric current is used to excite the atoms of helium and neon. Mirrors are used to control the direction of the laser light produced.

Lasers were first developed in 1960. Since then, their importance has grown greatly. For example, they are used to cut diamonds and weld metals. Eye doctors are using lasers to reattach torn retinas. Lasers are used in other kinds of surgery as well.

Figure 21.12 *left:* Using laser light to measure and align in the construction of a tunnel; *right:* Using laser light to cut a diamond

Lasers can produce three-dimensional photographs called **holograms** [HOH-luh-gramz]. A hologram shows all sides of a subject instead of just one. To make a hologram, a single beam of laser light is split into two beams by a mirror. One beam is directed at the subject of the photograph. When the laser light strikes the subject, it is reflected from the subject onto a photographic film. The second laser beam never strikes the subject. Instead, it is reflected by a mirror directly onto the same photographic film. The two beams of light meet on the photographic film. Interference occurs and creates a pattern on the film. The film is developed producing a hologram.

To see the hologram, you must direct laser light onto it. The laser light must be of the same wavelength that was used to produce the hologram. You see a three-dimensional image of the subject. In fact, if you change your viewing angle, you see another view of the subject.

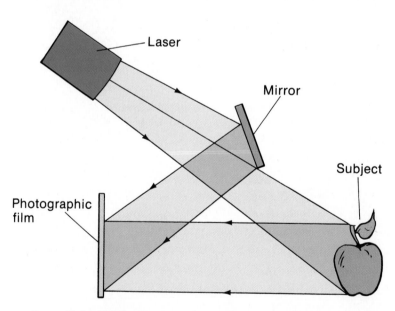

Figure 21.13 Producing a hologram

One of the biggest breakthroughs in the field of communications has been the use of laser light and ordinary light to carry messages. For example, laser light can carry 10,000,000 telephone messages at the same time! Conventional metal wires are able to carry far fewer messages.

Figure 21.14 Optical fibers

Signals and messages are carried by light waves along thin strands of glass called **optical fibers.** Using the principle of refraction, scientists have designed optical fibers so that light waves become trapped inside and are able to move along them. The light waves travel very quickly. They can carry a large amount of information in a short amount of time. Optical fibers using laser light carry messages over long or short distances. Ordinary light can also be used for short distances.

Optical fibers carrying ordinary light are used by doctors in a device called an **endoscope** [EHN-duh-skohp]. An endoscope can be inserted into the body. It allows a doctor to examine internal organs without having to perform surgery. Endoscopes are frequently used to examine the lungs and the digestive system.

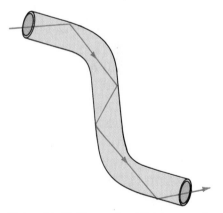

Figure 21.15 The path of light waves in optical fibers

Study Questions for 21.3

1. What is laser light?
2. What are the three basic components of a laser?
3. Name two uses of lasers.
4. What are optical fibers?

What Did You Learn?

- Lenses are curved pieces of glass or plastic that refract light waves.
- A picture formed by a lens is called an image.
- A convex lens has curved surfaces that bulge out at the middle to bring light waves together.
- A concave lens has curved surfaces that dip in at the middle to spread light waves apart.
- The focal length of a lens is the distance from its center to its focal point.
- A virtual image appears right side up and cannot be focused on a screen.
- A real image appears upside down and can be focused on a screen.
- The lens in your eye forms a real image on the retina.
- Muscles in your eye change the thickness of the lens so you can see both close and distant objects clearly.
- In farsighted people, the real image is formed behind the retina instead of on it.
- In nearsighted people, the real image is formed in front of the retina instead of on it.
- A camera, like your eye, uses a lens to form a real image on a surface.
- Microscopes and telescopes use convex lenses to form magnified images.
- Laser light is made up of light waves all of the same wavelength traveling in the same direction.
- Lasers involve a substance that can produce laser light, an energy source, and a way to control the direction of the laser light.
- Lasers are used to make holograms.
- Optical fibers are thin strands of glass that use light waves to carry signals and messages.

Key Terms

lenses
image
convex lens
concave lens
focal point
focal length
virtual image
real image
retina
refracting telescopes
reflecting telescopes
laser light
laser
holograms
optical fibers
endoscope

Career

Optometrist

Optometrists are health professionals who specialize in the diagnosis of vision problems and the prescription of lenses to correct those problems. Optometrists are the major providers of vision care. They are concerned with how general health problems affect vision, color vision, and depth perception and how well a person sees. Some optometrists work in private practice. Other optometrists work in groups with other health professionals to provide complete health care.

An office visit to an optometrist generally involves a 45-minute to 1-hour examination of the eye and vision capabilities. Since many instruments are used in the examination, a person planning to be an optometrist should have a good mechanical aptitude as well as an interest in physics, math, and biological science.

To become an optometrist, you need 5 to 6 years of study at a school of optometry. There are 10 accredited schools of optometry in the United States. The course of study includes the basic health sciences, optics and visual

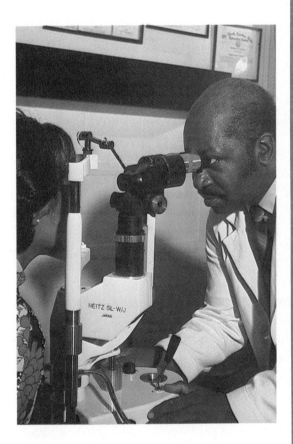

science, behavioral and community science, and clinical science and services. After graduation, you must take clinical and written examinations in order to obtain a license.

TO THINK ABOUT AND DO

Vocabulary

Number your paper from 1 to 10. Read each of the sentences. If the sentence is true, write *true*. If it is false, make it true by changing the underlined expression.

1. A <u>refracting telescope</u> uses a system of lenses and mirrors to view stars and planets.
2. The distance between a lens and the point where the light waves come together is called the <u>focal length</u> of the lens.
3. Photographic film in a camera is like the <u>lens</u> of the eye.
4. A <u>virtual image</u> can be focused on a screen.
5. A three-dimensional photograph produced by laser light is called a <u>hologram</u>.
6. A <u>concave lens</u> spreads light waves apart.
7. A magnifying glass has a <u>concave lens</u>.
8. <u>Images</u> are used to send telephone messages.
9. <u>Lenses</u> produce light waves of one wavelength that all travel in one direction.
10. A doctor can use an <u>endoscope</u> to see inside the lungs.

What Do You Remember?

1. What is a lens?
2. Name and diagram the two basic kinds of lenses.
3. How does a convex lens affect the light waves that pass through it?
4. How does a concave lens affect the light waves that pass through it?
5. What kind of image is found on the retina?
6. How do your eyes change to clearly see objects at different distances?
7. Why are some people nearsighted?
8. How is a camera like an eye?
9. What is laser light?
10. What are optical fibers?

Applying What You Have Learned

1. Lighthouses use lenses to concentrate light into a bright beam that is easily seen. What kind of lenses do they use?
2. You may have noticed some people holding a book or paper out at arm's length while reading. Who might do this and why?
3. How is a hologram different from an ordinary photograph?
4. Birdwatchers often use binoculars to enable them to examine birds from a distance. What kind of lenses are used in binoculars?

Research and Investigation

1. In 1982 Alan Scott, an ophthamologist, reported that a derivative of the poison that causes botulism can be used to correct eye defects. Investigate Scott's drug, Oculinum, and report on how it functions.
2. Some people wear glasses that are bifocal or trifocal. What are bifocal and trifocal glasses?

Unit Six

Energy
and
the Future

Energy and Society 22

Did an electric alarm clock wake you this morning? How was your breakfast cooked? Did you get to school by car or bus? Think for a moment about your life-style. You probably take for granted the use of cars, buses, heating systems, cooling systems, lights, and other things. Where does the energy come from to provide you with this life-style?

In this chapter you will learn about the two main sources of energy in the United States. You will find out how your life-style is maintained by these energy sources. You will also learn about what is being done to ensure that there will be enough energy available in the future. While these energy sources do answer the current need for energy, they also create problems. The solution to those problems should be an interest and a concern of everyone.

Figure 22.1 A supertanker entering Boston Harbor

22.1 Fossil Fuels

You will find out
- what fossil fuels are;
- how fossil fuels are obtained;
- what some of the problems associated with fossil fuels are.

Close to 90 percent of the energy used in the United States comes from coal, oil, and natural gas. These energy sources are called **fossil** [FAHS-uhl] **fuels.** Fossil fuels are fuels formed from the remains of plants and animals that lived millions of years ago. Energy from the sun was stored in the plants. When the animals ate the plants, they obtained and stored the energy. The energy was stored in the chemical bonds of molecules in the plants and animals.

After the plants and animals died, they were buried under heavy layers of mud and sand. They only partially decayed. The chemical bonds and the energy contained in them were preserved. Depending on the specific kind of material and the conditions, oil, coal, or natural gas was formed. These fossil fuels are used to do many things such as power cars, heat and cool buildings, and generate electricity.

Figure 22.2 Drilling for oil offshore

Do You Know?
The United States has 6 percent of the world's population and uses 35 percent of the total energy used in the world.

Figure 22.3 Strip mining

Coal is the most plentiful fossil fuel in the world. Some coal deposits are deep underground and must be taken out through tunnels, or shafts, cut into the earth. This method, called **shaft mining,** is expensive and can be dangerous. When the coal lies near the surface, tunnels are not needed. This surface coal can be exposed with explosives. It is then removed with giant shovels. This practice is called **strip mining.** Strip mining is the least costly and safest way to get coal. However, it completely destroys the environment in and around the area being mined. Mine operators are now required to repair the damage done to the environment.

Oil is found in many places around the world in underground pools. Sometimes the oil is mixed with other substances. Deposits of oil mixed with sand are called **tar sands.** Oil is also found in a rock called **oil shale** [SHAYL]. Scientists are working on ways to separate out and use the oil in tar sands and oil shale.

A lot of time, effort, and expense are involved in finding oil. Oil prospectors study aerial and satellite photographs. They use sound waves to study the earth's outer layer. This and other information is used to determine the kinds of rocks present in an area and the layering of those rocks. Certain rock structures are known to be associated with oil deposits. If the indications suggest that oil is present, a well may be drilled. Some wells strike oil. Others come up dry.

The oil that comes out of a well is called crude oil. The crude oil must be transported to a refinery. At a refinery, it is separated into gasoline, kerosene, diesel fuel, heating oil, and other products.

Crude oil is often transported over land through pipelines. The recently completed Alaskan pipeline covers 1,287 km. It goes from the Arctic Ocean to the southern coast of Alaska. It took 20,000 people three years to build. More than half of the pipeline is on stilts. If the

Figure 22.4 The Alaskan pipeline

Chapter 22 / Energy and Society

Figure 22.5 An LNG tanker

pipeline were buried, heat from the oil flowing through it could have a negative effect on Arctic plants and animals. If the pipeline were on the surface of the ground, it would block the path of migrating caribou and reindeer.

Giant ships called supertankers transport crude oil at sea. Some supertankers are over 350 m long. Crew members often use bicycles to get from one end of the ship to the other!

Like oil, natural gas is found deep underground. To make transportation easier, the natural gas is often cooled and compressed above ground to form a liquid. This liquid is called liquified natural gas or LNG. You may have heard of LNG tankers or seen trucks carrying LNG.

The chemical energy stored in the chemical bonds of fossil fuels is released when they are burned. Your lifestyle depends on this energy. Unfortunately, some unhealthy compounds are produced and released into the air when fossil fuels are burned. One such compound is carbon monoxide. Carbon monoxide is a deadly poison. It prevents your body from getting the oxygen it needs. People have died from breathing air having too high a concentration of carbon monoxide.

Figure 22.6 The burning of fossil fuels contributes to air pollution.

Figure 22.7 Much of the damage to this statue was caused by air pollution.

Two other unhealthy compounds produced by the burning of fossil fuels are oxides of sulfur and nitrogen. The breathing of these oxides can be harmful. When sulfur and nitrogen oxides combine with water in the atmosphere, they form acids. These acids fall to the ground as **acid rain.** Acid rain can damage both plant and animal life. It can also contaminate water supplies.

Small particles are also released into the air when fossil fuels are burned. These particles, together with the unhealthy compounds produced, create air pollution. People who breathe polluted air can suffer from eye, nose, and throat irritations, breathing problems, and even cancer.

Steps are being taken to control air pollution. Devices that control or prevent the release of pollutants into the air are being used in cars, factories, and other places where fossil fuels are burned. Even so, the problem is far from solved. It remains a concern for everyone.

The transportation of fossil fuels can also cause damage to the environment. Oil pipelines are designed to minimize their effects on the environment. Even so, their construction and mere existence change the natural state. Supertankers carrying crude oil sometimes accidentally spill their cargo. These oil spills cause serious damage to the sea and coastal environments. Much plant and animal life is destroyed. On land, plant and animal life are also destroyed by the practice of strip mining.

Another problem related to the use of fossil fuels is their availability. Fossil fuels are being used up much more quickly than they are forming. New fossil fuels are forming today. But the formation process takes millions of years! Clearly, at the rate fossil fuels are being used, there will certainly come a time when they are no longer available.

One possible solution to the problem of dwindling fossil fuel resources is the development of synthetic fuels. Scientists can make alcohol from sugar cane and other plants. They are currently exploring ways to use alcohol to fuel cars. Both alcohol alone and in combination with gasoline (gasohol) are possible energy sources for the future.

Do You Know?
Some oil wells extend more than 8 km into the earth.

Figure 22.8 Oil spills can cause serious environmental damage.

Study Questions for 22.1

1. What are fossil fuels?
2. Where are coal, oil, and natural gas found?
3. Name two problems associated with the use of fossil fuels for energy.

22.2 Nuclear Energy

You will find out
- how fission is used to generate electricity;
- what some of the problems associated with nuclear reactors are;
- why fusion reactors are difficult to design and operate.

Most of the electricity in the United States is generated with fossil fuels. Another energy source that is also being used to generate electricity is nuclear energy. Nuclear energy is released when the nucleus of an atom undergoes a nuclear reaction.

There are two main kinds of nuclear reactions. In fission, energy is released when a heavy nucleus is split into lighter nuclei. In fusion, energy is released when two light nuclei join together forming a heavier nucleus. Society's demand for energy is high and continues to grow. Use of the large amounts of energy released in nuclear reactions is one possible way to meet this growing demand.

Scientists continue to explore ways to obtain and use fission and fusion energy. So far, efforts involving fission have been more successful than those involving fusion. Fission-powered submarines, aircraft carriers, and space probes have been launched. In the United States and in other countries, electricity is being generated using energy from fission.

Figure 22.9 The Indian Point nuclear power plant in New York

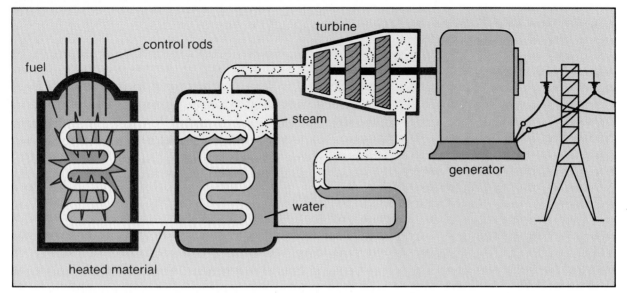

Figure 22.10 A nuclear power plant

A nuclear-fission power plant generates electricity. The power plant uses a fissionable material for fuel. A material that is fissionable is one that is able to undergo fission. The fuel most commonly used is uranium 235. The uranium fuel undergoes fission in a chain reaction. The energy released from the chain reaction is absorbed as heat by a material such as water. The heat is used to produce steam. The steam is directed at the blades of a turbine. The rotating turbine is used to generate electricity.

The chain reactions take place in a **nuclear reactor.** It is important to have effective control of chain reactions because they proceed very quickly and involve large amounts of energy. In the reactor, **control rods** made of steel mixed with another element, such as boron or cadmium, control the chain reaction. They control the reaction by absorbing neutrons.

To stop the chain reaction, control rods are lowered into the reactor. They absorb neutrons, preventing those neutrons from bombarding the uranium nuclei and continuing the chain reaction. As the rods are raised, fewer neutrons are absorbed and the chain reaction can proceed. By positioning the control rods at just the right level, the stopping, starting, and speed of a chain reaction can be controlled.

Do You Know?
A sample of uranium 235 the size of a golf ball can provide the same amount of energy as more than 500,000 liters of oil.

How much uranium is there on Earth? Scientists predict that if nuclear-fission reactors become widely used, the uranium supply could be used up in about a hundred years. The answer to this problem may be the **breeder reactor.** In a breeder reactor, plutonium 239 is produced from the fission of uranium. The plutonium can also be used as a fuel. In this way, the uranium supply could be made to last longer. However, plutonium fuel is especially dangerous to work with. So far, this problem has prevented any large-scale use of breeder reactors.

As with other energy sources, there are concerns about nuclear energy. Since radioactivity is involved, extreme care must be taken to insure the safety of people and the environment. Protection systems and back-up systems must be designed, thoroughly tested, and used.

The waste products of nuclear reactors are radioactive. These wastes will remain radioactive for thousands of years. How and where can they be safely discarded? Many people are concerned about the safety of radioactive waste dumps. Scientists and engineers are working on a solution to this problem.

Figure 22.11 The control room of a nuclear power plant

Enormous amounts of heat are involved in the production of nuclear energy. Water from a lake or river near a nuclear reactor is often used to absorb and take away excess heat. This practice raises the temperature of the water and the land around it. This unnatural increase in temperature is called **thermal** [THUR-muhl] **pollution.** Thermal pollution can damage or destroy plant and animal life.

Scientists are working on ways to produce useful energy from nuclear fusion. One kind of fusion reaction involves an isotope of hydrogen having one proton and one neutron. This isotope is called **deuterium** [doo-TIHR-ee-uhm]. The oceans contain a large supply of deuterium. The fusion of deuterium produces no radioactive wastes. It releases a large amount of energy. With the supply of deuterium plentiful, why isn't fusion energy being used?

For deuterium to undergo fusion, it must be in the plasma state. This state requires temperatures of many millions of degrees Celsius. Such a condition exists naturally on the sun but is very difficult to produce and control here on Earth. Scientists at the Princeton Plasma Physics Laboratory have succeeded in producing the plasma state in their experimental fusion reactor. Researchers at Princeton and elsewhere are making progress in the development of fusion energy.

Another problem with fusion energy is that a nuclear-fusion reactor becomes highly radioactive. It would require very expensive shielding to protect the environment. As a result, even the most optimistic scientists agree that it will be many years before a practical fusion reactor is built and operating.

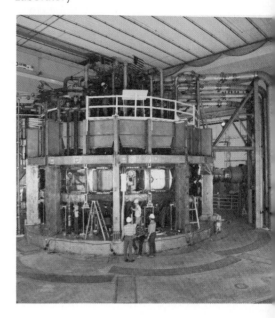

Figure 22.12 The fusion test reactor at the Princeton Plasma Physics Laboratory

Do You Know?
It has been estimated that there is enough deuterium in one cubic meter of seawater to produce an amount of energy equal to the energy produced from 1,500 barrels of oil.

Study Questions for 22.2

1. How is fission used to generate electricity?
2. Why are control rods important?
3. Name two problems that are associated with nuclear reactors.
4. What difficult problems do scientists face in designing fusion reactors?

22.3 Energy Conservation

You will find out
- why energy conservation is necessary;
- what is being done to conserve energy.

Scientists are exploring the oceans and examining data from satellites in their search for sources of energy. As present supplies of fossil and nuclear fuels are used, new supplies are needed. Fossil and nuclear fuels are **nonrenewable.** Something that is nonrenewable cannot be replaced. If you cut down a tree, you can plant a seed to grow a new tree. You can replace, or renew the tree. But if you burn coal or use uranium as a nuclear fuel, you have no way of replacing that coal or uranium.

The energy from fossil and nuclear fuels is becoming more and more expensive. This fact, together with the understanding that these fuels are nonrenewable, has made people realize they can't afford to waste energy.

Only a little more than a third of the energy from the fuel in an electric power plant is used to produce electricity. The rest of the energy is lost in the form of heat. Scientists and engineers are working on ways to reduce these energy losses. They are also trying to develop ways to use the energy that is lost.

Figure 22.13 Coal, like all other fossil fuels, is a nonrenewable resource.

ACTIVITY

Materials
meterstick
pencil
paper

Do You Have Too Many Windows?

Procedure

1. Copy the chart and use it to record your measurements and calculations.

2. Windows can account for a significant amount of heat loss. To see how much heat may be lost from your classroom, calculate the area of the classroom floor and of each window in the room. To calculate area, measure the length and width of the floor or window. Then multiply the two numbers together.

3. Find the total window area by adding together the area of each window in the room.

Questions

1. Experts have devised a formula that tells whether a large amount of heat could be lost through the windows of a room. Apply this formula to your classroom data.

$$\frac{\text{total window area}}{\text{floor area}} \times 100 = ?\%$$

2. The higher the percentage calculated from the formula above, the greater the potential for heat loss from the room. What steps could be taken to compensate for a large potential for heat loss?

3. Repeat the procedure for a room in your home and apply the formula in question 1 to your data for that room.

	Length (m)	Width (m)	Area (m²)
Floor			
Window A			
Window B			

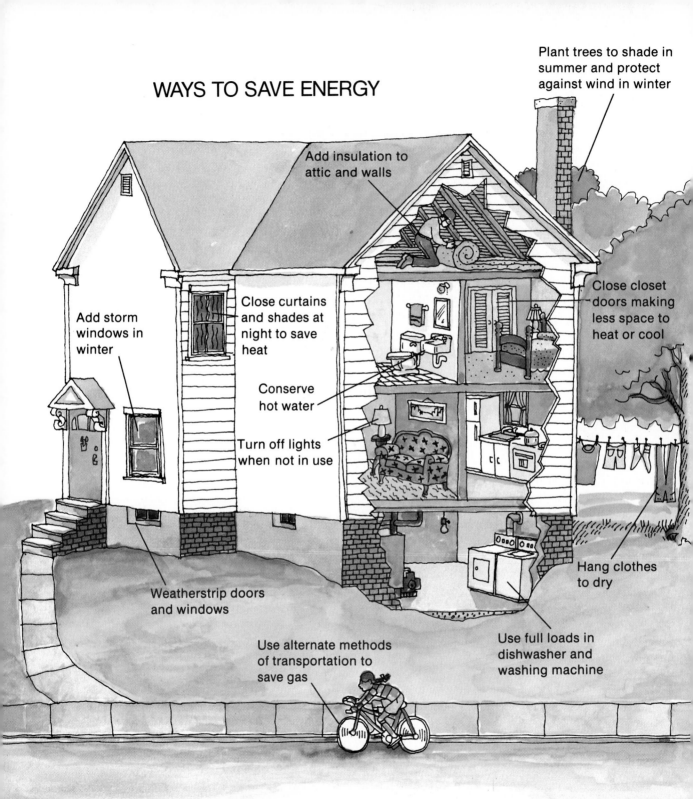

WAYS TO SAVE ENERGY

Plant trees to shade in summer and protect against wind in winter

Add insulation to attic and walls

Close closet doors making less space to heat or cool

Add storm windows in winter

Close curtains and shades at night to save heat

Conserve hot water

Turn off lights when not in use

Weatherstrip doors and windows

Hang clothes to dry

Use alternate methods of transportation to save gas

Use full loads in dishwasher and washing machine

Figure 22.14 Some cities have constructed special bicycle lanes, promoting the use of bicycles to save gasoline.

Government laws and recommendations encourage energy conservation. The highway speed limit is set at 88 kilometers per hour (55 mph) because higher speeds cause more energy to be wasted. The temperatures in government and public buildings are restricted to no more than 20°C in winter and no less than 25.5°C in summer. These restrictions cut down on the energy used for heating and air conditioning. Tax cuts have been made available to people who spend money to conserve energy in their homes.

Homeowners have discovered many ways to conserve energy. This conservation saves them money. Insulating a home keeps it warmer in the winter and cooler in the summer. Energy and money are saved. If the attic floor of a house has good insulation, and weather stripping, storm windows, and storm doors are used, fuel bills can be cut by up to 50 percent. Electric lights and appliances that were once carelessly left on are now being turned off when not needed. Also, energy-efficient appliances are now available.

Do You Know?
Most cars get about 21 percent better mileage at 8 km/h (55 mph) than at 113 km/h (70 mph).

Study Questions for 22.3

1. Why is energy conservation necessary?
2. How is energy waste being reduced?

What Did You Learn?

- Fossil fuels are formed from the remains of plants and animals that lived millions of years ago.
- Coal is obtained through shaft mining and strip mining.
- Oil is found in underground pools, tar sands, and oil shale.
- Natural gas is often cooled and compressed to form a liquid, called liquified natural gas.
- The burning of fossil fuels releases particles and unhealthy compounds such as carbon monoxide and sulfur and nitrogen oxides.
- The transportation of fossil fuels can damage the environment.
- Fossil fuels are being used up much more quickly than they are forming.
- A nuclear power plant uses the energy released from fission to produce steam that is used to generate electricity.
- The position of the control rods in a nuclear reactor controls the starting, stopping, and speed of the chain reaction.
- In a breeder reactor, uranium produces plutonium fuel.
- The protection of people and the environment from the radioactivity and thermal pollution associated with nuclear power plants is a serious problem.
- Scientists are making progress in the development of fusion reactors.
- Fossil and nuclear fuels are nonrenewable.
- The energy from fossil and nuclear fuels is becoming more and more expensive.
- Energy conservation is being encouraged and practiced at the governmental and the individual level.

Key Terms
fossil fuels
shaft mining
strip mining
tar sands
oil shale
acid rain
nuclear reactor
control rods
breeder reactor
thermal pollution
deuterium
nonrenewable

Biography

Chien–Shiung Wu (1912–   )

Chien–Shiung Wu is a well-known nuclear physicist. She has a keen understanding of the significance of theory in scientific research and a deep appreciation of the importance of experiments. Her methods and results are highly respected. One scientist said of her, "She has never made a mistake in her measurements."

Chien–Shiung Wu was born in China, near Shanghai. Her father, principal of the local school, encouraged Chien-Shiung to read about any subjects that interested her. After graduating from the National Central University in Nanking, China, she came to the United States to continue her studies. She earned her doctor's degree in physics from the University of California in 1940.

During World War II, Dr. Wu went to Columbia University in New York to work on the secret Manhattan Project for the development of the atom bomb. After the war she stayed at Columbia and continued her work in nuclear physics. Her reputation as a good experimenter grew.

In 1956, two young Chinese scientists, Dr. T. D. Lee and Dr. C. N. Yang, came to Dr. Wu with a new theory that

they wanted to test. The theory questioned one of the basic laws of nuclear physics. Dr. Wu and her co-workers proved that Lee and Yang were right. The news shocked physicists all over the world. This kind of work shows that science is always growing and changing. As Dr. Wu told a group of young science students, "It is the courage to doubt what has long been established . . . that has pushed the wheel of science forward."

TO THINK ABOUT AND DO

Vocabulary

Number a piece of paper from 1 to 10. Beside the appropriate number write the letter for the term that is described.

1. the exposure and removal of surface coal
2. a rock containing oil
3. an unnatural increase in temperature
4. an isotope of hydrogen
5. a reactor that produces plutonium
6. fuel formed from the remains of dead plants and animals
7. something that controls chain reactions
8. that which describes an energy source that cannot be replaced
9. that which is formed from sulfur and nitrogen oxides
10. a combination of oil and sand

a. nonrenewable
b. oil shale
c. deuterium
d. tar sands
e. breeder reactor
f. strip mining
g. thermal pollution
h. fossil fuel
i. shaft mining
j. control rods
k. acid rain
l. nuclear reactor

What Do You Remember?

1. In what position are the control rods of a nuclear reactor when the chain reaction is stopped?
2. How does strip mining affect the environment?
3. What problem may be solved by the use of breeder reactors?
4. How were fossil fuels formed?
5. What problem exists concerning the waste products of nuclear reactors?
6. How are fission and fusion different?
7. How can homeowners conserve energy?
8. How do prospectors locate oil?
9. How does the burning of fossil fuels affect the air you breathe?
10. What is a nonrenewable energy source?

Applying What You Have Learned

1. How would you describe a perfect energy source?
2. How is the energy in fossil fuels related to the energy of the sun?
3. People in the United States first used wood to heat their homes. Coal was used at the beginning of this century. Now people rely on oil and natural gas. Experts estimate that it takes approximately 50 years for the public to change from one energy source to another. Can you explain why this is so?

Research and Investigation

1. Throughout history, people have relied on many different energy sources. How many can you name? Give an example of how each energy source is or was used.
2. Do research and report on the dangers involved in shaft mining.

Energy Alternatives

23

The perfect energy source would be cheap, plentiful, efficient, easy to use, and would not cause pollution. Is there such an energy source? Maybe not, but there are things in the environment that do supply energy without showing signs of ever running out. What gives off heat and light every day? What causes a sailboat to move over the water? How does a raft get downstream?

People have used energy from the sun, wind, and water for centuries. Before the extensive use of fossil and nuclear fuels, these sources of energy were very important. Now the problems associated with fossil and nuclear fuels are becoming better known. As a result, people are beginning to think about using other energy sources.

In this chapter you will find out how the sun, the wind, and water are being used as sources of energy. You will also learn about other energy sources that are minor now but might become more important in the future.

Figure 23.1 An apartment building that has been modified to use solar energy

23.1 Solar Energy

You will find out
- why people are interested in solar energy;
- what devices are being used to collect solar energy;
- how solar energy can be used.

The idea of using energy from the sun, or **solar energy,** to answer people's energy needs is not a new one. Solar energy has been used to dry and bake foods for centuries. In the early 1600's, a French inventor reportedly used solar energy to heat air in an engine that pumped water. The Pueblo Indians built their homes out of adobe, a mixture of mud and sand. The adobe absorbed heat from the sun during the day and gave off that heat at night. Clearly, use of solar energy is not new. What is new, however, is an increasing and intensified interest in solar energy.

Why are people suddenly so interested in solar energy and other energy alternatives? They have come to recognize that while fossil and nuclear fuels can and do effectively answer their energy needs, these fuels are nonrenewable. They are also becoming more and more expensive. In addition, the use of fossil and nuclear fuels

Figure 23.2 The walls of these adobe homes absorb solar heat during the day and release that heat at night.

Figure 23.3 A solar home

creates some serious environmental problems. The question people are asking now is whether there is another energy source that could answer their energy needs without presenting the same serious problems. Many people believe that solar energy is the answer or, at least, part of the answer.

Solar energy is a **renewable** energy source. A renewable energy source is one that can be replaced. Every day the earth receives an enormous amount of solar energy. The use of solar energy does not appear to threaten the environment. Scientists and engineers are working on ways to collect, store, and change solar energy into other forms of usable energy. As ways to do these things become more practical, efficient, and affordable, more businesses and individual home owners are choosing to use solar energy.

The simplest way to use solar energy to heat a building is to allow sunlight in through windows or glass panels. If you have ever entered a car that had been closed up while sitting in the sun, you have surely noticed the results of this kind of solar heating. The temperature of a greenhouse can also be dramatically affected in the same way. This use of solar energy, while simple and relatively inexpensive, only affects areas that receive direct sunlight.

Do You Know?
If the sun's energy came from coal, it would shine at its present brightness for less than 5,000 years. By that time, all the coal would have been burned up.

Scientists have devised ways to collect solar energy in one area of a building and carry it to other areas. **Solar collectors** collect and change solar energy into heat energy. These devices are positioned on a building in a place that allows for maximum exposure to sunlight. Some can even be moved or tilted to follow the sun. Many collectors are flat metal plates painted black. They are painted black because a dark surface absorbs solar energy better than a light one. Water or air passing in pipes behind the plates is heated. The warm water or air is then pumped to places where it is needed. The same water or air can be used over and over to absorb and transport heat. Other solar collectors have curved mirrors that direct sunlight onto tanks or pipes carrying water or air. Like the flat plates, the tanks and pipes are often painted black for better absorption of solar energy.

Solar cells are used to collect solar energy and change it into electric energy. These devices are used on spaceflights. Large panels covered with thousands of solar cells provide electric power for the spacecraft. On Earth, solar cells are in use in homes and businesses. However, they are not in widespread use. One reason for this is the current high cost of making and installing the cells.

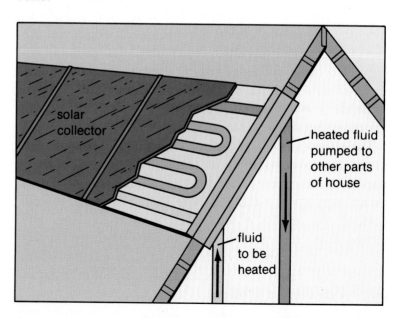

Figure 23.4 Using solar collectors in a solar home

Buildings using solar cells or solar collectors or both exist today. It is probable that more will be built in the future. However, the conversion of already existing buildings to solar energy is not realistic in most cases due to the expense involved. Also, most existing buildings are not located or positioned for maximum exposure to sunlight. Still, the use of solar energy to answer the energy needs of a single building is growing.

ACTIVITY

How Can You Make a Solar Collector?

Materials

shoe box
newspaper
black spray paint
rubber or plastic
    tubing with a
    small opening
    (about 1 m)
funnel to fit
    into tubing
tape
plastic wrap
2 beakers
graduated cylinder
thermometer

Procedure

1. Half fill the shoe box with crumpled newspaper. Spray paint on the newspaper and the inside of the box.

2. Punch a hole wide enough for the tubing at each end of the box. Arrange the tubing as shown in the diagram. Tape it in place. Cover the box tightly with plastic wrap.

3. Put 100 mL of water in a beaker. Measure and record the temperature of the water.

4. Place the box in direct sunlight. Rest one end on a thin book to slightly tilt the box. Set an empty beaker under the lower end of the tubing. Insert the funnel into the other end.

5. Pour the water into the funnel. Allow it to flow through the tubing and collect in the empty beaker.

6. Repeat step 5 fifteen times. After every fifth trial, measure and record the temperature of the water and the trial number.

Questions

1. Make a line graph to show the temperatures you measured.

2. How does the water temperature change?

3. How could you make your solar collector produce hotter water?

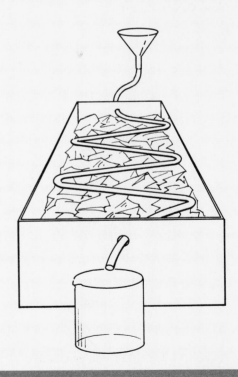

Figure 23.5 Collecting solar energy in a New Mexico desert

What about using solar energy on a larger scale to provide electricity, not just for a single home, but for a whole community? The problem here is that the sun's energy, although plentiful, is spread out over an enormous area. Suppose solar cells were being used to produce as much electricity as the amount currently being produced in the United States by other means. Experts estimate that this would require solar cells covering from 25,000 to 70,000 square kilometers of land! Where is there an area of land this size that is available? Not any area of land will do. The land must receive a consistently large amount of solar energy.

The most appropriate areas for collecting solar energy in large amounts are in the desert areas of the world near the equator. Within the United States, the desert areas of Arizona and New Mexico are most appropriate. However, the use of large areas of these states to collect solar energy would probably conflict with other interests.

Experts have suggested two possible ways to collect solar energy without taking over large land areas. One way would be to construct solar collection stations in ocean areas. The second way is to use solar collection satellites. As a satellite orbited Earth, the satellite would receive a constant, reliable supply of solar energy. This energy could then be sent down to Earth.

As the use of solar energy grows and is further investigated, more practical and effective applications of it will be developed. Although it does not seem to have a negative effect on the environment, there is a possibility that the widespread use of solar energy might bring about some change in the overall distribution of heat from the sun. However, at the present time, solar energy does appear to be a promising energy alternative. People should also remember that once they have paid the price for the purchase and installation of solar energy devices, the sunlight is free.

Figure 23.6 A solar music box

Study Questions for 23.1

1. What makes solar energy a desirable energy source?
2. What is a solar collector?
3. What is a solar cell?
4. What problem has prevented the use of solar energy to produce electricity for whole communities rather than single buildings?

23.2   Energy from Water

You will find out
- how hydroelectric power is produced;
- how hydroelectric power is related to solar energy;
- why hydroelectric power is not more widely used;
- how tidal energy is used.

For years people have used moving water to carry logs downriver to sawmills and paper mills. Rivers have also moved rafts of goods and people from place to place. The major application of moving water as an energy source, however, has been in the generation of electricity. When falling water strikes the blades of a turbine, a rotational motion is produced. This motion is used to generate electricity. The electricity generated by the use of moving water is called **hydroelectric power.**

Figure 23.7 Falling water can be used to generate electricity.

Do You Know?
One of the earliest hydroelectric power plants was built in Niagara Falls, New York, in 1896.

In order to produce hydroelectric power at a steady rate, the water in rivers is dammed up to make waterfalls. The largest hydroelectric power plant in the United States is at the Grand Coulee Dam across the Columbia River in the state of Washington. Although many states in the United States have hydroelectric power plants, the most productive ones are in Washington, Oregon, and California.

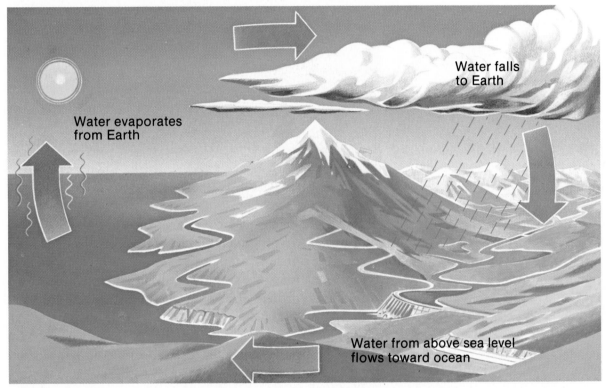

Figure 23.8 The water cycle

Hydroelectric power is related to solar energy. The sun heats water and causes it to evaporate from the surface of the earth. That water eventually falls back to the earth as rain or snow. If the water falls on a place that is above sea level, it runs downhill. It may eventually enter a river and flow to the ocean. While in a river, that water may be used to produce hydroelectric power. As long as there is sunlight to evaporate water so that it can fall back to earth and form rivers, the production of hydroelectric power will be possible.

Figure 23.9 A hydroelectric power plant at the Bonneville Dam on the Columbia River in the state of Washington

Hydroelectric power is renewable and does not cause pollution. Why, then, is it not more widely used? Not all rivers are appropriate for the production of hydroelectric power. Also, the damming up of rivers causes drastic changes in the environment. Plant and animal life both in and along a river are threatened. In some areas, plans for hydroelectric power plants have been considered and finally canceled due to environmental concerns.

Many of the world's large rivers are in undeveloped areas of South America, Africa, and Asia. The potential for hydroelectric power in these areas is high. But, so far, the countries with that potential have not made use of it.

Another kind of energy that involves water is **tidal energy.** Gravitational forces involving the earth, the sun, and the moon cause ocean tides. Tidewaters can be used to turn turbines that generate electricity. The Rance tidal power plant in France has been producing electricity since 1966.

Tidal energy is renewable and does not cause pollution. However, the tidal areas that are involved may suffer some of the same changes in their environment as the river areas around hydroelectric power plants. This problem has limited the development of tidal power plants. Another limiting factor is the availability of coastline areas that are suitable for tidal power plants. A suitable coastline would be a narrow bay or inlet where there is a great difference in the water levels at high and low tides.

Figure 23.10 The Rance tidal power plant

Study Questions for 23.2

1. How is hydroelectric power produced?
2. What is the relationship between hydroelectric power and solar energy?
3. How do the dams associated with hydroelectric power plants affect the environment?
4. How is tidal energy used?

23.3 Wind and Other Sources of Energy

You will find out
- how wind energy is used;
- what is meant by geothermal energy;
- what is meant by biomass.

The wind is a source of energy that people have been using for centuries. Wind once filled the sails of ocean-going ships. It also turned windmills to grind grain and pump water.

Wind is the movement of masses of air from one place to another. This movement is the result of temperature differences in the atmosphere. The temperature differences come from uneven heating of the atmosphere by the sun. Wind energy, like solar energy, is a renewable energy source. Also like solar energy, the use of wind energy does not appear to threaten the environment.

Today, windmills are being used to generate electricity. The blades of a windmill act like a turbine. Wind strikes the blades, causing them to turn. This rotational motion is used to generate electricity.

Figure 23.11 *left:* Wind results when warmer, less dense air rises and cooler, denser air moves in to replace it. *right:* Using wind energy to generate electricity

In some areas, one windmill provides the electricity for a single home or business. In other areas, a large number of windmills generate enough electricity to service many homes or businesses. There is, of course, one obvious limitation to the large-scale use of windmills to generate electricity. Many areas do not receive enough wind on a regular basis to make windmills practical.

ACTIVITY

How Can You Measure Wind Speed?

Materials
protractor
long needle
thread
Ping-Pong ball
wood (30 cm by 2 cm)
glue

Procedure

1. Make a handle by gluing the wood to the corner of the protractor at the 180° mark.

2. Thread the needle and push it through the Ping-Pong ball. Pull the thread through the ball and tie a knot at one end.

3. Glue the free end of the thread to the center of the straight side of the protractor. When the protractor is held level, the thread and ball should hang at exactly 90°.

4. Use your device to measure the wind speed in five different areas near your school. Compare the protractor reading in degrees with those on the chart to determine approximate wind speed.

Questions

1. Make a bar graph to show the wind speed in the areas you visited.

2. To be useful in generating electricity, wind must have a constant speed of at least 13 km/h. Could the wind in any of the areas you visited be used to generate electricity?

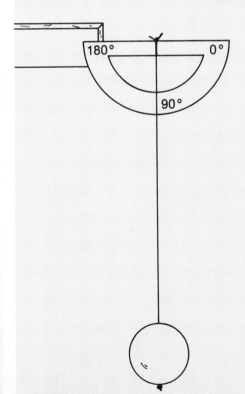

Angle	km/h
90°	0
80°	13
70°	19
60°	24
50°	29
40°	34
30°	42
20°	52

The interior of the earth is very hot. This fact may surprise you since people generally find basements and underground caves cool or even cold. However, this situation exists only in areas very near the earth's surface. If, for example, you were to go way down in the shaft of a deep coal mine, you would find it hot.

The high temperatures inside the earth can heat underground water supplies. This hot water and the steam it produces may come to or near the surface. It may erupt forcefully in geysers or flow into pools known as hot springs. The heat energy that comes from inside the earth is called **geothermal** [JEE-oh-thur-muhl] **energy.** Steam from geothermal energy can be used to spin turbines to generate electricity. Geothermal energy can also heat buildings and even cook food.

Geothermal energy is renewable and does not appear to seriously threaten the environment. However, the waters in geysers and hot springs do contain many minerals. In significant amounts, the distribution of these minerals could affect the environment.

Only certain locations are appropriate for the use of geothermal energy. Those areas have geysers or hot springs at or near the earth's surface. The Lardello area

Do You Know?
The steam wells tapped by The Geysers power plant are 2.5 km deep.

Figure 23.12 The Geysers power plant uses geothermal energy to generate electricity.

Figure 23.13 Wood, a form of biomass, is a renewable energy source.

of Italy has been using geothermal energy since 1904. Many areas of Iceland also rely on geothermal energy. In the United States, The Geysers power plant in California has been using geothermal energy since 1960.

Living things provide an energy source called **biomass** [BY-oh-mas]. Biomass includes all the materials in living things, their wastes, and their remains. Probably the most obvious use of energy from biomass is the burning of wood for heat. Other kinds of plant material can also be burned. In addition, efforts have been made to use garbage and other wastes for fuel.

Biomass is a renewable energy source. As long as there are living things there will be biomass. However, the burning of biomass does contribute to air pollution. Also, the careless cutting down of thousands of trees can drastically change the environment. Even if new trees are planted, it takes many years for them to grow. In the meantime, the area may lose topsoil due to the action of wind and running water. Food and shelter for animals are also lost when trees are cut down.

Study Questions for 23.3

1. How is wind energy used?
2. What is geothermal energy?
3. What is biomass?

What Did You Learn?

- Solar energy is renewable and does not appear to threaten the environment.
- Solar collectors collect and change solar energy into heat energy.
- Solar cells collect and change solar energy into electric energy.
- There are buildings today that use solar energy for heating and electric power.
- The electricity generated by the use of moving water is called hydroelectric power.
- To produce hydroelectric power, rivers are dammed up to make waterfalls.
- Hydroelectric power is related to solar energy.
- The dams involved in the production of hydroelectric power cause drastic environmental changes.
- Tidal energy can be used to generate electricity.
- Wind energy can be used to generate electricity.
- Geothermal energy is heat energy that comes from inside the earth.
- Geothermal energy can be used to generate electricity and to heat buildings.
- Biomass includes all the materials in living things, their wastes, and their remains.

Key Terms

solar energy
renewable
solar collectors
solar cells
hydroelectric power
tidal energy
geothermal energy
biomass

Career

Environmental Engineer

An environmental engineer studies the effects of human activity on the environment and develops methods to protect the environment. An environmental engineer may work in one or more of three general areas: air quality management, water quality management, or land reclamation. Land reclamation involves the restoration of an area that has been damaged by things such as strip mining, floods, or fire.

An example of the work of environmental engineers in the area of land reclamation can be seen at the Big Sky Mine in Montana. The Big Sky Mine was a strip mining operation. The land that was scraped away to gain access to the coal below has been shaped into rolling hills and seeded with oats, alfalfa, and a mixture of native grasses.

Some environmental engineers who work for industry design systems that reduce air and water pollution. For example, they may work to produce automobile engines that are less polluting. Or they may design ways to dispose of industrial wastes without contaminating water supplies.

Environmental engineers working for the government or other institutions may study the pollutants produced by industry or transportation. Or they may be called upon to study the expected harm to the environment of some new energy system, such as a large dam or mining operation.

The solution to environmental problems requires the skills and experience of people who know about health, sanitation, physics, chemistry, biology, meteorology, engineering, and many other fields. The energy systems you may take for granted have limitations and disadvantages as well as advantages. Many environmental engineers will be needed in the future to cope with the problems and maximize the advantages of all energy systems.

TO THINK ABOUT AND DO

Vocabulary

Number your paper from 1 to 10. Read each of the following sentences. If the sentence is true, write *true*. If it is false, make it true by changing the underlined term.

1. Solar collectors collect and change solar energy to electric energy.
2. The electricity generated with the use of moving water is called turbine power.
3. The generation of geothermal power requires the building of dams.
4. Wind energy and hydroelectric power are related to solar energy.
5. The use of tidal energy does not appear to threaten the environment.
6. Large land areas must be used in order to collect large amounts of solar energy.
7. The most obvious example of the use of energy from biomass is the burning of coal.
8. Solar cells collect and change solar energy to heat energy.
9. Geysers and hot springs contain geothermal energy.
10. The power plant at the Grand Coulee Dam produces hydroelectric power.

What Do You Remember?

1. Why are people interested in energy alternatives to fossil and nuclear fuels?
2. Name two ways a house can use solar energy.
3. Why are solar collectors usually painted black?
4. What is the difference between a renewable and a nonrenewable energy source?
5. Name three energy sources that do not appear to threaten the environment.
6. Name three energy sources that can be used to generate electricity.
7. What has limited the production of hydroelectricity?

Applying What You Have Learned

1. With all the sources of energy available on Earth, why do you think there is an energy crisis?
2. What kind of energy would you associate with lava from a volcano?
3. How is solar energy related to energy from biomass?
4. What source of energy do you associate with each of the following?
   (a) Hoover Dam in Nevada
   (b) a forest fire
   (c) Old Faithful in Yellowstone National Park
   (d) keeping a room cool by closing the drapes during the day
   (e) Skylab
   (f) a kite
5. How are fossil fuels and biomass related?

Research and Investigation

1. Make a map of the world. Indicate on the map geothermal hot spots and large rivers that could be used to produce hydroelectric power.
2. Two modern wind machines are the Savonius Rotor and the Helix Rotor. How are these machines different from ordinary windmills?

The Universe 24

What is the structure of the universe? How big is it? Are all the objects in the universe moving? Where are they going? These and many other related questions have been asked again and again over hundreds of years. The ancient Egyptians believed the sun was carried across the sky in a boat. An ancient Hindu myth explains that the universe came from an egg. One half of the egg was gold. It became the heavens. The other half of the egg was silver. It became the earth.

As time went by, some of the questions about the universe were answered, or partly answered. Others are still mysteries. In this chapter, you will find out how the scientific method and many of the principles of physical science have helped to answer some of the questions about the universe. You will also learn of questions that remain unanswered. Some of these questions may be answered as people venture out into one of the few remaining frontiers, the space frontier.

24.1 Investigating the Universe

You will find out
- how astronomers study the universe;
- what tools astronomers use.

Imagine that you want to study a very deep canyon. But the sides are so steep and the canyon is so deep that you cannot possibly climb down into it. How could you find out about the canyon? You could use instruments to make observations. You could send devices down to collect samples of the materials in the canyon and study the samples. You could compare your observations of the canyon with information about other canyons that are more accessible. You would have to piece together all these kinds of information to form an accurate picture of the canyon.

Scientists who study the universe, or **astronomers,** are faced with a similar challenge. They are studying objects and occurrences that they cannot visit or witness personally. They must study the universe the same way you would have to study the bottom of your imaginary canyon. To do this, astronomers use information gathered from many different sources.

Figure 24.2 *left:* Stonehenge, an ancient structure related to astronomical studies and observations; *right:* The modern complex at the Kitt Peak National Observatory in Arizona

You have already heard of one of the oldest and most important tools of astronomy. That tool is the telescope. Modern telescopes allow astronomers to carefully observe objects in the universe and monitor their motion. Some telescopes can pick up radio waves and other forms of radiation given off by objects in space. Information from telescopes continues to be very useful to astronomers.

ACTIVITY

What Is the Diameter of the Sun?

Materials
2 index cards
pin
meterstick
metric ruler
tape

Procedure

1. Label the index cards A and B. Use a pin to poke a hole in the center of card A.

2. Draw a square in the center of card B. The sides of the square should be 0.5 cm long.

3. Tape card A at the 20 cm mark on the meterstick as in the diagram.

4. Stand with your back to the sun. Hold the meterstick in one hand so that the sunlight shines directly on card A. Hold card B about 10 cm behind card A. Move card B slowly back and forth until a circle of light appears in the square on it. Measure the distance in centimeters between cards A and B when the circle appears in the square.

Questions

1. How far was card B from card A when the sun's image appeared in the square?

2. To find the diameter of the sun in kilometers, divide your answer from question 1 into 74,800,000.

3. The diameter of the earth is 12,640 km. How much larger in diameter is the sun?

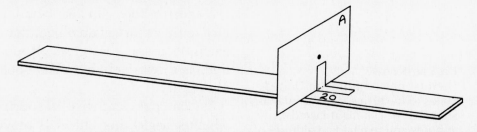

Figure 24.3 Astronauts and satellites have gathered large amounts of new information about the universe. *left:* An astronaut walks on the moon; *right:* A photograph of Jupiter taken from *Voyager*

Another important tool of astronomy is the **spectroscope** [SPEHK-truh-skohp]. A spectroscope is used to study the different wavelengths of light given off by a glowing object. It is known that different elements give off different wavelengths of light. By studying the light given off by glowing objects in space, astronomers can tell what elements are present in them.

A spectroscope can also be used to determine the surface temperature of an object that is giving off light. For example, a star that gives off more blue light than red light is a relatively hot star. Cooler stars give off more red light.

Astronomers can use a spectroscope to determine whether a glowing object is moving away from or toward the earth and how fast it is moving. For example, the light given off by a moving star may shift to include more of the longer red wavelengths. This is an indication that the star is moving away from the earth. The greater this shift to more red wavelengths, the faster the star is moving.

All the information astronomers have to work with has not been gathered from observations made only from Earth. The voyages of satellites, space probes, and the space shuttle have provided large amounts of new information. This information has been gathered by astronauts, cameras, and many specialized instruments.

Astronomers do not arrive at all their conclusions through direct observation and measurement alone. They apply the laws of gravitation, electricity, magnetism, nuclear reactions, and other principles of physical science to those observations and measurements. Then, following the steps of the scientific method, they develop theories to explain their observations and measurements. Thanks to recent advances in technology, astronomers can now call on computers to help them in their analysis of information about the universe.

Table 24–1 Milestones in Space Travel

Spacecraft	Launch Date	Length of Flight	Milestone
Vostok 1	April 12, 1961	1.8 h	First person in space
Freedom 7	May 5, 1961	15 min	First person from the U.S. in space
Friendship 7	Feb. 20, 1962	4.9 h	First person from the U.S. to orbit the earth
Vostok 6	June 16, 1963	70.8 h	First woman in space
Gemini 4	June 3, 1965	97.9 h	First person from the U.S. to walk in space
Apollo 11	July 16, 1969	195 h	First persons to walk on the moon
Skylab 1	May 25, 1973	672.7 h	First persons to travel in an earth-orbiting space station
Apollo-Soyuz Test Project	July 15, 1975	Apollo—216 h Soyuz—144 h	First cooperative space flight between the U.S. and the U.S.S.R.
Space Shuttle Columbia	April 12, 1981	54.4 h	First flight of a reusable spacecraft

Study Questions for 24.1

1. How do astronomers study the universe?
2. Name two important tools of astronomy.

You will find out
- how astronomers have determined the life cycle of stars;
- what some of the stages are in the life cycle of stars;
- what astronomers believe about black holes and quasars.

Stars are large masses of gases that give off energy. The closest star to the earth is the sun. Even so, the sun is 150 million kilometers away! The sun and all other stars pass through different stages. These stages are often referred to as the life cycle of stars.

Unlike the relatively short life cycles of living things on Earth, the life cycles of stars cover millions or even billions of years! Certainly no astronomer has been alive long enough to observe the life cycle of a particular star. How, then, can astronomers understand the sequence of stages in the life cycle of a star?

Figure 24.4 A painting of the laboratory of Tycho Brahe, a 16th-century Danish astronomer who analyzed the positions of more than 777 stars without the aid of a telescope

Figure 24.5 The McMath Solar Telescope at Kitt Peak is 30 meters high and extends 90 meters into the ground. It is specially designed to study the star nearest to Earth, the sun.

To understand the methods astronomers use to piece together a life cycle that covers millions of years, imagine that you are on a brief visit to Earth from another planet. During your visit, you explore a forest. You see oak trees in all stages of development. You see acorns on the ground, young sprouts coming out of the ground, and small trees. You also see tall, fully grown trees, dying trees, and dead trees. Your visit isn't long enough to allow you to watch a single oak tree grow from an acorn to a fully grown tree and then die. But you see many trees in many different stages. Using the scientific method, you develop a theory about the life cycle of trees. In much the same way, astronomers have studied many stars and developed a theory about the life cycle of stars.

The life cycle of a star begins when it forms from a cloud of dust and gases. The cloud is made up mostly of hydrogen. When the cloud gets very dense, all its atoms are pulled together by gravitational forces. The cloud shrinks, or collapses. Its center becomes very hot. Its temperature reaches several million degrees Celsius. Individual atoms are separated into electrons and nuclei, forming a plasma. Nuclear fusion reactions begin. Hydrogen nuclei join together, forming helium nuclei. These reactions release enormous amounts of energy. The cloud is now a star.

ACTIVITY

Materials
colored pencils
graph paper

How Far Away Are the Stars?

Procedure

1. Study the chart and arrange the stars in order of their distance from the earth. (A light-year is the distance that light travels in one year. That distance is 9,461,000,000,000 km.)

2. Make a bar graph to illustrate how far each star is from the earth. The names of the stars should go across the bottom of the graph. The distance from the earth in light-years should go up the side of the graph.

Questions

1. Which star is closest to the earth?

2. Which star is farthest from the earth?

3. Are any stars equally distant from the earth?

4. Which star is about twice as far away as Alpha Centauri?

5. Which star is three times as far away as Spica?

6. Which star is about four times as far away as Sirius?

The 20 Brightest Stars	Distance from Earth in Light–Years
Sirius	8.8
Canopus	98
Alpha Centauri	4.3
Arcturus	36
Vega	26
Capella	46
Rigel	900
Procyon	11
Betelgeuse	490
Achernar	114
Beta Centauri	290
Altair	16
Alpha Crucis	390
Aldebaran	68
Spica	300
Antares	250
Pollux	35
Fomalhaut	23
Deneb	1,630
Beta Crucis	490

Fusion reactions continue in the star. As the hydrogen is used up in fusion, the center of the star collapses. At the same time, its outer layers expand. The overall diameter of the star increases a hundred or more times. At this stage, the star gives off mostly red light and is, therefore, called a **red giant.** The red-giant stage lasts several million years.

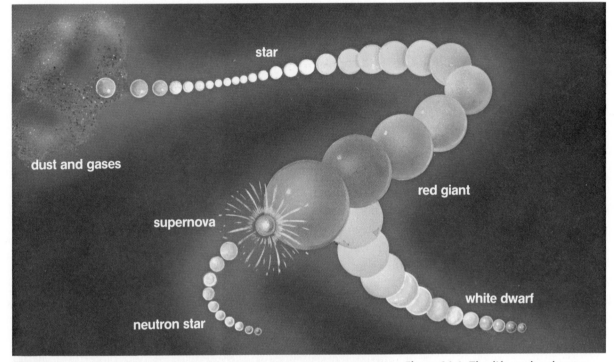

Figure 24.6 The life cycle of a star

Astronomers estimate that the sun will become a red giant in about five billion years. As a red giant, the sun's diameter would be so great that its outer surface would almost touch the earth! This situation would cause the earth's oceans to boil away!

What happens after the red-giant stage depends on the mass of the star. A star with a mass about equal to that of the sun will collapse to about the size of the earth. The result of this collapse is a very dense star called a **white dwarf.** The available hydrogen in a white dwarf is used up, so fusion reactions stop. No nuclear energy is released. However, white dwarfs are so hot that they glow for billions of years.

The events after the red-giant stage are different for a star that is much more massive than the sun. Such a star will have a violent explosion. The explosion of a massive red giant is called a **supernova.** In a supernova, the star's outer layers are blown into space.

The collapsed star left behind after a supernova is a **neutron star.** A neutron star is extremely dense. Its atoms are completely crushed. It is difficult to imagine just how dense neutron stars are. A ball of neutron-star material the size of a period on this page would have a mass of 40,000,000 kilograms!

Like the density of neutron stars, many other things in the universe are hard to imagine. For example, in the early 1970's astronomers found something they call Cygnus X-1. In Cygnus X-1, there seems to be a region in which gravity is so strong that nothing, not even light, can escape. Cygnus X-1 is called a **black hole.** Black holes are thought to be stars that have collapsed into a material that is so dense that its gravity allows nothing to escape. Since black holes allow no light to escape, they cannot be seen. Astronomers can only detect their existence by observing their gravitational influence on other objects.

Figure 24.7 This is an X-ray image of Cygnus X-1. The X rays are thought to be produced by hot gases falling into the black hole.

FIRST LIGHT
CYGNUS X-1 ENTERING HRI FOV
EXPOSURE = 164 SECONDS

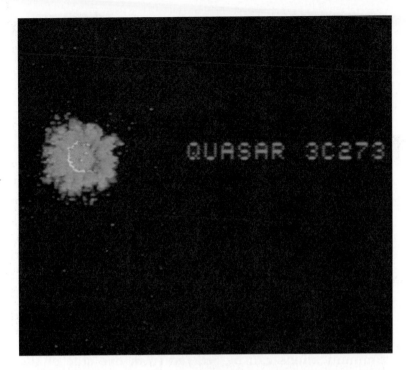

Figure 24.8 An X-ray image of a quasar

Astronomers discovered another unusual kind of object in space back in the early 1960's. These objects are called **quasars** [KWAY-zahrz]. Quasars appear to be extremely distant objects emitting radio waves, visible light waves, and X rays from a small area. This area may be associated with a very massive black hole. Quasars appear to be moving away from the earth at very high speeds. They also give off an amazingly large amount of energy. Astronomers are still puzzling over the source of this energy. Nuclear fusion reactions do not release enough energy to account for it. So far, this mystery remains one of the many unanswered questions about the universe.

Do You Know?
The term *quasar* is short for quasi-stellar radio source.

Study Questions for 24.2

1. How have astronomers pieced together the life cycle of stars?
2. Put the following stages in the life cycle of a star in order: red giant, neutron star, supernova, cloud of dust and gases.
3. What is Cygnus X-1?

24.3 The Space Frontier

You will find out
- how satellites are being used;
- what advantages there are to working in space;
- what space colonies might be like.

You are probably aware that the universe contains billions of objects and groups of objects such as stars, galaxies, comets, planets, and moons. But you are probably not consciously aware of most of these objects in your daily life. Your life centers mainly around one planet, the earth, and one star, the sun. However, many people believe that life could be very different in the future.

Things have been changing fast in recent years. People are now seriously thinking about venturing into space. Here on Earth, people are already benefiting from the use of satellites. Telephone and television communications can be relayed from one side of the earth to the other by satellites. Satellites equipped with telescopes and cameras gather information and relay it back to Earth. Such satellites are very useful in the study of weather patterns, air pollution, water and other natural resources, and movements of the earth's outer layer.

Figure 24.9 Information from satellites is used in making weather forecasts.

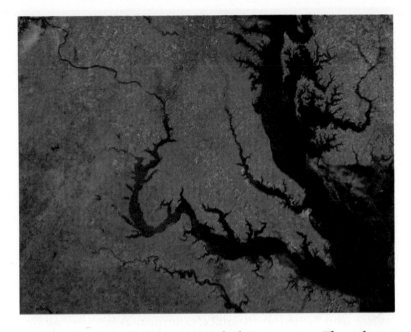

Figure 24.10 A satellite photograph of the Chesapeake Bay area of the United States

Already people have traveled in space. They have walked on the moon. So far, the main goal of such ventures has been to explore, experiment, and observe. However, many scientists believe that in the future people may venture into space not just to explore, but to actually live and work there. Groups of people living and working in space would form **space colonies.**

The limitations of working and living in space are obvious. A long list of essentials, including water and oxygen, would have to be supplied from Earth. Adjustments would have to be made for the absence of gravity. These and other practical aspects of life in a space colony pose many problems. Also, the funding of a space colony would require enormous amounts of money. Why, then, is anyone interested in space colonies? Many people are interested in them because there would be advantages to doing industrial and manufacturing work in space.

One advantage to doing work in space is the huge supply of solar energy available. In the United States, industry and manufacturing currently account for over 40 percent of the country's total energy consumption. The advantage to these businesses of a plentiful and relatively inexpensive energy source is obvious.

Many industrial and manufacturing processes require very high or very low temperatures. These temperatures are readily available in space. With the use of lenses and mirrors, solar energy could be concentrated to provide temperatures of thousands of degrees Celsius. Very cold temperatures are easy to come by in a space colony. The outside temperatures in places shielded from the sun would be lower than −200°C.

The materials used to make products such as electronic devices and drugs must be highly pure. Molecules and tiny particles in the air can affect that purity. To protect the purity of the materials involved, the products are made in a vacuum. It is expensive and difficult to produce a vacuum on Earth. A better vacuum exists naturally in space. And it is free.

The absence of gravity would pose problems to people living and working in space colonies. However, at the same time, it would be an advantage to the production of certain materials. It is easier to form many kinds of mixtures in the absence of gravity. The different substances in the mixture would stay evenly distributed. No substances would settle out.

Figure 24.11 An artist's conception of a space colony

Studies have shown that a new kind of steel, ten to a hundred times stronger than any made on Earth, could be made in space. One company has estimated that at least 400 new mixtures of metals could be produced in space. Mixtures of metals are used to make many kinds of machinery and equipment. The new and improved mixtures of metals would be very useful.

The absence of gravity and the vacuum that exists in space would make it possible to grow large, pure crystals. Such crystals could be used in computers, lasers, solar cells, and many other devices.

The advantages of a space environment to industry and manufacturing are significant. These advantages and a spirit of curiosity and adventure may eventually bring people into space colonies. Some scientists and engineers have even drawn up plans for space colonies. One popular design is a huge cylinder about 20 kilometers long and 10 kilometers in diameter. Another design details a doughnut-shaped structure of about the same size. An effective substitute for gravity could be produced by spinning the colony.

The planners suggest that the interiors of the space colonies could be landscaped with hills, valleys, water, whatever was desired. Weather could be controlled. The number of daylight hours could be controlled.

It is difficult to say whether people will ever live in space colonies. And, if they do, exactly what those colonies will be like is an unanswered question. But it is fun and useful to think about the frontier of space and the possibilities that exist. What may seem impossible or unbelievable now may some day be taken for granted. Remember, there was a time when people believed that the earth was flat and that no one would ever walk on the moon.

Do You Know?
In the absence of gravity, you would be two or three centimeters taller.

Study Questions for 24.3

1. How are satellites being used?
2. Give three advantages to doing industrial and manufacturing work in space.
3. How do some people think space colonies will be designed?

What Did You Learn?

- Astronomers use telescopes to observe objects and monitor their motion and to pick up radio waves and other forms of radiation given off by objects in space.
- A spectroscope can be used to study the surface temperature and the motion of objects in space.
- Astronomers develop theories by following the scientific method and applying the principles of physical science to the information they have gathered.
- Stars are large masses of gases that give off energy.
- Astronomers have studied many stars in many different stages and developed a theory about the life cycle of stars.
- Stars form from a cloud of dust and gases.
- Nuclear fusion reactions in stars release energy.
- A star with expanded outer layers that gives off mostly red light is called a red giant.
- A white dwarf is a collapsed red giant that glows for billions of years.
- The explosion of a massive red giant is a supernova.
- A neutron star is the collapsed star left behind after a supernova.
- A black hole is an object in which gravity is so strong that not even light can escape from it.
- Quasars appear to be extremely distant objects emitting radio waves, visible light waves, and X rays from a small area.
- Satellites are used to relay telephone and television communications and to gather information.
- There would be advantages to doing industrial and manufacturing work in space.
- Some scientists and engineers have drawn up plans for space colonies.

Key Terms

astronomers
spectroscope
stars
red giant
white dwarf
supernova
neutron star
black hole
quasars
space colonies

Biography

Beatrice Tinsley (1941–1981)

Beatrice Tinsley was an astronomer. In particular, she studied galaxies. She was interested in finding out how galaxies change as the stars in them change. Through her studies, Dr. Tinsley hoped to gain an understanding of what the future of the universe will be.

Early in her career, Dr. Tinsley had problems finding a permanent job. She had problems because it was difficult for a woman to get a permanent position at an astronomical observatory. She found a position at Yale University and remained there until her death.

While at Yale, Dr. Tinsley became a leader in her field. Just as important, she had a positive effect on the people she worked with. She took great joy in her own work and, at the same time, was interested in the work of others. She was happy and eager to help others with their work.

Dr. Tinsley became the Director of Graduate Studies at Yale. In this role she encouraged women to study science. Perhaps as a result of her work, Yale graduated several talented women scientists during the time that Dr. Tinsley was there.

TO THINK ABOUT AND DO

Vocabulary

Number your paper from 1 to 10. Beside each number write the word or words from the list that best complete each sentence.

1. Astronomers use a(an) _____ to study the different wavelengths of light given off by a glowing object.
2. _____ are large masses of gases that give off energy.
3. Cygnus X-1 is a(an) _____.
4. A(An) _____ is the explosion of a massive red giant.
5. Spectroscopes and telescopes are tools used by _____.
6. A large star that gives off mostly red light is called a(an) _____.
7. _____ appear to be extremely distant objects emitting radio waves, visible light waves, and X rays.
8. Many people believe that in the future people may live and work in _____.
9. A red giant with a mass equal to that of the sun will eventually collapse to form a(an) _____.
10. The collapsed star left behind after a supernova is called a(an) _____.

white dwarf
black hole
spectroscope
astronomers
neutron star
space colonies
supernova
red giant
stars
quasars

What Do You Remember?

1. How can astronomers tell what elements are present in a glowing object in space?
2. How does a star form?
3. What stage will follow the red-giant stage for a star the size of the sun?
4. How do astronomers detect black holes?
5. What information can be gathered by satellites?
6. Why are many people interested in space colonies?
7. Why would it be easier to make mixtures in the absence of gravity?

8. Why is it better to produce electronic devices in a vacuum?
9. What is a white dwarf?
10. How do astronomers develop theories about the universe?

Applying What You Have Learned

1. Why is the sun the only star that is visible during the day?
2. Imagine that you have discovered a new star. How will you study it?
3. The sun is the most important star in your life. What would the earth be like if the sun did not exist?
4. Do you think you would like living in a space colony? Why or why not?

Research and Investigation

1. People have always found comets interesting. Perhaps the most well-known comet is Halley's Comet. Write a report on Halley's Comet.
2. Report on the use of satellites in weather forecasting.

APPENDICES

SOME COMMONLY USED METRIC UNITS

LENGTH	meter (m) base unit	kilometer (km) 1,000 m = 1 km	centimeter (cm) 100 cm = 1 m	millimeter (mm) 1,000 mm = 1 m
MASS	gram (g) base unit	kilogram (kg) 1,000 g = 1 kg	centigram (cg) 100 cg = 1 g	milligram (mg) 1,000 mg = 1 g
VOLUME	liter (L) base unit	kiloliter (kL) 1,000 L = 1 kL	centiliter (cL) 100 cL = 1 L	milliliter (mL) 1,000 mL = 1 L cubic centimeter (cc) 1,000 cc = 1 L

You can easily convert from one metric unit to another by moving the decimal point to the right or the left a certain number of spaces. You can figure out how many spaces and which way to move the decimal point by studying the diagram and examples below. The diagram shows units of length. If you are working with units of mass or volume, simply substitute g or L for the m in each unit.

Example

How many km are in 837.0 m?
1. How many spaces from m is km and in what direction? three spaces to the left
2. Move the decimal point in 837.0 three spaces to the left.
3. 837.0 m = 0.8370 km

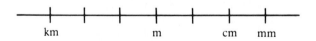

Example

How many mm are in 35.0 m?
1. How many spaces from m is mm and in what direction? three spaces to the right
2. Move the decimal point in 35.0 three spaces to the right.
3. 35.0 m = 35,000.0 mm

Example

How many mm are in 64.2 cm?
1. How many spaces from cm is mm and in what direction? one space to the right
2. Move the decimal point in 64.2 one space to the right.
3. 64.2 cm = 642.0 mm

THINKING IN METRIC TERMS

The following approximations will help you to get an idea of the sizes of some metric measurements.

LENGTH
1 km = the total length of 5 average city blocks
1 m = the length of a softball bat
1 cm = the width of the fingernail on your little finger
1 mm = the thickness of a dime

VOLUME
1 L = the total volume of about 4 single-serving milk cartons
1 mL = the total volume of 20 drops of water

MASS
1 kg = the mass of an average pineapple
1 g = the mass of a wire paper clip
1 cg = the mass of a flea

TEMPERATURE
Water freezes at 0°C.
Water boils at 100°C.
Normal human body temperature is about 37°C.
Room temperature is about 20°C.

THE LABORATORY BURNER

The Bunsen burner is the most common kind of laboratory burner. Some simple but important steps should be taken to light and use the burner safely and successfully. Remember, when near an open flame you should always roll up long sleeves, tie back long hair, and wear safety glasses.

1. Using an appropriate hose, connect the burner to the gas supply.
2. If you are using matches, light a match and then turn on the gas. Bring the match up along the side of the barrel to the top.
3. If you are using a sparker, turn on the gas and strike the sparker next to the top of the barrel.
4. Adjust the air supply so that the burner burns steadily with a light blue cone and without orange flames.

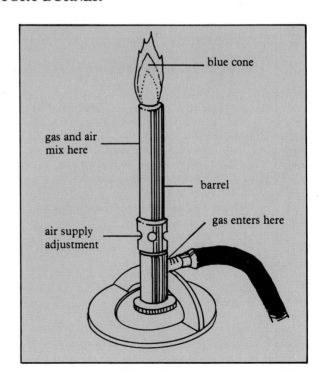

THE LABORATORY BALANCE

You use a balance to measure mass. There are many different kinds of balances.
Your school probably has either equal-arm balances or triple-beam balances.
No matter which kind of balance you use, the same general rules apply.

1. Always hold the balance with two hands at the base while carrying it.

2. Always place the balance on a level surface.

3. Always be sure the balance is zeroed before using it.
   If the pointer is still, the balance is zeroed when the pointer points to the zero mark.
   If the pointer is moving, the balance is zeroed when the pointer moves the same distance to each side of the zero mark.
   If the balance is not zeroed, ask your teacher to adjust it.

4. Never attempt to adjust or fix the balance yourself. Refer any problems to your teacher.

5. Never place chemicals directly on the balance.
   Place them on a paper. Then place the paper on the balance.

Using an Equal-Arm Balance

1. Place the object of unknown mass on the left pan.
2. Use the riders and the known masses to balance the object. The known masses should be placed on the right pan.
3. When the pointer moves the same distance to each side of the zero mark, the object is balanced.
4. The mass of the object is the total of the rider readings and the known masses on the right pan.

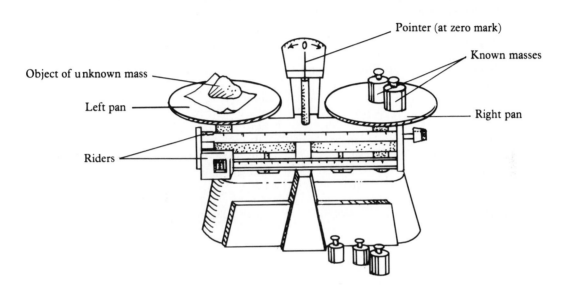

Using a Triple-Beam Balance

1. Place the object of unknown mass on the pan.
2. Use the riders to balance the object.
3. When the pointer moves the same distance to each side of the zero mark, the object is balanced.
4. The mass of the object is the total of the rider readings.

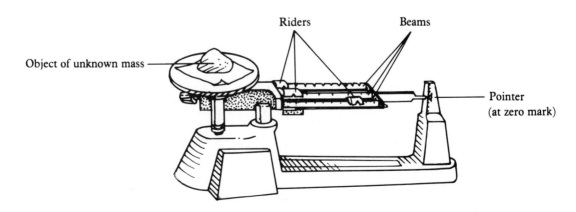

GLOSSARY

PRONUNCIATION KEY

The glossary contains all the Key Terms in *Heath Physical Science* and their definitions. Some of these Key Terms are followed by their phonetic spelling, which shows you how to pronounce them. The words are divided into syllables and respelled according to the way each syllable sounds. The syllable that has the emphasis when the word is spoken appears in capital letters. The guide below is based on the Key to Pronunciation in *The World Book Encyclopedia*.

Sound	Respelling of Sound	Example	
hat, map	a	animal	AN-uh-muhl
age, face	ay	space	spays
care, air	ai	hair	hair
father, far	ah	charge	chahrj
child, much	ch	chocolate	CHAWK-luht
let, best	eh	energy	EHN-uhr-jee
equal, see,	ee	leaf	leef
machine, city		dream	dreem
term, learn	ur	earthworms	URTH-wurmz
sir, work		turkey	TUR-kee
it, pin	ih	system	SIHS-tuhm
ice, five	eye, y	iodine	EYE-uh-dyn
coat, hook	k	cloud	klowd
hot, rock	ah	cotton	KAHT-n
open, go,	oh	program	PROH-gram
grow		row	roh
order, all	aw	corn	kawrn
		fall	fawl
oil, voice	oy	poison	POY-zn
house, out	ow	fountain	FOWN-tuhn
say, nice	s	soil	soyl
she	sh	motion	MOH-shuhn
cup, butter,	uh	bulb	buhlb
flood		blood	bluhd
full, put,	u	pulley	PUL-ee
wood		wool	wul
rule, move,	oo	dew	doo
food		shoe	shoo
pleasure	zh	treasure	TREHZH-uhr
		vision	VIHZH-uhn
about	uh	sofa	SOH-fuh
taken	uh	paper	PAY-puhr
pencil	uh	fossil	FAHS-uhl
lemon	uh	carbon	KAHR-buhn
circus	uh	syrup	SIHR-uhp
curtain	uh	mountain	MOWN-tuhn
section	uh	action	AK-shuhn

A

absolute zero: $-273°$ C; the lowest possible temperature

acceleration [ak-sehl-uh-RAY-shuhn]: the change in velocity divided by the time during which the change occurs

acid rain: rain containing the oxides of sulfur and nitrogen

acids: substances that produce positive hydrogen ions in liquid solution

actinide [AK-tih-nyd] **family:** the radioactive elements below the main body of the periodic table

activation energy: the energy that must be supplied to start a chemical reaction

alchemists: persons who established the laboratory and experimental approach of taking matter apart and analyzing it

alcohol: the compound formed when an OH group replaces a single hydrogen atom in a hydrocarbon

alkali [AL-kuh-ly] **metal family:** the family of very reactive elements with one valence electron

alkaline [AL-kuh-lyn] **earth metal family:** the family of elements that have two valence electrons

alpha particles: the form of nuclear radiation having two protons and two neutrons

alternating [awl-tur-NAY-tihng] **current:** current that is constantly switching directions

alternator: a generator that produces alternating current

amino acids: organic acids containing nitrogen

amperes [AM-pihrz]: the amount of electric current that passes a point in a conductor in one second

amplifier [AM-pluh-fy-uhr]: an electronic device that strengthens electronic signals

amplitude [AM-pluh-tood]: the height of a wave

analyze: to organize observations

Archimedes' principle: the principle that states that the buoyancy of any object is equal to the weight of the liquid that the object displaces

astronomers: scientists who study the universe

atmospheric pressure: the pressure exerted by the weight of the earth's atmosphere

atomic mass number: the sum of protons and neutrons in a nucleus

atomic number: the number of protons in a given nucleus

atoms: the smallest particles of individual elements

attract: to cause two oppositely charged objects to be pulled toward each other

B

bases: substances that produce a negative ion in liquid solution, usually the OH ion

beta particles: high-speed electrons that are a form of nuclear radiation

biomass [BY-oh-mas]: an energy source provided by all the materials in living things, their wastes, and their remains

black hole: an object thought to be a star that has collapsed into a material so dense that its gravity allows nothing to escape

boiling point: the temperature at which a liquid begins to boil

boron family: the family of elements with three valence electrons

breeder reactor: a nuclear reactor in which the fission of uranium produces plutonium 239, which can also be used as a fuel

buoyancy: the force that pushes an object up and makes it seem to lose weight in a fluid

C

calorie: the amount of heat required to raise the temperature of one gram of water one degree Celsius

carbon family: the family of elements that have four valence electrons

carburetor [KAHR-buh-rayt-uhr]: the part of a gasoline engine in which gasoline mixes with air

catalysts [KAT-uh-lihstz]: substances that affect the rate of a chemical reaction without being changed or used up in the reaction

cathode [KATH-ohd] **ray tube:** a vacuum tube in which a stream of electrons is directed onto a screen coated with a fluorescent material

center of gravity: the point around which an object's weight is evenly placed

519

chemical bond: the bond formed when atoms fit together, making a molecule

chemical changes: changes that affect the chemical properties of one or more substances

chemical equation [ih-KWAY-shuhn]: formulas and symbols that show what happens in a chemical reaction

chemical reaction: a process that results in chemical change

circuit breaker: a device that breaks or opens a circuit to stop electric current

coefficient [koh-uh-FIHSH-uhnt]: a number placed in front of a formula or symbol, indicating how many atoms or molecules of that substance are present

compounds: substances made of two or more elements chemically combined

compressional [kuhm-PRESH-uhn-ul] **wave:** a wave in which the disturbance occurs back and forth along the direction of wave motion

computer: a machine that can carry out a detailed set of instructions to perform a task

computer program: a set of instructions for a computer

concave [kahn-KAYV] **lens:** a lens with curved surfaces that dip at the middle and spread light waves apart

condensation [kahn-duhn-SAY-shuhn]: the change of a gas to a liquid

conduction [kuhn-DUHK-shuhn]: the process whereby heat energy is transferred from a hot object to a cooler one by collisions between particles

control rods: steel rods that control the rate of the chain reaction in a nuclear reactor

control unit: the unit that regulates the flow of information in a computer

convection [kuhn-VEHK-shuhn]: the spreading of heat energy by large movements of a liquid or a gas

convex [kahn-VEHKS] **lens:** a lens with curved surfaces that bulge out in the middle and bring light waves together

covalent [koh-VAY-luhnt] **bond:** a bond in which electrons are shared

crankshaft: the device connected to the rod of a heat engine and used to turn one or more wheels

crest: the highest point of a wave

crystals: solids in which the atoms are arranged in a regular pattern

cylinder: the part of a heat engine that confines a heated gas

D

deceleration: a change in velocity to a decreasing speed

decibels [DEHS-uh-behlz]: units that measure the intensity of sound

density: the mass of a substance in grams divided by its volume in cubic centimeters

deuterium [doo-TIHR-ee-uhm]: an isotope of hydrogen that has one proton and one neutron

diatomic [dy-uh-TAHM-ihk] **molecule:** a molecule in which only two atoms join together

diffraction [dih-FRAK-shuhn]: the bending of waves around the sides of a barrier

diffraction grating: a thin piece of glass with thousands of parallel slits close together

direct current: current that always flows in the same direction

distillation: the process by which a liquid is changed to a gas, then collected and cooled, returning the gas to a liquid state

Doppler effect: a change in the frequency of a wave as measured by an observer due to the motion of the wave source or the observer

double bonds: covalent bonds in which two pairs of electrons are shared

drag: the friction created when objects move in air

dry cell: a device that produces voltage as a result of chemical reactions between a moist paste and a metal

E

efficiency: a measure of the amount of work a machine puts out compared to the amount of work put into the machine

effort distance: the distance over which an effort force acts

effort force (F_E): the force that acts on a machine

electric charge: a characteristic of an object affected by electric forces

electric circuit [SUR-kiht]: the path of an electric current

electric current: the flow of electric charges from one point to another

electric discharge: the flow of an electric charge through a gas from a charged object to a conductor

electric forces: forces causing attraction or repulsion between two objects

electric generator: a machine that changes kinetic energy into electric energy

electric motor: a machine that changes electric energy into kinetic energy

electric power: the amount of electric energy that flows through a circuit at a given time

electrical ground: a very large conductor

electrically neutral objects: objects with equal numbers of positive and negative charges

electromagnetic induction: the creation of a current by a changing magnetic field

electromagnetic spectrum [SPEHK-truhm]: the range of all the kinds of electromagnetic waves

electromagnetic [ih-lehk-troh-mag-NEHT-ihk] **waves:** transverse waves that result from the action of electric and magnetic forces

electromagnetism [ih-lehk-troh-MAG-nuh-tihz-uhm]: the branch of physical science that involves the combined effects of electricity and magnetism

electromagnets: magnets in which magnetism is produced by an electric current

electron cloud: a three-dimensional area formed by the electron shells around the nucleus of an atom

electron dot diagram: a diagram in which the valence electrons are shown as dots

electronic [ih-lehk-TRAN-ihk] **devices:** devices that have rapid and accurate control of the flow of electrons

electrons: negatively charged particles surrounding the nucleus of an atom

electroscope: a device that detects the presence of an electric charge on an object

electrostatic induction [ih-lehk-truh-STAT-ihk in-DUHK-shuhn]: the production of an electric charge on an object by bringing it near a charged object

elements: substances that cannot be chemically broken down into simpler basic substances

endoscope [EHN-duh-skohp]: a device with optical fibers used by doctors to examine internal organs

endothermic [ehn-doh-THUHR-mihk] **reaction:** a chemical reaction in which energy is absorbed

energy: the capacity to move matter from one place to another, or to change matter from one substance to another

enzymes [EHN-zymz]: catalysts in living things

equilibrium [ee-kwuh-LIHB-ree-uhm]: a condition during which the net force is equal to zero

evaporation: the change from the liquid state to the gas state

exothermic [ehk-soh-THUHR-mihk] **reaction:** a chemical reaction that releases energy

experiments: measurements and tests under controlled conditions

F

facts: the building blocks of science

families: groups of elements with similar properties that appear in vertical columns in the periodic table

first law of motion: the law that states that every object stays in its equilibrium state unless it is acted on by outside forces

fluid: any substance that flows

fluorescent [floo-REHS-ehnt]: glowing when struck by electrons

focal length: the distance from the center of a lens to the focal point

focal [FOH-kuhl] **point:** the point at which light waves passing through a lens come together

force: a push or pull that is exerted on matter

fossil [FAHS-uhl] **fuels:** fuels formed from the remains of plants and animals that lived millions of years ago

fractional distillation: the process of distillation by which a substance is separated into many parts

freezing: the change of a liquid to a solid

frequency [FREE-kwuhn-see]: the number of crests of a wave that pass a point in a second

521

friction: a force that acts on a moving object in a direction opposite to the motion of the object

fulcrum: a fixed point of a lever

fuse: device that breaks or opens a circuit

G

gamma radiation: nuclear radiation in the form of energy without mass

gas: matter that has no definite shape or volume

geothermal [JEE-oh-thur-muhl] **energy:** heat that comes from inside the earth

gravitational force: the attraction between the earth and all objects on it

grounded conductors: conductors that are connected to very large conductors

H

half-life: the time it takes for half the nuclei in a sample of a radioactive isotope to undergo radioactive decay

halogen [HAL-oh-jehn] **family:** the family of elements that have seven valence electrons and are extremely reactive

heat energy: the total kinetic energy of all the molecules or atoms in a substance

heat engine: a device that uses heat energy to do work

heat of fusion: the amount of heat energy used to melt a substance without changing its temperature

heat of vaporization [vay-puhr-ih-ZAY-shuhn]: the amount of heat energy used to evaporate a liquid

heat pump: a machine that takes heat from outdoors and carries it indoors

hertz [hurts]: a unit of measurement for wave frequency

holograms [HOH-luh-gramz]: three-dimensional photographs

hydrocarbons [hy-droh-KAHR-buhnz]: compounds made of only carbon and hydrogen

hydroelectric power: the electricity generated by the use of moving water

hypothesis [hy-PAHTH-uh-sis]: an educated guess that explains observations

I

image: a picture produced by light waves passing through a lens

impurities: elements that are added to semiconductor crystals to increase conductivity

inclined plane: a simple machine that increases the effort distance through which an object is moved and decreases the effort force needed to move it

indicator: a special type of organic compound that changes color as the pH of a solution changes

induced [ihn-DOOST] **magnetism:** the magnetizing of a material by a magnet

inertia [ihn-UR-shuh]: the tendency for objects to continue in their state of motion or rest

input unit: the part of a computer that takes in information

insulators: poor conductors of heat and electricity

integrated [ihn-tuh-GRAYT-ehd] **circuits:** circuits that are put on a semiconductor chip by placing impurities in a very precise arrangement

intensity [ihn-TEHN-suh-tee]: the loudness of a sound

interference [ihn-tuhr-FIHR-uhns]: the combined effects of two or more waves coming together

ionic [eye-AHN-ihk] **bond:** the bond formed when one atom shifts one or more electrons to another atom

isomers [EYE-suh-muhrz]: compounds with the same molecular formulas but different structural formulas

isotopes: atoms of the same element that differ in the number of neutrons in their nuclei

J

joule (J): the unit of work equal to a newton-meter

K

kilogram: a unit of mass

kilowatt: a unit of measure of large amounts of electric power

kilowatt-hour: the amount of energy produced by one kilowatt of power in one hour

kinetic energy: the energy of motion

kinetic theory: the theory that states that particles of matter move to varying degrees in solids, liquids, and gases

L

laboratory: the workshop of science

lanthanide [LAN-than-yd] **family:** the family of elements below the main body of the periodic table

laser: a device that produces laser light

laser light: an intense narrow beam of light made up of light waves all of the same wavelength and traveling in the same direction

law of conservation of mass: the law that states that in a chemical reaction, no atoms disappear and no new atoms are formed

lenses: curved pieces of glass or plastic that refract light waves

lever: a bar or board that is free to pivot about a fixed point

lift: the upward force of air moving around an object

liquids: matter that has a definite volume but does not have a definite shape

liter: a unit of volume

live wire: any wire connected to a voltage

M

machine: a device that helps a person to do work

magnet: a magnetized object

magnetic domains [doh-MAYNZ]: clusters of many atoms present in materials that can be magnetized

magnetic field: the area around a magnet where its magnetic force can be experienced

magnetic poles: areas of greatest magnetic force

magnetism: a force produced by the motion of electric charges in a material

mass: the amount of material in an object

matter: anything that has mass and takes up space

measurements: observations expressed in numbers

mechanical advantage: the amount of force gained by using a machine

medium: the matter or space through which a wave travels

melting: the change of a solid to a liquid

melting point: the temperature at which a solid changes to a liquid

memory unit: the part of a computer that stores all programs and information that have been put into it

meniscus [men-NIS-kuhs]: the curve at the surface of a liquid in a narrow cylinder

metallic [muh-TAL-ihk] **bond:** a bond in which many electrons are shared by many metal atoms

metals: materials that are good conductors of heat and electricity and that can be pounded into different shapes

meter: a unit of length

metric system: a decimal system of measurement based on the meter, the kilogram, and the liter

microelectronics: a branch of electronics involving integrated circuits

mirage: an illusion caused by the refraction of light waves, making objects that are far away appear to be nearby, floating in air, or upside down

mixture: two or more elements or compounds that are not chemically combined

molecular formulas: representations of molecules using symbols

molecule [MAHL-uh-kyool]: a combination of two or more atoms

momentum [moh-MEHN-tuhm]: the mass of an object multiplied by its velocity

N

natural elements: elements found in nature

negative ion: an atom with more electrons than protons

negative terminal: the place on the zinc jacket of a dry cell where electric contact is made

net force: the sum of opposing forces

neutralization [nu-truh-luh-ZAY-shuhn] **reaction:** a reaction in which an acid and base combine to produce water and a salt

neutron: a particle with no charge in the nucleus of an atom

neutron star: a collapsed star left behind after a supernova

newton (N): a unit of force or weight

nitrogen family: the family of elements that have five valence electrons

noble gas family: the family of elements that mark the end of each period on the periodic table and have eight valence electrons, except for helium

noise pollution: an excess of unpleasant sounds

nonmetals: materials that break instead of bend and are poor conductors of heat and electricity

nonrenewable: not able to be replaced

north geographic pole: the northernmost point of the earth

north magnetic pole: the north pole of the imaginary magnet stuck in the earth

nuclear chain reaction: a reaction in which each fission reaction causes more fission reactions

nuclear fission [FIHSH-uhn]: a reaction in which a heavy nucleus is split apart into nuclei of lighter elements and neutrons

nuclear force: the force holding neutrons and protons together in the nucleus

nuclear fusion [FYOO-zhuhn]: a reaction in which the nuclei of light atoms join together to form a heavier nucleus

nuclear radiation: the products of radioactive decay (alpha particles, beta particles, and gamma radiation)

nuclear reaction: a reaction in which the nucleus of one kind of atom changes into the nucleus of a different kind of atom

nuclear reactor: the part of a nuclear power plant where uranium fuel is bombarded with neutrons to produce a chain reaction that releases energy

nucleus: the small, dense core of an atom

O

observe: to record mentally or in writing things that are noticed

octet [ahk-TEHT] **rule:** the rule that states that atoms form chemical bonds to reach a more stable condition with eight valence electrons

ohms: units used to measure resistance

Ohm's law: the law that states that the greater the voltage, the higher the resistance

oil shale [shayl]: rock containing oil

optical fibers: thin strands of glass that use light waves to carry signals and messages

organic acids: hydrocarbon chains with a COOH group

organic [ohr-GAN-ihk] **compounds:** compounds that contain carbon

oscillator [AHS-uh-layt-uhr]: an electronic device that produces electronic signals from direct current

output unit: the part of a computer that changes the results of the processing unit from computer language into words, numbers, and symbols, and then prints them

overtones: notes of multiple frequencies produced by musical instruments

oxygen family: the family of elements having six valence electrons

P

parallel circuits: circuits in which the current divides and flows in two or more separate paths, or branches

periodic table: a table of the elements arranged according to properties

periods: horizontal rows of elements with increasing atomic numbers in the periodic table

photons: tiny bundles of energy present in electromagnetic waves

pH scale: scale that measures the strength of an acid or base

physical changes: changes that affect the size, shape, or physical state of a substance but not its chemical properties and formula

physical science: the branch of science that searches for answers to questions about matter and energy

piston: the movable top of a cylinder in a heat engine

pitch: the highness or lowness of a sound that the ear hears

plasma: the state of matter in which the particles of a gas break apart into electrically charged pieces

polarizing [POH-luh-ry-zing]: allowing only light waves with crests and troughs at a certain angle to pass through a material

polymers [PAHL-uh-muhrs]: organic molecules containing a large number of atoms

positive ion: an atom with fewer electrons than protons

positive terminal: the place on the carbon rod of a dry cell where electric contact is made

potential energy: stored energy that can be released when matter moves

power: the measurement of the rate at which work is done

pressure: force that is applied over a certain area

prism: a triangular piece of glass that bends light waves

processing: the carrying out of instructions and performance of operations using information that has been put into a computer

processing unit: the unit that carries out a computer program

products: substances that result from a chemical or nuclear reaction

property: a quality or characteristic of a substance

proteins: amino acids joined together in long chains

proton: positively charged particle in the nucleus of an atom

pulley: a lever that rotates around a fixed point

Q

quarks: small particles that are believed to make up protons and neutrons

quasars [KWAY-zahrz]: extremely distant objects that emit radio waves, visible light waves, and X rays from a small area

R

radiation [ray-dee-AY-shuhn]: a form of energy transfer that occurs through matter and through empty space

radioactive: giving off high-energy particles

radioactive decay: a nuclear reaction in which the nucleus of one kind of atom spontaneously changes into the nucleus of another kind of atom

radioactivity: the energy given off when a nuclear change occurs

reactants [ree-AK-tuhntz]: substances that undergo a chemical reaction

real image: an image that appears upside down and can be focused on a screen

rectifier [REHK-tuh-fy-uhr]: an electronic device that changes alternating current to direct current

red giant: a large star that gives off mostly red light

reflecting telescopes: devices that use a curved mirror and a convex lens to reflect and refract light waves from distant objects to produce a magnified image

reflection [rih-FLEHK-shuhn]: the bouncing back of a wave when it hits a boundary

refracting telescope: a device that uses two convex lenses to concentrate and bend light waves from distant objects to produce a magnified image

refraction [rih-FRAK-shuhn]: the bending of waves due to a change in the medium

renewable: able to be replaced

repel: to cause two similarly charged objects to push each other apart

resistance [rih-ZIHS-tuhns]: the opposition a material offers to the flow of electric charges

resistance distance: the distance an object on which work is being done is moved

resistance force (F_R): the weight of an object to be moved

resonance [REHZ-uh-nuhns]: the amplification of sound by musical instruments

retina [REHT-uhn-uh]: the surface in the eye upon which a real image is formed

reverberations [rih-vur-buh-RAY-shuhnz]: mixtures of reflected sounds

S

salt: the compound produced in a neutralization reaction when the hydrogen in the acid is replaced with another element from the base

science: a method of organizing curiosity

scientific method: investigation using observation, analysis, synthesis, and testing

screw: a combination of an inclined plane and a cylinder

second: a unit of time

second law of motion: the law that states that an object acted on by a constant force will move with a constant acceleration in the direction in which the force is acting

semiconductors: solid materials that have a conductivity in the range between that of an insulator and that of a good conductor

series circuit: a circuit with only one path for the current

shaft mining: the removal of coal deposits by cutting tunnels or shafts in the earth

shells: specific energy levels around the nucleus where electrons can be found

short circuit: a situation that occurs when current flows over an unintended path that has very low resistance

signals: short bursts of electric energy to which electronic devices respond

simple machines: devices that increase forces

solar cells: devices that collect solar energy and change it into electric energy

solar collectors: devices that collect and change solar energy into heat energy

solar energy: energy from the sun

solid: matter that has a definite shape and volume

solid-state devices: transistors or equipment utilizing transistors

solutions: mixtures in which substances are uniformly distributed

sound waves: compressional waves produced by a back-and-forth motion

space colonies: structures in space where people could live and work

spark plug: the part of a gasoline engine that ignites a mixture of gasoline and air

specific heat: the amount of heat needed to raise the temperature of one gram of a substance one degree Celsius

spectroscope [SPEHK-truh-skohp]: a device used to study different wavelengths of light given off by a glowing object

speed: the measure of how fast an object is moving

stars: large masses of gases that give off energy

static electricity: an electric charge that builds up on an object

steam turbine [TUHR-byn]: an engine in which steam under pressure is used to produce a rotational motion

straight chain hydrocarbons: compounds in which carbon atoms are bonded together in a single line

strip mining: the exposure of coal deposits with explosives and removal of the coal with giant shovels

strokes: movements of the piston in a gasoline engine

structural formula: a chemical formula using dashes to represent covalent bonds

supernova: the explosion of a massive red giant

synthesize [SIN-thuh-syz]: to put observations together in a new way

synthetic [sihn-THEHT-ihk]: word describing substances produced in the laboratory

T

technology: a way of applying scientific discoveries to the real world

temperature: the measure of the average kinetic energy of the atoms or molecules that make up a substance

terminal velocity: the velocity at which a falling object will not accelerate anymore

test: the check of a theory's predictions against new observations

theories: ideas that explain groups of facts

third law of motion: the law that states that for every action by one object there must be an equal and opposite reaction on the other object

tidal energy: energy in tidewaters that can be used to generate electricity

transformer [trans-FAWR-muhr]: a device used to increase or decrease voltage

transistor [tran-ZIHS-tuhr]: a device that uses semiconductors to control the flow of electrons

transition metals: elements in which the next to the last shell is filled as the number of electrons increases

transverse [trans-VURS] **waves:** waves in which the disturbance occurs at right angles to the direction of the wave motion

triple bonds: covalent bonds in which three pairs of electrons are shared

trough [trawf]: the lowest point of a wave

visible light: light waves that can be seen

voltage: the difference in electric potential that causes current to flow

volts: units for measuring voltage

volume: the measurement of the amount of space an object takes up

U

ultrasonic: sound waves with very short wavelengths and frequencies above 20,000 Hz

universal law of gravitation: the law that states that the force of gravitation is present between any two objects in the universe

V

vacuum tubes: electronic devices made of glass tubes from which nearly all air has been removed

valence [VAY-luhns] **electrons:** electrons in the shell farthest from the nucleus

velocity [vuh-LAHS-uh-tee]: a measure of both the speed of a body and its direction of motion

vibration: a back-and-forth motion

virtual [VUR-choo-wuhl] **image:** an image that appears right side up and cannot be focused on a screen

W

watt: a unit of power equal to one joule of work done in one second

wave: a disturbance that travels through matter or space

wavelength: the distance from one crest of a wave to the next

wedge: an inclined plane that moves

weight: the amount of gravitational pull on an object

wheel and axle: a lever that can move around in a circle

white dwarf: a very dense, hot star formed as a result of the collapse of a red giant

white light: a mixture of all the colors of visible light

work: the application of a force moving an object a distance

INDEX

NOTE: Page number in **boldfaced** type indicates a definition.

Metals, **136**-137, **138**-139; bonding in, **174**-175; in periodic table, 142-145
Meter, **15**
Methane, 184
Metric system, **15**-17
Microelectronics, **361**
Microscope, 442-443
Microwaves, 419
Millimeter, 17
Mining, shaft and strip, **457**
Mirage, **427**
Mirrors, light and, 424-426
Mixture, **161**, 162, 163
Molecular formulas, **164**, 166
Molecule, **164**-165
Momentum, **40**-41
Motion, 9; first law of, **58**-59; force as a cause of, 48; net force and, 54, 55; second law of, **60**-61; third law of, **62**-63. *See also* Speed; Velocity.
Motors, electric, **344**-345
Music, sound of, 402-405
Musical instruments, 403-408

N
Natural elements, **121**
Nearsightedness, 441
Negative charge. *See* Electric charge.
Negative ion, **168**
Negative terminal, **317**
Net force, **54**
Neutralization reaction, **222**
Neutron, **124**, 125, 126, 232, 233
Neutron star, **504**
Newton, Isaac, 43, 65; gravitational force and, 49-51. *See also* Laws of motion.
Newton-meter, **71**
Newton (N), **51**
Newton's laws. *See* Laws of motion.
Nitrogen family, **147**
Noble gas family, **150**-151, 165, 167
Noise pollution, **406**-407
Nonmetals, **136**-137, **138**-139
Nonrenewable fuels, **466**
North geographic pole, **301**
North magnetic pole, **300**
Nuclear chain reaction, **245**
Nuclear energy, 462-465
Nuclear fission, **244**-245, 462-463
Nuclear force, **129**, 233

Nuclear fusion, **246**-247
Nuclear physicist, 471
Nuclear radiation, **235**-243
Nuclear reactions, 231, **232**-233, 234-247; types of, 462
Nuclear reactor, **463**-464
Nucleus, atomic, **123**, 124-127, 128, 232

O
Objects, falling, 37-39
Observations, **9**; expressed in numbers, 14-17; recording of, 12
Occupational Safety and Health Act (OSHA), 409
Oceanography, 389
Octet rule, **167**
Oersted, Hans Christian, 336-337
Ohm, George S., 321
Ohms, **323**
Ohm's law, **323**
Oil, distillation of crude, 189. *See also* Fossil fuels.
Oil shale, **457**-458
Optical fibers, **447**
Optometrist, career as, 449
Organic acids, **191**, 193
Organic compounds, **183**
Oscillator, **357**, 360
Output unit, computer, **364**
Overtones, **405**
Oxygen family, 119, **148**-149

P
Parallel circuits, **319**-320
Periodic table, **136**-140
Periods, **136**, 138-139
Phenolphthalein, **225**
Photographs, infrared, 418; three-dimensional, 446
Photons, **416**
pH scale, **223**
Physical changes, **206**
Physical science, **5**, 6-7, 8-11
Physical scientist, career as, 177
Physicist, 311, 471
Piston, **275**, 281
Pitch of sound waves, **397**-399
Planets, atomic structure and, 128; gravitational pull of, 50
Plasma state, **28**
Plastic, 197
Polarizing sunglasses, **429**
Poles, magnetic, **296**. *See also*

North magnetic pole.
Pollution, noise, **406**-407. *See also* Air pollution; Thermal pollution.
Polyethylene, 195
Polymers, **194**-195
Positive charge. *See* Electric charge.
Positive ion, **168**
Positive terminal, **317**
Potential energy, **29**, 30
Power, efficiency and, **84**-87; hydroelectric, **482**-485
Predictions, 4, 10
Property, **29**
Pressure, atmospheric, **104**-105; formula for, 94; in liquids, **94**-97
Prism, **420**
Processing computer, **364**
Processing unit, computer, **364**
Products, **208**
Properties of matter. *See* Boiling point; Melting point; Specific heat.
Proteins, **193**
Protons, **124**, 125, 126, 232, 233
Pulley, **82**-83

Q
Quarks, **127**
Quasars, **505**

R
Radar, 387
Radiant energy, 267
Radiation, **267**. *See also* Cancer and radiation; Nuclear radiation.
Radiation sickness, 237
Radioactive decay, **235**, 239
Radioactive elements, 152
Radioactive isotopes, 238-243
Radioactivity, **234**-243; nuclear reactors and, 464-465
Rain, acid, **460**
Rainbows, 420
Ramp. *See* Inclined plane.
Reactants, **208**; and chemical reactions, 215-216
Reactions, chemical, 205-**207**, 208-225; four types of, 208-209; neutralization of, **222**; nuclear, 231, **232**-247, 462; nuclear chain, **245**

ACKNOWLEDGEMENTS

Illustration

Michael Carroll   4, 127
Glenna Collett   138–139
James Conahan   109, 211, 235, 244–245
Genigraphics   17
David Hannum   463, 478
Walter Hortens   354, 416–417, 483, 503
Leonard Morgan   104, 143 bottom, 171, 208, 209, 233, 258, 284, 300, 344
Mike Prendergast   16, 21, 30, 56, 79, 83, 107, 108, 121, 142, 143 top, 145, 146, 147, 148, 149, 151, 153 top, 161, 162, 182, 185, 192, 213, 215 top, 237, 239, 240, 246, 259, 260, 261, 262, 265, 274, 275, 278, 279, 281, 285, 317, 322, 327, 338, 341, 353, 377, 379, 382, 384, 403, 420, 428, 429, 431, 442, 446, 447, 479, 497
Vytas Sakalas   16, 27, 45, 62, 76, 80, 86, 96, 120, 126, 129, 140, 144, 153 bottom, 157, 165, 167, 168, 170, 172, 184, 186, 212, 236, 238, 241, 271, 296, 297, 298, 309, 357, 364, 380, 416 top, 436, 437, 439, 444, 467, 487
Jeff Stock   33, 35, 95 bottom, 188
Will Tenney   14
Gary Torrisi   50, 51, 97, 99 bottom, 124, 169 top, 175, 440, 441
George Ulrich   2, 8, 13, 37, 38, 40, 41, 53, 58, 61, 78, 85, 94, 95 top, 99 top, 125, 141, 169 bottom, 190, 215 bottom, 223, 224, 240, 242, 266, 301, 304, 316, 318, 319, 320, 328, 336, 342, 345, 386, 394, 401, 417 center, 427, 438, 468, 486
Lily Yamamoto   359, 366, 399

Photography

Alpha: Jim Howard 227, 411; Richard Laird 462; D. C. Lowe 484; Alan McGee 407 left; James M. Mejuto 405; Blair Seitz 145; Al Zalon 406 top
Erik Anderson   viii, 9, 10, 12, 180, 256 bottom row, 516
Animals Animals: 283; Margot Conte 32; Robert Mitchell 28 top
Peter Arnold, Inc.:   Steve Allen 477; E. F. Bernstein 187 bottom; Cecile Brunswick 397 top; Richard Choy 259, 474; Jacques Jangoux 476; James H. Karales 269; Stephen J. Krasemann 496 right; Hans Pfletschinger 123; Mike Phillips 494; Clyde Smith 49
Atoz Images, Inc.:   George Mars Cassidy 214; Peter Fronk 334; Fred Leavitt 230; Carol Lee 321; William Mean 407 right; L. L. T. Rhodes 114; Leonard Lee Rue 329, 398 bottom; L. Starz 308
Bell Laboratories   6 top and bottom right, 177, 361
The Bettman Archive   119 top
Biblioteca Marucelliana   19
Dr. Jason Birnholz, Brigham and Women's Hospital   6 top left
Black Star: Andy Levin 435; John Lopino 415; Debra & Flip Schulke 452; Fred Ward 447
Lee Boltin   146
David Brownell   48 right
The Burndy Library   43
James N. Butler   185 bottom
California Institute of Technology   142
Camerique   26, 204; Ron Dahlquist 378; J. Pickerell 68;
A. James Casner   52 bottom, 55, 63, 74, 75, 163 bottom
Stuart Cohen   91

Dave Olson   202
Tom Pantages   409, 445 right, 506 right
Photofile International, Ltd.   175, 210, 252
Photo Researchers, Inc.:   Farrell Grehan 404 top
Phototake: Yoav Levy 116 top and bottom left
Photri: Don Davis 508
The Picture Cube: Ed Hof 412; Eric Roth 493;
   Steven M. Stone 261; R. Terry Walker 247;
   Richard Wood 347
Picture Group: Fredrik D. Bodin 29 bottom
Princeton Plasma Physics Laboratory   465
Rainbow: Coco McCoy 406; Dan McCoy 5 right,
   149, 384, 419; Hank Morgan 291, 360
Shostal Associates   389, 485; Tony Linck 445 left;
   William Hamilton 387
Smithsonian Institution 505
Tom Stack and Associates: 193; Gerald A. Corsi
   179, 486; William & Genny Garst 482; Bob
   McKeever 313; Gary Milburn 279
Stock, Boston: 421; Fredrik D. Bodin 255 right,
   404 bottom; Daniel Brody 464, 469; Anestis

Diakopolous 164, 397 bottom; Donald Dietz 87
left; Owen Franken 274, 356; Bill Gillett 457;
Edith G. Haun 352, 358; James R. Holland 255
center; Bohdan Hrynewych 459; Litchfield 39;
Mike Malyszko 254; Tony Mendoza 34 top; Peter
Menzel 46, 488; Eric Neurath 333; Stacy Pick
325; Jonathan Rawle 328; John Running 218,
349, 402; Lincoln Russell 307; Frank Siteman
199 bottom; Peter Southwick 103; Peter Van-
dermark 37; Harry Wilks 292; Cary Wolinsky
182, 280
Taurus Photos: Mrs. T. W. Bennett 496 left; L. L.
   Rhodes 451; Frank E. Toman 151
U.S. Air Force   150 right
University of California   152, 500
University of Pennsylvania   362
Woods Hole Oceanographic Institution:
   Rod Catanach 100
Yale University: J. D. Levine 511
Dick Zimmerman   365

GUIDE TO UNITS USED IN PHYSICAL SCIENCE

Unit	Chapter Where Introduced	Page Where Introduced	What It Measures
ampere	15	317	electric current
calorie	12	257	heat
decibel (dB)	19	396	sound intensity
degree Celsius (°C)	12	256	temperature
hertz (Hz)	18	379	wave frequency
joule (J)	4	71	work
	12	257	heat
kilogram (kg)	1	15	mass
kilowatt	15	324	power
kilowatt-hour	15	325	electric energy
liter (L)	1	15	volume
meter (m)	1	15	length, distance
newton (N)	3	51	weight
ohm	15	323	resistance
second (s)	1	17	time
volt	15	316	voltage
watt	4	84	power